Psychology of Sport Injury

Britton W. Brewer, PhD
Springfield College

Charles J. Redmond, MS, ATC, LAT, PT
Springfield College

HUMAN KINETICS

Library of Congress Cataloging-in-Publication Data

Names: Brewer, Britton W., author. | Redmond, Charles J., 1946- author.
Title: Psychology of sport injury / Britton W. Brewer, Charles J. Redmond.
Description: Champaign, IL : Human Kinetics, [2017] | Includes bibliographical references and
   index.
Identifiers: LCCN 2016030816 | ISBN 9781450424462 (print)
Subjects: | MESH: Athletic Injuries--psychology | Athletes--psychology | Psychology,
   Sports--methods | Sociological Factors
Classification: LCC RD97 | NLM QT 261 | DDC 617.1/027--dc23 LC record available at
   https://lccn.loc.gov/2016030816

ISBN: 978-1-4504-2446-2 (print)

The web addresses cited in this text were current as of August 2016, unless otherwise noted.

Senior Acquisitions Editor: Myles Schrag; **Developmental Editor:** Kevin Matz; **Managing Editors:** Stephanie M. Ebersohl and Anna Lan Seaman; **Copyeditor:** Tom Tiller; **Indexer:** Nancy Ball; **Permissions Manager:** Dalene Reeder; **Graphic Designer:** Whitney Milburn; **Cover Designer:** Keith Blomberg; **Photograph (cover):** © AP Photo/Joe Nicholson; **Photo Asset Manager:** Laura Fitch; **Photo Production Manager:** Jason Allen; **Senior Art Manager:** Kelly Hendren; **Illustrations:** © Human Kinetics, unless otherwise noted; **Printer:** Sheridan Books

Printed in the United States of America   10 9 8 7 6 5 4 3 2 1

The paper in this book is certified under a sustainable forestry program.

Human Kinetics
Website: www.HumanKinetics.com

United States: Human Kinetics
P.O. Box 5076
Champaign, IL 61825-5076
800-747-4457
e-mail: info@hkusa.com

Canada: Human Kinetics
475 Devonshire Road Unit 100
Windsor, ON N8Y 2L5
800-465-7301 (in Canada only)
e-mail: info@hkcanada.com

Europe: Human Kinetics
107 Bradford Road
Stanningley
Leeds LS28 6AT, United Kingdom
+44 (0) 113 255 5665
e-mail: hk@hkeurope.com

Australia: Human Kinetics
57A Price Avenue
Lower Mitcham, South Australia 5062
08 8372 0999
e-mail: info@hkaustralia.com

New Zealand: Human Kinetics
P.O. Box 80
Mitcham Shopping Centre, South Australia 5062
0800 222 062
e-mail: info@hknewzealand.com

E5665

Psychology of Sport Injury

Contents

Preface

A gymnast conceals intense ankle pain from her coaches and teammates so that she will not be prevented from competing in the conference championships.

After sustaining a season-ending injury, a basketball player withdraws from his friends and family and spends most of his time away from school locked in his room playing video games.

As soon as she returns home after her knee surgery, a skier vigorously undertakes her assigned rehabilitation exercises and devotes 15 minutes per day to meditating and imagining herself back on the slopes, fully recovered from her injury.

What do these scenarios have in common? Not only do they each involve an athlete with an injury, they also involve the interface between sport injury and psychological factors. Indeed, it can be argued convincingly that *every* sport injury affects or is affected by psychological factors. This involvement of psychological issues in sport injury creates a need to chronicle and integrate the latest theoretical, empirical, and applied developments in the field. This book meets that need by covering a full range of topics under the umbrella of the psychology of sport injury in a manner that is useful for scholars, practitioners, and students alike.

In the book's introduction, we argue in favor of a contemporary approach to preventing, treating, rehabilitating, and communicating professionally about sport injury; this approach takes into account both physical and psychological elements. The introduction also presents epidemiological data that frame sport injury within a broader public health context; in addition, it highlights the book's theme of integrating biological, psychological, and social factors to best understand and address sport injury by identifying disciplines for which the psychology of sport injury is relevant.

Chapter 1 presents an overview of the biopsychosocial approach that serves as the guiding framework for the book. The chapter opens

with a vivid example of the sociocultural context in which sport injury exists (specifically, the "culture of risk" inhabited by the gymnast depicted in the opening scenario of this preface), then summarizes biological, psychological, and social factors that play major roles in the prevention, treatment, and rehabilitation of sport injury.

For much of the ensuing exploration of psychological aspects of sport injury, we adopt a semi-sequential approach; in other words, we cover topics in the approximate order in which they are likely to occur. Consequently, chapter 2 addresses circumstances that *precede* the occurrence of a sport injury. Specifically, it discusses physical and psychosocial models of sport injury occurrence, identifies psychosocial predictors of sport injury, explores proposed mechanisms by which psychosocial factors are thought to precipitate sport injury, and examines methods (e.g., questionnaires, face-to-face interactions) that professionals can use to assess life stress, which is chief among the psychosocial factors that contribute to sport injury occurrence.

Chapter 3 applies principles covered in chapter 2 to address the question of whether certain psychological measures can be taken by athletes (and the professionals with whom they have contact) to decrease the likelihood of sport injury. In particular, the chapter reviews empirical support for psychosocial interventions to reduce the risk of sport injury and discusses practical implications for implementing such interventions.

Continuing the temporal sequence, we focus next on circumstances *after* the occurrence of a sport injury, beginning with cognitive, emotional, and behavioral responses to sport injury. These responses not only may influence sport injury processes and outcomes but also warrant clinical attention in their own right, as illustrated in the scenario about the basketball player depicted at the start of this preface.

More specifically, in chapter 4, we describe models of psychological response to sport injury and summarize empirical support for these models; along the way, we dispel a few myths about how athletes respond psychologically to injury. Another prominent psychological response to sport injury—pain—is the focal topic of chapter 5, which examines definitions, types, dimensions, measurement, theories, predictors, and treatments of pain associated with sport injury. This chapter addresses questions pertaining to athletes' pain tolerance, the distinction between pain and injury, playing through pain, and the treatment of sport-related pain through pharmacological means, physical therapies, and psychological techniques.

Another presumed critical influence on clinical outcomes is the extent to which an athlete adheres to the prescribed rehabilitation program. This important topic is addressed in chapter 6, which examines models, measures, predictors, and methods of enhancing adherence to sport injury rehabilitation. We adopt the stance that *before* making extensive efforts to boost adherence, we must understand the dose–response relationship between the amount of prescribed rehabilitation activity engaged in by the athlete (i.e., the dose) and the rehabilitation outcome (i.e., the response).

In chapter 7, we tackle the intriguing question of whether psychological factors are related to clinical outcomes in sport injury rehabilitation. We identify potential mechanisms by which psychological factors might influ-

ence sport injury rehabilitation outcomes and review research on personal, social, cognitive, emotional, and behavioral factors associated with such outcomes.

Chapter 8 extends chapter 7 by applying knowledge about the relationship between psychological factors and sport injury rehabilitation outcomes to the development and implementation of psychological interventions in sport-related health care. This chapter examines the potential utility of the approach taken by the skier in the third scenario that opened this preface by reviewing empirical support for psychological interventions in sport injury rehabilitation and discussing practical implications for implementing such interventions.

Successful professional practice in sport health care hinges on the practitioner's ability to communicate effectively; accordingly, the final two chapters of the book address communication between sport health care practitioners and their patients and professional colleagues. Chapter 9 examines interactions between practitioners and patients, with particular emphasis on informational and socioemotional communication and its effects on key processes and outcomes in sport health care. The chapter also introduces counseling skills as a means of enhancing patient–practitioner communication.

Finally, in the context of referral for psychological services, chapter 10 addresses communication between sport health care professionals and the other health care practitioners with whom they have frequent contact. Specifically, the chapter covers collaboration, networking, documentation, legal and ethical obligations, and decision making. In order to fully meet athletes' needs and optimize the rehabilitation process, practitioners must recognize when to refer an athlete for psychological services and know how to do so competently. To this end, and with particular emphasis on psychopathology, we identify common reasons for referral and provide practical guidance for setting up referral networks and making referrals.

In each of the book's 10 chapters, we present an overview of the topic at hand, define key terms, and review relevant theory and research. Throughout, specific Focus on Research boxes provide a sense of how we know what we know about the psychology of sport injury; similarly, Focus on Application boxes highlight practical applications of the knowledge base, and case examples illustrate the relevance of the material to professional practice. Thus this book can serve multiple purposes—as a reference source, an educational tool, and a springboard to new ideas for research and practice in the psychology of sport injury.

Because interest in the psychology of sport injury cuts across disciplines, we have consciously *not* tailored the book's content to any particular profession or constituency. Nevertheless, we recognize the potential utility of the text in athletic training education; therefore, as shown in the following table, we have ensured that the book addresses (in total or in part) the vast majority of topics relevant to the "Psychosocial Strategies and Referral" content area of the *Athletic Training Education Competencies* document (National Athletic Trainers' Association, 2011). In addition, we have used draft chapters from the book to teach a course

in the psychology of sport injury, and the feedback we received from students in diverse fields of study (including athletic administration, athletic training, counseling psychology, sport psychology, strength and conditioning, and student personnel in higher education) helped us present the material in a manner that carries broad-based appeal.

Category	Chapter(s)
PS-1	9
PS-2	4
PS-3	7
PS-4	9
PS-6	6, 9
PS-7	8
PS-8	8
PS-9	5
PS-11	Introduction, 10
PS-12	10
PS-13	10
PS-14	10
PS-15	10
PS-16	10
CIP-7	8
CIP-8	10

Acknowledgments

We gratefully acknowledge the contributions of many individuals in bringing this book to fruition. For laying the foundation on which the book is based, we thank the founders of the psychology of sport injury, Thomas Holmes and J. Crawford Little, and the first generation of psychology of sport injury scholars, including Mark Andersen, Steve Danish, Sandy Gordon, Bob Grove, Charles Hardy, John Heil, Steve Heyman, David Pargman, Mike Passer, Al Petitpas, Bob Rotella, John Silva, Ron Smith, Frank Smoll, Maureen Weiss, Diane Wiese-Bjornstal, and Jean Williams, whose pioneering efforts continue to impress and inspire.

We owe a debt of gratitude to the distinguished group of professionals from around the world with whom we have collaborated on projects and events involving the psychology of sport injury, including Mark Andersen, Mark Archer, Monna Arvinen-Barrow, John Brickner, Allen Cornelius, John Corsetti, Derick Cummings, Deborah Cupal, Thomas Deroche, Terry Ditmar, Thomas Dugdale, Kelley Emery, Lynne Evans, G. B. Giles, Meghan Granquist, Laura Jensen, Urban Johnson, Greg Kolt, Christopher Lena, Darwyn Linder, Ralph Maddison, Al Petitpas, Trent Petrie, Les Podlog, Mark Pohlman, Harry Prapavessis, Ignatius Reilly, Victor Rubio, Olivier Schmid, Josie Scibelli, Joe Sklar, Janel Shurrocks, Yannick Stephan, Tomasz Tasiemski, Dean Tripp, Judy Van Raalte, Samuel Zelazo, Gordon Zimmermann, and Ianita Zlateva. We thank the Springfield College Athletic Training staff and faculty for their support and insights, and the sizable crew of Springfield College graduate students who have served as research assistants, helped maintain our psychology of sport injury database, and provided classroom feedback on the content of the book.

To the talented, professional, and highly competent staff at Human Kinetics, particularly Stephanie Ebersohl, Kevin Matz, and the ever-patient author-whisperer, Myles Schrag, we express our sincere appreciation for bringing our manuscript to life. Finally, we thank our families for their encouragement, support, and tolerance over the course of writing this book.

Introduction

A Contemporary Approach to the Challenges of Sport Injury

On a warm, sunny afternoon in early autumn, an American football game has just begun at a large university's jam-packed stadium. The visiting team's running back has turned the corner on the defense and is just about to scamper down the sideline for a large gain when, out of nowhere, Tyrell, the home team's acclaimed senior middle linebacker, dashes across the field and drops the ball carrier for a two-yard loss, displaying the athleticism and competitive fire that have drawn the attention of pro scouts. The running back pops right up after the play and returns to his team's huddle, but Tyrell remains on the ground, clutching his left knee, with his helmet off and sweat and tears streaming down his face. He slaps the grass and yells, "No, no, no! Why, why, why?!" The athletic training staff help him off the field and through the tunnel to the locker room for evaluation and treatment.

Like millions of his athletic peers, Tyrell has sustained a sport injury. On the surface, his injury appears to resemble many others that occur in the rough-and-tumble world of competitive sport. A closer look, however, would reveal that Tyrell's injury was a unique, more personal event than a sport reporter's account of the game might suggest. What injury did he sustain? Why did he react to it in the way he did? What is the meaning of his cryptic shouts? Before answering these questions by delving more deeply into the circumstances of Tyrell's injury, let's take a step back and briefly explore the broader health context of sport injury in order to set the stage for the remainder of the book.

Health Context of Sport Injury

As illustrated by Tyrell's case, injury is a likely if not inevitable consequence of training and competing in the physically demanding—and sometimes combative and violent—environment of sport. A sport injury generally requires the athlete to seek medical attention and refrain from training and competing for a period of time, regardless of whether it is sustained in organized sport or in a recreational setting (Flint, 1998; F.E. Noyes, Lindenfeld, & Marshall, 1988). Therefore, sport injury is a concern not only for athletes and coaches but also for the general population; indeed, epidemiological studies have shown that sport injury is a significant public health concern.

In the United States, for example, people participating in sport, exercise, and other recreational forms of physical activity incur an estimated total of 7 to 17 million injuries per year (Booth, 1987; Conn, Annest, & Gilchrist, 2003), some 4 million of which result in an emergency room visit (Centers for Disease Control and Prevention [CDC], 2002). From a monetary standpoint, the 200,000 anterior cruciate ligament (ACL) tears sustained each year in the United States carry a total estimated lifetime burden of $7.6 billion to $17.7 billion; the cost for an ACL tear depends on whether it is treated through rehabilitation or surgical reconstruction (Mather et al., 2014). Similarly, in Australia, sport accounts for 18 percent of ER visits by adults and 20 percent of visits by children (C. Finch, Valuri, & Ozanne-Smith, 1998), and the annual cost of sport- and recreation-related injuries has been estimated at $1.8 billion (Medibank Private, 2004). And in another example, in the United Kingdom, approximately one-third of all injuries can be attributed to involvement in sport and exercise (Uitenbroek, 1996).

Thus we see that sport- and recreation-related injuries are common in the general population—more common, in fact, than injuries sustained during transportation-related accidents (Conn et al., 2003). In athletic populations, the odds of becoming injured are higher still. For example, estimates of the yearly incidence of injury among male U.S. high school athletes range from 27 percent to 39 percent (Patel & Nelson, 2000). The vast majority (80 percent) of sport injuries involve the musculoskeletal system (Zemper, 1993), and the most common forms of sport-related and recreation-related injury are strains, sprains, fractures, dislocations, contusions, abrasions, and lacerations (CDC, 2002, 2006; Conn et al., 2003; C. Finch et al., 1998). Most sport injuries are minor, but nearly a quarter of a million are deemed severe (Darrow, Collins, Yard, & Comstock, 2009), and approximately 38 "catastrophic" (Zemper, 2010) sport injuries are incurred per year by U.S. high school students. Most of the severe injuries are season ending, and about a quarter of them require surgery (Darrow et al., 2009); the catastrophic injuries are often fatal, and the vast majority involve damage to the head or spine (Zemper, 2010).

Injury frequency, type, and location vary considerably across sports and across demographic characteristics, such as sex and age (D.J. Caine, Caine, & Lindner, 1996). For example, the most common sources of sport injury are basketball and cycling in the United States (Conn et al., 2003), but cycling, Australian football, and basketball in Australia (C. Finch et al., 1998). Reflecting sex differences in sport participation, twice as many males as females experience sport injury (Conn et al., 2003; Knowles, 2010); among adolescents, more than six times as many males sustain sport-related fractures (Wood, Robertson, Rennie, Caesar, & Court-Brown, 2010). However, when injury rates are adjusted for amount of risk exposure in practice and competition, males and females are equally likely to become injured through involvement in comparable sports (CDC, 2006; Hootman, Dick, & Agel, 2007). In the United States, the injury rate is 1.5 times higher for whites than for blacks (Conn et al., 2003). Children and adolescents are especially vulnerable to sport injury; indeed, sport is the most common source of injury among adolescents (Emery, 2003), and injury rates are highest for people aged 5 to 14 and 15 to 24 years, respectively (Conn et al., 2003). Among adolescents in particular, overuse injuries are more common than injuries due to acute trauma (Patel & Nelson, 2000; Stracciolini, Casciano, Friedman, Meehan, & Micheli, 2013). For more on the epidemiology of sport injury, see this introduction's Focus on Research box.

Multiple Perspectives on Sport Injury

Returning to the case of Tyrell, what exactly happened to him? Based on his reaction, it would be reasonable to assume that he sustained a serious injury and was in severe pain. In reality, however, as confirmed by diagnostic testing, Tyrell incurred no structural damage; nor did he experience severe pain. His injury turned out to be a deeply bruised quadriceps, and his emotional display resulted largely from mental anguish. Why, then, did the appearance of the situation deviate so greatly from the reality of it?

The answer lies in the fact that sport injury is a complex phenomenon that defies simple explanation; therefore, in order to understand it, we must understand its potential contributors and consequences. In Tyrell's case, we need to know that he was in his senior year of college, that many of his friends and family members were at the game, and that he was playing in his first game since completing

Epidemiology of Sport Injury

Health care and sport administrators rely on data from epidemiological studies to allocate resources for the prevention and treatment of sport injury. Epidemiology is the scientific study of the occurrence, distribution, and control of disease in populations. In the context of sport injury, epidemiology focuses on describing how many injuries occur, who becomes injured, what types of injury occur, where and when injuries occur, and what outcomes are experienced, all for the purpose of identifying why and how the injuries occur (C.G. Caine, Caine, & Lindner, 1996).

Two key terms in the epidemiology of sport injury are *prevalence*, which refers to the number of injuries within a population at a single point in time, and *incidence*, which refers to the number of new injuries occurring within a population over a particular period of time (e.g., one year). Although informative, these frequency counts of injury do not tell the whole story of sport-injury risk. We can develop a more complete understanding through the concept of *exposure*, which refers to an instance of opportunity to become injured while participating in sport. Of course, the more an athlete is exposed to risk through involvement in sport, the more likely he or she is to experience injury. Beyond this generalization, we can illustrate the importance of accounting for exposure by examining sex differences in risk for sport injury.

Although the incidence of sport injury in adolescent athletes is sometimes two or more times higher in boys than in girls (Conn et al., 2003; Knowles, 2010), that difference can disappear or even be reversed when risk is expressed in terms of the number of injuries per athlete exposure—that is, an index that adjusts for exposure (for a review, see Knowles, 2010). Similarly, the oft-cited statistic that girls have a higher rate of ACL tear per athlete exposure than do boys (Prodromos, Han, Rogowski, Joyce, & Shi, 2007) means that within a population consisting both of equal numbers of male and female athletes and equal amounts of exposure to risk through training and competition, one could expect more females than males to incur an ACL tear. Thus, in populations in which more males than females

participate in sport—and therefore collectively expose themselves to a greater degree of risk, as is often the case in school settings—more males than females may experience an ACL tear, yet individual females still face elevated risk for the injury as compared with males.

Epidemiological investigators in sport often measure factors thought to confer risk for injury, (e.g., demographic, anthropometric, environmental, medical-history, and training variables) and record the athlete exposures (i.e., practices and competitions), sport injuries, and sport injury outcomes in a given population of athletes over a period of time. This research approach helps investigators not only determine prevalence and incidence of injury but also identify risk factors for the types of injury sustained by the athlete population during the period of study. In other words, investigators can use findings from epidemiological studies to trace patterns of injury and, when the research methods are strong, gain insights into the causes and mechanisms of injury; these insights can then be incorporated into injury prevention efforts (C.G. Caine et al., 1996).

Sport injury epidemiologists face numerous challenges, including the fact that their studies can be costly, time consuming, and logistically demanding. Fortunately, large-scale, computerized, Internet-based surveillance systems can help in the following ways:

- Determining what should be measured and how it should be measured
- Monitoring athlete exposures, injuries, and injury outcomes
- Centralizing data collected at multiple satellite locations
- Archiving the information obtained for the scientific community to examine

Although epidemiological findings are best viewed as estimates—perhaps even underestimates (Darrow et al., 2009)—of the magnitude of the sport injury problem, they are vitally important in gauging the relative risk of various sport activities and assessing the effectiveness of preventive practices and interventions.

Focus on Research

rehabilitation following reconstructive knee surgery. This information helps us understand why he reacted the way he did and can inform decisions about how best to treat his injury.

Sometimes sport injuries are just what they appear to be; at other times, however, there is more to the story than meets the eye. Tyrell had misinterpreted the initial blow to his knee and the immediate symptoms it produced as a repeat of the incident in which he had suffered an ACL tear. When this fear is coupled with the social pressure he felt while performing in front of his friends and family members—not to mention professional scouts—his response to the new injury makes sense.

Clearly, then, in order to thoroughly understand sport injury, we must adopt a broad, holistic approach that goes well beyond the immediate medical circumstances and incorporates multiple perspectives. Tyrell's response to his injury involved a wide variety of biological, psychological, and social factors. From a biological standpoint, his health status was affected by the collision he initiated with the opposing running back and the tissue damage he sustained as a result. Psychologically, his response to the injury encompassed the domains of cognition (i.e., thought, or his interpretation of the meaning of the injury), emotion (e.g., his tears and obvious distress), and behavior (e.g., his calling out and slapping the ground). Less obvious, but no less important, is the part played by social factors. Competing before pro scouts may have prompted Tyrell to play with even more disregard for his physical well-being than usual and, after being injured, to try to prove to spectators just how injured he thought he was.

In contrast, *failing* to consider biological, psychological, and social influences leaves us with an incomplete picture of an athlete's injury. Consequently, though this book focuses primarily on psychological aspects of sport injury, it should be assumed that in any given situation, psychological factors may be interacting with biological and social factors to affect the prevention, treatment, and rehabilitation of sport injury. Historically, however, this assumption has not been widely promoted in sport health care, which has evolved as a subspecialty over the past three-quarters of a century in response to the increased incidence of sport injury (which, in turn, is associated with a concomitant rise in sport participation).

More recently, scientific professional societies and scholarly publications have helped disseminate research findings that provide an empirical basis for professional training and clinical practice. Although most of the advances in the prevention, diagnosis, and treatment of sport injury have taken place in the physical realm, a parallel literature has emerged to address psychological aspects of sport injury. Over the past four decades, the psychology of sport injury has become a topic of scientific study across multiple disciplines (J.M. Williams & Andersen, 2007) and has been increasingly incorporated into the curricula of educational programs in sport health care.

Professionals Potentially Involved in the Prevention and Rehabilitation of Sport Injury

The broadening conception of the causes, consequences, and appropriate treatments for sport injury has resulted in an expanding array of professionals with whom injured athletes may come into contact. Today, Tyrell and other athletes in similar circumstances may encounter representatives of a panoply of disciplines on their journey through the sport health care system. Among the personnel identified by Kolt and Snyder-Mackler (2007) as potentially being involved in the prevention and management of sport injury are the following (in alphabetical order): athletic trainers, chiropractors, coaches, dentists, dietitians and nutritionists, fitness coaches, massage therapists, nurses, occupational therapists, optometrists, orthotists, physical therapists, physicians (family and primary care physicians, orthopedic surgeons, osteopaths, radiologists, sport physicians), podiatrists, psychologists and sport psychologists, and sport scientists (e.g., biomechanists, exercise physiologists). That list could easily be expanded to include acupuncturists, neurologists, neuropsychologists, physical therapy assistants, and strength and conditioning specialists.

Some of these professionals are likely to act as first responders to injury, whereas others are likely to be involved primarily in diagnosis, treatment, rehabilitation, or prevention. Of course, no single athlete is likely to see—and no single treatment team is likely to include—*all* of these professionals. The practitioners are involved mostly in the physical domain, but a perspective incorporating biological, psychological, and social aspects of sport injury can enable individuals from different disciplines to work together in service of a common goal—to provide athletes with comprehensive care.

Focus on Application

Understanding and Preventing Sport Injury

The chapters presented here provide a foundation for the biopsychosocial approach adopted throughout the rest of the book. They also offer a vivid illustration of how the approach can be used to address issues associated with the occurrence of sport injury. Specifically, part I outlines biological, psychological, and social aspects of sport injury and locates them within the pertinent sociocultural context. It then demonstrates the advantages of applying a biopsychosocial approach to the prediction and prevention of sport injury. It also shows that even for injury-related phenomena with substantial biological components, we can thoroughly understand them only if we consider the relevant psychological and social factors.

Chapter 1

Biopsychosocial Foundations of Sport Injury

Chapter Objectives

1. To identify biological, psychological, and social underpinnings of sport injury
2. To discuss and illustrate the implications of adopting a biopsychosocial approach to conceptualizing sport injury
3. To foster appreciation of the sociocultural context in which sport injury occurs

"I'll bet half of the half-million views are mine," Lisa thought to herself as she played the famous Kerri Strug video from the 1996 Olympic Games for the fifth straight time. "Just a few more days and the pain will stop." Like Strug, Lisa had hurt her ankle on the vault and was "toughing it out" for the team. Unlike Strug, however, Lisa's injury had not been viewed by millions on television. In fact, because Lisa had sustained her injury at the end of a practice, none of her coaches had seen it happen, and only she and her roommate even knew about it. After under-rotating the landing on her vault, she had known right away that her ankle was seriously damaged. Despite the intense pain, she had told the teammate observing her vault that she had merely twisted her ankle and was "fine."

Lisa had then avoided the athletic training room, knowing that the staff would take one look at her ankle and rescind her clearance to participate in the upcoming collegiate conference championships—the event that she had been training for all winter. Next, she had sworn her roommate to secrecy; not even her teammates could know what had happened, because word might get back to the coaches. She had also bought herself a little healing time by feigning a migraine, which had gotten her out of practice (and school) for a couple of days. Meanwhile, she had gobbled ibuprofen pills by the handful (and had the stomach pains to prove it), had her roommate procure large amounts of crushed ice from the dining hall, and watched the YouTube clip constantly for inspiration.

When Lisa could no longer avoid practice without arousing suspicion, she wrapped her ankle as tightly as she could stand and acted as healthy as she could while going through the motions of training. She went straight to her room after each practice and collapsed on her bed, mentally drained from the effort of concealing her injury and with her ankle howling in pain. "Just a few more days and the pain will stop . . . ."

Why would Lisa put herself through such an ordeal and risk permanent damage to her ankle? She was not at risk of missing the Olympics or even the national championships. What could she possibly have expected to gain by pulling such a stunt? Did she have any idea what could happen if her ankle became further traumatized? Was she stupid? As it turns out, Lisa was quite intelligent and, as an athletic training major, had a pretty good idea of what was wrong with her ankle (third-degree sprain and tendon damage, just like Kerri Strug) and what could happen if things went wrong at the conference championships. Yet, despite her intelligence and medical knowledge, she persisted in concealing her injury and participating in her sport. What would prompt an otherwise logical and insightful young woman to place her well-being at risk?

From a physical standpoint, it is easy to explain how Lisa's injury happened and why it might not be healing as quickly as it could. Her ankle was damaged due to the force it was exposed to in her under-rotated landing, and that damage was repeatedly aggravated by the stress placed on her ankle while she kept training for the conference championships. This purely physical perspective does not, of course, explain why Lisa concealed her injury and continued to traumatize her ankle by engaging in vigorous weight-bearing activity in spite of the intense pain. As with the case of Tyrell in this book's introduction, Lisa's situation is much easier to understand when psychological and social factors are brought into the equation.

Lisa had set a goal to compete and help her team in the conference championships. Not wanting to let her coaches and teammates down, she did what she thought was necessary to achieve her aims; in so doing, she adopted attitudes and behaviors that are common—indeed, glorified—in the world of sport. Therefore, although Lisa's actions might cause sport health care professionals to shake their heads, her case makes a strong argument for adopting the biopsychosocial approach to sport injury that is advocated in this book.

A Biopsychosocial Perspective

The idea that the mind influences health can be traced back more than two millennia to the medical systems of several ancient societies. In each of these systems, physical and psychological functioning were considered to be intertwined. For example, according to the humoral theory of Hippocrates—the Greek physician best known for his oath to practice medicine ethically—an individual's health status and personality were determined by the relative balance among four bodily fluids or humors (i.e., blood, red bile, black bile, and phlegm). Similarly, maintaining a harmonious internal balance between physical and mental aspects is considered crucial for health in the medical traditions of China (East Asian medicine) and India (Ayurvedic medicine).

For the past two centuries, however, the predominant perspective on health has been the biomedical model, which holds that the mind and the body are separate entities and that health is affected solely by physical factors (Straub, 2012). Even so, during the twentieth and twenty-first centuries, the mind has reemerged as a recognized potential contributor to health. Although the biomedical model has facilitated tremendous advances in the diagnosis and treatment of physical disorders, it has been unable to explain either the effectiveness of treatments with no apparent biological mechanism (e.g., the placebo effect) or the occurrence of medical conditions with no obvious biological cause.

Sigmund Freud referred to these latter conditions as "conversion disorders" and attributed them to the conversion of unconscious psychological conflicts into biological disturbances. Elaborating on this position, the field of psychosomatic medicine was founded on the notion that faulty mental processes could cause a wide variety of physical problems, such as bronchial asthma, essential hypertension, migraine headache, rheumatoid arthritis, and ulcers. On the positive side, research showed that people can gain willful control over physiological functions (e.g., blood pressure, resting heart rate) by applying learning principles in the form of biofeedback. These findings spurred the advent of behavioral medicine, an interdisciplinary field that involves the biomedical, psychological, and social sciences and focuses both on treating illness and on promoting health. These developments set the stage for the emergence in the 1970s of the branch of psychology known as health psychology and—central to the purpose of this chapter—the biopsychosocial model (Straub, 2012).

Engel (1977, 1980) proposed the biopsychosocial model specifically to address the limitations of the biomedical model and to incorporate a full array of factors that contribute to health. As its name suggests, the biopsychosocial model posits the joint influence of biological, psychological, and social factors on health. It is not a true model in the strict scientific sense of the word, because it does not specify which factors should contribute to a given health problem or how those factors relate to each other; that is, it does not generate the testable predictions required of a scientific model. Rather, the biopsychosocial model offers a general framework that encourages us to examine biological, psychological, and social

factors when we attempt to explain and treat medical conditions. As a result, this book uses the term "biopsychosocial *approach*" rather than "biopsychosocial *model*."

As depicted in figure 1.1, adopting a biopsychosocial approach has two main implications for understanding sport injury. First, the occurrence of sport injury is influenced by interactions between biological, psychological, and social variables. As shown in chapter 2, even when a biological factor (e.g., a blow to the leg) is ultimately responsible for an injury, psychological and social factors (e.g., distracted attention, stressful life events) may help create the situation that puts the athlete in a position to sustain the injury (i.e., blow to the leg). The second implication is that sport injury can affect not only physical functioning but also psychological and social functioning (for more on this topic, see chapter 4). This potential is vividly illustrated, for example, in the chapter-opening scenario about Lisa's risky decision making and her patterns of interaction with her peers and coaches after her ankle injury.

In this way, each subcategory of the biopsychosocial approach—that is, the biological, the psychological, and the social—includes

Figure 1.1 A biopsychosocial approach to sport injury.

an abundance of factors potentially related to sport injury. These many factors constitute the biological, psychological, and social foundations of sport injury.

Biological Foundations

At its core, sport injury is a biological phenomenon. When an athlete sustains an injury, a biological structure is damaged, and recovery is achieved through a biological process. Therefore, although the biological events involved in a sport injury may affect—and be affected by—psychological and social factors, we cannot deny the primacy of biological factors. The biological foundations of sport injury include the characteristics of injury, the healing and rehabilitation processes, and the associated body systems.

Characteristics of Sport Injury

A sport injury can be classified along multiple biological dimensions, including mechanism, location, type, and severity. In terms of mechanism, an injury can be classified as either traumatic or involving overuse. Traumatic injury results when external or internal forces place excessive strain on body tissue, thus causing deformation that persists after the forces have been removed (Prentice, 2011). Such "macrotrauma" injuries can usually be traced to a single, identifiable, pathomechanical incident in which an athlete notices that he or she has sustained an injury. Overuse (or "microtrauma") injury, on the other hand, occurs when repeated pathomechanical overloading over an extended period of time produces microscopic breakdown in body tissue; examples include tendinitis and stress fracture (Flint, 1998; L. Peterson & Renström, 2001).

Classification of sport injury by location is performed at multiple analytical levels. At the most general level, an injury is distinguished by whether it involves the head, the torso, an upper extremity (i.e., something above the hips, typically a shoulder, arm, wrist, or hand) or a lower extremity (i.e., something from the hips to the toes). As the level of analysis becomes more specific, injury location can be designated with increasing precision, progressing from specific body parts within the upper or lower extremity (e.g., knee, shoulder) to structures within a given body part (e.g., anterior cruciate ligament, glenohumeral joint) and then to locations detectable only with a microscope or other enlarging technology.

Injury location is related closely to type of injury, which depends at least partly on which body parts are vulnerable and which kinds of tissue inhabit those parts. Fractures, for example, can occur in bones but not in muscles. In addition to fractures, common types of injury include muscle strains; ligament sprains; joint dislocations; ruptures in muscles, ligaments, and tendons; and various soft-tissue injuries, such as hematomas (including contusions [bruises] and more serious blood clots under the skin), abrasions (scratches that affect primarily the epidermis [skin]), and punctures (which occur to the epidermis and proximal tissues) (Flint, 1998; L. Peterson & Renström, 2001).

Classifying sport injuries on the basis of severity carries intuitive appeal. Presumably, of course, injuries graded as severe involve more extensive tissue damage than those graded as mild, and this assumption holds true for some parts of the body. Injuries to the lateral ligaments of the ankle, for example, range from grade I (partial rupture of the calcaneofibular ligament, the anterior talofibular ligament, or both) to grade III (full rupture of both). For such ankle injuries, grade of injury may figure in treatment decisions (Bahr, 2004). For other injuries, however, severity classification depends on criteria that are more behavioral than biological. When factors such as function and time loss (i.e., time away from sport participation) are incorporated into determinations of injury severity, it is less clear how much of the severity assessment involves damage to biological structures and how much it involves psychological and social variables (e.g., motivation, pain tolerance, and coach influence) (Flint, 1998).

Healing and Rehabilitation Processes

In contrast to the destructive nature of sport injury, healing and rehabilitation processes perform restorative functions within the body. It is widely thought that these processes involve three nondiscrete, overlapping phases through which athletes pass on the way to recovery:

1. Inflammatory response phase
2. Fibroblastic repair (proliferation) phase
3. Maturation-remodeling phase

Various terms have been used to label the phases, which refer primarily to soft tissue. Although the chronology, treatment goals, and underlying processes of the phases vary considerably across injury locations and types, healing is also characterized by some cross-injury constants. During the first phase, interactions between chemicals (e.g., histamine, leukotrienes, and cytokines) initiate an inflammatory response, in which phagocytes are attracted to the injured area to clean the wound. During the second phase, fibers of collagen protein are deposited, and a firm scar is formed. Finally, during the third phase, collagen is realigned (or "remodeled"), and the normal appearance and function of the affected tissue is restored (Prentice, 2011).

Like healing, rehabilitation restores the structure and function of injured body tissue. In the context of sport injury, rehabilitation also involves maximizing the injured athlete's functional capacity, fitness, and performance. As with healing, we can identify three phases of sport injury rehabilitation. During the first phase, rehabilitation aims to limit tissue damage, relieve pain, control inflammation, and protect the injured area. During the second phase, it focuses on limiting impairments (e.g., atrophy, weakness, range-of-motion restrictions) that could lead to loss of functions that are critical to sport performance (Frontera, 2003). Rehabilitative activities during this phase are intended to increase flexibility, strength, proprioception, coordination, and endurance (Frontera; L. Peterson & Renström, 2001). These activities typically include a major psychological component in that they consist of behavior (i.e., performing exercises). The third phase involves preparing athletes for a return to sport training and competition (Frontera); as with the second phase, behavior figures prominently in this phase as athletes work to reacquire sport-specific skills (L. Peterson & Renström).

Body Systems

In keeping with this book's holistic approach of integrating disparate influences on—and consequences of—sport injury, let us now consider the various body systems associated with sport injury. For the most part, the systems are interrelated, such that changes in one system initiate changes in one or more other systems. Unquestionably, the body system most substantially involved in sport injury is the musculoskeletal system, which gives the body its shape, protects vital organs, executes movement commands given by the somatic nervous system, and provides the body with support and stability. Consisting of bones, cartilage, muscles, joints, and connective tissues (e.g., tendons, ligaments), the musculoskeletal system is affected in about 80 percent of sport injuries (Zemper, 1993). In fact, it is not only the most common location of sport injury but also can facilitate rehabilitation (through completion of prescribed exercises) and signify recovery (through return to a suitable level of functional performance).

Other body systems associated with sport injury include the circulatory, digestive, endocrine, epidermal, immune, nervous, reproductive, and respiratory systems. Of these, the nervous system has the most pronounced association with sport injury, because it is not only a common site of sport injury (e.g., concussion, compressed nerve) but also a means to achieve injury prevention and recovery. For example, cognitive and behavioral interventions for preventing and rehabilitating sport injury are generally mediated by the central nervous system—specifically, the brain and spinal cord. The other body systems are occasionally, but not typically, injured in the course of sport participation. As shown in table 1.1, they do, however, play active parts in injury prevention and recovery.

Psychological Foundations

As with its biological foundations, sport injury affects and is affected by multiple interrelated psychological aspects. In particular,

TABLE 1.1   Examples of Potential Connections Between Body Systems and Sport Injury

Body system	Examples of potential connection with sport injury
Circulatory	Contributes to success of inflammatory phase; delivers nutrients for tissue repair
Digestive	Delivers nutrients essential for healing to cells
Endocrine	Experiences changes in response to stress (before injury) and to injury itself
Epidermal	Is often an injury location; is a point of contact for therapeutic modalities
Immune	Facilitates inflammatory response to injury
Musculoskeletal	Is often an injury location; executes rehabilitation activities; signifies recovery through functional behavior
Nervous	May be an injury location; mediates cognitive and behavioral interventions for prevention and rehabilitation
Reproductive	Transmits inherited somatic weaknesses from parents to offspring
Respiratory	Declines in efficiency due to postinjury detraining; enables breathing exercises as part of psychological intervention for prevention and rehabilitation

psychological areas that are directly relevant to sport injury include perception, cognition, motivation, emotion, behavior, and several integrative concepts (see table 1.2 for a summary).

Perception

Perception—the process of interpreting or making sense of sensory input—is associated with sport injury at a fundamental level. Indeed, the perceptual level is often where athletes first determine that their sensations indicate injury rather than mere discomfort, soreness, fatigue, exertion, or other benign causes. More objective methods may be used to confirm the initial diagnostic impressions of athletes, coaches, and sport health care professionals, but perception plays a primary role in the process.

Cognition

Cognition consists of the mental activities associated with thinking and knowing. Cognitive aspects relevant to sport injury include structure, content, and process.

Cognitive Structure

Cognitive structure relates to the way in which thoughts are organized. Typically, one's

thoughts are not scattered randomly about one's mind; instead, like thoughts are often grouped together in structures known as schemas or beliefs. Each time we see a car, for example, we process information about that car in relation to what we already know about automobiles (e.g., made of metal and plastic, guided by a steering wheel, propelled by an engine, rolled on rubber tires). Our automobile schema allows us to streamline the process of perceiving and thinking about cars (which can be mighty convenient during a traffic-filled commute!).

In the context of sport injury, cognitive structures can produce either facilitative or debilitative effects, depending on the particular beliefs that are activated. For example, an athlete who perceives physical symptoms as indicating injury might seek treatment from a sport health care professional based on the belief that one should obtain medical assistance upon sustaining an injury. In contrast, if an athlete perceives dealing with physical symptoms as part of an athlete's responsibility to be mentally tough and battle adversity, she or he might delay seeking treatment from a sport health care professional. In both cases, the athlete's behavior is guided not by the physical symptoms themselves

TABLE 1.2   Examples of Psychological Aspects Relevant to Sport Injury

Psychological aspect	Example of relevance to sport injury
Perception	An athlete distinguishes injury from soreness.
Cognition	
· Cognitive structure	An athlete fails to seek treatment due to a belief that athletes should be tough.
· Cognitive content	An athlete encourages herself to do her rehabilitation exercises.
· Cognitive process	
· Memory	An athlete forgets how to do his rehabilitation exercises.
· Attention	An athlete fails to notice bodily symptoms of injury.
· Attribution	An athlete blames her coach for her overuse injury.
· Decision making	An athlete decides to seek treatment for pain.
Emotion	An athlete experiences sadness following injury.
Motivation	An athlete feels driven to complete his rehabilitation before the season starts.
Behavior	An athlete's aggressive style of play increases her risk of injury.
Learning	An athlete acquires skills to reduce stress and thereby decrease vulnerability to injury.
Personality	An optimistic athlete perseveres throughout a lengthy rehabilitation.
Psychopathology	An athlete replaces the thrill of sport participation with persistent high-stakes gambling while recovering from injury and continues gambling thereafter.

but by beliefs about physical symptoms and what they mean.

Cognitive Content

Cognitive content refers to *what* a person is thinking about; therefore, it encompasses people's thoughts, images, and internal dialogue (self-talk). This aspect of cognition is important to sport injury because in some cases it is a person's thoughts themselves—*not* how those thoughts are organized (i.e., not their cognitive structure)—that influence the person's functioning. Cognitive content can vary in terms of both valence (tone) and function. Self-talk characterized by a prominent positive or negative tone can directly affect emotions, thus coloring a person's inner world in a certain way. A negative internal dialogue, for example, can leave a person feeling sad or depressed, whereas positive self-talk can boost a person's mood. With respect to function, some cognition is purely informational (e.g., "I am supposed to do three sets of my rehab exercis-

es each day"), whereas other cognition serves a motivational purpose (e.g., "Come on—push it and finish strong"). From an applied standpoint, cognitive content is often used as a point of entry in psychological interventions for sport injury prevention and rehabilitation.

Cognitive Process

Cognitive process involves *how* people think, know, and pertain to input, storage, transformation, and output of information within a cognitive system. Processes of particular relevance to sport injury include memory, attention, attribution, and decision making. Memory involves retaining and recalling information; it affects sport injury when, for example, an athlete remembers the details of an injury episode, forgets to do (or how to do) his or her rehabilitation exercises, or experiences postconcussive amnesia. In contrast, attention involves selectively concentrating or focusing on aspects of the internal or external environment. One's attention level can play a role in sport injury in various ways. For example, distractedness can place an athlete at greater risk of injury during sport performance; it can also decrease an athlete's awareness of painful sensations during rehabilitation. Attribution is the process by which people explain the causes of behaviors and events. Athletes engage in attributional thought, for instance, when they generate explanations for injuries and assign responsibility (e.g., to themselves, others, or factors beyond anyone's control) for their recovery.

Decision making—the process of determining a course of action from among multiple options—is relevant to sport injury from the time before the injury occurs through the athlete's return to sport after rehabilitation. Examples include athletes' decisions about whether to inform their coaches and sport health care professionals about their physical symptoms, whether to train with a painful body part, whether to adhere to prescribed rehabilitation regimens, and whether to resume sport training. Athletes have varying levels of decision-making autonomy, depending on the situation, the setting, and the particular decision in question; the process may, or may not, be shared with parents, coaches, sport health care professionals, or administrators. For example, scholastic and collegiate athletes generally have less input into decisions about returning to play after sustaining a concussion than after incurring a blow to the thigh that produces no detectable damage other than a large bruise.

Emotion

Emotions are psychophysiological states characterized by physiological arousal, expressed actions, and experienced feelings. In terms of sport injury, emotions are most relevant to athletes' adjustment to injury and their approach to the hurdles they encounter on the way to recovery. Emotion may be triggered, for example, by the injury occurrence itself and then by surgery, rehabilitation setbacks, and a successful return to sport. As discussed in chapter 2, emotions may also be involved in the occurrence of injury.

Motivation

Motivation is the force that drives and directs behavior, whether derived from outside the individual (extrinsic motivation) or inside the individual (intrinsic motivation). Motivation is relevant to sport injury from before the occurrence of injury through the conclusion of rehabilitation and the return to sport. More specifically, it prompts athletes to put themselves into risky sport situations that produce injury, to complete rehabilitation programs after injury, and to attempt to resume sport participation after recovering from injury.

Behavior

Like motivation, behavior, which consists of observable actions, is relevant across the full sport injury time line. For example, athletes who train excessively or play recklessly place themselves at increased risk for injury. On the other hand, athletes who adhere to postinjury activity restrictions and take prescribed medications may accelerate their recoveries; similarly, athletes who transition gradually back into full training may reduce the likelihood of reinjury. One might view these factors—excessive training, risky play, adherence to restrictions, medication compliance, and gradual resumption of training—as physical variables, but they do not exist in the absence of behavior. Ultimately, then, though the physical properties or results of the behavior affect an athlete's injury risk, recovery time, and reinjury risk, these physical effects are delivered by the vehicle of behavior.

Integrative Concepts

Several key psychological foundations of sport injury are integrative in that they combine multiple psychological aspects; three examples are learning, personality, and psychopathology. Learning refers to relatively permanent changes in behavior and mental processes as a result of experience. Like motivation and behavior, learning is ubiquitous across the sport injury time line. Learning can exert either positive or negative effects. For example, athletes can learn ways of coping with stress that reduce their injury risk. On the other hand, athletes can also learn technical or tactical "bad habits" that predispose them to injury, as well as associations between certain cues and pain, strategies to rationalize avoidance of rehabilitation exercises, and "bracing" or "guarding" responses to return-to-sport activities.

Personality consists of stable patterns of cognition, emotion, and behavior that are characteristic of a person—that is, a given individual's consistent ways of thinking, feeling, and acting. Personality is not thought to be *directly* related to sport injury outcomes (e.g., injury occurrence, recovery rate). It is, however, viewed as a facilitator of cognitions, emotions, and behaviors that are more closely tied to such outcomes.

Psychopathology involves abnormal behavior and mental processes. Common psychopathological conditions (e.g., depression, anxiety) are marked by prominent cognitive, emotional, behavioral, and physiological components that can impair an athlete's ability to avoid injury, stick with a rehabilitation program, and return successfully to sport participation.

Social Foundations

On the surface, it might appear that, as compared with biological and psychological factors, social factors are far removed from the immediacy of sport injury. After all, sport injuries happen within the bodies of athletes who sustain damage to biological structures and experience the mental and physical repercussions of that damage. To the extent that social factors are located outside of athletes, it can indeed be argued that those factors are more distant than are biological and psychological factors. Nonetheless, the influence of the social domain on sport injury should *not* be underestimated, because it permeates every aspect of sport injury—from the athlete's preinjury state to his or her postinjury return to sport. In particular, social influences on sport injury are exerted both through the cultural context in which sport exists and through athletes' social relationships.

Culture of Risk

Beginning with their first experience in the sport environment, athletes are socialized into a culture marked by distinctive values, norms, roles, and expectations. From coaches, teammates, parents, and the media, athletes

The Interrelated Psychological Foundations of Sport Injury

Sport injury affects, and is affected by, a variety of psychological aspects, which are themselves interrelated—a fact that carries important practical implications. Just as medical interventions targeting one body system can produce consequences (intended or unintended) for other body systems, interventions directed at one psychological element can affect other psychological elements. In other words, a treatment designed to modify the cognitive content of athletes may affect not only the athletes' cognitive functioning but also their emotional and behavioral functioning. For example, increasing the positivity of an athlete's cognitive content may also improve her mood and energize her behavior. Professionals who regularly implement psychological interventions not only anticipate such interrelationships—they count on them! Thus, the integration of the major components of the biopsychosocial approach is mirrored by interrelationships between its subcomponents, and it plays out to noticeable effect in applied practice.

Focus on Application

learn—and in many cases internalize—what has been referred to as the "sport ethic." According to Hughes and Coakley (1991), this ethic or value system sets forth criteria for being what is thought of as a "real athlete." In this definition, "real" athletes are those who make sacrifices for sport, strive for distinction in sport, accept risks and play through pain, and refuse "to accept limits in pursuit of possibilities" (p. 310).

Each of these criteria carries implications for sport injury. The sacrifices that athletes make for sport may well include their health and well-being. For example, in trying to distance themselves from competitors and achieve distinction, athletes may willingly risk their safety and play through pain in training and competition. By refusing to accept their limitations—and, instead, doggedly pursuing their sport goals against all odds—they may also expose their bodies to overuse. Such sacrifices, and the single-minded pursuit of goals, are reinforced by the sport community and are in fact characteristic of a culture in which risk is commonplace (Frey, 1991; Nixon, 1992).

Characteristics

Nixon (1992) described high-level sport as inhabiting a "culture of risk" in which athletes are

- socialized to accept pain and injury as normal parts of sport participation,
- encouraged to ignore pain and play hurt, and
- reinforced for concealing their injuries and those of their teammates.

As part of the largely closed social environment of sport, athletes spend considerable time interacting with other members of the sport system. In this setting, they are exposed to messages that glorify the courage of athletes who sacrifice themselves for the good of the team and play through pain and injury. Such glorification of risky behavior has been tied to affirmation of a masculine identity in male athletes (Messner, 1990, 1992; K. Young, 1993; K. Young, White, & McTeer, 1994). These athletes, particularly those who participate in violent contact sports (e.g., American football, boxing, rugby, wrestling), often affirm their manhood through sport by displaying toughness and concealing pain (K. Young et al., 1994). Male athletes who express pain overtly, or miss a competition due to an injury perceived as insufficiently severe, run the risk of being called "soft" (or worse) or having their masculinity (or sexual orientation) questioned. This tendency was infamously illustrated, for example, when legendary National Football League coach Bill Parcells referred to injured wide receiver Terry Glenn as "she."

Even so, the culture of risk is not limited to male sports and male athletes. Like male athletes, female athletes have been found to push stoically through pain and injury in order to demonstrate courage and character, gain playing time, and adhere to the behavioral expectations of sport (Madrigal, Robbins, Gill, & Wurst, 2015; Malcom, 2006; K. Young & White, 1995). At the same time, differences do exist in the ways that men and women approach pain and injury in sport. Specifically, as compared with male athletes, female athletes may be more likely to experience injury and its bodily effects as threats to their attractiveness and gender identity (in this case, femininity), and share their experiences of pain and injury with their teammates (Charlesworth & Young, 2006).

Transmission

Researchers have yet to thoroughly investigate the process by which athletes become aware of and adopt the values and beliefs of the sport ethic and, more specifically, the culture of risk. It is clear, however, that the relevant cultural information is transmitted in large part by both the media and the people in athletes' social networks; both groups also play key roles in helping athletes internalize that cultural information. With respect to the media, Nixon (1993a) analyzed the contents of more than 22 years of articles from the popular U.S. magazine *Sports Illustrated* and identified 243 separate items addressing issues associated with pain, injury, and disability. Based on this analysis, along with the magazine's wide circulation, Nixon concluded that "athletes are exposed to . . . messages that tell them they must play as long as possible with pain and injuries and must try to come back as soon as possible after serious injuries" (p. 188). Beyond the print media, of course, athletes are also exposed to similar messages through television, movies, and Internet content.

Athletes also receive more direct and more personal messages about the sport ethic and the culture of risk from fellow members of the sport community with whom they interact on a regular basis. Nixon (1992) used the term *sportsnets* to refer to the "webs of interaction" that link members of a social network in a given sport setting. According to Nixon, these sportsnets provide the means by which information about the culture of risk is communicated to athletes. Typical sportsnets in high-level sport consist of people in four general roles: sport administrator, coach, sport health care professional, and athlete. Although members of a given sportsnet pursue some goals in common (e.g., competitive success for the sport organization), they are also likely to form divergent motives based on their respective roles in the sportsnet. Let us now explore these roles.

Sport Administrator   Sport administrators play powerful roles in sportsnets—for example, athletic director, executive board member, general manager, and owner. They may have little direct contact with athletes, but they establish institutional policies and procedures and generally exert considerable control over what happens in the sport environment. Despite this control, Nixon (1992) has argued that sport administrators (and the institutions they represent) are risk averse and therefore seek to shift responsibility for sport's inherent risks to athletes. As a result, athletes are exposed to risk in the arena of play on the grounds that it is "just part of the game" (Frey, 1991, p. 142), whereas sport administrators are insulated or protected from such hazards.

Coach   In contrast to sport administrators, coaches typically have extensive contact with athletes. They also play a central role in sportsnets because they simultaneously report to sport administrators and guide the participation of athletes and teams. Their incentives are often aligned with those of the athletes they coach, in that both coaches and athletes are rewarded when athletes and teams perform well. However, because coaches' fates can be tied to the competitive success (i.e., winning) of the athletes and teams under their supervision, situations can arise in which a coach's best interests may diverge from prioritizing the health and well-being of athletes. As a result, the coach may encourage athletes who are considered vital to competitive success to play hurt or return from injury too quickly. Because coaches hold power over athletes' playing time and status on the team, such situations put athletes in positions where they may feel compelled to risk damage to their health by playing (Nixon, 1992).

The idea that coaches' behavior regarding pain and injury is subject to the influence of competitive circumstances is supported by a study from Flint and Weiss (1992). The study found that high school and college basketball coaches made decisions about whether to re-

turn a hypothetical injured player to a game as a function of the player's status and the game situation. Specifically, coaches tended to return injured starters to the game when the score was close but keep them on the bench when the game's outcome was not in doubt (regardless of whether they were winning or losing). An opposite finding was obtained for injured nonstarters; that is, coaches tended to return injured reserves to the game when the score was not close and to keep them on the bench when the outcome of the game remained in doubt. These results reflect the portion of the coach's role that involves allocating playing time in a way that achieves the best possible competitive outcome.

To learn more about the role of coaches in the culture of risk, Nixon (1994a) surveyed 26 coaches of collegiate teams about the extent to which they agreed with 31 statements pertaining to risk, injury, and pain in sport. Consistent with an environment in which pain and injury are normalized in athletes, a majority of the coaches expressed either full agreement or agreement "with reservations" for 20 of the 31 statements, which included, for example, the following: "No pain, no gain." "Athletes who endure pain and play hurt deserve our respect." "Playing with injuries and pain demonstrates character and courage." However, the substantial number of statements for which respondents indicated either agreement with reservations or disagreement with reservations prompted Nixon to conclude that many of the coaches were ambivalent about pain and injury in sport and that they were subject to a "risk–pain–injury paradox," in which they "say they must push athletes to their physical limits but . . . do not want athletes to take excessive risks with their bodies" (p. 85).

Nixon (1994a) was careful to note that the findings in this study were based on coaches' reported beliefs rather than on their behavior per se, which may or may not have been consistent with their survey responses. Considering this caveat along with the results of the Flint and Weiss study (1992), it appears that although coaches may have noble intentions regarding the extent to which athletes should risk their health for the sake of sport, they may also alter their standards in situations where sport performance outcomes are on the line.

Sport Health Care Professional Health care personnel who work with athletes face a variant of the risk–pain–injury paradox (Nixon, 1994a) that is even more acute than the bind experienced by coaches. Charged with ensuring athletes' health, sport health care professionals are encouraged not only to restore health in injured athletes but also to return them as quickly as possible to the arena in which they were injured. This apparent paradox has been documented through qualitative research involving a variety of sport health care professionals. Specifically, interviews with sports medicine physicians, physiotherapists (Safai, 2003; Waddington, 2006), and student athletic trainers (Walk, 1997) suggest that acceptance and tolerance of risk, pain, and injury in sport are ubiquitous among sport health care professionals. Thus, the culture of risk is considered "part of the game" for this segment of sportsnets, too.

Some sport health care professionals have described experiencing pressure from coaches to expedite an athlete's return to sport competition faster than might be medically advisable, and in some cases they report making medical compromises with which they were not entirely comfortable (Waddington, 2006). Despite such pressure, which may also be exerted by athletes themselves, sport health care professionals have also reported that they are able to maintain focus on providing services in the best medical interests of athletes (Safai, 2003; Walk, 1997). Experimental backing for these claims of clinical objectivity was obtained by Flint and Weiss (1992), who administered the same procedures described earlier for research with coaches to athletic trainers working with high school and college basketball teams. Unlike the coaches' decisions, however, the athletic trainers' decisions about a hypothetical basketball player's return to play after an injury were *not* influenced by either the player's status or the game situation.

In addition, Safai (2004) concluded that physicians and physiotherapists in sports medicine are not only influenced *by* the prevailing social climate in sportsnets but also are able to *influence* that social climate through their behavior. Indeed, Safai (2004) proposed that sport health care professionals could counteract the culture of risk by establishing a "culture of precaution" that resists the culture of risk and promotes an environment in which "sensible risks" are taken after careful consideration. In fact, a culture of precaution is already somewhat evident in the case of head and brain injuries, regarding which a zero-tolerance approach is often taken to playing hurt (Safai, 2003). For more on sociocultural aspects of sport injury, see this chapter's Focus on Research box.

Athlete As noted by Nixon (1992) in his initial description of sportsnets and their role in the culture of risk, athletes learn that they must "be able to play hurt and come back from serious injuries . . . and accept or ignore the risks of pain and injuries" (p. 128). This assertion has been consistently supported by research examining the behaviors and beliefs of elite and nonelite athletes in Canada, the United Kingdom, and the United States in regard to risk, pain, and injury in sport (Liston et al., 2006; Nixon, 1994b; Safai, 2003; K. Young et al., 1994). The idea that pain and injury are normal parts of sport participation appears to be widely accepted among athletes.

Nixon (1992) also proposed that athletes receive a "biased" set of messages reaffirming the values and beliefs associated with the culture of risk from other members of the sportsnet, who collectively constitute a "collusive, closed system that attempts to isolate them from external social contact" (p. 130) and conspires to have them play in pain. Evidence supporting the first part of this claim—regarding messages that athletes receive about risk, pain, and injury—was obtained in a survey of 156 collegiate athletes (Nixon, 1994b). Nearly half of the athletes (49 percent) reported feeling pressured by coaches to play hurt; in addition, 41 percent reported feeling such pressure from teammates and 17 percent from athletic trainers.

The second (and more controversial) portion of the claim made by Nixon (1992)—regarding collusion by sportsnet members to isolate athletes from outside influences—remains without empirical support. In fact,

Documenting the Culture of Risk

From the mid-1980s through the mid-1990s, the sociocultural aspects of pain and injury were hot topics in the sociology of sport. During that fertile period, articles on the subject appeared regularly in professional journals. In particular, a trio of prolific scholars published multiple papers examining various sociological issues associated with pain and injury in sport, thereby laying a theoretical and empirical foundation on which subsequent investigators could build. Timothy Jon Curry (1986, 1993; Curry & Strauss, 1994; Strauss & Curry, 1983) got the ball rolling with a series of studies examining social factors, pain, and injury among competitive wrestlers. Kevin Young (1991, 1993; K. Young & White, 1995; K. Young et al., 1994) followed Curry's lead and brought gender roles into the discussion of risk and injury in sport. In addition, Howard L. Nixon II (1992, 1993a, 1993b, 1994a, 1994b, 1996a, 1996b) published a flurry of seven articles on pain and injury in sport from a sociological perspective over a five-year period. Best known for explicating the "culture of risk" that permeates sport, Nixon enjoyed an incredible run of scholarly productivity.

Subsequent research (e.g., Liston, Reacher, Smith, & Waddington, 2006; Safai, 2003; Walk, 1997) validated Nixon's ideas regarding the extent to which athletes and other members of their sport-related social networks (or "sportsnets") endorse the values and beliefs associated with the culture of risk. These endorsements emphasize the idea that risk, pain, and injury should be accepted, tolerated, and played through (Nixon, 1992). Some of Nixon's original assumptions about how sportsnets operate and impart the culture of risk to athletes have been questioned (e.g., Roderick, 1998) and challenged empirically, prompting him (Nixon, 1998) to note that "Walk's (1997) research concerning student athletic trainers casts some doubt on the idea of insulated, culturally homogenous, and conspiratorial sportsnets of athletes and student trainers" (p. 82).

In the ensuing dozen years or so, the sociocultural dimension of pain and injury in sport has remained a staple in the sociology of sport, as evidenced by the publication of a single-author book (Howe, 2004) and two edited volumes (Loland, Skirstad, & Waddington, 2006; K. Young, 2004) on the subject. Indeed, though the rate of scholarly productivity may have slowed since the mid-1990s, the topic is now being explored by a more diverse group of researchers. For example, the latter of the two edited volumes (Loland et al., 2006) featured scholars from seven nations, thus reflecting widespread interest in the topic. Most recently, attention to sociocultural issues has accompanied the explosion of scientific research on—and public awareness of—sport-related concussion, as multiple investigations have examined factors associated with athletes' level of willingness to disclose concussion symptoms (e.g., Davies & Bird, 2015; Z.Y. Kerr, Register-Mihalik, Kroshus, Baugh, & Marshall, 2016).

Although investigators have long recognized the psychological implications of sociocultural phenomena in sport injury (e.g., Flint & Weiss, 1992; Wiese-Bjornstal, Smith, Shaffer, & Morrey, 1998), few studies have examined the subject from a psychological perspective, and many important questions remain unanswered. Here are a few examples: By what developmental process do athletes internalize the culture of risk? How do athletes learn to balance the requirements of their sport with measures that help ensure their health and well-being? What cognitive processes underlie athletes' decisions to play hurt, as well as coaches' and sport administrators' decisions to allow athletes to do so? Can the culture of risk be modified without fundamentally altering the nature of sport? Answers to these and other key questions ramify in the realm of professional practice and therefore warrant attention from sport scientists.

Focus on Research

Walk (1997) presented evidence that athletes sometimes seek medical attention outside of their sportsnet and that although athletes may experience pressure from coaches to play hurt, such pressure is not implemented in a coordinated, consistent way across the sportsnet. Examining the relevant data, Roderick (1998) likewise rejected the notion that sportsnets conspired and colluded against athletes stating that "the risks of pain and debilitating injury . . . cannot be explained simply in terms of the planned intentions of coaches, management, owners, and other 'powerful' individuals" (p. 77).

On the whole, although athletes are firmly entrenched in the culture of risk and subject to its influences, they are also capable of acting autonomously in the face of risk, pain, and injury. Walk (1997) stated that "we should not view athletes as 'dupes' in minimizing the roles and responsibilities they may play in exercising sovereignty over the treatment of their own bodies" (p. 54). Toward this end, Walk showed that by willfully disregarding medical recommendations and hiding injuries from coaches and sport health care professionals, athletes testified "to their relative freedom to use athletic training services at their own discretion" (p. 51). Similarly, athletes interviewed by Safai (2003) reported engaging in "intrapersonal negotiation" (i.e., internal discussions) about when and under which circumstances to seek treatment for conditions that are painful but not severe enough to preclude sport participation.

Social Support

Of course, not all of an athlete's social interactions pertain to the culture of risk; in fact, most of an athlete's contact with other people involves matters other than risk, pain, and injury. Moreover, a portion of an athlete's relationships can generally be labeled as *social support*. This type of relationship has been evaluated in many ways, including the number of one's social relationships; the assistance one perceives as being available from others; the assistance one actually receives (House & Kahn, 1985); the exchange of resources between two or more people resulting in enhanced well-being for the recipient (Richman, Rosenfeld, & Hardy, 1993; Shumaker & Brownell, 1984); and companionship that provides emotional comfort, material help, or informational feedback (Straub, 2012). Despite the variability in how social support is defined, it is generally agreed that social support can involve multiple dimensions, providers, and functions.

Dimensions of Social Support

Various schemes have been proposed to describe the ways in which people provide support to one another. Common elements in these schemes include three kinds of support: emotional, informational, and tangible (Hardy, Burke, & Crace, 1999). Emotional support involves caring for, comforting, instilling a sense of belonging in, listening to, reassuring, and showing concern and empathy for another person. Informational support provides advice, guidance, and, of course, information; tangible support, in contrast, provides material goods, monetary assistance, and personal services. Athletes receive these forms of social support from a variety of providers.

Providers of Social Support

Providers of social support for athletes include both the members of their sportsnets (i.e., coaches, sport administrators, sport health care professionals, and other athletes) and people *outside* of their sportsnets (in particular, partners and significant others, friends, and family members). Different providers may give athletes different kinds of support (Rosenfeld, Richman, & Hardy, 1989). For example, a collegiate softball player might receive emotional support from her partner or significant other and her friends, informational support from her coach and athletic trainer, and tangible support from her parents and other family members.

Functions of Social Support

Social support is widely recognized as benefitting both physical and psychological well-being (Hardy et al., 1999). These benefits are thought to occur both directly, through health-enhancing effects (Wills, 1985), and indirectly, through stress-buffering effects (Cohen & Wills, 1985). More specifically, and consistent with a biopsychosocial perspective, social support is positively associated with health-enhancing behavior and with cardiovascular, immune, and neuroendocrine functioning (Uchino, Cacioppo, & Kiecolt-Glaser, 1996; Uchino, Uno, & Holt-Lunstad, 1999)—all of which may contribute to improved health and well-being. Social support also reduces the effects of stressors on physical and mental health, both by making stressors themselves less potent (e.g., by providing financial assistance to relieve debt) and by empowering individuals to better handle stressful situations (e.g., by demonstrating how to view a problem in a new and constructive way). As shown in the chapters ahead, the relationship between social support and well-being carries important implications for sport injury occurrence, response, and recovery.

Biopsychosocial Analysis

Let us now review this chapter's key concepts by returning to the case of Lisa, which opened the chapter, and examining it from a biopsychosocial perspective. Lisa experienced an injury in her ankle due to macrotrauma from forces generated when she under-rotated her vault landing. Fueled by her strong motivation to participate in the conference championships, Lisa then repeatedly traumatized the injured area by continuing to participate actively in gymnastics. The ongoing stress in her ankle prevented her from getting past the inflammatory-response phase, to which she responded with repeated icing and copious amounts of ibuprofen. Healing could not begin in earnest for Lisa until she stopped abusing her ankle and sought treatment for her injury from a qualified practitioner.

Given Lisa's academic background, she understood the painful signals she was receiving from her ankle; however, she willfully chose to ignore the symptoms and conceal them from her coaches, teammates, and sport health care professionals. In attempting to play through her painful injury, Lisa seems to have internalized the sport ethic and decided that competing in sport at a high level was worth the potential long-term risks to her musculoskeletal health. Outside of the tangible assistance she received from her roommate, Lisa eschewed social support due to fear that her secret would be discovered and her progress toward her goal would be thwarted. Thus biological, psychological, and social factors converged in influencing the situation in which Lisa found herself and her responses to it.

Summary

In order to best prevent and treat sport injury, we must look beyond the physical perspective and consider psychological and social factors as well. The biomedical model, which holds that the mind and the body are separate entities and that health is affected only by physical factors, has persisted for some time; however, appreciation has also emerged of the mind's role in contributing to health. With origins in ancient medical systems, a biopsychosocial approach encourages us, as its name indicates, to examine biological, psychological, and social factors when considering health issues. This approach carries important implications for understanding how sport injuries occur, how athletes respond psychologically and socially to sport injury, and how athletes recover physically from sport injury.

Sport injuries can be classified along multiple biological dimensions, including mechanism (e.g., macrotrauma, microtrauma, overuse), type (e.g., sprain, strain), location (e.g., upper or lower extremity), and severity. Healing of a sport injury typically includes three stages: inflammation, fibroblastic repair (scarring), and tissue remodeling. Rehabilitation of a sport injury generally involves limiting tissue damage while decreasing pain and swelling, restoring normal function of the tissue and structures involved (e.g., range of motion, strength, balance), and returning to sport functioning.

In the holistic approach that characterizes this text, we must understand the role of both physical and psychosocial factors in supporting an athlete's healing and safe return to full sport participation. In particular, we must attend to biological systems (e.g., musculoskeletal, cardiovascular, nervous), psychological aspects (e.g., cognition, motivation, perception), and social influences (e.g., social support). We must also account for interactions between the biopsychosocial factors, which include reciprocal influences on each other.

Although social influences exist outside of athletes, their role should not be underestimated in the occurrence of sport injury or in athletes' short- and long-term responses to injury. Social support can take the form of emotional support (e.g., listening to, comforting), informational support (e.g., providing advice and guidance), or tangible support (e.g., providing monetary assistance and personal services). Common providers of social support to athletes include teammates, coaches, sport health care professionals, sport administrators, friends, partners, and family members.

Research suggests that both male and female athletes are socialized into a culture of risk that encourages them to minimize pain, conceal injury, and play hurt; in fact, these actions are treated as regular elements of sport participation and are considered to be acceptable behaviors. The process by which athletes adopt the sport ethic (which involves making sacrifices, striving for distinction, accepting risks, playing through pain, and refusing to accept limits) and the factors (e.g., coaches, teammates, parents, administrators, sport health care professionals, media) that can influence an athlete's adherence to the culture of risk are not fully understood and, therefore, warrant further investigation.

Discussion Questions

1. How does a biopsychosocial approach to sport injury differ from that of the biomedical model?
2. Why is it sometimes difficult to determine the severity of a sport injury?
3. How do perceptions of sport injury differ from cognitions about sport?
4. What is the "sport ethic"?
5. What roles do sport administrators, coaches, sport health care professionals, and athletes play in the "culture of risk"?

Chapter 2
Antecedents of Sport Injury

Chapter Objectives

1. To introduce contemporary models of sport injury occurrence
2. To identify psychosocial factors predictive of sport injury
3. To explore potential mechanisms by which psychosocial factors can contribute to the occurrence of sport injury

It was only mid-April, but it was already shaping up to be a bad year for Alex, a junior starter on his university's perennial top-10 lacrosse team. In just a few short months, Alex had experienced enough misery to last a lifetime. The year had begun innocently enough, with Alex and Michele, his girlfriend of two years, sharing a champagne "forever" toast to their relationship as they watched the New Year's Eve ball drop at Times Square. From that point on, however, things had unraveled quickly. A mere five weeks later, Alex's father had died. Though he had been sick for a long time and Alex hadn't been particularly close to him, Alex had nevertheless been shaken by the fact that he would never get to speak with his father again. The following week, on Valentine's Day, Michele had broken up with Alex out of the blue. Alex had suspected infidelity but had found no proof and had not even really cared anymore, given how many other things he had been dealing with at that point.

Meanwhile, Alex's mother had been struggling to get by since her husband's death, and she now spent most of her time drinking alcohol to excess. As a result, she relied on Alex to manage the family's household affairs, even though his university was located more than 90 miles away. On top of all that, Alex was doing a semester-long internship and taking a pair of challenging courses in his major. With everything that was going on, Alex was getting only four or five hours of sleep per night and eating only one sit-down meal per day.

"At least I have lacrosse again," thought Alex as he warmed up for the day's game, reflecting on the shoulder injury he had incurred last year with just four games left in the season. A mere 30 minutes later, Alex was flat on his back after colliding with a player on the opposing team. The diagnosis? Dislocated shoulder. What was already a bad year for Alex had just gotten worse.

As Alex was unfortunate enough to learn, injury is a common by-product of sport participation; as a result, sport health care professionals have long sought strategies for preventing (or at least minimizing) the occurrence of injury among athletes. In order to develop such interventions, professionals must thoroughly understand the processes by which athletes become injured (W. van Mechelen, Hlobil, & Kemper, 1992). Knowing the etiology of sport injury helps professionals determine when, where, and how to intervene in order to achieve maximal prevention. To that end, this chapter addresses models of sport injury occurrence, psychosocial predictors of sport injury, and mechanisms of psychosocial influence on sport injury occurrence.

Models of Sport Injury Occurrence

At first glance, explaining Alex's injury would seem to be a simple task. He collided with another player, fell to the ground, and dislocated his shoulder as a result of the impacts he sustained. End of story, right? Not necessarily. Contemporary models of sport injury occurrence suggest that although the physical forces Alex absorbed may have delivered the final blows, other culprits may have contributed to his injury. More specifically, models of sport injury occurrence have been proposed by two schools of thought—the multifactorial model of sport injury etiology, which is based primarily in sports medicine and epidemiology, and the stress–injury model, which is based predominantly in sport psychology. Despite a shared recognition that multiple biological, psychological, and social factors may contribute to sport injury occurrence, these two models have evolved in large part independently of each other. Both models have made important contributions to contemporary understandings of the etiology of sport injury and therefore warrant further exploration.

Multifactorial Model of Sport Injury Etiology

Developed over the past four decades, the multifactorial model is less a single, unified conceptualization of the causes of sport injury than a series of related representations of the processes by which sport injury is thought to occur. As described by W. van Mechelen et al. (1992), the earliest versions of the model focused on identifying both internal (i.e., intrinsic or personal) factors and external (i.e., extrinsic or environmental) factors that contribute to the occurrence of sport injury. These early versions of the model posited that internal factors determined an athlete's capacity to deal with the stress produced by environmental factors and that injury was most likely to occur when stress exceeded the individual's capacity.

Among the internal factors thought to affect this capacity were biological variables (e.g., previous injury, physical defect, height, weight, joint stability, body fat, age, sex), psychological variables (e.g., self-concept, locus of control, risk acceptance, personality), and physical fitness variables reflecting the interaction between psychological states (e.g., motivation, behavior) and physiological parameters (e.g., aerobic endurance, strength, speed, sport skill, coordination, flexibility). External factors thought to confer stress (and, ultimately, injury risk) on athletes included sport-related variables (e.g., type of sport, exposure, nature of event, opponent and teammate behavior [a social factor!], rules, referees' application of rules), venue (e.g., state of floor or ground, lighting, safety features), equipment (e.g., sport implements, protective gear, shoes, clothing), and weather conditions (e.g., temperature, relative humidity, wind).

Limitations were noted in this stress-capacity conceptualization of sport injury etiology by W. van Mechelen et al. (1992). As a result, they added a dynamic element, introduced the concept of strain, and incorporated an active role for the athlete into the process in order to explain the occurrence of acute and overuse injuries. Specifically, they suggested that

- stress from external factors produces strain, which, if substantial enough in relation to capacity, produces acute injury;
- repetitive and accumulated strain over time results in overuse injury;

- capacity can change over time and can be affected by external stress, such as when fatigue impairs motor skills; and
- athletes can reduce external stress by altering their involvement in the sport activity.

The multifactorial model was next expanded by Meeuwisse (1994), who made several key modifications. As shown in figure 2.1, he retained the temporal component added by W. van Mechelen et al. (1992), as well as the concepts of internal and external risk, but abandoned the stress–strain–capacity terminology and introduced in its place the concepts of predisposed athlete, susceptible athlete, and inciting event. In this iteration of the model, an athlete is predisposed to injury if her or his vulnerability is increased by one or more internal risk factors that are necessary, but typically not sufficient, to produce injury. Such an athlete is susceptible to injury when exposed to external risk factors.

This susceptible athlete is considered more vulnerable to injury than a predisposed athlete, but generally not so vulnerable that injury happens without an inciting event. Meeuwisse (1994) described the inciting event as "the straw that breaks the proverbial camel's back" (p. 169), in that it is not sufficient to cause an injury on its own but wreaks havoc on a susceptible athlete and tips the balance from susceptibility to injury. Inciting events are applicable to both acute and overuse injuries, but

events that incite acute injury (e.g., colliding with another athlete) may differ in nature from those that incite overuse injury (e.g., excessive training volume).

More recently, the multifactorial model has been further modified in important ways by Bahr and Krosshaug (2005) and by Meeuwisse, Tyreman, Hagel, and Emery (2007). Bahr and Krosshaug focused their efforts on the inciting-event portion of the model, with an eye toward describing more fully the mechanisms of sport injury. Specifically, they proposed that descriptions of inciting events should address

- the playing situation,
- the behavior of athletes and their opponents,
- gross biomechanical characteristics, and
- detailed biomechanical characteristics.

In this version of the model, both internal and external risk factors were considered as potentially interacting with the characteristics of inciting events to make injury more or less likely. For example, a volleyball player with poor neuromuscular control (an internal risk factor) who collides with a teammate (an inciting event) is more vulnerable to an ankle injury than an athlete who experiences a similar collision but possesses better neuromuscular control.

Meeuwisse et al. (2007) advanced the model even further by building on an elaboration

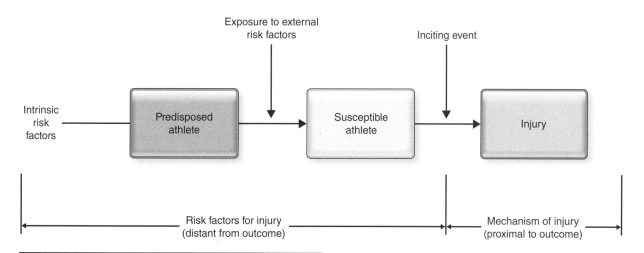

Figure 2.1 Multifactorial model of sport injury etiology.
Meeuwisse, 1994

of the inciting event proposed by Bahr and Krosshaug (2005) and on the following suggestions by Gissane, White, Kerr, and Jennings (2001):

- Internal risk factors can vary over time.
- The model should address what takes place after the occurrence of injury.
- The process by which athletes sustain injuries is not linear, as posited in an earlier version of the model (figure 2.1), but cyclical.

As displayed in figure 2.2, this updated model contains a number of modifications of the version shown in figure 2.1. First, among the sample intrinsic factors, it replaces flexibility and somatotype with neuromuscular control and strength; this change is mostly cosmetic. Second, this version depicts the possibility that susceptible athletes may encounter potentially injurious situations and *not* get injured. For example, injury may be

averted due to tissue adaptation, use of protective equipment, or another factor (internal or external) that modifies the athlete's injury risk. Third, the updated version incorporates the possibility that athletes who sustain an injury may not recover sufficiently to return to sport participation. Fourth, and perhaps most important, the "dynamic, recursive" nature of the model is highlighted by the arrows indicating the continuance of sport participation after noninjury or the return to sport after recovery from injury.

When an athlete continues or returns to sport participation, he or she does so with the strong possibility that internal or external risk factors have changed since the athlete last progressed through the cycle. For example, as noted by Meeuwisse et al. (2007), fatigue that lingers to the next day of sport participation can alter an athlete's neuromuscular control and therefore constitutes a change in the athlete's

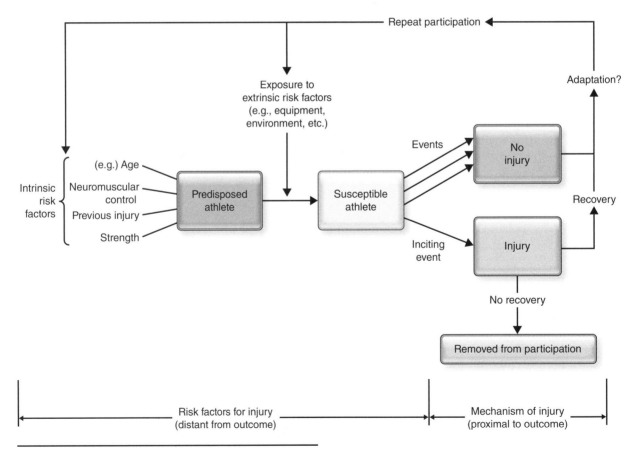

Figure 2.2 Updated multifactorial model of sport injury etiology.
Based on Meeuwisse et al. 2007

internal risk profile entering the second day of participation. Therefore, if all other factors in the model remain the same as they were on the first day of participation, the athlete's risk of injury is greater on the second day than it was on the first day.

Stress–Injury Model

In response to the proliferation of research on psychological and social predictors of sport injury in the 1960s, 1970s, and early 1980s, M.B. Andersen and Williams (1988) proposed a model of sport injury occurrence that incorporated the accumulated research findings and provided a framework to guide subsequent research. As shown in figure 2.3, the central thesis of their model posits that the stress response is a proximal cause of sport injury. Furthermore, the model hypothesizes that contributors to the stress response include three broad categories of psychosocial factors—personality, history of stressors, and coping resources—each of which acts either directly or through its relations with the other two categories. (The same investigators later updated the model [J.M. Williams & Andersen, 1998] by making the

arrows between the three categories bidirectional.) Interventions directed at the stress response are thought to alter the likelihood of injury occurrence.

The centerpiece of the stress–injury model is the stress response, a process in which people cognitively appraise the environmental demands placed on them in potentially stressful situations (i.e., stressors), the resources they possess to manage those demands, and the consequences of succeeding or failing at managing the demands. These cognitive appraisals are thought to influence and be influenced by physiological and attentional changes (e.g., general muscle tension, narrowing of visual field, distractibility) that place athletes at increased risk for injury. Thus, according to the model, athletes who perceive themselves as overwhelmed and helpless in the face of a stressful sport situation may experience tense muscles, "tunnel vision," or inattention to the sport environment—all of which make them more susceptible to injury. On the other hand, athletes who perceive themselves as possessing the resources necessary to manage the demands of a potentially stressful sport situation are considered less likely to experience

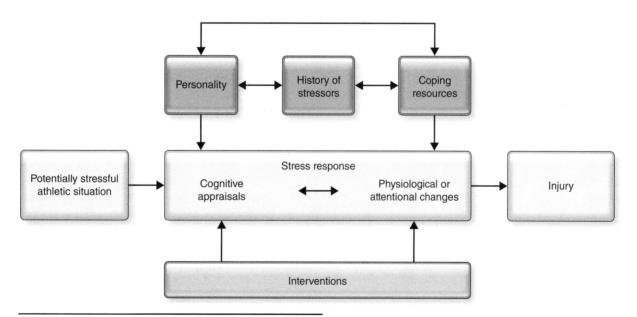

Figure 2.3 The stress–injury model.

Adapted, by permission, from M.B. Andersen and J.M. Williams, 1988, "A model of stress and athletic injury: Prediction and prevention," *Journal of Sport & Exercise Psychology* 10: 294-306.

the physiological and attentional changes that increase the risk of injury.

Let us now examine the three interrelated categories of psychosocial factors—personality, history of stressors, and coping resources—that are hypothesized to contribute to the stress response. Personality consists of enduring, stable patterns of thinking, feeling, and behaving. The personality characteristics that M.B. Andersen and Williams (1988) considered relevant to the stress response, and to sport injury occurrence, include locus of control (how much control one perceives oneself as having over life events), competitive trait anxiety (tendency to get anxious in competitive situations), and hardiness (resilience). Presumably, these characteristics interact with an athlete's history of stressors and coping resources to affect the athlete's cognitive appraisals of stressors, as well as his or her physiological and attentional changes in response to stress.

An athlete's history of stressors consists of the threatening or challenging events that he or she has experienced, whether recently or in the more distant past. Stressors typically involve change of some sort, and change can occur on multiple levels. The broadest level of stressors is made up of catastrophes—large-scale, cataclysmic events that generally affect many people at the same time (e.g., war, natural disaster, nuclear accident). The intermediate level consists of major life events that exert a pronounced effect, whether positive or negative; examples include divorce, death of a close friend or relative, high school and college graduation, and legal trouble. The micro level consists of minor life events, which might be referred to as daily hassles when negative and as daily uplifts when positive. Examples of daily hassles include encountering heavy traffic, waiting in line at the grocery store, and getting a bad grade on a school assignment. Examples of daily uplifts include acing an exam, receiving an unexpected gift, and getting praised by a colleague.

In formulating the stress–injury model, M.B. Andersen and Williams (1988) focused primarily on the latter two types of stressor—specifically, major life events and daily hassles—as most relevant to the stress response and to sport injury occurrence. The model also specifies previous injury as a stressor of particular importance. For one thing, incomplete rehabilitation increases an athlete's risk of reinjury; in addition, past injury experiences can promote negative cognitive appraisals and fear of reinjury, both of which can exacerbate the stress response and elevate the likelihood of reinjury.

The third category of variables posited to influence the stress response is that of coping resources, which includes behaviors and social networks that help athletes handle stress. For example, athletes can cope better with stress if they engage in behaviors such as getting enough sleep, eating nutritious foods, and managing time effectively. It is also helpful to use cognitive strategies for calming anxiety, maintaining focus, and appraising stressors in ways that prompt adaptive physiological and attentional responses. Along with the use of stress management techniques (e.g., relaxation, imagery, and meditation), another important coping resource is social support—that is, athletes' relationships with people who care about them, both inside and outside of the sport environment. These relationships are thought to affect injury vulnerability both by dampening the effects of stressful events and by directly altering an individual's stress response. Thus, having a close friend to rely on can make stressful events less stressful and minimize maladaptive physiological and attentional responses, all of which, theoretically, can reduce an athlete's injury risk (M.B. Andersen & Williams, 1988).

Since its unveiling in 1988, the stress–injury model has guided numerous investigations into the relationship between psychosocial factors and sport injury occurrence, and several modifications have been proposed. Wiese-Bjornstal (2004), for instance, adapted the model to youth sport participants by tailoring its variables in developmentally appropriate ways. Petrie and Perna (2004), meanwhile, added elements to the physiological portion of the model's stress-response component and advocated expanding that component to include affective and behavioral aspects. More specifically, they noted that chronic, prolonged, or repeated stress—in the form of a history of stressors from life events, training, and competition—can increase general muscle tension and narrow the visual field (which overlaps with the cognitive and attentional components of the stress response). It can also increase activation of the body's short-term (i.e., sympathoadrenal medullary, or SAM) and long-term (i.e., hypothalamic–pituitary–adrenal, or HPA) stress-response systems. These changes, when followed by the release of stress hormones (e.g., cortisol), are thought to raise the risk of illness, injury, and other deleterious health consequences by suppressing the immune system, disrupting the tissue-repair process, and interfering with the restorative effects of sleep.

Model Integration

On the surface, although the multifactorial model and the stress–injury model are both intended to explain the process by which athletes sustain injuries, they appear to differ greatly not only in their terminology but also in their depictions of the process of sport injury occurrence. A closer look, however, reveals that the two models are wholly compatible and that the stress–injury model represents a specific pathway within the more general multifactorial model. Specifically, the stress–injury model's personality component, as well as the cognitive and behavioral aspects of its coping-resources component, can be viewed as internal risk factors (or, more accurately, internal risk mitigators) in the multifactorial model. Similarly, the history of stressors in the stress–injury model dovetails nicely with the category of external risk factors in the multifactorial model.

The biggest question in this integration is whether the stress-response component of the stress–injury model is part of the susceptible-athlete phase of the multifactorial model— "where the intrinsic and extrinsic risks and the interactions between all the risks accumulate" (Meeuwisse et al., 2007)—or if it occurs after,

or as part of, an inciting or other event immediately before the injury and when there are no injury outcomes. In other words, is the heightened stress response that confers an elevated risk of injury on athletes a relatively chronic state experienced by individuals made susceptible by their personality, history of stressors, and coping resources? Or is it an acute state manifested only by individuals under stressful circumstances?

The answer is not as straightforward as it may seem. The stress–injury model clearly indicates that a "potentially stressful athletic situation" triggers the stress response that places athletes at increased risk for injury. For example, research has shown that a stressful sport situation (e.g., playing in an important game) causes a narrowing of the peripheral visual field (T.J. Rogers, Alderman, & Landers, 2003), which is positively associated with sport injury (T.J. Rogers & Landers, 2005). These findings might seem to support the view that a stressful situation beyond an athlete's history of stressors is needed in order to elicit the stress response that heightens injury risk. However, the vast majority of studies that have found components of the stress–injury model to predict the occurrence of sport injury (for a review, see J.M. Williams & Andersen, 2007) have *not* included measures of the stress response *under stressful conditions*. Therefore, it may not be necessary for an athlete to encounter a stressful sport situation over and above the ones experienced in his or her history of stressors (which includes the physical training stressors described by Petrie & Perna, 2004) in order to experience a maladaptive stress response sufficient to contribute to injury occurrence.

Instead, as suggested by the physiological responses to chronic stress identified by Petrie and Perna (2004), the independent and interactive influences of personality, history of stressors, and coping resources may be sufficient in combination to create a state of vulnerability—corresponding with the multifactorial model's susceptible-athlete phase— that needs only an inciting event or series of inciting events. This event or series of events could involve a stressful sport situation and subsequent exacerbated stress response that bring about injury. Removing the "potentially stressful athletic situation" as a *necessary* condition for the occurrence of sport injury better reconciles the stress–injury and multifactorial models. It also allows for the occurrence of overuse injuries and acute injuries in seemingly nonstressful circumstances such as training sessions and friendly competitions.

Psychosocial Predictors of Sport Injury

More than four decades' worth of research has identified numerous psychological and social factors that are predictive of sport injury outcomes, such as injury occurrence and time lost from sport participation due to injury. Many of these factors were specified by the developers of the stress–injury and multifactorial models, and predictive factors that are not explicitly mentioned in the two models can invariably be placed in an appropriate component of one or both of the models. Some of the psychosocial factors presented in this section have been linked to sport injury in a single study, whereas others have been repeatedly associated with sport injury in research investigations.

The quality of the studies varies widely. Some are retrospective (i.e., measuring psychosocial factors *after* injury occurrence), but most are prospective (i.e., measuring factors *before* the injury). Because almost all of the studies are correlational, it cannot be concluded that any of the psychosocial factors is *causally* related to sport injury. Indeed, if a positive correlation is found between a given personality factor and the number of days lost to injury during the season after personality was measured, it is possible that the personality factor caused the time lost due to injury, that another variable caused both the personality factor and the time loss, or, more likely, that the relationship between the personality factor and the time loss is mediated by one or more other variables. For example, in studies finding a relationship between trait anxiety and time loss, the tendency to be anxious

across situations may elevate other risk factors (e.g., muscle tension, distracted attention) that are more proximal to injury occurrence in the stress–injury and multifactorial models. For more on injury-prediction research, see this chapter's Focus on Research box.

Having acknowledged the limitations of the research base on sport injury prediction, we now turn to an overview of psychosocial factors associated with sport injury outcomes. Particular attention is given to personality, history of stressors, coping resources, mood states, miscellaneous factors, and interactive relationships.

Personality

As one of three categories of psychosocial variables proposed to affect the stress response in the stress–injury model, personality has been the focus of numerous investigations aimed at identifying predictors of sport injury. However, no "injury-prone" personality has been documented, and the association between individual personality characteristics and injury outcomes has generally been weak at best (for reviews, see Prieto, Labisa, & Olmedilla [2014] and J.M. Williams & Andersen [2007]). In the initial description of the stress–injury model (M.B. Andersen & Williams, 1988), five personality characteristics were hypothesized as potential contributors to the stress response: hardiness, locus of control, sense of coherence, competitive trait anxiety, and achievement motivation.

Of the five characteristics, competitive trait anxiety has shown the most consistent association with sport injury outcomes; specifically, higher levels of competitive trait anxiety are related to more or longer-lasting injuries. This finding, which seems to hold only when competitive trait anxiety is assessed with a measure specific to the sport environment (J.M. Williams & Andersen, 2007; Yang, Cheng, et al., 2014), makes sense in that athletes who tend to be anxious about sport competition in general would be expected to enter particular sport settings with elevated anxiety that could exacerbate the stress response and heighten the risk of

How We Know What We Know About Sport Injury Occurrence

Research on the general causes and precise mechanisms of sport injury is not likely to yield a smoking gun—not now, and not ever! This is not merely the opinion of guarded, appropriately skeptical scientists; it is an accurate reflection of the limitations of research on the etiology of sport injury. Under ideal circumstances, researchers would manipulate variables hypothesized to cause injury in athletes and then observe the effects on athletes' injury status. However, although this approach might be desirable from a scientific standpoint, it is impermissible on ethical grounds. Besides, who would sign up to participate in a study like that? This is not to say that experimental studies are *never* carried out in which sport injury occurrence is the dependent variable; they *are*. It's just that those studies typically involve experimental manipulations proposed to *decrease* the occurrence of sport injury. Therefore, they are covered in chapter 3, which pertains to the prevention of sport injury.

With experimental methods essentially off the table, investigators interested in the etiology of sport injury have relied heavily on correlational research designs that examine associations between sport injury and purported risk factors. Correlational studies do not enable researchers to draw causal inferences, but they can increase one's confidence that the hypothesized risk factors *might* exert a causal influence on sport injury occurrence—if the research design is not retrospective but prospective. In retrospective studies, proposed injury-risk factors are measured *after* the occurrence of sport injury. For instance, in a typical retrospective study, a group of athletes with injuries and a group of athletes without injuries complete a series of risk-variable measures. Comparisons between the two groups will reveal little about the causes of the athletes' injuries, because any differences between the two groups could just as easily be the *consequence* of sport injury as they could be the cause. In contrast, *prospective* studies administer measures of risk variables to asymptomatic athletes *before* the occurrence of injury, thereby making it less likely that the proposed risk factors are the effects rather than the causes of injury (Petrie & Falkstein, 1998).

The inability to conduct experimental etiological research with injury as the primary dependent variable has made it exceedingly difficult for investigators to identify the mechanisms by which sport injury occurs. Even if a researcher happened to observe an unfortunate athlete in the act of being injured, the occurrence would likely be uninformative unless the researcher had been monitoring relevant etiological parameters for a period of time before the injury was sustained. However, rather than throw their hands in the air and surrender to these difficulties, resourceful researchers have devised creative strategies to explore mechanisms of sport injury occurrence.

Specifically, Krosshaug, Andersen, Olsen, Myklebust, and Bahr (2005) indicated that researchers have examined the inciting events of sport injury in the following ways:

· Interviewing athletes about the circumstances under which they were injured

· Conducting clinical studies to analyze the pathology of an injury and related damage

· Systematically analyzing video representations of athletes incurring injuries

Focus on Research

(continued)

injury. It is possible that an even more pertinent form of anxiety—"sport injury trait anxiety"—may fare even better than competitive trait anxiety in predicting injury, but researchers have not yet ascertained the relationship between the first scale to assess the construct (Sport Injury Trait Anxiety Scale; Kleinert, 2002) and injury.

In addition, two studies have found negative associations between hardiness and sport injury occurrence outcomes (Ford, Eklund, & Gordon, 2000; Wadey, Evans, Hanton, & Neil, 2012a). Empirical support for the other three personality characteristics is either weak or nonexistent, whether because they have not

· Performing laboratory motion analyses in which typical injury situations are mimicked and loading patterns are assessed

· Measuring in vivo strain or force of muscles, tendons, or other tissues

· Documenting accidental injuries that occur during biomechanical experiments

· Simulating the effects of potential inciting events on cadavers and dummies

· Developing mathematical models that estimate what is likely to happen in situations with high risk for injury

Although these methods do not fully replace live human experimentation, they do shed an abundance of light on a critical part of the process of sport injury occurrence.

In sport injury prediction research, as in much of life, timing can be everything. In a typical study of sport injury prediction, risk factors for injury are assessed at the beginning of the season, and athletes' injury outcomes are recorded over the course of the season. Given the increased recognition that susceptibility to injury is a dynamic condition, researchers have recommended moving away from the standard preseason assessment and making more measurements of injury risk factors that can change during the study period (Meeuwisse et al., 2007; Petrie & Falkstein, 1998). Repeated assessment of such factors (e.g., history of stressors; social support; environmental conditions; and cognitive, affective, and behavioral responses to stress) at regular intervals enables more accurate representation of the risk for injury and therefore should enhance the predictive power of models of sport injury occurrence. Of course, the ability to manipulate the timing of data collection about risk factors may be limited by practical considerations, such as the willingness of athletes and coaches to participate.

been tested or because they have not shown consistent results when they have been tested.

M.B. Andersen and Williams (1988) also recognized that sport injury occurrence might be related to personality characteristics other than the five noted in their initial presentation of the stress–injury model. Of particular note, manifestations of the type A personality pattern—characterized by driven, hostile, hypercompetitive, hurried, and impatient behavior—has been positively associated with the occurrence of overuse injuries in runners in multiple studies (Diekhoff, 1984; Ekenman, Hassmén, Koivula, Rolf, & Fellander-Tsai, 2001; K.B. Fields, Delaney, & Hinkle, 1990). Similar results were reported by McClay, Appleby, and Plascak (1989), who found that young cross country runners who scored high on self-motivation were more likely than those who scored low to incur severe injuries. In addition, Kazarian, Thompson, and Clark (1995) showed that the positive association between type A behavior and both number of injuries and time lost due to injury extended beyond overuse injuries incurred by runners to more acute injuries experienced by American football players. The generalizability of the positive relationship between type A behavior and number of injuries was further demonstrated in a study of 2,164 collegiate athletes in Japan (Nigorikawa et al., 2003).

Associations with sport injury occurrence have also been documented for many other personality characteristics, but some of these associations seem to be contradictory, and most were reported in single, isolated studies and have not been replicated. For instance, a negative correlation was found between optimism and injury occurrence for athletes in a variety of sports (Wadey, Evans, Hanton, & Neil, 2013). Factors found to correlate positively with sport injury occurrence include dominance (W. van Mechelen et al., 1996), ego orientation (Steffen, Pensgaard, & Bahr, 2009), external locus of control (Pargman & Lunt, 1989), internal locus of control (Kolt & Kirkby, 1996; Plante & Booth, 1997), narcissism (Plante & Booth), perfectionism (Krasnow, Mainwaring, & Kerr, 1999), stress susceptibility (Ivarsson & Johnson, 2010), tendermindedness (D.W. Jackson et al., 1978; Valliant, 1981), toughmindedness (Wittig & Schurr, 1994), and trait irritability (Ivarsson & Johnson). In addition, in a study of elite youth ice-hockey players, low athletic identity was associated with increased risk for a first injury, but high athletic identity was associated with increased risk for subsequent injuries (McKay, Campbell, Meeuwisse, & Emery, 2013).

Potentially more important than these associations are the contributions of personality factors to the prediction of sport injury occurrence in the interactive relationships described in the following paragraphs. Personality may also contribute to behaviors that increase an athlete's risk of injury. For example, Webbe and Ochs (2007) found that elite male soccer players who scored high on extroversion (i.e., tendency toward assertive, enthusiastic, outgoing behavior) reported heading the ball more frequently than did those who scored low on extroversion. More recently, Akehurst and Oliver (2014) found that in their sample of 100 professional dancers, obsessive passion was positively associated with the tendency to report engaging in behavior that placed the dancer at increased risk for injury and that this relationship was mediated by dependence on dance.

History of Stressors

Seminal research by Holmes (1970) documented a positive association between injury and life-event stress in a sample of collegiate football players. Since then, history of stressors has been the most studied and most consistently supported psychosocial predictor of sport injury. In a review of more than 40 studies that examined the relationship between life stress and sport injury, J.M. Williams and Andersen (2007) "found that approximately 85 percent of the studies found some correlation between life event stress and injury risk" (p. 383). Indeed, the association between life

stress and sport injury is remarkably robust, having been demonstrated across a wide variety of sports and levels of competition (e.g., youth, elite) in studies that varied in their definitions of injury and in their measures of life stress. Support for a relationship between life stress and sport injury is strongest for *negative* life-event stress and *total* life-event stress (i.e., stress from life events perceived as negative plus those perceived as positive). Associations have also been reported between *positive* life-event stress and sport injury occurrence but with less consistency than for total and negative life-event stress (J.M. Williams & Andersen, 2007).

Since the review by J.M. Williams and Andersen (2007), ongoing research has provided additional documentation for the association between sport injury occurrence—as well as time lost due to injury—and both negative-life event stress (Dunn, Smith, & Smoll, 2001; Gunnoe, Horodyski, Tennant, & Murphey, 2001; Johnson & Ivarsson, 2011; Sibold, 2005) and total life-event stress (Dvorak et al., 2000; Galambos, Terry, Moyle, & Locke, 2005; Gunnoe et al.; Olmedilla, Prieto, & Blas, 2011; Steffen et al., 2009). For example, Dunn et al. reported that stress attributable to sport-specific negative life events predicted time lost due to injury over and above general negative life-event stress for male athletes but not for female athletes. On the other hand, a history of one specific type of stressor—physical abuse—has been associated with an elevated risk for injury among female athletes but not among male athletes (Timpka, Janson, et al., 2014).

In contrast to the volumes of research addressing the relationship between sport injury occurrence and major life-event stress, relatively little attention has been paid to the role of daily hassles (i.e., minor negative life events). The literature review performed by J.M. Williams and Andersen (2007) noted that because of the ever-changing nature of daily hassles, they must be assessed frequently over the course of a sport season. These researchers further observed that in studies where daily hassles were measured on only one occasion, no significant relationship was found between daily hassles and sport injury occurrence.

However, a different pattern has been found in studies that assessed daily hassles on multiple occasions. For example, in studies where measures of daily hassles were administered on a weekly basis, athletes who became injured had experienced either a significant increase in daily hassles during the week just before injury (Fawkner, McMurray, & Summers, 1999) or a near-significantly higher (p = .085) level of daily hassles before injury (Ivarsson & Johnson, 2010) as compared with athletes who did not become injured. Thus, it is possible that stress from minor life events affects sport injury risk but that this risk is short lived.

A consistent positive association has been documented between the third type of stressor identified in the stress–injury model—previous injury—and the occurrence of sport injury. In general terms, previous injury has been positively correlated with subsequent injury in numerous studies (e.g., Emery, Meeuwisse, & Hartmann, 2005; Kucera, Marshall, Kirkendall, Marchak, & Garrett, 2005; Lysens et al., 1984; Marshall, Covassin, Dick, Nassar, & Agel, 2007; Timpka, Jacobsson, et al., 2014; W. van Mechelen et al., 1996; J.M. Williams, Hogan, & Andersen, 1993). Previous injury has also been positively correlated with subsequent injury among athletes with specific injuries. Among youth soccer players, for example, injury to a given region of the body has been positively correlated with subsequent injury to that same region (Steffen, Myklebust, Andersen, Holme, & Bahr, 2008). Similarly, hip and groin injuries incurred by youth and junior soccer players have been correlated with the same types of injury in the players' adult and senior soccer years (Gabbe, Bailey, et al., 2010).

In other sports, concussions experienced during the competitive years have been correlated with concussions experienced in retirement by American football players (Guskiewicz et al., 2007), previous hamstring injuries have been correlated with subsequent hamstring injuries in Australian football players (Gabbe, Bennell, Finch, Wajswelner, & Orchard, 2006), and previous ankle sprains have been correlated with subsequent ankle sprains in elite badminton players (Yung, Chan, Wong, Cheuk, & Fong, 2007). Moreover, *not* sustaining an injury in the previous year has been found to be protective against injury among nonelite netball players (McManus, Stevenson, & Finch, 2006).

Among events in an athlete's history of stressors, previous injury is unique in at least one important way. Namely, it is unclear whether the elevated risk associated with previous injury results from a *fear* of reinjury that induces a magnified stress response or from an *actual* reinjury attributable either to incomplete healing or to somatic weakness in the injured area (M.B. Andersen & Williams, 1988). In cases where the current injury occurs in a location different from that of the previous injury, the fear-of-reinjury pathway is a tenable explanation. In cases where the current injury occurs in the same location as the previous injury, the actual-reinjury pathways seem more likely to be involved insofar as the current injury may simply be either a continuation of an unhealed previous injury or a new injury to a site that is especially vulnerable for anatomical, biomechanical, or other reasons. The matter is complicated by the finding that previous injury is associated with elevated perceptions of injury risk (Reuter & Short, 2005; Short, Reuter, Brandt, Short, & Kontos, 2004)—a variable that is, in itself, *inversely* related to the occurrence of sport injury (Kontos, 2004). Thus, it appears that a previous injury may elicit a cognitive response of wariness that helps protect against subsequent injury but is insufficient to offset the vulnerability to injury that an injury history confers on the athlete. Unfortunately, the research designs of the studies examining previous injury as a predictor of sport injury occurrence do not allow for any conclusions about *how* previous injury is related to current injury.

Coping Resources

Of the three major categories of stress-response predictors in the stress–injury model, coping resources have received the least attention from researchers and, not surprisingly, shown the fewest associations with the occurrence of sport injury. Coping-resource variables for

Assessing Life Stress

Among the psychosocial factors that may contribute to the occurrence of sport injury, one stands out from the pack: life stress. This factor has been studied the most in relation to sport injury and has been most consistently associated with sport injury occurrence. Given the importance of life stress as a predictor of sport injury, professionals who are charged with maintaining athletes' health are well advised to know their athletes' life-stress levels.

Assessment of athletes' life stress can be traced back to groundbreaking studies of the relationship between life stress and health conducted at the University of Washington by Thomas Holmes and his colleagues. Holmes and Rahe (1967) interviewed more than 5,000 people about life events they had experienced that seemed to be related to health problems they had incurred. Based on the interview data, the investigators developed the Social Readjustment Rating Scale (SRRS) to measure people's experience of stressful life events. Using the scale, respondents were asked to indicate which of a list of 43 major life events they had experienced during the previous year. On the assumption that life changes are stressful, each event in the SRRS was assigned a weighted value of "life-change units" (LCUs); higher values were assigned to events deemed more stressful. For instance, the two most heavily weighted events—death of a spouse and divorce—were assigned LCU values of 100 and 73, respectively, whereas being fired from a job was assigned 47 LCUs. Life-change values were also assigned to events generally considered positive, such as marriage (50 LCUs), outstanding personal accomplishment (29 LCUs), vacation (13 LCUs), and Christmas (12 LCUs).

Although Holmes (1970) used the SRRS to document a positive association between life stress and injury in collegiate football players, the applicability of the SRRS for athletes was limited because it excluded many events that can produce substantial stress in an athlete's life. Consequently, Bramwell, Masuda, Wagner, and Holmes (1975) developed a sport-specific version of the SRRS called the Social and Athletic Readjustment Rating Scale (SARRS), which eliminated a few irrelevant life events and added 20 new ones relevant to athletes, such as being dropped from a team (52 LCUs), having trouble with a head coach (35 LCUs), and making a major error in a competition (27 LCUs). Thus the SARRS was better equipped than the SRRS to capture the sorts of stressors typically encountered by athletes. In a prospective study, Bramwell et al. found that collegiate football players who sustained an injury during the competitive season had significantly higher scores on the SARRS than did players who did not sustain an injury.

The approach to measuring life stress used in the SRRS and the SARRS fell out of favor due to criticisms about combining positive and negative life events into a single index of life stress and about preassigning point values for each event. For instance, Sarason, Johnson, and Siegel (1978) argued that the processes of adapting to positive and negative events may not be the same and that individuals may differ in their perceptions of the degree of stress associated with a given event. Therefore, in their own Life Experience Survey (LES), Sarason et al. separated positive and negative life events and allowed respondents to provide their own ratings of the level of stress involved in life events experienced in the recent past. In turn, using a version of the LES modified for the sport setting, Passer and Seese (1983) investigated positive and negative life stress as independent predictors of injury among

(continued)

which significant correlations have been obtained include coping resources (Hanson, McCullagh, & Tonymon, 1992; J.M. Williams et al., 1986), coping skills (Noh, Morris, & Andersen, 2005; T.J. Rogers & Landers, 2005), coping strategies (Ivarsson & Johnson, 2010), and social support (Hardy, Richman, & Rosenfeld, 1991). As one would expect, higher levels of coping resources and coping skills were negatively associated with injury frequency (i.e., were associated with the occurrence of fewer injuries).

In contrast, coping strategies and social support were *positively* associated with injury frequency. In other words, greater reported use of self-blame (Ivarsson & Johnson, 2010; Timpka,

Focus on Application

collegiate male football players. However, in a study comparing the ability of the SARRS and the LES to predict the occurrence of injury in gymnasts, neither instrument gained a distinct advantage over the other; in fact, scores on neither instrument were associated with the occurrence of injury (J.M. Williams, Tonymon, & Wadsworth, 1986).

In a later attempt, Petrie (1992) developed a measure of life stress that borrowed the LES approach of separating positive and negative life events and asking respondents to rate their own level of stress associated with each of a lengthy list of events. Some of the events were drawn from the LES and other existing inventories, but the remainder were derived from lists generated by collegiate athletes—for example, suspension from the team for nonacademic reasons, receipt of an athletic scholarship, continual poor team performance. The resulting instrument, the Life Events Scale for College Athletes (LESCA), contained 21 sport-specific events (as compared with 16 on the SARRS). It outperformed the SARRS in predicting injury among female collegiate gymnasts and has become the standard means of assessing history of stressors among collegiate athletes in research investigations. The LESCA can be used to

screen for elevated levels of life stress in both team and individual-athlete settings. Although norms are not available for the instrument, athletes with high scores (e.g., one or two standard deviations above the mean for the team) can be identified for follow-up and possible intervention.

When working with individual athletes, LESCA responses can be used to generate face-to-face discussion with athletes about recent sources of stress (e.g., "What kinds of difficulty have you been having with your roommate?"), biopsychosocial responses to stress (e.g., "How have these challenges affected your sleep? Your schoolwork? Your relationships with your teammates?"), coping attempts (e.g., "What have you done to try make things less stressful?"), and, if deemed appropriate, approaches to stress management. Conversations of this sort should, of course, be carried out in private. Although it is possible to use an inventory such as the LESCA and an interview to assess athletes' stress levels at any time, the logical point for conducting a stress screening is during the preseason so that areas of vulnerability can be addressed preventively before athletes have been exposed to substantive risks on the field of play.

Jacobsson, et al., 2014), behavioral disengagement, and acceptance coping strategies (Ivarsson & Johnson)—as well as greater reported number of social support providers (Hardy et al., 1991)—were related to greater frequency of sport injury. Although unexpected, the result for coping strategies could result not from athletes' use of coping strategies per se but from athletes who were under a great deal of stress tending to adopt more coping strategies in order to deal with that stress but still experiencing more injuries as a result of the stress (and its consequences). The result for social support is more difficult to explain. Regardless, the counterintuitive findings for both coping strategies and social support are more the exception than the rule for coping resources as a whole. This reality is indicated, for example, in the upcom-

ing section on interactive relationships between variables, wherein coping resources are shown to moderate relationships between other psychosocial risk factors and sport injury occurrence in ways that make more intuitive sense.

Mood States

Although not explicitly part of the stress–injury model, mood states have been examined as potential predictors of sport injury occurrence. Studies have consistently found a positive association between indexes of sport injury occurrence and negative emotions, such as anger (Galambos et al., 2005; Lavallee & Flint, 1996; Plante & Booth, 1997; N.J. Thompson & Morris, 1994; Yang et al., 2014), cognitive anxiety (Kolt & Kirkby, 1994), confusion (Galambos et al.), depression (Galambos et al.; Lavallee & Flint), fatigue (Galambos et al.; Kleinert, 2007; Kolt & Kirkby, 1994), and tension (Galambos et al.; Lavallee & Flint). In addition, inverse relationships have been documented between sport injury occurrence and the positive emotion of vigor (Galambos et al.; Lavallee & Flint). The exact nature of the observed relationships between mood states and sport injury occurrence has not been determined, because both positive and negative moods can influence the stress response and can be influenced by personality, history of stressors, and coping resources.

Miscellaneous Factors

Several additional psychosocial variables have been identified as predictors of the occurrence of sport injury. These variables, which do not fit neatly into the categories of the stress–injury model, include attention-deficit/hyperactivity disorder (ADHD; Tan et al., 2014), hyperactivity (Timpka, Jacobsson et al., 2014), neurocognitive functioning (Swanik, Covassin, Stearne, & Schatz, 2007), perceived motivational climate (Steffen et al., 2009), physical self-perceptions (Janelle, Kaminski, & Murray, 1999), positive states of mind (J.M. Williams et al., 1993), sociability (Kleinert, 2007), and sport-specific tactical skills (Soligard, Grindem, Bahr, & Anderson, 2010). Elevated risk of injury is associated with high levels of perceived mastery climate, perceived sport competence, sociability, and sport-specific tactical skills. Elevated risk is also associated with slow reaction time, slow processing speed, and low levels of *perceived* physical strength, positive states of mind (i.e., ability to stay focused and relaxed), visual memory, and verbal memory. The importance of these findings will be determined as they are replicated (or not) and interpreted within the stress–injury and multifactorial models.

Interactive Relationships

As depicted in figures 2.2 and 2.3, the multifactorial and stress–injury models show that

the process by which athletes become injured includes a complex series of events involving multiple risk factors. Given this complexity, it is not surprising that many key findings about using psychological and social variables to predict sport injury occurrence involve interactive relationships. In the simplest type of interaction in this particular context, the relationship between a given risk factor (e.g., life stress) and the occurrence of sport injury differs depending on the level of a second risk factor (e.g., social support). For example, Petrie (1992) found a significant positive relationship between negative life stress and sport injury occurrence for athletes with low social support but a nonsignificant relationship for athletes with high social support. In this case, then, social support *moderated* the relationship between life stress and the occurrence of sport injury. Similarly, coping strategies were found to moderate the relationship between self-efficacy and sport injury; specifically, self-efficacy was positively associated with both emotional calming and risky behavior, the former of which was negatively associated with injury occurrence and the latter of which was positively associated with injury occurrence (Rubio, Pujals, de la Vega, Aguado, & Hernández, 2014).

A more complex type of interaction effect—conjunctive moderation—has also been identified as relevant to the prediction of sport injury in a study by R.E. Smith, Smoll, and Ptacek (1990). In the context of sport injury, conjunctive moderation involves two or more moderating variables that, when occurring simultaneously in a particular combination or pattern, maximize the relationship between a given risk factor and the injury outcome of interest. The study by Smith and colleagues demonstrated conjunctive moderation in which the association between negative life stress and time lost due to injury was greatest for athletes who were low in both social support and psychological coping skills.

In fact, the literature abounds with examples of interactive relationships in the prediction of sport injury occurrence with psychosocial factors. Studies in which a personal attribute acted as a moderating variable include those of R.E. Smith, Ptacek, and Smoll (1992) and Petrie (1993). Smith and colleagues reported that sensation seeking—a personality variable involving the extent to which a person seeks out and tolerates emotionally arousing situations—moderated the relationship between negative life-event stress and time lost due to injury in a sample of high school athletes. Specifically, the association was significant and positive for athletes who were low in sensation seeking but nonsignificant for athletes who were high in sensation seeking. In Petrie's study of American football players, two moderating effects were identified:

1. Trait anxiety was positively associated with injury occurrence for starters but unrelated to injury occurrence for nonstarters.

2. Positive life-event stress was directly related to time lost due to injury for players with high trait anxiety but unrelated for players with low trait anxiety.

In a study by N.J. Thompson and Morris (1994), the moderating variable was life-event stress, and a personal attribute (attentional vigilance) was the factor whose relation with injury was moderated. Specifically, attentional vigilance was negatively related to injury occurrence in American football players if a major stressor had been experienced in the previous 12 months; the association was positive, however, if a major stressor had *not* been experienced in the past 12 months. Thus, although personal attributes generally serve as moderators of the relationships between other variables and sport injury, their relationships with injury outcomes can also be moderated by other factors.

Coping resources have also been found to moderate relations between life-event stress and sport injury outcomes. In particular, social support has emerged as a frequent moderator. For example, in findings similar to those of Petrie (1992), as just described, Patterson, Smith, Everett, and Ptacek (1998) reported that social support moderated the relationship between life stress and injury. Specifically, high levels of negative life stress were associated with elevated risk for injury among ballet dancers with low social support but were unrelated to injury among ballet dancers with high social support. Complementary results were reported by Hardy et al. (1991), who found that when male athletes had high levels of negative life stress, they experienced fewer injuries when they had high levels of social support than when they had low levels of social support. The findings of Hardy et al. did not apply, however, to female athletes or to other types of life stress (e.g., total life change, positive life stress).

In addition, the conjunctive moderating effect involving social support reported by R.E. Smith et al. (1990), discussed earlier, was bolstered by Maddison and Prapavessis (2005). They found that the positive relationship between negative life stress and time lost due to injury in male rugby players was maximized when social support was low and when both avoidance coping and previous injury were high. This finding suggests that negative life stress exerts its greatest adverse effect on athletes' well-being when a host of other risk factors are present.

It is likely that the interactive relationships identified to date among psychosocial predictors of sport injury merely scratch the surface of potential moderating effects. Indeed, given the full spectrum of biopsychosocial variables included in the multifactorial model, numerous possible combinations of factors may confer injury risk on athletes. To uncover such combinations, we need large-scale research studies that measure extensive arrays of prospective contributors to injury repeatedly over time.

Mechanisms of Psychosocial Influence on Sport Injury Occurrence

Given the general nature of the multifactorial model and the multitude of ways in which athletes can become injured, it is no surprise that the model is silent with respect to the mechanisms by which psychosocial factors influence sport injury occurrence. On the other hand, the stress–injury model is a psychosocially oriented framework, and it speaks more explicitly about the role of psychosocial factors in sport injury occurrence. As argued earlier in this chapter, using the terminology of the multifactorial model, psychosocial factors contribute to athletes becoming both predisposed to injury (i.e., possessing a typically distal element of risk that makes injury more likely) and susceptible to injury (i.e., being on the verge of becoming injured, pending the presence of an inciting event). Psychosocial factors can even feature prominently in the inciting events that represent the last step in the causal chain—for example, when an angry opponent delivers a "cheap shot" to an athlete or when an athlete makes a fateful decision to push on despite experiencing a muscle twinge during competition.

In their original article on the stress–injury model, M.B. Andersen and Williams (1988) proposed three primary proximal mechanisms by which psychosocial factors contribute to sport injury occurrence: muscle tension, distracted attention, and narrowed peripheral vision. Each of these mechanisms is thought to result directly from the stress response, which itself is thought to be influenced by personality, history of stressors, and coping resources.

Empirical support for the proposed mechanisms varies. Despite the widespread notion that muscle tension emerges from the stress response, disturbs coordination, reduces flexibility, and contributes to the occurrence of a variety of musculoskeletal injuries (e.g., strains, sprains), these assertions are supported by remarkably little evidence. In contrast, there is some support for the idea that athletes become distracted under stressful conditions, whereupon they fail to attend to vital cues in the sport environment and sometimes become injured when a missed cue leads to an inciting event (e.g., collision, misstep). For example, as noted earlier, American football players who had experienced a major stressor in the past year experienced elevated risk for injury if they were low in attentional vigilance

(N.J. Thompson & Morris, 1994). Similarly, although the finding was not linked directly to the stress response, Swanik et al. (2007) found that collegiate athletes who sustained a noncontact injury to the anterior cruciate ligament (ACL) scored more poorly on a preseason test of visual attention than did a matched group of their peers who did not incur such an injury.

The strongest empirical support for a proposed mechanism by which a psychosocial factor affects sport injury occurrence involves narrowed peripheral vision. M.B. Andersen and Williams (1988) argued that "during stress, narrowing of the visual field may occur, leading to a failure to pick up vital cues in the periphery and thus increasing the likelihood of injury (e.g., getting blind-sided)" (p. 299). In fact, athletes have been shown to experience narrowing of peripheral vision during stressful conditions involving both laboratory stressors (J.M. Williams & Andersen, 1997; J.M. Williams, Tonymon, & Andersen, 1990, 1991) and real-life stressors (T.J. Rogers et al., 2003). For example, M.B. Andersen and Williams (1999) reported that among a sample of collegiate athletes with low social support, those who were high in negative life stress and peripheral narrowing sustained more injuries than did those who were low in negative life stress and peripheral narrowing. More recently, T.J. Rogers and Landers (2005) demonstrated that peripheral narrowing mediated 8 percent of the relationship between negative life stress and sport injury in a sample of high school athletes.

Elaborating on the physiological and psychological aspects of the stress response, Petrie and Perna (2004) extended the hypothesized influence of the stress response to include the following prospective and interrelated mechanisms:

- Suppressed immune system
- Disrupted tissue-repair process
- Compromised sleep
- Altered self-care behavior

Empirical links have been documented between stress and each of these four proposed mechanisms. For instance, immunosuppressive effects are well documented for long-lasting chronic stress (Segerstrom & Miller, 2004). Moreover, coupling life stress with rigorous physical training, both of which involve the secretion of the stress hormone cortisol, further suppresses the immune system (Perna & McDowell, 1995) and can inhibit processes vital to healing muscle and other body tissues (Kiecolt-Glaser, Page, Marucha, MacCallum, & Glaser, 1998; Petrie & Perna, 2004).

Stress can also interfere with sleep duration and quality (Cartwright & Wood, 1991; Van Reeth et al., 2000; W.F. Waters, Adams, Binks, & Varnado, 1993), which can bring about conditions conducive to the occurrence of injury—for example, compromised immune functioning, diminished concentration, slowed reaction time, hampered perception, increased aggressiveness, impaired decision making, and reduced secretion of growth hormone (Orzel-Gryglewska, 2010), which is a contributor to healing. In addition, stress can interfere with one's ability or inclination to take care of oneself (Heatherton & Penn, 1995; Steptoe, Wardle, Pollard, & Canaan, 1996), which, for athletes, may contribute to neglecting to eat nutritious meals, hydrate sufficiently, or engage in adequate stretching, strengthening, or other preventive activities (Petrie & Perna, 2004). Taking stock, although logical and theoretical connections can be drawn between these four mechanisms and the occurrence of sport injury, the hypothesized relationships have not been tested empirically and are therefore currently without research support.

Another potential mechanism by which psychosocial factors might influence the occurrence of sport injury lies in the behavior of athletes and their opponents in the competitive sport setting. Although this mechanism has been largely neglected in scientific literature on the psychosocial antecedents of sport injury, Bahr and Krosshaug (2005) identified player and opponent behavior as one of four categories of inciting events that could bring about injury in susceptible athletes. This cat-

egory could also include the cognitive and emotional underpinnings of athletes' actions toward and interactions with their opponents, because in some cases an athlete's decision to behave in a particular way (e.g., to initiate hard contact) is what sets in motion a course of events that culminates in an injury. At the same time, a player's behavior need not involve interaction with an opponent; it could simply reflect a decision made in the heat of competition (e.g., attempting a sharp turn without braking). Opponent behavior could be either intentionally or unintentionally (i.e., accidentally) injurious.

Although little is known about athlete (and opponent) behavior as a mechanism of sport injury, insight may be provided by several lines of research. For example, Bredemeier and her colleagues (e.g., Bredemeier, 1985; Bredemeier, Weiss, Shields, & Cooper, 1987) have extensively examined intentionally injurious acts in sport from the perspective of moral reasoning. This research may prove helpful in identifying athletes who are likely to attempt to injure opponents intentionally, why they might choose to do so, and which opponents they might attempt to injure. With regard to the latter issue, Soligard, Grindem, et al. (2010) found that high levels of technical skill, tactical skill, and physical strength were associated with an elevated risk of injury in soccer players. This finding suggests the possibility that strong players in some sports may be targets of opponent behavior that confers an increased risk of injury.

In another area of inquiry, fine-grained, video-based analyses have enabled researchers to determine the events immediately preceding injury in professional soccer players (T.E. Andersen, Larsen, Tenga, Engebretsen, & Bahr, 2003). In one study, the vast majority of ankle sprains observed were attributable to illegal tackles from the side in which the medial portion of the injured player's lower leg was struck by an opponent's foot (T.E. Andersen, Floerenes, Arnason, & Bahr, 2004). Thus, the influence of opponent behavior as an inciting event can be observable, quantifiable, and subject to analysis.

Biopsychosocial Analysis

Let us now return to the case of Alex, which led off the chapter. In hindsight, it is not surprising that he incurred an injury during the lacrosse season. Indeed, he (unintentionally, of course) collected risk factors for sport injury like they were going out of style. In addition to his previous injury to the same body part (shoulder) the year before, he experienced a series of major life events (the death of his father; the breakup of his romantic relationship; his mother's alcohol abuse; and increased responsibilities for household tasks, an internship, and a heavy course load) that compromised his health behavior (e.g., insomnia, poor eating habits) and left him weakened, distracted, and unfocused on the sport tasks at hand.

The circumstances of Alex's injury are highly consistent with prominent models of sport injury etiology. In terms of the multifactorial model, Alex's previous shoulder injury made him predisposed to subsequent injury; in turn, the stressful life events and their consequences increased his vulnerability until, finally, he sustained an injury upon encountering an unspecified inciting event, which may have been made more likely by his lack of focus. In terms of the stress–injury model, Alex had several risk factors that could have led to his injury. Little is revealed about his personality, but he had a history of stressors (i.e., major life events, previous injury) and an erosion of coping resources (at least in terms of social support, as evidenced by the dissolution of his romantic relationship and the death of his father) that appear to have affected his cognitive, behavioral, and, perhaps, physiological responses in ways that may have amplified his susceptibility to injury.

One of the primary benefits of models of sport injury etiology is that they suggest points of entry for preventive interven-tion. Although Alex's previous injury could not have been undone, his predisposition to future injury could conceivably have been modified by ensuring complete rehabilitation of his prior injury (if it was not). Similarly, although the stressful events he experienced might also have been unavoidable, he might have benefited from stress management training, academic support services, and social support. These measures might have helped Alex develop coping skills and given him resources to alter his reactions to life stressors, minimize his stress response, and, potentially, reduce his odds of incurring the new injury. Preventive efforts of this sort are addressed at length in chapter 3.

Summary

When we seek to develop strategies and interventions for preventing (or at least minimizing) and managing injuries, it is helpful to examine models of why and how athletes are injured and to know the psychosocial predictors of sport injury. To that end, this chapter presents two schools of thought regarding sport injury occurrence:

1. The multifactorial model of sport injury etiology
2. The stress–injury model

The multifactorial model proposes that factors in sport injury include both intrinsic or personal items (e.g., previous injury, joint stability, age, physical conditioning level) and extrinsic or environmental factors (e.g., nature of chosen sport, exposure to injury-enabling situations, coaching, equipment, environmental influences). Modifications of the model have added the concept of the inciting event, which includes the playing situation, the behavior of the athlete and opponents, and biomechanical characteristics.

The stress–injury model, on the other hand, posits the stress response as the proximal cause of sport injury. The stress response is described as resulting from the cognitive appraisals that athletes make in stressful competitive sport situations. Cognitive appraisals are influenced by three broad categories of psychosocial factors: personality (i.e., well-learned patterns of thinking, feeling, and behaving), history of stressors (e.g., minor and major life events, previous injury, daily hassles), and coping resources (e.g., stress management techniques, proper rest and nutrition, social support). Cognitive appraisals affect both physiological and attentional processes that can influence the occurrence of sport injury.

Although these two models evolved independently and appear to be quite different, they are in fact complementary; more specifically, the stress–injury model represents a specific pathway within the multifactorial model. Both models have been the source of considerable research and have made important contributions to understanding the etiology of sport injury. Consistent with the tenets of these models, numerous psychosocial factors have been identified as predictors of sport injury occurrence and time lost due to injury. Some factors have been linked to sport injury in a single study, whereas others have repeatedly emerged as predictors across multiple studies.

Although no "injury-prone" personality has been identified, personality is one psychosocial category connected to injury occurrence. Personality factors associated with injury include hardiness, locus of control, competitive trait anxiety, and achievement motivation. For example, higher levels of competitive trait anxiety are related to more and longer-lasting injuries. In addition, several studies have found a positive association between the type A personality pattern and overuse injuries in runners.

The most studied and consistently supported psychosocial predictor of sport injury is history of stressors. Total life-event stress (i.e., total stress from negative and positive life events) has frequently been correlated positively with subsequent injury. In contrast, little research has been conducted on the relationship between minor life events (e.g., daily hassles) and sport injury occurrence.

Coping resources have received the least attention from researchers and have demonstrated the fewest associations with sport injury occurrence. Studies examining the relationship between coping resources (e.g., coping strategies, social support) and sport injury occurrence and severity have been inconclusive. Additional psychosocial variables that have been identified as predictors of sport injury include neurocognitive functioning, perceived motivational climate, physical self-perceptions, positive states of mind, and sociability. High levels of perceived mastery climate, perceived sport competence, and sociability are associated with elevated risk of injury, whereas low levels of neurocognitive functioning and positive states of mind are inversely related to injury risk.

Relatively little is known about the mechanisms by which psychosocial factors affect sport injury occurrence. A variety of mechanisms have been proposed, including muscle tension, distracted attention, narrowed peripheral vision, suppressed immune functioning, disrupted tissue-repair process, compromised sleep, altered self-care behavior, and athlete and opponent behavior. Collectively, these factors may serve as a bridge between psychosocial factors and the occurrence of sport injury.

Discussion Questions

1. What similarities and differences exist between the multifactorial model of sport injury and the stress–injury model?

2. Why is it not possible to definitively determine the processes that cause sport injuries?

3. What are some proposed mechanisms by which psychosocial factors may contribute to the occurrence of sport injury?

4. What implications do theory and research about psychosocial antecedents of sport injury have for the prevention of sport injuries?

Chapter 3
Sport Injury Prevention

Chapter Objectives

1. To outline types and contemporary models of sport injury prevention
2. To describe the following methods of sport injury prevention: training, equipment, regulation, and psychosocial intervention

Members of a collegiate swim team met with a sport psychology consultant after each weekday practice from the beginning of the season in September through the end of the season in March. Each session included 10 minutes of progressive relaxation exercises, which were followed by 5 minutes of guided imagery focused on swimming skills. At the conclusion of this season-long intervention, 12 swimmers earned All-American honors, whereas only 1 had done so in the preceding season. In addition, although injury was not a focus of the sport psychology intervention, the team experienced 52 percent fewer injuries than in the previous year.

A similar program was implemented with a collegiate (American) football team at a major university. The format was essentially the same as for the swimmers—10 minutes of relaxation followed by 5 minutes of sport-specific imagery training—all conducted after a water break in the middle of practice five times per week during the preseason and twice per week during the competitive season. In the first year of the intervention, the team experienced its most successful season in 20 years. The intervention's second year, however, was disastrous from the standpoint of performance because a scandal rocked the football program and got the coaching staff fired. Even so, as with the swimmers, the team experienced fewer serious injuries (as compared with the results for typical preintervention and postintervention years) for the duration of the two-year sport psychology intervention (33 percent fewer in the first year and 28 percent fewer in the second year).

These cases, reported by Davis (1991), were not the randomized, controlled clinical trials necessary to demonstrate causation. They do, however, suggest that a sport psychology intervention consisting of relaxation and imagery might have a beneficial effect on injury rate in competitive athletes. In both cases, the goal of the intervention was not to prevent injury but to enhance performance. Even so, reduction in the occurrence of injury appears to have been an unintended favorable by-product.

Sport injury is a public health problem that exacts enormous personal and social costs, and prevention has been advocated as one means of addressing the issue (Emery, 2010; Klügl et al., 2010). As a result, recent years have brought increased emphasis on prevention of sport injury in both research and clinical practice (Klügl et al.; Matheson, Mohtadi, Safran, & Meeuwisse, 2010). The upswing in preventive efforts has also been reflected in the staging of a quartet of world congresses on sport injury prevention, which were held in 2005, 2008, 2011, and 2014.

To prevent sport injury, we must first understand how it occurs. Fortunately, as shown in chapter 2, an understanding of the antecedents of sport injury is emerging, and that understanding informs efforts to prevent the occurrence of sport injury. Because sport participation carries inherent risks, it is unlikely that we will ever completely prevent sport injury. However, learning about the factors that are related to—or, better yet, contribute to—sport injury occurrence can help us identify points of entry for preventive intervention. With that fact in mind, this chapter examines sport injury prevention with a particular emphasis on psychosocial aspects. It reviews types, models, and categories of prevention and addresses practical considerations for implementing preventive interventions.

Types of Prevention

The surest way to prevent sport injury is for people not to participate in sport. Of course, this solution is neither viable nor desirable—people will choose to participate in sport and expose themselves to the resulting risks. We focus, therefore, on sport injury prevention, which can be categorized into three types: primary, secondary, and tertiary. Primary prevention involves actions taken prior to the occurrence of sport injury, and these preventive efforts are extended to the entire population of interest (e.g., all athletes in a given league or in a certain club), regardless of individual members' level of risk. For example, if a requirement for hockey players to wear a mouth guard were implemented as a form of primary prevention, even players with no teeth would have to wear a mouth guard. Most preventive interventions that target sport injury fall into the category of primary prevention.

Secondary prevention involves actions taken prior to injury occurrence among individuals deemed to be at elevated risk for sport injury within a larger population of interest. Individuals possessing one or more of the risk factors for sport injury identified in chapter 2 are targeted for intervention, thus enabling the concentration of preventive resources on those who need them the most. For example, Maddison and Prapavessis (2005) implemented a stress management intervention with rugby players who were low in social support and high in avoidance coping—factors that the researchers had previously demonstrated as placing the players at increased risk for injury.

Tertiary prevention is not prevention at all in the traditional sense of the word. Rather, in tertiary prevention, athletes are treated as soon as possible after injury occurrence in an attempt to minimize the damage to the injured body part. Efforts are also made to rehabilitate injured athletes to the maximum extent possible. Most of the treatment that athletes receive for their injuries from sport health care professionals can be classified as tertiary prevention.

Models of Sport Injury Prevention

Several frameworks have emerged to guide sport injury prevention efforts. These frameworks serve as models to ensure that sport injury research and practice proceed in an organized, scientific manner. Models of sport injury prevention have been proposed by W. van Mechelen, Hlobil, & Kemper (1992), Finch (2006), and Van Tiggelen, Wickes, Stevens, Roosen, and Witvrouw (2008). The model put forward by W. van Mechelen et al. proposed a four-step framework. The first step involves identifying the magnitude of the sport injury problem and describing the incidence and severity of sport injury. The second step involves determining the etiology and mechanisms of sport injury, and the third step involves introducing preventive measures. The final step involves assessing the effectiveness of the preventive measures introduced in the third step by essentially repeating the first step—that is, checking whether the incidence and severity of sport injury have changed as a result of the preventive efforts.

Finch (2006) acknowledged that the model proposed by W. van Mechelen et al. (1992) had been valuable in guiding research on sport injury prevention and aligning it with public health approaches to injury prevention outside of sport, but she also identified a major shortcoming of the model. Specifically, it failed to consider challenges in implementing injury-prevention measures in sport settings; in fact, it completely neglected factors contributing to the adoption (or nonadoption) of preventive behavior. To remediate this deficiency, Finch proposed the six-step TRIPP framework, which is short for Translating Research into Injury Prevention Practice.

The first four steps of TRIPP resemble the four steps of the model put forth by W. van Mechelen et al. (1992). Specifically, step 1 of TRIPP consists of injury surveillance—an ongoing process of monitoring the occurrence of sport injuries in order to establish the extent of the problem and gauge progress toward achieving prevention aims. Step 2 is identical to the second step of the van Mechelen model—establishing the etiology and mechanisms of injury. Step 3 involves using a multidisciplinary approach based on theory and research to identify possible solutions to the sport injury problem and develop corresponding preventive interventions. Step 4 consists of subjecting the preventive measures generated in the third step to evaluation under "ideal

conditions"—that is, laboratory or controlled clinical or field settings in which researchers deliver interventions to coaches and athletes who have been convinced and helped to participate through incentives and reminders.

In the fifth and sixth steps of TRIPP, Finch (2006) departs from the model of W. van Mechelen et al. (1992). The purpose of TRIPP step 5 is to "describe intervention context [in order] to inform implementation strategies" (p. 4). This process involves getting a sense of the real-world sport contexts in which to apply the preventive measures developed in step 3 and evaluated in step 4. Doing so requires gathering information about athletes', coaches', and administrators' knowledge, attitudes, and current behaviors regarding sport safety practices. Ultimately, the critical tasks of step 5 are to determine how likely the target sport populations are to accept and adopt preventive interventions and to plan for the implementation of the interventions. In step 6, based on the information gathered in step 5, the preventive measures are implemented and evaluated in naturalistic sport settings under real-world conditions. In addition, whereas step 4 examined the *efficacy* of interventions, step 6 assesses their *effectiveness* (for more on the distinction between these two terms, see this chapter's Focus on Research box). Despite their importance, steps 5 and 6 are underrepresented in the research literature (Klügl et al., 2010).

Van Tiggelen et al. (2008) agreed with the contention of Finch (2006) that, contrary to the model of W. van Mechelen et al. (1992), merely showing that a preventive measure reduces the incidence or severity of injury is insufficient to demonstrate the effectiveness of that measure. As depicted in figure 3.1, they argued that for a preventive measure to be found effective, additional criteria must be satisfied. Specifically, after finding the preventive measure *efficacious* in the fourth steps of the W. van Mechelen et al. and Finch models, it is also necessary to show that the measure displays *efficiency*, is complied with adequately, and does not adversely affect risk taking.

The first criterion, efficiency, is demonstrated when those involved in adopting and

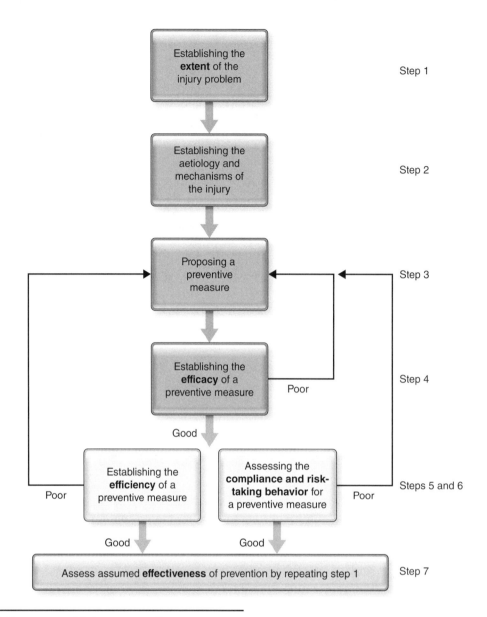

Figure 3.1 Sequence of injury prevention.

Reproduced from *British Journal of Sports Medicine*, "Effective prevention of sports injuries: A model integrating efficacy, efficiency, compliance and risk-taking behavior," D. Van Tiggelen et al., 42: 648-652, 2008, with permission from BMJ Publishing Group Ltd.

implementing preventive measures (e.g., administrators, coaches, athletes) deem that the benefits (e.g., fewer injuries, lower medical costs, fewer lost training hours, less postinjury distress) outweigh the costs (e.g., monetary expenses of prevention-related goods and services, time required to implement measures, discomfort or restricted movement when wearing protective gear). The second criterion, compliance, is satisfied when the preventive measures are introduced and are adhered to by intervention recipients. As discussed in chap-

ter 6, the extent to which people adhere to interventions related to sport injury is influenced by a multitude of personal, social, cognitive, emotional, and behavioral factors. Compliance with preventive measures cannot be assumed, even for highly motivated athletes.

The third criterion, which involves risk-taking behavior, is satisfied by the avoidance of "risk homeostasis" (Wilde, 1998), in which the beneficial effects of prevention are offset by a corresponding increase in risk taking. It can be challenging to avoid risk homeostasis (also

Efficacy Versus Effectiveness

The TRIPP framework (C.F. Finch, 2006) highlights the distinction between efficacy studies and effectiveness studies pertaining to the prevention and treatment of sport injury. Whereas efficacy research examines an intervention's success in preventing or reducing sport injury occurrence under controlled experimental conditions, effectiveness research evaluates success in a naturalistic, real-world environment. In essence, efficacy research addresses whether the intervention *can* work, whereas effectiveness research addresses whether it *does* work in the real world.

Both types of study are vital to the eventual success of interventions designed to prevent or reduce sport injury occurrence. Once researchers have identified factors that cause or contribute to the incidence of sport injury, they can develop interventions that alter those causal or contributing factors in an attempt to decrease the injury rate. Newly developed interventions are then subjected to scientific scrutiny in efficacy studies, first simply to demonstrate that the intervention is feasible (i.e., "proof of concept") and later to show that the intervention has the intended effect on the occurrence of sport injury. The gold standard for intervention research is the randomized controlled trial (RCT), in which eligible participants are randomly assigned to a treatment or no-treatment group. RCTs are often used in efficacy research because they allow for a critical test of the intervention's potency. In providing the critical test of the intervention, however, an artificial study environment can be created in which extraneous, real-world influences are minimized. Interventions are typically delivered, by the investigators themselves, to participants (e.g., athletes) whose involvement in the study is encouraged, supported, and reinforced by the researchers and by coaches and administrators (Finch, 2006).

Effectiveness studies are needed because interventions that succeed in the controlled environment of efficacy studies sometimes fail miserably when put into practice in the real world. For a vivid example outside of the domain of sport injury prevention, one need look no further than interventions pertaining to physical activity. Evidence abounds of the beneficial effects of exercise on a wide variety of physical and mental health outcomes. *If* people exercise with the appropriate frequency, duration, and intensity for a long enough period of time, they are likely to reap benefits. But that's a big *if*, because dropout rates for exercise programs stand at about 50 percent (Buckworth & Dishman, 2007).

Presumably, the same question applies to programs aimed at sport injury prevention. As emphasized by Van Tiggelen et al. (2008), preventive measures shown to be *efficacious* will be *effective* only to the extent that athletes complete the efficacious measures. An athlete may fail to complete a sport injury prevention program for any of many reasons. For example, coaches may not provide adequate time or support, the intervention may not be delivered with fidelity to the original, or the athlete might simply fail to adhere to the requirements of the program. Steps 5 and 6 in the TRIPP framework (Finch, 2006) are devoted to understanding and overcoming the barriers to successful implementation of efficacious interventions to prevent sport injury. In the end, interventions that are not efficacious are highly unlikely to be effective, and interventions that *are* efficacious still may be either effective or ineffective. Additional research efforts beyond efficacy studies are needed to help translate promising preventive methods into real-world practice.

Focus on Research

known as "risk compensation"), as illustrated by the following research findings: Skiers and snowboarders who wore a helmet went nearly 5 kilometers per hour faster than those who did not wear a helmet (Shealy, Ettlinger, & Johnson, 2005); children who wore safety gear proceeded through an obstacle course featuring various hazards faster and more recklessly than those who did not wear safety gear (Morrongiello, Walpole, & Lasenby, 2007); and athletes in collision sports (e.g., hockey, rugby) reported that they play more aggressively when wearing protective gear (C.F. Finch, McIntosh, & McCrory, 2001; Woods et al., 2007). The dangerous behavior that characterizes risk homeostasis may be underlain by erroneous beliefs about the protective capabilities of safety gear (Chaduneli & Ibanez, 2014).

Content Categories of Sport Injury Prevention

Given the many factors associated with the occurrence of sport injury, efforts to prevent sport injury vary widely in focus. Still, Klügl et al. (2010) have identified three main categories of content in sport injury prevention:

1. Training
2. Equipment
3. Regulation

These categories are described in the following sections, along with an additional category that is a mere blip on the radar screen of sport injury prevention: psychosocial intervention.

Training

Training intervention, which is currently the dominant form of sport injury prevention in research investigations (McBain et al., 2011), consists of "all forms of physical preparation for sport and exercise" (Klügl et al., 2010, p. 408). Common targets of training include agility; balance; sport-specific skills; and muscular strength, endurance, and power. One popular preventive approach in this category is "neuromuscular training," which "incorporates general (e.g., fundamental movements) and specific (e.g., exercises targeted to motor control deficits) strength and conditioning activities, such as resistance, dynamic stability, core-focused strength, plyometric, and agility, that are designed to enhance health and skill-related components of physical fitness" (Myer et al., 2011, p. 157). The rationale for neuromuscular training holds that

- biomechanical and other physical deficits underlie many sport injuries;
- neuromuscular training helps reduce the deficits that underlie the injuries; and, therefore,
- completing neuromuscular training reduces the occurrence of sport injuries.

These assertions have been supported by empirical evidence. For example, screening of neuromuscular characteristics (e.g., certain patterns of electrical activity in the knee flexor and extensor muscles) has been found to predict the occurrence of ACL rupture (Zebis, Andersen, Bencke, Kjær, & Aagaard, 2009). In addition, neuromuscular training can lower the levels of sport injury risk related to biomechanics, flexibility, and strength (e.g., Lim et al., 2009). Research also suggests that neuromuscular training is an efficacious strategy for decreasing injury risk among both youth and adult sport participants (Aaltonen, Karjalainen, Heinonen, Parkkari, & Kujala, 2007; Abernethy & Bleakley, 2007; Campbell et al., 2014; Gagnier, Morgenstern, & Chess, 2013; Laursen, Bertelsen, & Andersen, 2014; O'Malley, Murphy, Gissane, McCarthy-Persson, & Blake, 2014; Parkkari, Kujala, & Kannus, 2001; Pasanen et al., 2008).

One primary advantage of neuromuscular training is its adaptability; specifically, it can be readily tailored to the age and chosen sport in the population of interest. For example, efficacious neuromuscular training programs have been developed specifically for youth sport participants (Myer et al., 2011); basketball players (e.g., Emery, Rose, McAllister, & Meeuwisse, 2007); soccer players (e.g., Emery & Meeuwisse, 2010; Mandelbaum et al., 2005); and prevention of injury in certain parts of the body, such as the ankle (e.g., Bahr & Lian, 1997; Stasinopoulos, 2004; E. Verhagen et al., 2004) and the ACL (e.g., Caraffa, Cerulli, Projetti, Aisa, & Rizzo, 1996; Mandelbaum et al.; Myklebust et al., 2003). As with any intervention, the success of neuromuscular training programs presumably depends at least in part on adherence to program requirements (Hägglund, Atroshi, Wagner, & Waldén, 2013; Soligard, Nilstad, et al., 2010; Sugimoto et al., 2012).

One prime example of a widely disseminated neuromuscular training program can be found in the "11 + " prevention program (as well as its predecessor, "The 11"). Developed with the support of the Fédération Internationale de Football Association (FIFA), the worldwide governing body for soccer, the 11 + program consists of a series of soccer-specific running, strengthening, jumping, and balancing exercises that can be completed as a warm-up in about 20 minutes by players who are familiar with it (Soligard et al., 2008). Freely available on the web, the 11 and 11 + programs have been subjected to extensive evaluation in Switzerland (Junge et al., 2011; Junge, Rosch, Peterson, Graf-Baumann, & Dvorak, 2002), Norway (Soligard et al., 2008; Soligard, Nilstad, et al., 2010), the Netherlands (A. van Beijsterveldt, Krist, van de Port, & Backx, 2011b), Canada (Steffen, Emery, et al., 2013; Steffen, Meeuwisse, et al., 2013), and the United States (Silvers, Mandelbaum, Bizzini, & Dvorak, 2014). Research findings have generally supported the programs' efficacy and effectiveness.

In Switzerland, where soccer injuries account for annual health care costs of approximately $130 million, the 11 program was used as part of an ambitious countrywide campaign to reduce the incidence of soccer injuries by 10 percent. All coaches of amateur teams in the national soccer association were given instruction in how to implement the program in their training. Four years later, more than half of the coaches reported that their teams were still performing all or most of the program. Players on these teams experienced 12 percent fewer match injuries, 27 percent fewer noncontact match injuries, and about 25 percent fewer training injuries than did players on teams whose coaches reported that they were not performing the program. Teams performing the program also experienced 17 percent fewer match injuries and 19 percent fewer training injuries relative to their own experience of four years earlier (Junge et al., 2011). Thus, it is possible to develop a sport-specific neuromuscular training program, implement it on a large scale, and achieve a demonstrable favorable effect on injury outcomes.

Comparable success was achieved with a neuromuscular warm-up program similar to the 11 + among 1,500 girls participating in high school basketball and soccer in Chicago. About half of the 95 coaches in the study were randomly assigned to a control condition, and the remaining coaches were randomly assigned to the intervention group. Coaches in the control group used their usual warm-up, whereas coaches in the intervention group received two hours of instruction on how to implement a 20-minute neuromuscular warm-up program with their players; they were also given a DVD and printed materials with specific information about the program. Intervention-group coaches reported that they used the prescribed warm-up in more than 80 percent of their training sessions. As compared with control-group players, players in the intervention group experienced 65 percent fewer gradual-onset lower-extremity injuries; 56 percent fewer acute-onset, noncontact, lower-extremity injuries; and 66 percent fewer noncontact ankle sprains (LaBella et al., 2011). Thus, in this study, as with the 11 program in Switzerland, a minimal neuromuscular training intervention exerted a substantial favorable effect on the occurrence of sport injury (for more on this topic, see this chapter's Focus on Application sidebar).

Equipment

Until the past decade, equipment interventions were the most studied form of sport injury prevention (Klügl et al., 2010; McBain et al., 2011). Preventive activities in this category focus on getting athletes to play on safer surfaces (e.g., gymnasium floors) or use protective equipment (e.g., helmets, mouth guards) or devices (e.g., braces, orthotics). The impetus to get athletes to play on certain surfaces (and not on others) comes from research showing that injury rates vary as a function of playing surface. For example, one study found that ACL injuries in female team handball players occurred with greater frequency on floors with artificial surfaces than on floors with wooden surfaces (Olsen, Myklebust, Engebretsen, Holme, & Bahr, 2003). In another study, when high school American football players competed on Field-Turf rather than on natural grass, they sustained *more* low-severity noncontact injuries, muscle injuries, surface or epidermal injuries, and injuries in high temperatures but *fewer* short-term injuries (one- to two-day time loss), long-term injuries (22 or more days of time loss), head or neural injuries, and ligament injuries (Meyers & Barnhill, 2004).

Is the Juice Worth the Squeeze?

"An ounce of prevention is worth a pound of cure." So says an adage ultimately credited to the Dutch humanist Erasmus, who observed half a millennium ago that "prevention is better than cure" (Van Tiggelen et al., 2008, p. 648). Is this in fact true in the realm of sport injury? Does the value of prevention truly exceed that of treatment? Can such a comparison even be made? The evidence discussed in this chapter certainly suggests that a variety of interventions can be effective in reducing the occurrence of sport injury, but how does one go about establishing the worth of preventive activities?

One way of evaluating the merits of preventive interventions for sport injury is to examine the "bottom line"—the financial impact. In this vein, McGuine, Hetzel, Wilson, and Brooks (2012) argued persuasively that despite its initial cost, providing all high school American football players with lace-up ankle braces would result in substantial savings against the total comprehensive costs of ankle injuries suffered by high school American football players nationwide. Similarly, J. Williams (2011) conducted a cost analysis of the LaBella et al. (2011) study, in which a neuromuscular intervention akin to the 11+ program (discussed in this chapter's main text) reduced the injury risk in a sample of high school soccer and basketball players. Based on the reported cost of training coaches to implement the program ($80 per coach), Williams reasoned that all of the varsity and junior varsity coaches in the league could be trained for $960. Furthermore, in light of data indicating that one ACL tear could be prevented for every eleven coaches trained, this investment of less than $1,000 could

save in excess of $17,000 in medical costs associated with the surgical repair of a torn ACL. A subsequent investigation provided additional support for the cost-effectiveness of neuromuscular training for the prevention of ACL injuries in young athletes (Swart et al., 2014). Clearly, then, one can make a monetary argument for implementing sport injury prevention programs; in other words, an ounce of sport injury prevention may indeed be worth a pound of sport injury cure.

If sport injury prevention programs accomplish their intended aims in a cost-effective fashion, then why are they not implemented on a more widespread basis? Despite progress in developing, evaluating, and refining interventions to reduce the occurrence of sport injury, many barriers to widespread implementation remain. These obstacles involve issues of time, money, education, and motivation. With respect to time, even sport health care professionals whose job duties include sport injury prevention are often distracted from implementing preventive interventions by more pressing matters, such as treating acute injuries and directing rehabilitation activities. Coaches also face limitations on the time available in which to implement preventive interventions, and their access to training facilities and to the athletes they coach may also be restricted. Fortunately, some equipment interventions require little extra time, and some training and psychosocial interventions can enhance sport performance even as they help prevent injury.

Preventive interventions can also be limited by money concerns when the costs of equipment or services

Although insufficient evidence is available to conclude that using protective equipment and devices is efficacious in preventing sport injury in adolescents (Abernethy & Bleakley, 2007), data from randomized clinical trials indicate beneficial effects of protective equipment and devices on injury outcomes in older participants (Aaltonen et al., 2007). For example, the use of ankle supports can decrease injury occurrence in basketball and soccer; similarly, wearing shock-absorbing insoles can reduce the incidence of lower-limb stress frac-

tures (Parkkari et al., 2001). Helmets and other forms of headgear have been widely promoted as means of preventing head injury in sports as varied as American football, baseball, bicycling, cricket, equestrianism, rugby, skiing, snowboarding, and soccer. And the available evidence suggests that helmet use is associated with substantial reductions in concussions and other head injuries for most of the sports tested (McIntosh et al., 2011).

Despite positive perceptions of the benefits of wearing protective gear (Kahanov, Dusa, exceed the budget—whether of a sport health care professional, a coach, a parent, or an athlete—allocated for injury prevention. The issue is further complicated by the fact that one group of financial stakeholders in sport injury prevention—insurance companies—is not heavily involved in implementing preventive interventions in sport settings. As with time restrictions, monetary concerns can be eased by interventions that serve the purposes of both performance enhancement and risk reduction.

Lack of education can also be a barrier to implementing preventive interventions. This is the case when people in the best positions to implement interventions (or to make it possible to do so)—such as sport administrators, sport health care professionals, coaches, and even athletes themselves—are unaware of appropriate interventions or lack knowledge of how to put them into practice (Orr et al., 2013). Fortunately, the web provides an effective, low-cost vehicle for disseminating information, such as the following:

· The rationale for introducing preventive interventions to athletes

· The content of relevant interventions

· Strategies for implementing interventions with specific populations

However, unless the appropriate parties are motivated to seek out such information, even the best online resources may go unused (Vriend, Coehoorn, & Verhagen, 2015). Complicating matters further, the quality of online educational resources varies. For example, a study of mobile applications (i.e., apps) for sport injury prevention revealed that the vast majority were not scientifically sound (D.M. van Mechelen, van Mechelen, & Verhagen, 2014). Thus, even when motivation is adequate, exposure to supposedly educational materials may not translate into adoption of evidence-based practices.

Motivation is central not only to education about sport injury prevention but also to successful implementation of preventive interventions. Without sufficient motivation, sport governing bodies will not change rules to protect athletes' health, sport administrators will not authorize funds to purchase protective equipment or enable staff to deliver preventive interventions, sport health care professionals will not devote adequate attention to prevention as compared with treatment, coaches will not dedicate training time to preventive activities, and, perhaps most important, athletes will not adhere to preventive interventions. The motivation to facilitate or engage in preventive action can derive from a variety of sources, including the threat of litigation, a sense of professional responsibility, a need to keep top athletes healthy and available for competition, and a desire to stay injury free in pursuit of one's sport goals. Reminding stakeholders in the sport system of their role-specific incentives for adopting a preventive stance may increase the likelihood of realizing the promise of sport injury prevention.

Wilkinson, & Roberts, 2005) and its demonstrated efficacy (e.g., Janssen, van Mechelen, & Verhagen, 2014; McIntosh et al., 2011; Parkkari et al., 2001; Schieber et al., 1996) and cost-effectiveness (Janssen, Hendriks, van Mechelen, & Verhagen, 2014) in preventing sport injury, use of protective gear varies and can be extremely low. Among in-line skaters, for example, wrist guards and elbow pads can reduce wrist and elbow injuries by more than 80 percent, but less than 10 percent of skaters wear them (Schieber et al.). As with neuromuscular training programs, the effectiveness of protective equipment is contingent on adequate adherence to the preventive intervention. In simpler terms, even the strongest battle armor fails to protect soldiers if it goes unworn. Therefore, regulatory action is sometimes needed in order to bring about change.

Regulation

The regulation category is an infrequently examined (and enacted) form of sport injury prevention. It involves efforts to curb injury by changing the rules, regulations, and even laws that govern sport (Klügl et al., 2010). Despite the rarity of regulatory change as a means of injury prevention, and as a topic of scholarly inquiry, there is no shortage of success stories in which the modification of a rule or a law was followed by a decrease in the occurrence of sport injury. For example, in a study of junior ice-hockey players, the use of fair-play rules—in which teams receive points, regardless of whether they win or lose, for staying below a designated number of penalties per game—was associated with the athletes experiencing nearly five times fewer "notable" injuries and incurring only about half the previous number of penalties (Roberts, Brust, Leonard, & Hebert, 1996).

Similarly, in American football, a rule change made in 1976 at the collegiate and scholastic levels to decrease head-down contact and spearing was followed by a steady decrease in catastrophic cervical spine injuries (Heck, Clarke, Peterson, Torg, & Weis, 2004). Decreases in several types of injury have also followed rule changes in Australian football (Orchard, McCrory, Makdissi, Seward, & Finch, 2014). In baseball and softball, data show that the use of breakaway (quick-release) bases is associated with dramatically fewer sliding injuries (for a review, see Janda, 2003); as a result, Little League Baseball and Little League Softball mandated the use of breakaway bases for all league games. In karate, both injuries to the head and injuries to young competitors dropped significantly after the world governing body made rule changes that instituted heavy penalties for uncontrolled blows (Macan, Bundalo-Vrbanac, & Romic, 2006). And in youth cricket, the injury rate dropped markedly following the introduction of rules requiring every player to wear a helmet (Shaw & Finch, 2008).

In what is arguably the most comprehensive attempt to reduce sport injury occurrence in the general population, an entire municipality was targeted for an intervention as part of the World Health Organization (WHO) Safe Community program and then evaluated in relation to a comparably sized control mu-

nicipality that did not receive the intervention. The intervention initiated fair-play rules in team sports, supervision of youth during horseback activities, and use of protective gear and warm-up activities in soccer. No changes in injury rate were observed for the control community over the six-year study period. For the intervention community, however, a reduction in the injury rate was found among males under the age of 65 years from households in which the "vocationally important" member was employed. Especially noteworthy is the fact that the study was conducted in the mid to late 1980s (Timpka, Lindqvist, Ekstrand, & Karlsson, 2005)! Nevertheless, rule changes alone may be insufficient to reduce the occurrence of sport injury without appropriate regulatory enforcement (Klügl et al., 2010).

Psychosocial Intervention

Were it not for the restriction of training interventions to *physical* preparation for sport or exercise, psychosocial intervention could just as easily be placed in the training category because it generally involves training in an area of direct relevance to sport—for example, stress management. Support for the use of psychosocial intervention for sport injury prevention has been obtained through two lines of evidence: anecdotal and case reports and experimental studies.

Anecdotal and Case Reports

The earliest documentation of the potentially beneficial effects of psychosocial intervention on sport injury occurrence appeared in a series of anecdotal and case reports in which the primary intervention focus was not injury prevention but sport performance (Davis, 1991; DeWitt, 1980; S.M. Murphy, 1988; Schomer, 1990). DeWitt conducted two studies examining the effects of a combined intervention featuring cognitive and electromyographic (EMG) biofeedback training on muscle tension, heart rate, and ratings of sport performance in male collegiate football and basketball players. The cognitive training program included techniques such as cognitive restructuring, mental rehearsal, and relaxation. In postexperimental interviews, participants who received the intervention reported that they experienced a decrease in minor injuries over the course of the study (DeWitt).

In another case, S.M. Murphy (1988) reported that in his role as a sport psychology consultant at the U.S. Olympic Festival, he led a series of relaxation sessions with a team of 12 players (7 of whom were injured) during the period prior to the competition. In an apparent case of tertiary prevention for the athletes with injuries and secondary prevention for the athletes without injuries, the entire team was able to participate in the Festival (S.M. Murphy).

In yet another example, Schomer (1990) trained 10 marathon runners to use an associative cognitive strategy that involved monitoring bodily symptoms and other internal, task-related processes. The primary goal was to optimize performance, but Schomer reported that the runners were also able to run at high intensity while avoiding overuse injury thanks to the ongoing attention they paid to their bodies.

In the case described at the beginning of this chapter, Davis (1991) implemented a stress management intervention featuring progressive relaxation and mental rehearsal of sport skills with collegiate swimming and American football teams for the purpose of performance enhancement. Both teams experienced not only competitive success but also reduced injury rates relative to the year before the intervention was introduced. As in the studies by DeWitt (1980) and S.M. Murphy (1988), sport injury prevention thus appears to have been an unanticipated bonus of a psychosocial intervention.

Experimental Studies

From the time of DeWitt's (1980) anecdotal report, 16 years passed before the publication of an experimental study designed a priori—before the fact—to test the efficacy of psychosocial intervention in preventing sport injury. In that study, G. Kerr and Goss (1996) examined the effects of a stress management program on stress and time lost to injury in a sample of 16 male and 8 female gymnasts who ranged in age from 14 to 25 years and competed at the national or international level. After

being matched into pairs on the basis of age, gender, and performance level, participants were randomly assigned to either the experimental group or the control group. The study monitored participants' injury status (number of injuries and time lost from sport due to injury) and obtained measures of positive general stress, negative general stress, positive athletic stress, and negative athletic stress before the competitive season, at midseason (four months after the preseason assessment), and at the national championships (eight months after the preseason assessment). Participants in the experimental group received 16 individual, one-hour, biweekly sessions based on stress inoculation training (Meichenbaum, 1985), which addressed topics such as negative thought replacement, relaxation, and imagery. Participants in the control group received no treatment.

Over the course of the study, all participants sustained at least one injury. Participants in the experimental group had significantly lower levels of both negative athletic stress and total (general plus athletic) negative stress than those in the control group. Although the mean "injury incidence score" was only half as large for the experimental group as for the control group at the final assessment, the difference was not statistically significant. Therefore, although the stress management intervention was effective in reducing stress, it appeared not to have been effective in reducing the occurrence of injury.

However, in reviewing the report by G. Kerr and Goss (1996), M.B. Andersen and Stoové (1998) noted that the researchers "were probably too cautious in interpreting the results of an innovative and exploratory study" (pp. 168–169). Specifically, Andersen and Stoové argued convincingly that although the difference between the experimental and control groups in injury incidence was not statistically significant, the *effect size* (a measure of the magnitude of the difference between the two groups that, in this case, was independent of sample size) was underestimated and was likely to have been indicative of a substantial influence by the stress management intervention on the occurrence of injury. Thus the study may have been hampered by the low statistical power afforded by the small sample size.

In another study that appears to have been adversely affected by low statistical power, Kolt, Hume, Smith, and Williams (2004) investigated the effects of a stress management program similar to that of G. Kerr and Goss (1996) on injury and stress in a sample of 17 girls and 3 boys who had competed in gymnastics at the national or international level. The program was implemented with gymnasts in the experimental group in a series of 12 one-hour sessions over a 24-week period. Gymnasts in the control group received a placebo treatment in which anthropometric measurements were taken and lectures on nutrition were given. Injury status was assessed by self-report on a weekly basis over the course of the nine-month study, and measures of general and athletic stress were administered at the start of the study and at three-month intervals thereafter. The study found no statistically significant effects of the intervention on either stress or injury, although a medium to high effect size was reported for injury, which suggests that a clinically meaningful preventive effect on injury may have been obscured by the study's small sample size and concomitant lack of statistical power.

An unambiguous preventive effect of a stress management intervention on sport injury occurrence was documented by Perna, Antoni, Baum, Gordon, and Schneiderman (2003) in a study of 20 female and 14 male collegiate rowers. The rowers were stratified by gender and competitive level and randomly assigned to either the experimental group or the control group. Rowers in the experimental group received a seven-session, athlete-specific stress management intervention based on the stress inoculation training approach of Meichenbaum (1985) over a four-week period. In contrast, rowers in the control group participated in a single two-hour session that presented information about stress management. The investigators assessed frequency and duration of injury and illness by reviewing the rowers' medical charts. They administered measures of life stress, mood, and serum cortisol directly before and after the intervention.

Over the course of the study, participants in the experimental group experienced significantly fewer days injured or ill and significantly fewer medical office visits for injury or illness than did participants in the control group. Negative affect was found to partially mediate the relationship between receiving the intervention (or not) and the number of days injured or ill; specifically, receiving the stress management intervention was inversely related to negative affect, which, in turn, was positively related to number of days injured or ill. Thus, the intervention may have exerted a protective effect on injury and illness at least in part by helping the rowers cope with stressors and regulate their mood.

Johnson, Ekengren, and Andersen (2005) built on these findings in a study of elite soccer players. After administering measures of life stress, personality, and coping resources to 132 male players and 103 female players, Johnson et al. identified players scoring in the highest 50 percent for life stress and the lowest 50 percent for coping resources as being at elevated risk for injury. Players in the high-risk subsample were then matched on the basis of age, gender, and level of competition and randomly assigned to either the experimental group or the control group. Players in the experimental group received a brief intervention in six individual in-person sessions and two telephone contacts over a 19-week period. The intervention featured "somatic and cognitive relaxation . . . stress management skills . . . goal setting skills . . . attribution and self-confidence training . . . and . . . identification and discussion about critical incidents related to their [athletes'] soccer participation and situations in everyday life" (p. 34). Players in the control group received no treatment.

To make it more likely that the intervention would produce changes in psychosocial variables that would in turn substantially alter players' injury risk, the researchers introduced the intervention only to players with the greatest psychosocial risk for becoming injured. (This approach accords with the differential effects of neuromuscular training on ACL injury-risk factors of athletes at high versus low risk of ACL injury as demonstrated by Myer, Ford,

Brent, & Hewett [2007].) Over the course of the study, injury frequency data were collected from coaches six times, and the results were quite striking. In the control group, 13 of 16 players sustained at least one injury, whereas in the experimental group only 3 of 13 players were injured. In other words, the control group averaged 1.3 injuries per player, whereas the experimental group averaged only 0.2 injuries per player. This difference was both clinically and statistically significant.

Like Johnson et al. (2005), Maddison and Prapavessis (2005) targeted the most psychosocially vulnerable athletes for receipt of their cognitive-behavioral stress management intervention based on stress inoculation training (Meichenbaum, 1985). The investigators identified 48 rugby players as being at elevated risk for injury due to low scores on social support or high scores on avoidance coping or previous injury, then randomly assigned each player to either an experimental group or a control group. They delivered the stress management intervention to members of the experimental group in six 60- to 90-minute sessions over a four-week period during the preseason; players in the control group received no treatment. Players in both groups recorded the number of injuries they sustained and the number of days of rugby participation they lost due to injury on a weekly basis. The investigators obtained measures of sport-specific competitive anxiety and coping resources before and after the competitive season.

The study results indicated that relative to players in the control group, players who received the stress management intervention reported less worry, higher coping resources, and fewer days of rugby lost due to injury. The effects of the intervention on worry and coping resources did not, however, account for the smaller amount of time lost. Therefore, although the intervention had a favorable effect on an important injury outcome (time loss), it is not known how the intervention produced the salubrious effect.

More recently, Tranaeus and her colleagues (Tranaeus, Johnson, Engström, Skillgate, & Werner, 2014; Tranaeus, Johnson, Ivarsson, et al., 2014) investigated the effects of a stress management intervention on injury occurrence in elite male and female floorball players. With a total of 346 players, the study possessed adequate statistical power. The intervention consisted of six one-hour sessions designed to furnish the players with skills to reduce the stress response; players in the control group received no intervention. Although players in the intervention group experienced fewer injuries than did players in the control group over the two seasons monitored, the small effect was not statistically significant.

Only one experimental study of a psychosocially based preventive intervention featured an approach other than that of attempting to reduce injury risk through stress management. In that study, Arnason, Engebretsen, and Bahr (2005) attempted to prevent or minimize injury occurrence among male soccer players by fostering an awareness of the risk, types, and mechanisms of injury in soccer. Members of nine elite and first-division teams viewed a 15-minute video presentation and discussed with a teammate each of the 12 commonly occurring injury incidents depicted in the video. Specifically, they addressed the playing situation that led up to the incident, the incident's cause or causes, and potential strategies for preventing it. In contrast, control-group members of eight elite and first-division teams received no intervention. Team physical therapists recorded injury outcomes, coaches recorded training exposure, and official records were consulted to obtain match exposure.

The results indicated that the intervention and control groups did not differ from each other in injury incidence in either training or match play over the course of the study. Although the findings suggested that awareness of factors associated with sport injury occurrence is not sufficient to reduce the incidence of injury, it should be noted in this case that the validity and use of the injury-avoidance strategies offered by the players was not evaluated. Awareness is likely useful in preventing injury only when it translates into action taken by athletes, but this study involved no sustained effort to translate the intervention content into behavior on the field.

Biopsychosocial Analysis

Effective prevention of sport injury involves biological, psychological, and social components. From a biological standpoint, training interventions can reduce injury risk by acting directly on biological parameters, and equipment interventions can decrease susceptibility to injury by protecting anatomical structures. The psychological component is evident not only in psychosocial interventions themselves, which influence psychological and physiological processes underlying injury occurrence, but also in the adherence behavior that is vital to the success of all kinds of intervention (via training, equipment, regulation, and psychosocial approaches). Regulatory interventions are initiated at the social (i.e., organizational) level, and social factors can also affect the extent to which training-based, equipment-based, and psychosocial interventions are adopted.

The case histories reported by Davis (1991) and summarized at the beginning of this chapter serve as examples of primary prevention of sport injury through psychosocial intervention. Because the apparent injury-reducing effects of the intervention were discovered serendipitously, the sequence of events in documenting the effectiveness of stress management interventions departed from the models of sport injury prevention proposed by W. van Mechelen et al. (1992), C.F. Finch (2006), and Van Tiggelen et al. (2008). Issues normally associated with implementing preventive interventions may have been minimized by the fact that the stated purpose of the intervention was to enhance performance rather than prevent injury.

Summary

Informed by research on predictors of sport injury occurrence, preventive interventions have been developed to address the public health problem of sport injury. In general, preventive interventions either target all athletes in a given population (i.e., primary prevention), target only the athletes in a given population who are deemed at elevated risk for injury (i.e., sec-

ondary prevention), or focus on athletes who have sustained injuries in an attempt to minimize the damage (i.e., tertiary prevention).

Prevention models have been proposed that are specific to sport injury. In one four-step model, for example, prevention of sport injury involves identifying the magnitude (i.e., incidence and severity) of the sport injury problem, determining the causes of injury, introducing preventive measures, and assessing their effectiveness. A second model, the TRIPP framework, involves six steps:

1. Conducting surveillance of sport injury
2. Establishing the etiology and mechanisms of injury
3. Using theory and research from multiple disciplines to devise potential interventions
4. Implementing the preventive intervention under ideal conditions
5. Describing the context of the intervention to facilitate planning for implementation in real-world conditions
6. Implementing the intervention in real-world conditions and evaluating its effectiveness

These models, particularly the TRIPP framework, highlight the distinction between efficacy (whether the intervention works in a controlled setting) and effectiveness (whether it works in a real-world setting).

Preventive interventions can be placed into four main content categories:

1. Training
2. Equipment
3. Regulation
4. Psychosocial interventions

Preventive training interventions focus on building attributes such as agility; balance; sport-specific skills; and muscular strength, endurance, and power. Neuromuscular training programs have been shown to be both effective and cost-effective in preventing sport injury. One training program in particular, named 11 + , has been widely disseminated via the web. Equipment interventions involve having athletes play on safer surfaces, wear protective gear, and use protective devices. Regulatory interventions involve changing rules and regulations in sport. In keeping with the stress–injury model, psychosocial interventions focus primarily on managing stress; they have received preliminary research support. Adoption of preventive interventions—even ones that have been proven effective—can be limited by factors such as lack of time, money, education, or motivation.

Discussion Questions

1. What is the connection between psychosocial interventions to prevent (or reduce) sport injury occurrence and the models of sport injury occurrence discussed in chapter 2?

2. What are some challenges in implementing interventions designed to prevent sport injury in real-world settings?

3. How much of a threat is "risk compensation" to the effectiveness of sport injury prevention programs?

4. How is psychology involved in the potential success of training-based, equipment-based, and regulatory interventions to prevent sport injury occurrence?

Consequences of Sport Injury

Beyond its physical effects, sport injury can produce a wide array of psychological consequences. The chapters in part II address ways in which athletes respond psychologically to injury. Chapter 4 examines common cognitive, emotional, and behavioral reactions displayed by athletes after sustaining an injury. Chapter 5 focuses on pain—a complex sensory and emotional phenomenon frequently experienced by athletes after injury, as well as at other times during their sport involvement.

Chapter 4

Psychological Responses to Sport Injury

Chapter Objectives

1. To compare models of psychological response to sport injury
2. To examine cognitive, emotional, and behavioral effects of sport injury

The sport careers of Danielle and Nicole have been intertwined since they were eight-year-olds playing on rival U11 club soccer teams on different sides of the same state. Both are center midfielders, and when they played together on the state Olympic Development Program team, Danielle, the taller of the two girls, was the defensive center midfielder and Nicole was the attacking center midfielder. Over the years, they became friends and enjoyed playing with and against each other. Midway through last summer, their lives—sometimes parallel, sometimes crossing—converged once again in a disastrous way. After nearly 12 consecutive months of full-on competitive soccer without a significant break, Danielle and Nicole were both playing in the group phase of a national tournament. They were on different teams—Nicole playing on a U17 team ranked in the top five in the nation and Danielle starring on a U16 team that had gone to the national finals the year before. Both girls, though playing effectively, were running on fumes. And then it happened: Less than an hour apart, on different fields at the same sport complex, Danielle and Nicole both sustained noncontact injuries in which they each tore an ACL. However, except for a few facial grimaces as they were taken from the field, that's about as far the similarity went.

For the first few weeks after the injury, Danielle was devastated. She tried to put on a brave face and maintain her composure, but she often found herself sobbing uncontrollably in her room after school for what seemed like hours. She withdrew from her family and friends, and her school performance suffered markedly as she was unable to concentrate on her work because her thoughts kept drifting back to the events surrounding her injury. Danielle's mental outlook improved considerably as her surgery date approached. She seemed to be mobilizing her resources for the operative and postoperative struggles that lay ahead. However, about 10 days after her surgery—and after having embarked gamely on her rehabilitation program—she withdrew once again as the reality hit that she was going to miss her junior year of high school soccer and was unlikely to be anywhere near her best for the all-important spring club season. Having yet to make a college commitment, Danielle saw her goals and dreams crashing in front of her and felt powerless to do anything about it.

Nicole's response to her injury bore little resemblance to Danielle's. She experienced some pain for the first week or two after the injury but did not seem to be bothered by the physical limitations caused by the injury. In fact, her mental state seemed so normal that her parents felt concerned that something was wrong. Nicole reported feeling a sense of "lightness," as if a heavy weight had been lifted off of her shoulders. She was, in her words, a "grump" after her surgery because of the challenges associated with getting around on crutches and the pain she experienced when she forgot to take her medication. But her grumpiness passed quickly, and she balanced her school and rehabilitation efforts with social activities that she had not previously had time to engage in due to her heavy soccer commitments. She knew that her chances of playing collegiate soccer at a top Division I school were essentially nil, but she was comfortable with that prospect and felt determined to make the most of what life had to offer in the days, weeks, and months ahead.

Danielle and Nicole each experienced a severe physical injury that, in addition to the extensive physical consequences, can exact a psychological toll. However, despite sustaining essentially the same injury under similar circumstances, Danielle and Nicole reacted psychologically in ways that differed dramatically. Why, given their apparent similarities, did these two young athletes respond so differently to the challenges of injury? This chapter tackles that question and addresses cognitive, emotional, and behavioral responses to sport injury, as well as factors thought to influence those responses. First, however, it describes models of psychological response to sport injury and summarizes the available empirical support for those models.

Models of Psychological Response to Sport Injury

In order to provide athletes with the best psychological help in the wake of injury, we must understand the process of psychological adjustment to sport injury. Since the earliest published report (Little, 1966) indicating that at least some athletes might experience psychological difficulties after sustaining an injury, researchers have proposed models of psychological response to sport injury and evaluated those models scientifically. Early attempts, faced with an absence of relevant sci-

entific data, borrowed heavily from other areas of psychology. Over time, two main types of psychological-adjustment models have been developed: stage models (inspired by the literature on grief reactions) and cognitive appraisal models (drawing on theory and research about stress and coping).

Stage Models

Two main assumptions underlie stage models of psychological adjustment to sport injury. The first assumption is that when athletes become injured, they lose part of themselves (Peretz, 1970). Given that athletes can derive a sense of identity and a social role from participating in sport (Brewer, Van Raalte, & Linder, 1993), they can experience a state of loss when injury deprives them of these benefits. The second assumption is that when athletes become injured, they follow a predictable, immutable sequence of psychological responses on the way to achieving satisfactory adjustment. In positing this sequence, several sport psychologists (e.g., Astle, 1986; Lynch, 1988; B. Rotella, 1985) adapted a popular model of adjustment to terminal illness (Kübler-Ross, 1969); specifically, they suggested that athletes progress sequentially through the stages of denial, anger, bargaining, and depression before reaching acceptance. Other sport-specific stage models have also been proposed, and they vary somewhat in the number, names, and content of stages (L. Evans & Hardy, 1995).

Stage models carry enormous practical appeal (Rohe, 1988) because they imply that knowing the stages enables us to understand what an athlete has experienced and predict what lies ahead. Consistent with the tenets of most stage models, research has shown that some athletes do experience psychological responses akin to grief reactions after sustaining a serious injury (Macchi & Crossman, 1996). They also show a general trend in which an athlete's psychological responses become more favorable over time (e.g., McDonald & Hardy, 1990; A.M. Smith, Scott, O'Fallon, & Young, 1990). These findings, however, are not uniquely supportive of stage models. Indeed, it is not necessary to invoke the concept of developmental stages in order to accept the idea that some athletes may feel quite distressed after sustaining an injury and that, with time, they are likely to show improved psychological functioning.

In addition, in summarizing the criteria of explanatory stage models as defined by Piaget (1971), Rape, Bush, and Slavin (1992) noted that "stages must follow an invariant sequence such that (a) the sequence is culturally universal, (b) it occurs in the same order for everyone, (c) all individuals reach the last stage, and (d) there is never regression from a higher to a lower stage" (pp. 10–11). However, research has not supported the claim that athletes respond psychologically to injury by going through a stereotypic, invariant sequence of reactions (Brewer, 1994). Instead, as shown later in this chapter, athletes vary extensively in terms of how they respond to injury; in other words, no uniform pattern of response to injury has been documented. Athletes may experience responses aligned with some of the stages but not with others, and they may do so in an order that differs from those proposed in stage models (Tracey, 2003). Exhaustive reviews of research on adjustment to other threatening events, including terminal illness, have also reached the conclusion that the assumptions of stage models are not tenable (Silver & Wortman, 1980; Wortman & Silver, 1987; see also the cogent analysis by R. Friedman & James, 2008).

To illustrate the difficulties of applying stage models to the full range of circumstances surrounding sport injury, consider that these models make no distinction between a relatively minor injury that keeps an athlete out of action for a few weeks and a severe injury that signals the end of an athlete's competitive career. According to stage models, both injuries would be expected to trigger the same set of adjustment stages even though the degree of loss differs dramatically. Nor do stage models account for differences in athletes' circumstances. This rigidity has made it difficult for stage models to establish a scientific foundation.

It is possible to recognize the potential relevance of the grief response to sport injury while still rejecting the notion that athletes follow a universal pattern of psychological response to sport injury (L. Evans & Hardy, 1995, 1999). If we uncritically accept the existence of adjustment stages following sport injury, we run the risk of assuming that athletes are or will be distressed following injury and that athletes who experience emotional disturbance following injury will inevitably achieve resolution or acceptance if left alone. In reality, postinjury psychological distress should be neither expected nor dismissed (Brewer, 1994), lest the stages become "iron-plated pigeonholes into which human experience must somehow be made to fit" (Hopson, 1981, p. 37) or lest we fail to recognize and respond to an athlete's experience of distress.

Cognitive Appraisal Models

Whereas stage models were not designed to account for individual differences in psychological response to sport injury, cognitive appraisal models were explicitly intended to fulfill that very function. Instead of expecting all athletes to respond to injury in a predictable way, cognitive appraisal models posit that athletes' appraisals or interpretations of their injuries—along with the contexts in which they occur—play central roles in determining how athletes respond cognitively, emotionally, and behaviorally.

One example can be found in the integrated model of psychological response to sport injury (Wiese-Bjornstal, Smith, Shaffer, & Morrey, 1998), which evolved over several iterations and is displayed in figure 4.1. This model views sport injury as a stressor that initiates a process in which athletes appraise both the nature of the injury and their ability to cope with it. Cognitive appraisals are thought to be influenced by numerous personal and situational factors, including the psychosocial factors posited in the stress–injury model as potential contributors to sport injury occurrence (i.e., personality, history of stressors, coping resources). Personal factors consist of dispositional and historical characteristics of the individual, whereas situational factors consist of characteristics of the physical, social, and sport environments. In turn, cognitive appraisals are thought to affect three primary, interrelated domains of psychological response to sport injury: cognitive, emotional, and behavioral. More generally, the process of psychological adjustment to sport injury is considered to be dynamic, reflecting the ongoing reciprocal influence of potentially ever-changing thoughts, feelings, and actions. Psychological responses are also thought to affect psychosocial and physical recovery outcomes (these associations are discussed in detail in chapter 7).

In the predictions of stage models, predictions generated by cognitive appraisal models have received abundant research support. For example, evidence has been obtained that

- athletes find injury to be a significant source of stress (Bianco, Malo, & Orlick, 1999; Brewer & Petrie, 1995; L. Evans, Wadey, Hanton, & Mitchell, 2012; Ford & Gordon, 1999; Gould, Udry, Bridges, & Beck, 1997a; Heniff, 1998);
- various personal and situational factors are related to psychological responses to sport injury (for a review, see Brewer, 2007); and
- psychological responses are associated with sport injury rehabilitation outcomes (for a review, see Brewer, 2010).

Also in contrast to the stage approach, the cognitive appraisal framework is marked by inherent flexibility and inclusiveness that allow the model to consider a multitude of possible predictors of psychological adjustment.

Psychological Consequences of Sport Injury

As illustrated by the cases of Danielle and Nicole, presented at the beginning of this chapter, sport injury can exert a dramatic effect not only on physical functioning but also on psychological functioning. Although investigating the psychological consequences of sport injury has presented researchers with a unique set of challenges (for more information, see this chapter's Focus on Research box), a sizable body of empirical literature has accumulated over the past three decades. The following sections examine cognitive, emotional, and behavioral responses to sport injury; where relevant, they also identify personal and situational predictors of those responses.

Cognitive Responses to Sport Injury

Beginning with cognitive appraisals of the injury and proceeding through rehabilitation into the return to sport, cognition is a vital and omnipresent part of the process. The following aspects of cognition are especially involved in the psychological response to sport injury:

- Cognitive appraisals
- Attributions for injury
- Cognitive content
- Self-related cognition
- Cognitive coping strategies
- Perceived benefits of injury
- Injury-related perceptions
- Cognitive performance

Cognitive Appraisals

As noted earlier, injury-related cognitive appraisals initiate the process by which athletes respond psychologically to injury. Stress and coping theory (Lazarus & Folkman, 1984) suggests that the way in which people interpret (or

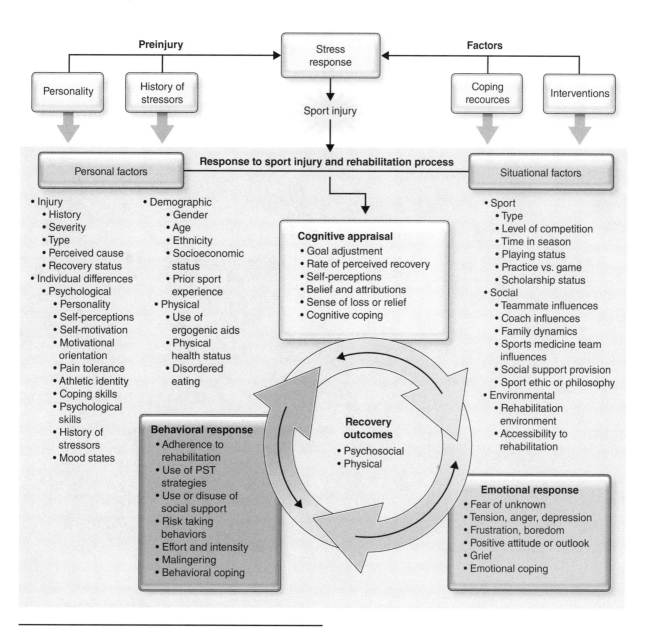

Figure 4.1 Integrated model of psychological response to sport injury.
Wiese-Bjornstal et al. 1998.

appraise) an environmental event or situation determines their emotional and behavioral reactions to it. Three basic forms of cognitive appraisal are postulated: primary appraisal, secondary appraisal, and reappraisal. In primary appraisal, the environmental event or situation (e.g., a sport injury) is assessed in terms of its implicati`ons for the individual's well-being. An event may be considered irrelevant (e.g., "the injury is unimportant"), benign-positive (e.g., "I needed a rest anyway"), or stressful (e.g., "the injury could not have come at a worse time").

Appraisals of an event or situation that is deemed stressful include interpretations of harm (or loss), threat, and challenge. Appraisals of threat and harm (or loss) are especially likely in the context of sport injury, which involves physical damage (Clement & Arvinen-Barrow, 2013; Ford & Gordon, 1999; Gould et al., 1997a). Threat appraisals in particular involve anticipation of future harm, whereas challenge appraisals imply that the injury offers an opportunity for growth. Different kinds of appraisal are not necessarily mutually

Priorities, Pitfalls, and Pragmatics in Postinjury Psychological Research

Researching the psychology of sport injury is not for the weak of will. Studying the prediction and prevention of sport injury involves numerous challenges and potential frustrations. It requires researchers to gather psychological data and deliver psychological interventions to large numbers of athletes before they sustain an injury, then record athletes' sport exposures on an ongoing basis, monitor their injury status, and collect pertinent injury and time-loss data. Conducting research on the psychological consequences of sport injury can be even more challenging. Consider first that the theoretically optimal method for examining the psychological effect of sport injury—experimentation—is neither ethical nor feasible (and even if it were, it might be difficult to recruit participants for a study in which they could be randomly assigned to the injury condition!). With experimentation off the table, prospective investigators face three major threats to the validity of their findings:

· Athletes' preinjury psychological characteristics

· Psychological characteristics of the sample from which the injured athletes originate

· Characteristics of the injuries experienced

Cognizant researchers design their studies to address these issues as best they can, given the specific questions for which they are seeking answers. Pragmatic concerns usually dictate that compromises be made on one or more of the issues.

Athletes' preinjury psychological characteristics are important because, as shown in chapter 2, psychological factors can cause or contribute to the occurrence of sport injury. Without assessing athletes' preinjury psychological characteristics, we cannot determine whether their postinjury psychological characteristics are causes or consequences of sport injury. Similarly, we need to know the psychological characteristics of the sample from which an injured athlete is drawn, because the athlete's postinjury psychological characteristics could be influenced by something in his or her sport experience other than the injury, and this influence (e.g., losing season, team disharmony) could be shared by teammates or coparticipants.

Leddy, Lambert, and Ogles (1994) addressed these issues—that is, psychological characteristics of individual athletes before injury and of the sample from which injured athletes are drawn. They did so in a single study with a prospective research design in which a large sample of male collegiate athletes ($n = 343$) was assessed on measures of anger, depression, and self-esteem during the preseason. When athletes became injured, they (and a set of matched controls) completed

exclusive (Lazarus & Folkman, 1984). For example, an athlete might simultaneously interpret an injury as causing harm or loss and as presenting a challenge. This response acknowledges the injury's effect but views the rehabilitation process as a chance to apply personal resources toward recovery.

In secondary appraisal, individuals assess what can be done to manage the stressful event; this type of appraisal takes into account both outcome expectancy and efficacy expectations (Lazarus & Folkman, 1984). Outcome expectancy involves the belief that a particular behavior will produce certain outcomes, whereas efficacy expectations involve the belief that one can perform the given behavior to bring about certain outcomes (Bandura, 1977, 1982). Thus, in secondary appraisal, the athlete considers what can be done about the injury, whether it can be treated, and whether he or she can do what is required to bring about recovery.

The third basic form of cognitive appraisal is reappraisal, which involves modifying an appraisal based on new information (Lazarus & Folkman, 1984). For example, learning of an effective treatment technique might lead an athlete to change her or his appraisal of an injury's effects. Reappraisal emphasizes the ongoing nature of the appraisal process; indeed, an athlete's perceptions of an injury are subject to change throughout the rehabilitation period.

Cognitive appraisals are influenced by a variety of personal and situational factors. With respect to sport injury, cognitive appraisals are the psychological measures within one week of injury and again two months later. The preinjury assessment controlled for the potential influence of preinjury psychological characteristics on postinjury psychological characteristics and on the postinjury assessments. The postinjury assessments controlled for any sample- or team-specific trends (independent of injury status) in the psychological characteristics that were measured. Unfortunately, studies as thorough and methodologically rigorous as this one are few and far between.

The third potential threat to the validity of data collected on the psychological consequences of injury involves the characteristics of the injuries experienced. Psychological responses to sport injury may be greatly affected by the nature of the injury itself—for example, location, severity, duration, and symptoms. There is evidence, for example, that emotional responses of athletes who experience musculoskeletal injuries differ from those of athletes who sustain concussions (Hutchison, Comper, Mainwaring, Richards, & Bisschop, 2011; Mainwaring, Hutchison, Bisschop, Comper, & Richards, 2010). Even in carefully controlled studies, such as the one conducted by Leddy et al. (1994), the sample is typically heterogeneous with respect to the injuries experienced. One way in which researchers attempt to deal with this issue is to collect data from a group of athletes with a common injury *after* the injuries have occurred.

Of course, taking such an approach results in a trade-off with respect to the first two threats to the validity of the postinjury data because it does not collect preinjury or peer-versus-control data. Researchers sometimes collect longitudinal psychological response data starting with the occurrence of the injury or an equalizing event, such as surgery, and use the individual athletes as their own controls. For example, multiple assessments of emotional functioning have been made following ACL reconstructive surgery in several studies (e.g., Brewer, Cornelius, et al., 2007; Langford, Webster, & Feller, 2009; Morrey, Stuart, Smith, & Wiese-Bjornstal, 1999).

Even with imperfect studies that do not address most or even all of the three threats to the validity of self-reports, useful information can still be gleaned from the data. Of particular note, findings from case studies (e.g., Carson & Polman, 2008; McArdle, 2010), qualitative investigations (e.g., Bianco et al., 1999; Carson & Polman, 2012; Johnston & Carroll, 1998), and action research projects (e.g., L. Evans, Hardy, & Fleming, 2000) can enhance our understanding of the consequences of sport injury in terms of psychological functioning.

especially influenced by the characteristics of the injury, such as its location and symptoms. Two personal factors thought to be particularly influential on cognitive appraisals are the athlete's commitments and his or her beliefs about control. The commitments that a person makes to certain goals have important cognitive and motivational implications (Klinger, 1977; Lazarus & Folkman, 1984). First, they influence appraisal by directing the individual's behavior regarding potentially threatening (and potentially beneficial) situations. For instance, in order to succeed at sport, athletes frequently elect to forego other activities that could provide their lives with greater balance. Second, an athlete's commitments heighten her or his sensitivity to cues that may be relevant to those commitments. For example, as compared with their nonathlete peers, athletes may have greater sensitivity, or give greater weight, to physical information due to the importance of physical functioning in sport. Third, and most important, commitments are closely related to psychological vulnerability. Given that commitments determine what is important to an individual, events that threaten those commitments are appraised as particularly meaningful. In terms of sport injury, Lazarus and Folkman noted that "the extent to which . . . *physical* vulnerabilities . . . have implications for *psychological* vulnerability depends on the importance of the commitments that the physical disabilities threaten" (p. 51, emphasis added). For example, a severely sprained ankle is more likely to be appraised as a major life disruption by a tennis player than by an office manager (unless, of course, the office manager is also an avid athlete).

Cognitive appraisals can also be affected by both general and situational beliefs about control. General beliefs about control—which involve the extent to which one thinks that he or she can control important events and outcomes—are thought to contribute most strongly to appraisals in ambiguous or novel situations (Rotter, 1966). Therefore, athletes with an internal locus of control (i.e., who believe they generally can act to control environmental events) are viewed as more likely to appraise an ambiguous injury situation as controllable than are athletes with an external locus of control (i.e., who believe that outcomes are not generally contingent on their actions). Sport injuries, however, often occur in *unambiguous* or familiar situations; therefore, situational beliefs about control, which are very similar to secondary appraisals, are especially relevant to injury-related appraisals (Lazarus & Folkman, 1984).

The primary situational factors thought to affect cognitive appraisals are novelty, predictability, event uncertainty, temporal (time) factors, ambiguity, and timing of the event in the athlete's life cycle (Lazarus & Folkman, 1984). Even for athletes who have not previously been injured, an injury is likely to be appraised as a kind of harm or loss due to the well-known debilitating effects of injury on sport performance. Knowledge of the course of an injury may increase both predictability and the athlete's feelings of control and thus lead to a less threatening appraisal of the situation. An appraisal is likely to be influenced by event uncertainty when the athlete is unsure whether an injury has occurred (e.g., "Is my leg pain symptomatic of a fractured bone?"). The temporal factor that is most relevant to appraisals associated with sport injury is duration; for instance, a short-term injury might be less likely than a chronic condition would be to produce a stress appraisal. As noted earlier, ambiguous situations invoke appraisals based on general beliefs about control. Finally, the appraisal process may be particularly influenced by the timing of an injury in the athlete's life cycle. Consider the example of an athlete

whose sport career is ended in its prime by an injury. If the athlete had planned on participating in sport for many more years, an appraisal of harm and loss might be especially likely.

Attributions for Injury

When people encounter unexpected events, they tend to think about what might have caused them (Wong & Weiner, 1981). In other words, they tend to make attributions for the causes of the events. Among other things, this kind of attributional cognitive activity is stimulated by the usually unanticipated and often traumatic experience of sustaining a sport injury. Athletes generally have little trouble generating attributions for the causes of their injuries. For example, athletes in two studies (San José, 2003; Tedder & Biddle, 1998) tended to identify behavioral factors as causing their injuries, whereas athletes in a third study (Brewer, 1999a) tended to attribute their injuries to mechanical or technical factors. Because causal attributions are essentially situational beliefs about control, it would be expected that locus of control (i.e., general beliefs about control) and situational factors (e.g., social context) influence athletes' causal explanations for their injuries.

Cognitive Content

The generally unanticipated, often traumatic nature of sport injury may also produce images associated with the injury event that recurringly invade the athlete's mental space and are experienced by the athlete as disturbing (McArdle, 2010; Newcomer & Perna, 2003; Shuer & Dietrich, 1997; Vergeer, 2006). In one study (Shuer & Dietrich), athletes with chronic injuries reported having intrusive thoughts at a level below that of people who had been in an earthquake but comparable to that of people who had been in a fire. In addition, the athletes reported trying to avoid thoughts associated with their injuries to a greater extent than people who had been in a fire or earthquake did with thoughts about their respective traumatic events. Although one might expect intrusive injury-related thoughts—and the avoidance of such thoughts—to dissipate over time (Vergeer, 2006), Shuer and Dietrich reported no significant differences in intrusion and avoidance among athletes with injuries of different durations, ranging from less than one week to more than a year. Intrusive injury-related images can have ramifications for both psychological and physical functioning. Appaneal, Perna, and Larkin (2007) demonstrated that relative to athletes without injuries, athletes who had recently sustained a severe sport injury responded with greater self-reported distress and skin-conductance reactivity when exposed to video content related to traumatic injury.

Self-Related Cognition

For many athletes, sport serves as a source of self-worth and self-definition (Brewer, Van Raalte, & Linder, 1993), and injury—which poses a threat to sport involvement—can affect thoughts about the self. With respect to self-esteem, studies have shown that injured athletes have lower global self-esteem than do athletes without an injury (Chan & Grossman, 1988; Kleiber & Brock, 1992; Leddy et al., 1994; McGowan, Pierce, Williams, & Eastman, 1994) and that athletes experience decreased global and domain-specific physical self-esteem after becoming injured (Leddy et al.). In addition, athletes with chronic injuries have reported lower levels of global self-esteem than athletes with acute injuries (Wasley & Lox, 1998), a finding which suggests that injury duration (a personal or injury-related factor) is associated with self-related cognitions. Similarly, illustrating the potential relevance of personal factors to self-perceptions following injury, Kleiber and Brock (1992) found that among athletes who had incurred a career-ending injury, those who were highly invested in playing professional sport had lower self-esteem than those without that aspiration. Presumably, the athletes who were highly invested in playing sport professionally were more likely to appraise their injuries as threatening or stressful.

Changes over time after injury have been documented for the related concepts of sport self-confidence and self-efficacy. Quinn and Fallon (1999) found that injured athletes began the rehabilitation period high in sport self-confidence, declined in confidence during rehabilitation, and experienced an increase in confidence as they recovered from injury. Similarly, athletes with knee injuries (some of whom had reconstructive surgery) have reported increases in knee-specific self-efficacy across the rehabilitation period (Thomeé et al., 2007a). Other personal and injury-related factors are also (positively) associated with knee-specific self-efficacy, including internal locus of control and perceived knee functioning (Thomeé et al., 2007a, 2007b).

Another aspect of self-related cognition that can be affected by sport injury is self-identity. Brewer, Cornelius, Stephan, and Van Raalte (2010) reported that people who underwent reconstructive surgery after an ACL tear decreased their identification with the athlete role over the first two years after surgery. The decline in athletic identity was greatest between 6 and 12 months after surgery, and the largest reductions were reported by athletes who experienced the least rehabilitation progress during that period. Such modification of self-image may have been a protective response to the fact that the ACL injury threatened the athlete's sport participation and to any difficulties experienced during postoperative rehabilitation activities. Research has documented similar changes in self-image—in which an exclusive (or at least very narrow) identification with the athlete role was replaced by a current or desired self-image reflecting a diminished focus on sport as a source of self-worth and self-description—among athletes whose physical functioning was severely hampered by injury (Vergeer, 2006) or another disabling medical condition (Sparkes, 1998).

Cognitive Coping Strategies

As indicated by the apparently self-protective changes in self-identity described in the preceding section, athletes need not be merely passive recipients of the physical and psychological trauma associated with experiencing a sport injury. Instead, they can initiate efforts to cope with the adverse effects of injury, and some of the coping strategies are clearly cognitive in nature. Results of qualitative research have suggested that the use of cognitive coping strategies is commonplace among injured athletes and is characterized by themes such as accepting injury, focusing on getting better, disengaging mentally, thinking positively, and using imagery (Bianco et al., 1999; Carson & Polman, 2008, 2010; Gould et al., 1997b; Rose & Jevne, 1993; Ruddock-Hudson, O'Halloran, & Murphy, 2014; Tracey, 2003; Udry, Gould, Bridges, & Beck, 1997; Wadey, Evans, Hanton, & Neil, 2012b). The findings from qualitative investigations are complemented by those from quantitative studies, in which athletes from a broad range of sports report using a similar set of cognitive coping strategies to deal with the consequences of injury (El Ali, Marivain, Heas, & Boulva, 2008; Quinn & Fallon, 1999; Udry, 1997).

Consistent with cognitive appraisal models, the use of cognitive coping strategies has been found to vary as a function of two injury-related factors (injury type and phase of rehabilitation) and one personal factor (hardiness). With respect to injury type, Wasley and Lox (1998) found that athletes with chronic injuries reported using more escape-avoidance coping, which includes "wishful thinking," than did athletes with acute injuries. In terms of phase of rehabilitation, Udry (1997) found that the amount of negative-emotion coping and palliative coping (both of which include substantial cognitive components) varied over the course of rehabilitation in a sample of athletes who had undergone knee surgery. Complementing these findings, Johnston and Carroll (2000) documented a steady decrease in the use of logical analysis, positive reappraisal, cognitive avoidance, and acceptance coping strategies over the course of injury rehabilitation. Thus, it appears that athletes may adjust their use of cognitive coping strategies in accord with fluctuations in injury symptoms and the demands of rehabilitation. Regarding the personal factor—hardiness—Wadey et al. (2012b) found that athletes who were low on that dimension tended to report using ineffective, avoidance-based strategies to cope with their injuries.

Perceived Benefits of Injury

Despite the frequency with which athletes make appraisals of threat and harm or loss with respect to sport injury (Ford & Gordon, 1999; Gould et al., 1997a)—and despite the psycho-

logical turmoil that such appraisals can elicit—the effects of injury on cognition do not appear to be uniformly negative. Qualitative research has revealed that amidst the negativity, which can be pervasive in the cognition of injured athletes, perceptions of benefit from injury can also emerge (Almeida, Luciano, Lameiras, & Buceta, 2014; Crawford, Gayman, & Tracey, 2014; Ford & Gordon, 1999; Hurley, Moran, & Guerin, 2007; Podlog & Eklund, 2006a; Rose & Jevne, 1993; Ruddock-Hudson et al., 2014; San José, 2003; Tracey, 2003; Udry et al., 1997; Wadey, Clark, Podlog, & McCullough, 2013; Wadey, Evans, Evans, & Mitchell, 2011; Wadey et al., 2012b; J.A. Young, Pain, & Pearce, 2007). Most of the benefit-oriented themes articulated by injured athletes can be classified into the three main categories identified by Udry et al.:

1. Personal growth benefits
2. Psychologically based performance enhancement
3. Physical and technical development

Personal growth benefits include gaining perspective on sport involvement, developing interests outside of sport, and becoming a more understanding person. Psychologically based performance enhancement involves benefits such as improved mental toughness, increased tactical awareness, and increased motivation. Benefits associated with physical and technical development include improved technique, enhanced health, and increased strength.

Many of the perceived benefits of injury do not occur automatically upon sustaining an injury; instead, they require effort and may be realized only over time (Udry, 1999). Injury offers opportunities for benefits to be perceived and realized by athletes; it is up to them—and those who assist them—to take advantage of those opportunities. It is critical, therefore, to identify common perceived benefits of injury and determine the paths that athletes can follow to obtain them.

In an exceptionally thorough investigation of perceived benefits of sport injury, Wadey et al. (2011) examined the perceived antecedents and underlying mechanisms of perceived benefits of sport injury with a sample of 10 team-sport athletes who had sustained a severe injury. The athletes identified perceived benefits, as well as antecedents of those benefits, across three temporal phases: injury onset, rehabilitation, and return to sport competition. Regarding injury onset, the athletes reported that their cognitive, emotional, and physical responses to injury prompted them to seek out resources relevant to their injuries, mobilize their social support networks, and seek help from others. Such actions were said to have beneficial effects on body- and injury-related knowledge, self-understanding, emotion regulation, and the strength of their social network.

During rehabilitation, relevant antecedents included free time, inability to train and compete with the team, and involvement in a rehabilitation program with an approved professional. These antecedents were thought to allow the athletes to spend more time with their family, meet new people, devote more time to academics and other work, reflect on their experience, attend training sessions to spectate or play, work on sport-specific skills not impaired by the injury, adhere to their rehabilitation program, and learn about injury prevention. Among the numerous perceived benefits reported to accrue during rehabilitation were stronger social network, better academic performance, improved tactical awareness, increased confidence, better technique, enhanced strength, and reduced overall risk of injury. Later, when returning to sport competition, the athletes reported that factors such as reflecting on their recovery and interacting with other injured athletes enabled them to gain perspective on their injury and handle the adversity they encountered. In turn, these factors facilitated the development of resilience, empathy, and sympathy in their dealings with others and the situations in which they find themselves.

Although further research is needed to assess the validity of the paths to perceived benefits described by the athletes in the Wadey et al. (2011) investigation, the findings of Salim, Wadey, and Diss (2015) provide a step in that direction. Salim et al. found that previously injured athletes who were high in hardiness reported the most growth as a result of their injuries. As compared with their counterparts who were low in hardiness, the high-hardiness athletes seemed better able to mobilize social support for emotional purposes and to construe their injuries in positive terms—both of which coping strategies may have facilitated their growth.

Injury-Related Perceptions

Another area of cognition that appears to be affected by sport injury involves perceptions of sport injury itself. As compared with athletes who have not sustained an injury in the past year, athletes who have done so tend to report experiencing greater perceived risk of injury, more worry or concern about becoming injured, and less confidence in their ability to avoid becoming injured (Reuter & Short, 2005; Short, Reuter, Brandt, Short, & Kontos, 2004). It may not even be necessary for athletes to experience an injury in order for their injury-related cognition to be affected; indeed, simply having a teammate who incurs a serious injury may be sufficient to increase an athlete's fearful thinking about injury (O'Neill, 2008). Thus, awareness of injury occurrence—through either direct or vicarious experience—seems to be associated with increased sensitivity to the prospect of sustaining an injury.

Cognitive Performance

Evidence exists that sport injury can affect not only the content of cognition but also its quality. In particular, a substantial body of literature has documented the adverse effects of sport-related concussion on neurocognitive performance (Broglio & Puetz, 2008). Concussion, which is a relatively mild form of traumatic brain injury, can impair cognitive functions including attention, memory, processing speed, and reaction time (Moser, 2007). Findings are equivocal, however, for subconcussive blows to the head, such as those experienced in heading the ball in soccer; in carefully conducted studies, consistent relationships between soccer heading (frequency and intensity) and neurocognitive performance have not been documented (Webbe & Salinas, 2011).

Preseason neurocognitive assessment is now commonplace, especially for athletes in contact sports and other sports with a high possibility of concussion (see this chapter's Focus on Application box). As a result, it has become feasible to examine the effects of all kinds of injury—not just brain injury—on cognitive performance. In a study of collegiate athletes that featured neuropsychological assessment both in the preseason and after injury (within 72 hours), athletes who sustained musculoskeletal injuries did not differ significantly from athletes who experienced concussions on any of the seven cognitive subtests administered, and they scored significantly lower than the athletes who sustained no injury on one of the cognitive subtests. The concussion group scored significantly lower than the no-injury group on three of the seven cognitive subtests. The reasons for the difference between the musculoskeletal injury group and the no-injury group are not clear, but the psychological disturbance that can accompany musculoskeletal injury (see the section on emotional consequences of sport injury later in this chapter) may have disrupted the ability of the athletes who incurred musculoskeletal injuries to process information effectively (Hutchison, Comper, Mainwaring, & Richards, 2011).

Emotional Responses to Sport Injury

Emotions lie at the heart of psychological responses to sport injury. Indeed, from the seminal work of Little (1969) to the present day, the one psychological consequence of sport injury that has generated the most attention from researchers is the athlete's emotional reaction. In this research, both qualitative and quantitative methods have been used to investigate how sport injury occurrence influences athletes' affects, moods, and emotions.

Qualitative Studies of Emotional Responses to Sport Injury

Investigators using qualitative methods have operated under the assumption that if one wants to know how athletes respond emotionally to injury, one should simply ask them to talk about it. As a result, qualitative inquiry

has yielded rich "in their own words" accounts of the emotions that athletes experience after sustaining a sport injury; how these emotions unfold over time during rehabilitation; and what personal, situational, and injury factors are associated with postinjury emotions.

Athletes' descriptions of their emotional state during the early postinjury period and the initial phases of rehabilitation have consistently been characterized by a preponderance of negative emotions in reaction to the disruption of their physical functioning and their pursuit of sport-related goals. These negative emotions include anger, anxiety, bitterness, confusion, depression, disappointment, devastation, fear, frustration, helplessness, resentment, and shock (Bianco et al., 1999; Carson & Polman, 2008; Gordon & Lindgren, 1990; Johnston & Carroll, 1998; Mainwaring, 1999; McArdle, 2010; Ruddock-Hudson et al., 2012, 2014; Sparkes, 1998; Stoltenburg, Kamphoff, & Bremer, 2011; Tracey, 2003; Thatcher, Kerr, Amies, & Day, 2007; Udry et al., 1997; Wadey et al., 2012b). More specifically, athletes who have undergone ACL reconstruction surgery have described it as a substantial source of stress (Carson & Polman, 2008; Heijne, Axelsson, Werner, & Biguet, 2008) and indicated that they sometimes experience apprehension (as well as anger, depression, and frustration) before surgery and feel relief (and anxiety) after surgery (Carson & Polman, 2008).

In contrast, athletes' accounts of the middle phases of rehabilitation are marked by a trend toward more positive emotions (Carson & Polman, 2008; Stoltenburg et al., 2011; Thatcher et al., 2007), albeit with periodic experiences of depression and frustration reported in association with the rigors and setbacks of rehabilitation (Bianco et al., 1999; Carson & Polman, 2008; Johnston & Carroll, 1998). Regarding the latter stages of rehabilitation, athletes have noted that, with full recovery and a return to sport on the horizon, they have experienced a mix of positive and negative emotions, including apprehension, anticipation, anxiety, confidence, depression, encouragement, fear of reinjury, and frustration (Bianco et al., 1999; Carson & Polman, 2008, 2012; Johnston & Carroll, 1998).

For head injuries, emotional aftereffects may occur well beyond the point of apparent

Consensus on Concussion Consequences

It is difficult to think of an area of sport injury with a higher public profile than that of sport concussion. In response to an explosion of research on the subject—and a groundswell of public interest in it—a group of experts met in Zurich in late 2012 to discuss the definition, evaluation, management, prevention, investigation, and other key aspects of sport concussion. The meeting yielded a document, the "Consensus Statement on Concussion in Sport" (McCrory et al., 2013), that summarizes the state of sport concussion science. The panel unanimously defined concussion as "a complex pathophysiological process affecting the brain . . . [and] induced by traumatic biomechanical forces" (p. 250). It also noted these other key definitional issues:

· Concussion is usually caused by a blow to the head, neck, or face or by a blow to another part of the body that reverberates in the head.

· Concussion produces symptoms that typically, but not always, arrive rapidly and depart spontaneously.

· The acute symptoms of concussion tend to be functional in nature and are not typically due to structural damage (structural abnormalities are not detected in neuroimaging studies).

· Concussion may or may not result in loss of consciousness.

· Although the symptoms of concussion are usually graded and tend to resolve in a sequential pattern over a short period of time (7 to 10 days), the recovery process is sometimes prolonged.

It is recommended that evaluation for concussion begin on-site at the first sign of a head injury in a manner that adheres to emergency management principles and attends initially to first-aid issues. Accurate diagnosis of acute concussion requires assessment of clinical symptoms (e.g., dizziness), physical signs (e.g., unconsciousness), behavior (e.g., anger), cognition (e.g., reaction time), and sleep (e.g., drowsiness). The panel developed the Sport Concussion Assessment Tool 3 (SCAT3) to assist with rapid diagnosis and made the instrument freely available to sport health care professionals via the web (McCrory et al., 2013).

The panel's consensus recommend that athletes who sustain a head injury should be monitored for a period of hours after the incident (some athletes experience delayed onset of symptoms) and that athletes receiving concussion diagnoses should not be permitted to return to play on the day of the injury (McCrory et al., 2013). Many jurisdictions and leagues have enacted laws or policies addressing concussion management and establishing protocols for allowing a return to play. The Zurich panel noted that the initial on-site evaluation should be followed up off-site with a more formal and thorough evaluation conducted by medical personnel. These practitioners should take a detailed medical history and complete an in-depth neurological examination that assesses balance, cognitive functioning, gait, and mental status. Findings from the evaluation should be used to determine current clinical status and assess whether neuroimaging (e.g., CT scan, MRI) is needed to rule out a more serious brain injury involving structural damage (McCrory et al., 2013).

The panel also advised neuropsychological testing and interpretation (ideally from a neuropsychologist) to help with concussion management and return-to-play decisions; this consideration can take into account preseason neuropsychological data where available (McCrory et al., 2013). Such preseason data, which are increasingly required as a condition of participation in high school sport, can contribute to concussion management by serving as a baseline against which to judge postconcussion performance.

According to the panel, the initial key ingredient in concussion management is symptom-determined physical and cognitive rest. Once symptoms remit, a protocol should be implemented featuring a gradual progression from no activity to (in sequence) light aerobic exercise, sport-specific exercise, noncontact training drills, full-contact practice, and, finally, return to play. Stepwise advancement can be made as long as symptom abatement continues. The panel also recognized potential roles for psychological and pharmacological treatments and suggested possible strategies for reducing the occurrence of sport concussion—for example, encouraging the use of protective gear (e.g., helmets), promoting fair play, minimizing violence, and advocating for rule changes that increase athlete safety (McCrory et al., 2013).

Focus on Application

recovery and the return to sport. In a study of retired American football players (Guskiewicz et al., 2007), those who reported experiencing three or more concussions were approximately three times more likely than players who reported no history of concussion to have been diagnosed with clinical depression in their lifetime. For players who reported having one or two concussions, the risk for clinical depression was approximately 1.5 times higher than for players with no history of concussion.

Athletes' postinjury narratives have identified several cognitive, personal, situational, and injury-related factors perceived as contributing to their emotional responses to injury. In terms of cognitive factors, postinjury emotional functioning has been perceived as being affected by cognitive appraisals (Clement & Arvinen-Barrow, 2013; Johnston & Carroll, 1998; Ruddock-Hudson et al., 2014) and by attributions of injury cause (i.e., mental explanations for why the injury occurred). The latter factor was described by McArdle (2010) in the context of an athlete who, three months after injury, was "visibly angry" at the opposing player whom he perceived as causing his severe knee injury; in fact, he was sufficiently angry that "he expressed a desire to injure the culpable party once he was playing competitive soccer again" (p. 74). One personal factor mentioned as potentially influencing an athlete's postinjury emotional state is athletic identity, which involves the extent to which an individual identifies with the athlete role (Brewer et al., 1993). Athletes high in athletic identity described themselves as having difficulty adjusting emotionally to their injuries (Sparkes, 1998; Stoltenburg et al., 2011). In the final two categories—situational and injury-related—that have been described as contributing to emotional responses to sport injury, potential factors include previous injury experience, injury severity, injury type, time of the season, and rehabilitation progress (Bianco et al., 1999; Johnston & Carroll, 1998; Ruddock-Hudson et al., 2012; Sparkes; Stoltenburg et al.).

Quantitative Studies of Emotional Responses to Sport Injury

As indicated in the preceding section, information obtained from a relatively small group of *qualitative* studies has illustrated the wide range of potential emotional responses to sport injury, identified temporal trends in emotional responses to sport injury, and suggested an array of potential predictors of emotional reactions to sport injury. These qualitative findings have been brought into clearer focus by *quantitative* investigations that have achieved the following advances:

- Allowing calculations to estimate the prevalence of clinical levels of emotional disturbance among injured athletes

- Enabling the testing of models of psychological response to sport injury

- Expanding the list of variables that are predictive of emotional adjustment to sport injury

In much of the quantitative research on emotional responses to sport injury, the key construct—emotional response—has been measured with either the Profile of Mood States (POMS; McNair, Lorr, & Droppleman, 1971) or the Emotional Responses of Athletes to Injury Questionnaire (ERAIQ; A.M. Smith, Scott, & Wiese, 1990). Using the POMS, the ERAIQ, and other instruments, researchers have shown that injured athletes report experiencing an array of negative emotions similar to those identified in qualitative studies (e.g., anger, anxiety, depression, fear, frustration, total mood disturbance; for reviews, see Wiese-Bjornstal et al. [1998] and Brewer [2001]).

Although positive emotions may also be experienced by athletes after an injury, they have been less well documented than negative emotions. This difference likely depends to some extent on the fact that for most athletes, injury is incompatible with their pursuit of important sport-related goals—a circumstance that does not lend itself to experiencing positive emotions. In addition, the emotional-response measures that have been used in research tend to emphasize negative emotional states. For example, the Psychological Responses to Sport Injury Inventory (PRSII), developed by L. Evans and her colleagues (Evans, Hardy, Mitchell, & Rees, 2008; Evans, Hardy, & Mullen, 1996) specifically to assess psychological responses common to athletes with injuries, includes a preponderance of negative emotional states (e.g., devastation, dispiritedness, feeling cheated, restlessness) rather than positive emotional states (e.g., reorganization).

The best available evidence suggests that sport injury adversely affects emotional functioning. As compared with uninjured athletes, athletes who are injured have tended to display both higher levels of emotional disturbance (Abenza, Olmedilla, & Ortega, 2010; Appaneal, Levine, Perna, & Roh, 2009; Brewer & Petrie, 1995; C.S. Chan & Grossman, 1988; Johnson, 1997, 1998; Leddy et al., 1994; Mainwaring et al., 2004; Mainwaring et al., 2010; Pearson & Jones, 1992; A.M. Smith et al., 1993) and greater subjective distress when exposed to video footage related to orthopedic trauma (Appaneal, Perna, & Larkin, 2007). Similarly, athletes have shown higher levels of emotional disturbance after injury than before injury (Appaneal et al., 2009; Leddy et al., 1994; Mainwaring et al., 2004, 2010; A.M. Smith et al., 1993). Although most of the emotional disturbance experienced by injured athletes is not severe or long-lasting enough to qualify for a clinical diagnosis (Heil, 1993a), data obtained through research with self-report symptom checklists (Appaneal et al., 2009; Brewer, Linder, & Phelps, 1995; Brewer, Petitpas, Van Raalte, Sklar, & Ditmar, 1995; Brewer & Petrie, 1995; Leddy et al., 1994; Manuel et al., 2002) and clinical interviews (Appaneal et al., 2009) suggest that 5 percent to 27 percent of injured athletes experience clinically meaningful levels of psychological distress.

The tendency of injured athletes to experience emotional disturbance (particularly anger and depression) to a greater extent than uninjured athletes is consistent with what would be predicted in stage models of adjustment to sport injury (e.g., Astle, 1986; Lynch, 1988; Rotella, 1985). Contrary to stage-model expectations, however, such emotional disturbance is not universal (i.e., not every athlete experiences it). In addition, there is no evidence that anger precedes depression in sequence (they often occur together), and athletes' emotional responses to injury are incredibly varied, both within and across athletes. For example, some athletes experience a variety of postinjury emotions, whereas other athletes are steadier or more "even-keeled" in their emotions after injury.

Across many studies, the general trends among injured athletes are for negative emotions to become less intense and for positive emotions to become more intense over the course of rehabilitation (Appaneal et al., 2009; Brewer, Cornelius, et al., 2007; Crossman, Gluck, & Jamieson, 1995; Dawes & Roach, 1997; Manuel et al., 2002; Mainwaring et al., 2004, 2010; Leddy et al., 1994; Macchi & Crossman, 1996; McDonald & Hardy, 1990; Quackenbush & Crossman, 1994; Quinn & Fallon, 1999; Olmedilla, Ortega, & Gómez, 2014; A.M. Smith, Scott, O'Fallon, & Young, 1990). However, these general trends have been shown to partially reverse—with a slight increase in negative emotions and a slight decrease in positive emotions—near the end of rehabilitation after ACL reconstructive surgery, as athletes prepare for a return to sport (Morrey et al., 1999). This change is inconsistent with ideas set forth in stage models, but it is compatible with the influence of situational factors—in this case, the prospect of returning to sport—on psychological responses to sport injury as posited by cognitive appraisal models.

Temporal (time) factors alone do not fully account for the tremendous variability observed in athletes' postinjury emotions. As proposed in the cognitive appraisal model (depicted in figure 4.1), personal and situational factors are also thought to affect emotional responses to sport injury through cognitive appraisals. Most research on this topic, however, has examined the direct relationship between postinjury emotions and various personal and situational factors, bypassing the presumed role of cognitive appraisals themselves.

With respect to personal (and injury-related) factors, higher levels of emotional disturbance following injury have been documented among athletes who are young (Brewer, Linder, & Phelps, 1995; A.M. Smith, Scott, O'Fallon, & Young, 1990), lower in hardiness (Wadey et al., 2012a), higher in neuroticism (Brewer et al., 2007), lower in optimism (Wadey, Evans, Hanton, & Neil, 2013), higher in pain catastrophizing (Baranoff, Hanrahan, & Connor, 2015), less fully recovered (McDonald & Hardy, 1990; A.M. Smith, Young, & Scott, 1988), more impaired in their ability to perform daily activities (Crossman & Jamieson, 1985), more acutely injured (Alzate, Ramírez, & Artaza, 2004; Brewer, Linder, & Phelps, 1995), experiencing more pain (Brewer, Cornelius, et al., 2007), more severely injured (Alzate et al., 2004; Malinauskas, 2010; Manuel et al., 2002; A.M. Smith, Scott, O'Fallon, & Young, 1990; A.M. Smith et al., 1993), more self-identified with the athlete role (Baranoff et al., 2015; Brewer, 1993; Manuel et al., 2002), more invested in playing professional sport (Kleiber & Brock, 1992), or less accepting of uncomfortable experiences (Baranoff et al., 2015).

Regarding situational factors, higher levels of emotional disturbance are more likely to occur among injured athletes who commit a large number of hours to sport training and competition (Salvador, 1985); participate at a lower level of sport competition (Crossman et al., 1995); report a high level of life stress (Albinson & Petrie, 2003; Brewer, 1993; Brewer, Cornelius, et al., 2007; Malinauskas, 2010; Manuel et al., 2002); or indicate low levels of social support for their rehabilitation (Brewer, Linder, & Phelps, 1995; Rees, Mitchell, Evans, & Hardy, 2010), of social support in general (Malinauskas, 2010), or of overall satisfaction with their social support (S.L. Green & Weinberg, 2001; Manuel et al., 2002). Moreover, social support has been shown to buffer the effects of life stress on psychological adjustment; specifically, the negative association between life stress and psychological adjustment (high life stress is associated with poor psychological adjustment) is reduced for athletes with a high level of social support (Malinauskas, 2010; Rees et al., 2010).

In accord with cognitive appraisal models of psychological response to sport injury, several cognitive factors have been found to predict emotional responses to sport injury. Specifically, greater postinjury emotional disturbance has been reported by athletes who report perceiving themselves as unable to cope with their injuries (Albinson & Petrie,

2003; Daly, Brewer, Van Raalte, Petitpas, & Sklar, 1995), using more avoidance-focused (Gallagher & Gardner, 2007) and fewer instrumental (Wadey, Evans, et al., 2013) coping strategies, possessing early maladaptive schemas (i.e., dysfunctional cognitive structures that affect how people process information about themselves and the world in which they live) (Gallagher & Gardner), and being low in physical self-esteem (Brewer, 1993). Attributions for the cause of sport injury also appear to be related to postinjury emotions, but the nature of this relationship is unclear. In one study (Brewer, 1999a), attribution of injury to internal and stable factors was associated with lower levels of emotional disturbance, whereas another study (Tedder & Biddle, 1998) found that attribution of injury to internal factors was associated with higher levels of emotional disturbance.

One particular emotional response to sport injury—fear of injury—warrants brief mention here because even though it occurs *after* sport injury, it is less a reaction to a previous injury than an anxious anticipation of a prospective *future* injury. Nevertheless, as with the perceptions of injury risk described earlier, athletes who have experienced an injury have been shown to report higher levels of fear of injury than those who have not experienced an injury (Reuter & Short, 2005). Similarly, in an investigation of triathletes, sport injury anxiety has been positively associated with both number and severity of previous injuries (Habif, 2009). More recently, a pair of studies of collegiate competitors found that athletes returning to participation from major injuries expressed greater fear of reinjury than did athletes returning from moderate or minor injuries (Deitrick, Covassin, Bleeker, Yang, & Heiden, 2013) and that athletes who had experienced an injury in the past year reported higher preseason levels of kinesiophobia (fear of movement) than did athletes with no recent injury history (Rivet, Brewer, Van Raalte, & Petitpas, 2013). It may not even be necessary to sustain an injury in order to experience elevated fear of injury; for example, skiers displayed increased use of "fear words and phrases" after a teammate incurred an injury on the slopes (O'Neill, 2008).

Whether fear results from direct or vicarious experience, it may in part underlie the spike in negative emotions that can occur near the end of rehabilitation, when a return to sport is imminent (Morrey et al., 1999).

Behavioral Responses to Sport Injury

As suggested in figure 4.1, sport injury can influence not only cognition and emotion but also behavior. Behavioral responses to sport injury are important because they can directly affect rehabilitation outcomes (Brewer, Andersen, et al., 2002; Wiese-Bjornstal et al., 1998). The postinjury behavior that is most relevant to the rehabilitation process is that of adherence to rehabilitation programs, which is considered in depth in chapter 6. Also important is coping behavior. Just as athletes may try to cope with their injuries by initiating cognitive strategies, they may engage in behaviors intended to achieve the same ends.

In one study (Gould et al., 1997b), for example, skiers reported using a variety of behavioral coping strategies in response to their injuries: (a) "driving through," which involves trying to do things as normally as possible despite the injury and working hard to achieve rehabilitation goals; (b) distracting oneself, which involves staying busy and potentially seeking a change of scenery to keep one's mind off of being injured; (c) seeking and using social resources; and (d) avoiding others or isolating oneself. Skiers in a second study (Bianco et al., 1999) indicated that they tried to cope with their injuries by using a variety of strategies, including several methods that are akin to driving through: (a) taking an aggressive approach to their rehabilitation; (b) acquiring information about their injuries; (c) trying alternative therapies; and (d) strengthening their bodies. Instrumental methods of this sort were the coping strategies endorsed most frequently in an investigation of athletes undergoing rehabilitation following knee surgery (Udry, 1997). More recently, Australian Football League players described disengaging from their club and seeking social support as strategies for coping with a long-term in-

jury (Ruddock-Hudson et al., 2014), and athletes from a variety of sports reported using both problem-focused behavioral strategies (e.g., pursuing goals) and emotion-focused or avoidant behavioral strategies (e.g., watching television, going out drinking) to cope with their injuries (Wadey, Evans, Hanton, & Neil, 2012a, 2012b).

There is some question as to whether athletes' use of behavioral coping strategies varies over the course of rehabilitation in the same way that their use of cognitive coping strategies appears to fluctuate in response to changes in the nature and intensity of their physical symptoms and the demands of rehabilitation. Although one study (Udry, 1997) found no changes in the use of instrumental coping strategies over the course of rehabilitation, three other studies (Bianco et al., 1999; Johnston & Carroll, 2000; Quinn & Fallon, 1999) found differences over time in coping behavior after injury. Unfortunately, there was no consistency in the differences observed. Quinn and Fallon found that athletes reported making more active coping efforts (i.e., attempting to deal with stressors directly by initiating action) toward the end of rehabilitation than they did near the beginning (Quinn & Fallon, 1999). Johnston and Carroll, on the other hand, found that athletes reported making less use of multiple coping behaviors (e.g., seeking support, problem solving, discharging emotions) as their rehabilitation progressed. Additional research is needed to clarify the role of time and the phase of rehabilitation in the use of behavioral strategies to cope with sport injury. Athletes also seem to report using active behavioral coping strategies when they appraise their injuries as stressful and difficult to cope with and when they are experiencing mood disturbance (Albinson & Petrie, 2003), which suggests that distress serves as a "cue to action" during sport injury rehabilitation (Brewer, 2007).

Some behavioral responses to sport injury can be problematic in and of themselves. Suicidal behavior, for example, has been documented among athletes with severe postinjury emotional disturbance (A.M. Smith & Milliner, 1994). Sport injury may also trigger disordered eating (Sundgot-Borgen, 1994) or prompt the consumption of alcohol (M.P. Martens, Dams-O'Connor, & Beck, 2006) and banned substances, such as anabolic steroids, amphetamines, ephedrine, and marijuana (National Collegiate Athletic Association, 2012). These maladaptive responses underscore the need to adopt a biopsychosocial approach when considering the effects of injury on athletes.

Of course, as illustrated by the more adaptive behavioral coping strategies described in this section, not all behavioral responses to sport injury are problematic. For example, driving through, adhering to rehabilitation protocols, acquiring injury-related information, and gaining physical strength can all presumably exert a favorable influence on an athlete's recovery and return-to-sport outcomes. Some postinjury behaviors may even provide benefits that extend beyond adjustment to the injury; for example, spending time with family members and friends, building social support networks, and devoting time to academic and occupational pursuits (Stoltenburg et al., 2011; Wadey et al., 2011) are behavioral responses that can provide adaptive value outside the realm of sport. In some cases, over the long term, athletes whose sport careers have been decimated by injury find a "silver lining" amid the devastation and end up pursuing a career in health, medicine, or a related field in which they can use professional skills to help other athletes (Wiese-Bjornstal, 2009).

Biopsychosocial Analysis

The cases of Danielle and Nicole, described at the beginning of this chapter, highlight some key aspects of the psychological consequences of sport injury. In particular, the intensity, volatility, and variability of Danielle's responses to her ACL injury and rehabilitation illustrate the following realities:

- The breadth and depth of an injury's potential effects on an athlete's cognitive, emotional, and behavioral functioning

- The interrelationships between physical and psychological functioning throughout the processes of injury, rehabilitation, recovery, and return to sport

- The influence of situational factors on psychological responses to sport injury

In contrast, Nicole's decidedly less dramatic responses to her ACL injury show that athletes' reactions to injury are not necessarily negative and that other people's expectations about how an athlete *should* respond to injury may bear little resemblance to what the athlete actually experiences.

The contrast between the responses of Danielle and Nicole is especially revealing. Their injury and sport situations were substantially similar, yet their responses differed dramatically. This difference makes readily apparent the fact that there is no universal pattern of psychological response to sport injury. In the differences between these two athletes' responses, a central role was played by their respective cognitive appraisals of the injury and its ramifications for the pursuit of their goals. Whereas Danielle viewed the injury as devastating and saw herself as having little control over what happened to her, Nicole chose a more benign interpretation of the injury and viewed herself as having a degree of control over her fate. It is unclear how much of the two athletes' responses to injury can attributed to stable underlying characteristics (i.e., personality), but there is some suggestion that Nicole's social support system may have helped her experience a more satisfactory adjustment to her injury.

Summary

Research has documented a wide array of cognitive, emotional, and behavioral responses to sport injury. Attempts to explain how athletes respond psychologically to injury have primarily involved the stage and cognitive appraisal approaches. Inspired by literature on reactions to grief, stage models hold that injury creates a state of loss, in response to which athletes proceed through a sequential series of psychological stages. Despite their practical appeal, stage models have not withstood empirical evaluation; in reality, psychological responses to sport injury are highly variable and do not seem to follow a set pattern. In contrast, with roots in the stress and coping literature, cognitive appraisal models hold that injury is a stressor and that athletes' cognitive, emotional, and behavioral responses to sport injury are influenced largely by the ways in which they appraise or interpret their injuries. The interpretations that athletes form regarding their injuries are thought to depend in part on personal and situational factors. Aspects of cognitive appraisal models have received consistent research support.

In addition to interpreting an injury's implications for their well-being and their ability to manage the situation, athletes respond cognitively to injury in various ways. For example, they may make attributions for the cause of the injury, endure intrusive thoughts and images related to the injury, experience changes in self-related cognition (e.g., self-esteem, self-confidence, self-efficacy, self-identity), initiate

cognitive coping strategies, note benefits of injury occurrence, perceive an increased risk of injury occurrence, and experience diminished cognitive performance.

In terms of athletes' emotional responses to injury, qualitative and quantitative research has documented a variety of postinjury responses, including anger, confusion, depression, fear, frustration, helplessness, and shock. Negative emotions tend to be most pronounced shortly after injury and to abate over time, with a possible spike in responses (e.g., anxiety, fear) as the return to sport approaches. Predictors of emotional responses to sport injury include personal, situational, and injury-related factors. A small portion of athletes with injuries experience emotional disturbance to a degree that is considered to be clinically meaningful.

Behavioral responses to sport injury include coping strategies that athletes deploy to deal with injury and its effects, such as immersing themselves in rehabilitation tasks, engaging in activities to distract themselves, seeking social support, and learning about their injuries. Problematic behavioral responses to sport injury include disordered eating, substance use, and suicidal behavior.

Discussion Questions

1. How well do stage and cognitive appraisal models of psychological response to sport injury fit the research findings on psychological consequences of sport injury?

2. What are some common ways in which athletes try to cope with sport injury and its consequences?

3. What are some examples of positive and negative cognitive, emotional, and behavioral consequences of sport injury?

4. How might media attention to the effects of concussion on athletes' behavior and cognition affect the public's appreciation and understanding of psychological responses to sport injury?

Chapter 5
Pain, Sport, and Injury

Chapter Objectives

1. To present an overview of pain in the contexts of sport and sport injury
2. To examine sport-related pain in terms of its definitions, types, dimensions, measurement, theoretical explanations, and associated factors
3. To highlight issues pertaining to how sport-related pain is interpreted and acted on

The pain hit Veronica like a blinding white light and took her breath away. She fell beside home plate stunned, the bat still touching her outstretched right hand. Veronica's eyes filled with tears as she struggled to catch her breath and find her bearings. As the wooziness began to subside, she was left with a searing pain in her upper left leg. After being led from the field by her coach and a teammate while a pinch runner took first base, Veronica was evaluated by the team's athletic trainer, who concluded that no structural damage had been done and that Veronica was going to have a nasty bruise on the big red spot that bore the imprint of a softball. Although the pain had abated somewhat, Veronica was extremely surprised when she heard her coach say, "Hey, Ronnie, you gonna be ready to go back in the field when the inning is over?"

Luis was wobbly as he crested Agony Hill for the tenth and final time of the afternoon. His lungs were burning and his quads were shot as a result of his hardest-ever session of hill repeats (he had never before done more than eight). With his chest heaving, he gasped and said, "That hurt so bad . . . it was awesome!"

Not yet 23 years of age, Kijuan felt like an old man. His knee ached constantly after practices and games, and he could even tell when it was going to rain by how his knee felt—something his 93-year-old great-grandfather hadn't been able to do until he hit 82. Ice and anti-inflammatories dimmed the pain somewhat, but Kijuan's knee hurt even during the off-season when he was doing hardly anything at all. The orthopedic surgeon told him that he wasn't currently injured but that due to repeated trauma and injuries to his knee earlier in his sport career, scar tissue had built up and his knee had become arthritic. The surgeon said there wasn't much he could do to help at this point, and the best Kijuan could hope for would be to manage the symptoms.

With a slight sense of dread, Roberta walked down the long ramp toward the athletic training room. Her shin splints had been feeling better since she had started receiving treatments before practice, but that didn't make her any more eager to get her daily friction massage. Roberta reminded herself that the temporary pain of the treatments was absolutely worth the longer-term relief from the constant throbbing in her shins.

Reflecting back on the day he had torn his hamstring, Scott knew that all the warning signs of impending injury had been there and that he had ignored them. His hamstring had been tight, tired, and tender for a few days just before the injury, but he had thought that analgesic cream, compression shorts, and light stretching would be enough to get him through the preliminary and final rounds of the 4 × 400-meter relay in the championship meet. Obviously not.-

Pain is woven tightly into the fabric of sport participation. In combat sports (e.g., boxing), competitors try to inflict pain (and possibly injury) on their opponents as an integral part of the activity (Parry, 2006). In other sports (e.g., American football), players' pursuit of instrumental objectives within the activity often produces behaviors that cause an opponent to experience pain. In some sport situations, such as the one encountered by Veronica in the chapter-opening scenario, the nature of the sport dictates that athletes put themselves in risky positions where events that lead to pain are possible if not probable. In other cases, vigorous attempts to achieve sport-related goals lead athletes such as Luis (intentionally) and Scott (unintentionally) to engage in behaviors that are likely to cause them pain. Clearly, then, the culture of risk that permeates the world of sport (as described in chapter 1) did not evolve by accident; furthermore, it could just as easily be characterized as a culture of pain.

As pain is closely related to sport participation, it is also closely tied to sport injury. Pain often precedes or signals the occurrence of injury (as in Scott's experience), and injury often precipitates the experience of pain (as in Veronica's case). However, the correspondence between pain and sport injury is not one to one. Pain can occur in the absence of current injury (as in Kijuan's experience), and it does not necessarily indicate that injury is imminent. Conversely, in some circumstances, sport injuries—even severe ones—do not produce pain (at least not right away). Nevertheless, pain exists in an unusual, perhaps even unique, cultural and clinical context in relation to sport injury.

Against a cultural backdrop in which pain is glamorized, glorified, celebrated, and even sought after, the vast majority of sport-related pain is largely preventable, escapable, avoidable, or reducible. For one thing, when athletes experience pain that is caused or aggravated by sport participation, they can simply elect not to participate. Granted, they may experience monetary, social, or personal pressures to participate in spite of pain—as well as monetary, social, or personal costs associated with not participating—but the choice does exist. Still, although the prospect of experiencing pain may deter some people from being involved in sport, many individuals choose to participate despite (and sometimes because of) the likelihood of encountering pain.

Given the ubiquity of pain in sport, as well as the close connection between pain and sport injury, the primary purpose of this chapter is to provide an overview of pain in the contexts of sport in general and sport injury in particular. The chapter examines sport-related pain through its definitions, types, dimensions, measurement, theoretical explanations, and associated factors. It also highlights issues pertaining to how sport-related pain is interpreted and acted on—for example, distinguishing between pain and injury, playing hurt, performing while experiencing pain, seeking treatment, and managing pain.

Definitions of Pain

As a concept, pain is elusive and difficult to define. Although most people have a good sense of what pain is, and what it is like to experience it, numerous definitions of pain have been proposed. Here is one definition used frequently in relation to sport health care: "an unpleasant sensory and emotional experience associated with actual or potential tissue damage, or described in terms of such damage" (International Association for the Study of Pain, 1979, p. 249). Though brief, this definition contains an abundance of information. For starters, pain is considered unpleasant and involves both sensory and emotional components. It is also something that is experienced and therefore does not exist independently of the person experiencing it. Furthermore, though pain is often experienced after the occurrence of tissue damage, it can also occur in anticipation of or even in the complete absence of tissue damage. Other definitions of pain address some additional aspects: experience of a noxious stimulus; behavior designed to escape, avoid, or destroy the stimulus; and influential factors such as current social and environmental context, previous experiences, learning history, and cognitive processes.

Pain occupies a crowded landscape of related terms which, as depicted in figure 5.1, are sometimes overlapping and sometimes distinct. For example, pain is distinguishable from *nociception*, which involves the impingement of mechanical, thermal, or chemical energy on specialized peripheral nerve endings known as nociceptors (generally, small-diameter A-delta and C nerve fibers), thus signaling the brain about the occurrence of an aversive event (Fordyce, 1988; E. Mann & Carr, 2006). Although nociception and pain often occur together, pain can occur without nociception (e.g., when the thought of a previous collision causes a sharp twinge of pain to radiate through an athlete's torso); similarly, nociception can occur without pain (e.g., when an athlete who is "in the zone" fails to notice bodily sensations during a record-setting performance).

Another related term is *anguish*, which refers primarily to the emotional component of pain, in which the individual experiences emotional distress whether in the presence of or in

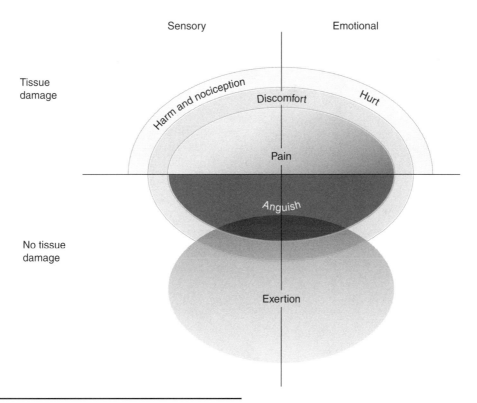

Figure 5.1 Conceptual depiction of pain-related terms.

the absence of any injury or tissue damage. *Discomfort*, in contrast, refers to experiencing mild distress or feeling uncomfortable due to pain, nociception, anguish, or a related condition. Another term, *hurt*, refers to the experiencing of circumstances that cause pain or distress, whereas *harm* occurs when injury or tissue damage is sustained. Thus harm can produce hurt, but hurt cannot produce harm (Parry, 2006).

The term that is probably the farthest afield conceptually from the other pain-related terms addressed here is *exertion*, which, ironically, is also the term most directly associated with sport participation. It refers to the act of putting forth great mental or physical effort. Finally, perhaps the most all-encompassing of the terms is *suffering*. In one conceptualization (Parry, 2006), suffering can include any of the preceding experiences—nociception, anguish, discomfort, hurt, harm, or exertion. However, in another conceptualization (Fordyce, 1988), suffering consists simply of the affective or emotional component of responses triggered by nociception or some other aversive stimulus.

Types of Pain

The generic nature of pain definitions serves as an umbrella under which a wide variety of phenomenal experiences reside. Attempts have been made to identify various types of pain by clustering experiences with similar symptoms, symptom durations, and symptom sources. Perhaps the simplest distinction that can be made is between acute pain and chronic pain. Based solely on symptom duration, acute pain lasts less than three months, whereas chronic pain lasts longer than three months or exceeds the expected healing time (International Association for the Study of Pain Subcommittee on Taxonomy, 1986). Acute pain is temporary and generally occurs as a result of a specific injury (e.g., fracture, overused muscle) and the ensuing tissue damage. Chronic pain, on the other hand, can be further divided into three subtypes:

1. Chronic-recurrent pain, which is benign (i.e., harmless) and episodic (i.e., involves repeated periods of pain alternating with periods of no pain)

2. Chronic-intractable-benign pain, which is ongoing, harmless, and resistant to treatment

3. Chronic-progressive pain, which is ongoing, increasing in intensity over time, and due to a malignant (i.e., harmful) underlying cause (Turk, Meichenbaum, & Genest, 1983)

Other types of pain include causalgia, phantom-limb pain, and referred pain, each of which highlights the potential lack of correspondence between tissue damage and pain. Causalgia involves sustained burning pain that can result after a wound has healed and the nerves have regenerated. For example, a lacrosse player might experience causalgia after recovering from an injury caused by being struck by a fast-moving ball. Phantom-limb pain occurs when a person who has had an amputation experiences pain that seems to be located in the missing body part. This kind of pain might be encountered by an athlete with an amputation participating in the Paralympic Games. Referred pain typically has a physiological basis and starts at tissue in one part of the body but is experienced in another part of the body. For example, an athlete with a hip injury might experience knee pain rather than hip pain and obtain relief only after the hip problem is addressed.

Although the distinctions between acute pain, chronic pain, causalgia, phantom-limb pain, and referred pain are useful, they do not fully capture the types of pain experienced by people involved in sport and exercise. To address this gap, several classification schemes—all of which are in need of further empirical validation—have been proposed to identify types of pain relevant to sport involvement and sport injury. For example, Miles and Clarkson (1994) discussed three types of pain associated with physical activity:

1. Pain encountered during or shortly after engaging in exercise

2. Delayed-onset muscle soreness (DOMS), which occurs 24 to 48 hours after engaging in vigorous exercise

3. Pain resulting from muscle cramps

This framework helps foster appreciation of several common forms of pain experienced in association with sport and, more specifically, sport injury.

In another scheme, elaborating on the work of Heil (1993b), J. Taylor and Taylor (1997) distinguished performance pain from injury pain and distinguished benign pain from harmful pain. *Performance pain* is viewed by athletes as positive, acute, short lasting, voluntarily produced, controllable, and readily reducible. *Injury pain*, on the other hand, is viewed by athletes as negative, chronic, uncontrollable, indicative of bodily harm, and signaling a need to protect the injured body part. In the other distinction, *harmful pain*, as compared with *benign pain*, is thought to be sharper, more localized, longer lasting after exertion, and accompanied to a greater extent by swelling, tenderness, and soreness.

On the basis of face-to-face interviews conducted with 12 elite athletes, Addison and Kremer (1997) identified six types of sport-related pain that vary in terms of valence (value), intensity, and threat level. *Positive training pain* involves the feelings of muscle fatigue and noxious cardiorespiratory sensations that athletes encounter while training vigorously. It is perceived as benign and beneficial to sport performance, and it can be considered synonymous with performance pain as defined in the scheme put forward by J. Taylor and Taylor (1997). *Negative training pain* involves the same sorts of nonthreatening symptoms as positive training pain, but in this case those symptoms are not perceived as beneficial to sport performance. *Discomfort* involves symptoms of exertion that are not strong enough to be considered painful. *Negative warning pain* is like negative training pain but adds an interpretation of threat in which the sensations are viewed as possibly indicating injury. *Negative acute pain* results directly from a specific event or injury and involves sensations perceived as intense, harmful, and sudden in onset. *Numbness* involves an absence of sensation that is perceived as potentially threatening.

Dimensions of Pain

Pain can be evaluated in terms of two main dimensions—quality and intensity. *Quality* re-fers to the descriptive aspect of pain. Although there are limits on how well a phenomenon as subjective as pain can be described verbally, words can be used to convey some sense of the pain experience. For example, is the pain sharp, or is it dull? Is it constant or throbbing? Diffused or focused? As suggested by Heil (1993b) and J. Taylor and Taylor (1997), different types of sport-related pain may be characterized by different qualities.

Intensity refers to the strength or magnitude of the pain experienced. Pain intensity can be expressed both qualitatively (e.g., "hurts a lot more than it did yesterday") and quantitatively (e.g., "7 on a scale of 0 to 10"). The intensity dimension of pain is closely tied to the concepts of pain threshold and pain tolerance, which, as discussed in this chapter's Focus on Research box, have been investigated extensively through a variety of laboratory pain-induction methods. Pain threshold is the intensity of stimulation required for a given stimulus to be perceived as painful. For example, a pat on the back generally falls below the recipient's pain threshold, whereas a slap on the back is likely to be above the pain threshold. For hand-on-back contact, then, the pain threshold for most people lies somewhere between a pat and a slap.

Pain tolerance, on the other hand, is the intensity of stimulation at which a person refuses further exposure to the stimulus. It typically corresponds to a higher level of stimulation than does the pain threshold; for example, a person might notice a slap on the back as painful yet be willing to tolerate it. A point is likely to come, however, when the recipient of hand-to-back contact is no longer willing to accept the stimulation. That point is the person's pain tolerance for this particular stimulus. Whereas pain threshold is influenced primarily by physiological factors, pain tolerance is affected mainly by psychological factors (DiMatteo & Martin, 2002). As indicated in chapter 6, pain tolerance is relevant to the rehabilitation of sport injuries because higher pain tolerance is associated with better adherence to sport injury rehabilitation regimens (Byerly, Worrell, Gahimer, & Domholdt, 1994; Fields, Murphey, Horodyski, & Stopka, 1995; Fisher, Domm, & Wuest, 1988).

Experimental Pain Induction

Much of what is known about pain tolerance comes from laboratory research in which participants are exposed to increasing levels of stimulation from devices or procedures designed to induce pain. To qualify as a prospective means of inducing pain in humans in laboratory studies, a device or procedure must be safe, ethically acceptable, and capable of producing gradations of noxious stimulation that permit distinctions to be made between the absence of perceived pain, the pain threshold, and the pain tolerance (Friedman, Thompson, & Rosen, 1985; Pen & Fisher, 1994). Over the past five decades, numerous methods have been used to induce pain in laboratory research, including those involving hot, cold, ischemic, electrical, and pressure-related stimuli.

Among the most widely used means of laboratory pain induction is thermal stimulation, in which participants are exposed to heat-producing stimuli such as hot water, hot objects, infrared light sources, carbon dioxide and argon lasers, heating elements (Naidu, Reddy, Rani, & Rao, 2011), and capsaicin cream (Petersen & Rowbotham, 1999). Another common means of inducing pain in laboratory research is cold stimulation, typically through the cold pressor test. In this test, the participant immerses one hand in cold water and notifies the experimenter upon first noticing the cold as painful (pain threshold) and when the participant wishes to remove the hand from the water (pain tolerance). The utility of this test is limited by the fact that some people experience numbness before they experience the stimulus as painful or wish to withdraw their hand from the water (Pen & Fisher, 1994). Even so, the ability to tolerate cold stimuli (e.g., ice) can be useful in sport injury rehabilitation, and the results of the cold pressor test may be relevant for athletes who are prescribed cryotherapy.

Ischemic pain is induced by obstructing blood flow to a body part. In one ischemic procedure, for example, a slow-growing, lingering, aching form of pain is induced by having participants complete a series of hand grip exercises while the arm is occluded with a standard sphygmomanometer (blood pressure cuff; Sternbach, Deems, Timmermans, & Huey, 1977). In electrical stimulation, electric current of increasing intensity is applied to a body part (e.g., arm, finger, tooth pulp) to obtain quantitative indexes of pain threshold and tolerance.

As one would expect, pressure pain is induced by applying pressure to a body part. One example of a pressure-pain-induction device is the strain gauge pain stimulator (Forgione & Barber, 1971), in which a dull knife edge applies pressure to the second phalanx of a finger and produces pain that builds from light pressure to a dull ache. Another example is the gross pressure device introduced by E.D. Ryan and Kovacic (1966), in which a football cleat secured to a curved fiber plate (or soccer shin guard) is affixed to the anterior border of the tibia, halfway between the ankle and the knee, and secured with the sleeve of a sphygmomanometer. Pain is induced by gradually inflating the blood pressure cuff at a constant rate (5 mmHg/sec), and quantitative indexes of pain threshold and tolerance are provided, respectively, by the amount of pressure (measured in mmHg) at which the participant decides that the pressure is painful and the amount at which he or she elects to cease the exposure. The gross pressure device has been used fairly extensively in sport-related pain research.

The pain-induction methods used in most laboratory studies are limited chiefly by the fact that the pain is typically short in duration, the pain may not be similar to clinical pain, and participants know they are safe and unlikely to experience bodily harm as a result of the pain, thereby minimizing their fear (Pen & Fisher, 1994). In an attempt to lengthen the duration of laboratory pain and enhance the ecological validity of the pain experience, some researchers have begun to use delayed-onset muscle soreness (DOMS) as an alternative means of inducing pain in experimental studies. In a standard DOMS induction, participants are asked to complete a series of strength-training exercises, ideally involving an eccentric (lowering) component performed with untrained muscles (Pen & Fisher, 1994; Sullivan et al., 2002). Muscle soreness emerges about 24 hours after exercise, peaks about 48 to 72 hours after exercise, and diminishes slowly before subsiding completely over the next five to eight days (Clarkson, Nosaka, & Braun, 1992). The pain produced through DOMS induction is thought to replicate more closely the pain encountered in sport than does the pain generated through other common induction methods. It is not possible to assess pain threshold and pain tolerance in DOMS inductions, but they do permit measurement of the pain level experienced and of the participant's tolerance of the physical activity (Pen & Fisher, 1994).

Measurement of Pain

Pain is a complex, subjective phenomenon that is difficult to measure objectively and cannot be assessed directly. Nevertheless, effective treatment and meaningful research require accurate, thorough, dependable, and valid measurement of the pain experience. Sport-related pain is assessed through psychophysiological, behavioral, and self-report measures.

Psychophysiological Measures

Psychophysiological measures presumably tap the bodily changes that occur in response to the sensory and emotional aspects of pain. Physiological parameters that can be affected by pain—and can therefore be assessed as indexes of pain—include muscle tension, autonomic activity, and electrical activity in the brain (Sarafino & Smith, 2011). Muscle tension is customarily measured with an electromyograph (EMG). Autonomic activity includes physiological responses such as heart rate, respiration rate, blood pressure, skin temperature, and skin conductance. Electrical activity in the brain is typically assessed with an electroencephalograph (EEG).

The chief advantage of psychophysiological measures is that they provide objective data not subject to self-report bias. Their utility as "stand-alone" indexes of pain is limited, however, because they have shown inconsistent relationships with other measures of pain and can be influenced by psychological factors other than pain, such as attention and stress (Chapman et al., 1985; Flor, 2001). Nevertheless, recent research offers encouragement that assessment techniques (e.g., functional magnetic resonance imaging [fMRI] and muscle microdialysis) can be used to identify, respectively, biological markers of laboratory pain (Wager, Atlas, Lindquist, Roy, & Woo, 2013) and of clinical pain (Gerdle, Ghafouri, Ernberg, & Larsson, 2014).

Behavioral Measures

Although pain can be thought of as a subjective, internally experienced phenomenon, people in pain often engage in overt behavior that conveys information about the extent of their pain. These "pain behaviors" include, for example, limping, wincing, moaning, groaning, complaining vocally, remaining in bed, and requesting painkillers. In sport, pain behaviors are sometimes suppressed or minimized in accordance with the sport ethic (Hughes & Coakley, 1991). On the other hand, as any spectator of a Serie A soccer match can attest, athletes are also capable of demonstrating flamboyant pain behaviors when the potential for reinforcement (e.g., a foul call against an opponent) is high.

Behavioral assessment of pain typically involves monitoring pain behaviors and recording details such as the circumstances under which the behaviors occur, the duration of the behaviors, and their consequences (e.g., how others react or what happens as a result). This information can be useful in determining what precipitates pain, how pain affects a person's functioning, and what factors may maintain pain (Sarafino & Smith, 2011). In sport settings, an athlete's pain behaviors may be monitored by a parent, coach, or sport health care professional. Observed pain behaviors are more likely to correspond with self-reports of pain intensity when the pain being assessed is acute and when the two indexes of pain are taken close in time to each other (Labus, Keefe, & Jensen, 2003).

Self-Report Measures

To accurately and thoroughly assess a phenomenon as subjective as pain, we must obtain the perspective of the person being examined. The perceptions of people in pain are typically documented with self-report measures. Self-reports can be gathered through interviews, rating scales, diaries, and questionnaires. Interviews are especially useful for gaining background information on the following subjects (Karoly, 1985; Sarafino & Smith, 2011):

- Origins and progression of the pain complaint (When did it start? What precipitated it? How has the pain changed over time?)
- How the person has functioned physically and psychologically before and after the onset of pain (What changes in activity have you made as a result of the pain? How does the pain affect your emotions?)

- Attempts the person has made to cope with the pain (What treatments have been tried, and how well have they worked? What strategies have you used to deal with the pain, and how well have they worked?)
- Social aspects of the pain (How do you behave toward others, and how do others behave toward you, when you are experiencing pain at its worst?)
- Factors that may trigger, exacerbate, or reinforce the pain

Rating scales are used most frequently to address the intensity dimension of pain. Respondents are typically asked to indicate where their pain falls on a continuum from "no pain" to "pain as bad as it could be" (or the like). Responses can be given by marking a point on a line between the two endpoints (i.e., a visual analogue scale); writing a number between 0 and 100, where 0 means "no pain" and 100 means "pain as bad as it could be," on a line (a numerical rating scale); checking a box with an assigned numerical value, such as 0 to 10, between the two endpoints (a box scale); or selecting a word or phrase (e.g., "no pain," "some pain," "considerable pain," "pain that could not be more severe") from among several escalating alternatives (a verbal rating scale). The validity of rating scales is well established for assessing pain intensity (Jensen, Karoly, & Braver, 1986; Jensen, Karoly, O'Riordan, Bland, & Burns, 1989).

Pain ratings provide a snapshot of a person's pain at a given point in time. It can also be helpful to place pain ratings into the broader context of the person's pain experience. One means for doing so is a pain diary, in which the person records information about the intensity and other aspects of the pain, once per day or more frequently. Such a diary can furnish a richly detailed account of how a person's pain varies over time and, potentially, of the factors associated with those variations.

For example, Brewer, Cornelius, Van Raalte, Brickner, Tennen, et al. (2004) obtained daily ratings of current, worst, and average pain intensity for the first 42 days after ACL reconstructive surgery. Retrospective ratings of worst and average daily pain were taken for two 7-day periods and one 30-day period over the course of 42 days after surgery. Results indicated that although the retrospective ratings were strongly related to the daily ratings, the retrospective ratings slightly overestimated the amount of pain reported on a daily basis. That is, when the men and women in the study were asked to report on the intensity of pain that they experienced during the past week or month, they gave higher ratings than they did while rating their pain on a daily basis over the comparable period of time. As shown in figure 5.2, the diary data obtained from the study participants (Brewer, Cornelius, Van Raalte, Brickner, Tennen, et al., 2004) indicate that although the amount of average daily pain reported as a group decreased steadily over the first six weeks after surgery, the pain ratings given by some participants fluctuated greatly from day to day (Brewer & Van Raalte, 2009). The ability to track such fluctuations with pain diaries support their use in sport injury rehabilitation.

As compared with rating scales and pain diaries, pain inventories or questionnaires offer a more comprehensive glimpse at people's pain. The first pain inventory developed (and still the most broadly used) is the McGill Pain Questionnaire (MPQ; Melzack, 1975), which addresses the location, qualities, changeability, and intensity of the respondent's pain. In terms of location, respondents indicate where they are experiencing pain on a drawing of a human body and note whether the pain is internal, external, or both. To measure qualities of pain—sensory, emotional, and evaluative—the inventory provides 20 clusters of two to six adjectives each and asks respondents to select one word from as many clusters as are relevant to and descriptive of their pain. For example, in a cluster representing the sensory quality of pain, respondents can select one word from the following six escalating descriptors: flickering, quivering, pulsing, throbbing, beating, pounding.

To assess the changeability of pain, the MPQ (Melzack, 1975) uses a series of questions asking respondents to indicate a word

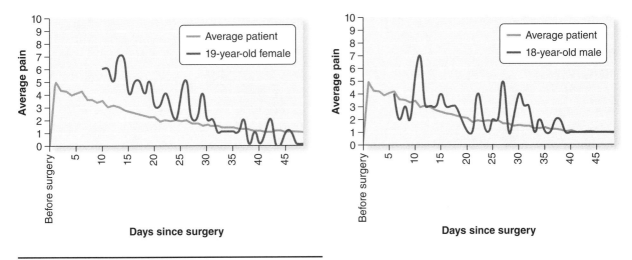

Figure 5.2 Pain-diary data after ACL surgery.

Reprinted, by permission, from Brewer, B., & Van Raalte, J. (Executive Producers). (2009). Conquering ACL surgery and rehabilitation. [CD-ROM]. (Available from Virtual Brands, LLC, 10 Echo Hill Road, Wilbraham, MA 01095)

or words that describe the pattern of their pain and to note what relieves or increases their pain. Pain intensity is assessed through a series of questions asking respondents to describe their pain in terms of a number (from 1 for mild to 5 for excruciating) at the present moment, at its worst, and at its least. For comparison purposes, respondents are also asked to rate the amount of pain experienced with their worst toothache, headache, and stomachache. Scoring the MPQ can be complicated, and completing it can be difficult for those without an extensive English vocabulary (Karoly, 1985), but it can yield valuable information about the pain of persons who are able to respond to it. Other pain inventories are also available, including the West Haven-Yale Multidimensional Pain Inventory (WHYMPI; Kerns, Turk, & Rudy, 1985).

Models and Theories of Pain

Due to the challenges of defining and measuring pain, there is no universally accepted explanation for the occurrence of pain. Models and theories of pain have evolved markedly over the past 60 years, incorporating new knowledge with each subsequent explanation. Let us now examine five of these models and theories: the sensory model, the

sequential components model, the parallel processing model, gate control theory, and neuromatrix theory.

The early *sensory model* held that mechanical, thermal, or chemical stimuli produced tissue damage, which triggered impulses in so-called "pain nerve pathways" and resulted in the sensations and behavioral responses commonly interpreted as pain. Thus, the amount of pain experienced was thought to be directly proportional to the magnitude of the injury to body tissue. The sensory model was characterized by several shortcomings. First, there is no such thing as a "pain nerve pathway" in which neurons are responsible solely for transmitting information about pain. Second, as illustrated vividly by athletes who sustain injuries in the heat of competition but fail to notice them until much later (after the competition), the amount of pain experienced is not simply a function of the magnitude of tissue damage incurred. In fact, an athlete's perception of pain may be modulated by factors such as focus on the sport activity, motivation to succeed at the sport task, and concomitant elevation in physiological arousal. Third, the assumption that tissue damage is a prerequisite for the occurrence of pain is fallacious. Just as athletes sometimes experience little or no pain after incurring injury, others experience pain in the absence of injury (e.g., an inexplicable sharp twinge of pain while quietly resting). Because of the shortcomings of the sensory model, it fell out of favor and was replaced by other models that attempted to better explain the process by which pain occurs (Leventhal & Everhart, 1979).

The *sequential components model* viewed pain as more than a mere sensory phenomenon. Beecher (1959) argued that pain consists of a sensory component and an emotional reaction component. As in the sensory model, the sensory component was thought to be activated by an injury or wound. The observed pain response, in turn, was thought to be a consequence of the emotional reaction triggered by the pain sensations (e.g., distress, fear) and any memories associated with those sensations. Of particular note, the sequential components model recognized that emotional and cognitive factors could influence the process of pain perception.

The relevance of this model to sport injury is clear. For example, athletes who, based on experience, recognize that certain pain sensations are linked to injuries that result in substantial restriction of sport participation may display a stronger pain response than athletes who have not previously encountered the pain sensations and therefore may interpret them more optimistically. The opposite may also be true (and is also compatible with the sequential components model); that is, athletes with prior experience of certain pain sensations may show a *more benign* response to the sensations than do athletes who experience them for the first time. Although this model was a clear improvement on the sensory model, it still required an injury or wound in order for pain to be experienced; it also considered pain as being proportional to the amount of sensory stimulation experienced, and it could not be reconciled with data indicating that emotional factors could influence the sensory response to noxious stimuli (Leventhal & Everhart, 1979).

To address the limitations of the sensory model and the sequential components model, researchers proposed the *parallel processing model*, which places sensation and emotion on equal footing and underscores the role of attention in the perception of pain. In this model, sensory information and emotional responses pertaining to a given stimulus are processed preconsciously—without conscious awareness—and (conscious) attention to the informational and emotional cues determines what the person is aware of, how much pain the person reports, how much distress the person displays, and how she or he responds physiologically. Depending on the locus of attentional focus, people exposed to potentially painful stimulation could become aware of the nature of the stimulus (in a neutral, unemotional way), of their stimulus-related distress (which would ordinarily be considered "pain"), or of anything else that captures their attention. Attention can be directed willfully, such as when a strategy of distraction is implemented intentionally, or, more frequently, guided by schemata, which are cognitive representations of previous experiences (in this case, experiences with noxious stimuli). Schemata incorporate information about sensory (e.g., visual, auditory, tactile) properties, pain qualities (e.g., bright, pricking), and emotional experiences (e.g., distress) associated with a given pain episode.

In the parallel processing model, an injury does not necessarily produce pain, and pain can be experienced in the absence of injury. The model explains how athletes, intently focused on the demands of training or competition, can be subjected to noxious stimulation and report experiencing no pain. It also accommodates situations in which athletes display signs of experiencing intense pain in response to benign stimulation (e.g., a tight muscle) because they attend to their emotional reaction to the prospect of being injured (e.g., fear associated with reinjury of the same muscle) rather than to purely informational sensory cues (i.e., muscle tension). Although the parallel processing model is not explicit with respect to the interface between biological and psychological factors in shaping pain experiences, Leventhal and Everhart (1979) described ways in which it is wholly compatible with *gate control theory* (Melzack & Wall, 1965)—a prominent neurophysiological approach to understanding pain that has important ramifications for psychological factors.

In gate control theory (Melzack & Wall, 1965), which was formulated through a collaboration between a psychologist (Melzack) and a physiologist (Wall), pain is viewed as both a bottom-up and a top-down phenomenon in that both sensory (bottom) and psychological (top) factors play key roles. The theory posits that information pertaining to noxious stimuli detected by nociceptors is *not* transmitted directly to the brain but instead flows through the dorsal horns of the spinal cord, where a neurological "gate" mechanism operates. An open gate allows messages pertaining to the noxious stimulus to go through, thus leading to the perception of pain, whereas a closed gate prevents such messages from getting through to the brain and thus diminishes or eliminates the experience of pain. The amount of pain that a person experiences in response to a given noxious stimulus is thought to be determined primarily by the amount of activity in A-delta and C (small-diameter) nerve fibers, by the amount of activity in A-beta (large-diameter) nerve fibers, and by messages from the brain based on interpretation of the noxious stimulus. Activity in A-delta and C nerve fibers tends to open the gate and is influenced primarily by the strength of the noxious stimulus (stronger stimuli generally elicit more pronounced pain responses). Activity in the A-beta nerve fibers, on the other hand, tends to close the gate and can be stimulated chemically (e.g., by medication), electrically (e.g., by transcutaneous electrical nerve stimulation [TENS]), physically (e.g., by massage), or thermally (e.g., by heat).

The gate can be either opened or closed by messages from structures in the brain (e.g., hypothalamus, thalamus, cerebral cortex), depending on how the stimulus is interpreted. Consistent with the parallel processing model (Leventhal & Everhart, 1979), attention diverted either away from a noxious stimulus (e.g., by distraction) or toward informational (rather than emotional) aspects of that stimulus would be expected to close the gate and thus either diminish or eliminate the experience of

pain associated with the stimulus. The prominent role ascribed to schematic processing in the parallel processing model is also compatible with gate control theory. For experienced endurance athletes, interpretation of the symptoms associated with a high level of exertion sustained over a long period of time would likely be guided by a schema suggesting that such symptoms are expected, commonplace, benign, and acceptable in light of the goals being pursued. An interpretation of that sort would likely close the gate; in contrast, in a novice or inexperienced endurance athlete or exerciser, interpretations of fear, panic, or distress might help keep the gate open and allow pain to be experienced.

Going beyond gate control theory, Melzack (1999) proposed *neuromatrix theory*, which ascribes an active role in pain perception to a widely distributed network of neurons in the brain. This neural network, labeled a "body–self neuromatrix," consists of an expansive set of feedback loops between the limbic system and the cerebral cortex. It is both genetically determined and subject to modification as a consequence of experience in the form of inputs from a variety of sources, including the senses (e.g., visual, auditory, tactile), body systems (e.g., endocrine, immune, autonomic), biochemical factors (e.g., cytokines, endogenous opioids), and manifestations of psychological processes (e.g., attention, anxiety, expectation, knowledge, personality) in the brain. The body–self neuromatrix produces a "neurosignature," which is a characteristic way of experiencing and responding behaviorally to pain. Neuromatrix theory recognizes the complexity of pain and acknowledges the multitude of prospective influences on the phenomenon (Melzack, 1999).

Although none of the models discussed in this chapter were designed with sport-related pain in mind, Addison and colleagues (Addison & Kremer, 1997; Addison, Kremer, & Bell, 1998) adapted principles from the parallel processing model, gate control theory, and the primary and secondary cognitive appraisal processes (Lazarus & Folkman, 1984) discussed in chapter 4 to the sport setting. The pain process is initiated in this model when, during the course of routine sport performance, an action brings about a physiological sensation that is subject to the influence of individual differences in age, fitness, physiology, and somatic attention. The resulting sensation is appraised first (primary appraisal) in terms of whether it constitutes a threat to the person and then (secondary appraisal) in terms of which of the six types of sport-related pain it represents: positive training pain, negative training pain, discomfort, negative warning pain, negative acute pain, or numbness. According to this model, the appraisal process is affected by a wide variety of extrinsic factors (e.g., culture, gender roles, past experience, significant others, situational context) and intrinsic factors (e.g., affective state, expectation, pain tolerance, personality, self-efficacy). Athletes' responses to the primary and secondary appraisals are thought to be affected by factors such as culture, motivation, and social exchange (i.e., rewards and costs). These responses include various options—for example, proceeding as normal, proceeding with caution, stopping the activity, seeking help, and implementing a cognitive coping strategy, the latter of which may influence subsequent perceptions and appraisals of physiological sensations. Although research is needed to evaluate the merits of the model, it represents a preliminary attempt to conceptualize pain in the context of sport participation.

Factors Associated With Pain in Sport

The contemporary models and theories of pain reviewed in the previous section are consistent in positing that a variety of factors outside of sensory inputs contribute to the experience of pain. Across the various forms of acute and chronic pain covered in the health psychology literature, factors identified as relevant to the pain experience include an array of variables pertaining to demographic and individual differences (e.g., age, race and ethnicity, sex, personality), cognition (e.g., attention, distraction, expectations, perceived control), emotion (e.g., anxiety), and social learning processes

(DiMatteo & Martin, 2002; Straub, 2012). Some of these factors have been examined in association with sport and with sport injury.

Demographic and Individual Differences

The variable that has garnered the most attention in this category with respect to sport-related pain is athlete status or, more specifically, whether a person is an athlete or a nonathlete. Tesarz, Schuster, Hartmann, Gerhardt, and Eidt (2012) identified 62 studies comparing the pain perceptions of athletes and nonathletes (or "normally active controls," as they were labeled in this investigation), then conducted a meta-analysis of the 15 studies that satisfied rigorous inclusion criteria. The analysis found that athletes demonstrated elevated levels of pain tolerance and pain threshold relative to nonathletes. The athlete–nonathlete differences in pain *tolerance* held for each of the five types of pain examined (cold, heat, ischemic, electrical, and pressure), whereas athletes showed higher pain *thresholds* than nonathletes for cold and pressure pain but not for electrical, heat, or ischemic pain. In addition, athletes who participated in game and endurance sports displayed higher levels of pain tolerance than nonathletes, but athletes who participated in strength sports did not. Similarly, game- and strength-sport athletes had higher pain thresholds than nonathletes, but endurance-sport athletes did not. After the potential for study bias was taken into account, the findings for pain tolerance were considered more reliable than those for pain threshold (Tesarz et al., 2012).

The results of this meta-analysis (Tesarz et al., 2012) do *not* shed light on the questions of whether people with the ability to tolerate pain are attracted to sport participation or whether participation in sport increases people's ability to tolerate pain. It is likely that both explanations are valid: People who do not tolerate pain well or are especially averse to the prospect of experiencing pain may shy away from sport participation (or at least away from participation in sports with a high probability of encountering painful stimuli); in addition, chronic involvement in sport may help people habituate to sensations potentially perceived as painful. Unfortunately, evidence in support of the former argument is sparse, because the necessary prospective longitudinal studies (measuring pain tolerance before the initiation of sport participation) have not been conducted. However, the latter argument—that sport participation can increase pain tolerance—is bolstered by research indicating the following:

- Acute bouts of physical activity (particularly activity of high intensity) can have hypoalgesic effects that include increased pain tolerance and pain threshold (Koltyn, 2000, 2002).
- Twelve weeks of aerobic fitness training can improve pain tolerance in unfit men (Anshel & Russell, 1994).

Thus, there are compelling reasons to suggest that both acute and chronic sport participation can result in elevated pain tolerance. The mechanisms by which this increase develops have not been identified, although biological, psychological, and social factors may be involved. In regard to potential biological factors, findings from research with laboratory animals has implicated endogenous opiates and neurotransmitters (e.g., serotonin, norepinephrine) in the analgesic effects of physical activity (for a review, see Koltyn, 2000). Psychological factors that may help increase pain tolerance include reducing fear of pain (Geva & Defrin, 2013; Rhudy, 2013), expecting that pain can be tolerated, reinterpreting pain in more positive terms (e.g., as exertion rather than pain), and assuming that pain will be of limited duration (Heil & Podlog, 2012). These psychological factors are potential consequences of exposure to and immersion in the sport ethic (Hughes & Coakley, 1991), which is a likely social source of increased pain tolerance among athletes as compared with nonathletes.

Another demographic and individual-difference factor—gender—has also been examined with some frequency in relation to pain in sport, albeit not nearly to the extent of athlete status. Outside the realm of sport,

in comparison with women, men have been found to report lower levels of clinical pain for several chronic conditions (Robinson, Wise, Riley, & Atchison, 1998) and to display higher thresholds and greater tolerance for several types of experimental (laboratory) pain (for a review, see Riley, Robinson, Wise, Myers, & Fillingim, 1998). Evidence suggests that at least some of these gender differences in pain perception are underlain by traditional gender-role stereotypes, with those endorsing traditional masculine gender roles more strongly displaying lower levels of pain dysfunction (Alabas, Tashani, Tasabam, & Johnson, 2012).

In order to reduce the variability of participants' responses, many of the research investigations on pain in sport have focused on a single gender (Tesarz et al., 2012); as a result, it is not possible to make reliable conclusions about gender differences in pain perception in sport populations. The findings of the small percentage of studies that have included both female and male athletes—thereby enabling direct gender comparisons—suggest that gender differences in pain perception are minimal for athletes. For example, Jaremko, Silbert, and Mann (1981) found no gender differences in ischemic and cold pressor pain, and Manning and Fillingim (2002) reported that male athletes had high higher pain tolerance and pain threshold values than female athletes for cold pressor pain but observed no gender differences for ischemic and pressure pain. Similarly, in a clinical setting, no gender differences in daily pain were found for physically active individuals undergoing rehabilitation after reconstructive ACL surgery (Brewer, Cornelius, et al., 2007).

What can be said with confidence about gender in terms of sport-related pain is that the robust athlete–nonathlete differences documented in the meta-analysis by Tesarz et al. (2012) are especially pronounced in women. Female athletes were significantly higher than female nonathletes in both pain tolerance and pain threshold, whereas male athletes exceeded male nonathletes only for pain tolerance (Tesarz et al., 2012). It appears, then, that women athletes as a group tend not to adhere to traditional gender roles with respect to pain.

However, as with general athlete–nonathlete differences in pain perception, it is unclear whether girls and women with nontraditional gender roles regarding pain gravitate to sport (Encarnacion, Meyers, Ryan, & Pease, 2000) or whether the process of sport socialization instills nontraditional roles in girls and women (Paparizos, Tripp, Sullivan, & Rubenstein, 2005). It is possible, of course, that both selection and participation factors contribute to the development of female athletes' attitudes and behaviors associated with pain. Individual-difference factors *positively* associated with pain in sport include history of exercise-related pain (Reinking, Austin, & Hayes, 2010; H. Walker, Gabbe, Wajswelner, Blanch, & Bennell, 2012), history of traumatic injury (Tate et al., 2012), training and competition exposure (Sein et al., 2010; Tate et al., 2012), biomechanical abnormality (H. Walker et al., 2012), and selected genotypes (George et al., 2014). Individual-difference factors *negatively* associated with pain in sport include muscle strength, flexibility, and endurance (Tate et al., 2012).

Cognitive Factors

Cognitive processes are viewed as playing important roles in both the parallel processing model (Leventhal & Everhart, 1979) and gate control theory (Melzack & Wall, 1965). Specifically, they are posited by the parallel processing model as determining the extent to which pain stimuli reach focal awareness and by gate control theory as exerting top-down influence on the pain-gating mechanism. As a result, cognitive factors have been examined extensively in relation to pain in sport. In general, these efforts have targeted athletes' attentional focus and cognitive content.

Attentional Focus

It is common for athletes not to notice that they have sustained scratches, bruises, and even more severe injuries during competition until after the event is over. With athletes' attention focused intently on the sport activity, pain stimuli associated with injurious events simply fail to reach focal awareness. After-

ward, however, without the distraction provided by the attentional demands of sport competition, the pain stimuli enter conscious awareness and athletes experience the injuries as painful. The efficacy of distraction is well documented as a means of minimizing the experience of pain in response to noxious stimulation (McCaul & Malott, 1984). Of course, due to their intensity or persistence, some noxious stimuli inevitably command one's attention; in such instances, distraction is not likely to prove fruitful. At the same time, having one's attention directed to prospective pain stimuli need not always be an aversive experience. Consistent with the parallel processing model (Leventhal & Everhart, 1979), an individual may reduce the level of pain experienced by attending to the sensory—rather than the emotional—aspects of a stimulus.

For example, in a study of direct relevance to sport injury rehabilitation (Pen, Fisher, Storzo, & McManis, 1995), physically active young adults completed a baseline assessment of quadriceps and hamstring strength and endurance performance—an exercise protocol designed to induce muscle soreness. Two days later, two additional assessments of quadriceps and hamstring strength and endurance performance were conducted three hours apart, the second of which was performed under one of several attentional conditions. In one group, participants were asked to focus all of their attention on a distracting task (e.g., repeating a phrase with each repetition of the strength and endurance task and counting their repetitions). Participants in a second group were instructed to focus their attention on their pain and to transform it into a bright light that symbolized motivation to perform the strength and endurance task. A control group was given no instructions. The strength performance of participants in the group instructed to focus on their pain decreased significantly from the first (baseline) assessment to the second assessment, but it increased significantly from the second (postsoreness, preattentional manipulation) assessment to the third (postattentional manipulation) assessment, returning to baseline level. The strength performance of participants in the other two groups also decreased significantly from the first trial to the second trial but failed to increase from the second trial to the third trial. Thus, attention focused on pain was more adaptive than distraction from pain with respect to strength performance.

Cognitive Content

Athletes' experience of sport-related pain is associated not only with the locus and direction of their attentional focus but also with the content of their cognitions. Athletes report that when they encounter painful circumstances, a variety of thoughts may cross their minds. Some of the thoughts are reactions to the pain itself, whereas others are planful attempts to cope with the aversive stimulation. For example, athletes sometimes respond to sport-related pain by catastrophizing, which involves thinking negatively in circumstances of actual or anticipated pain and may involve ruminating about, magnifying, and feeling helpless about pain (Sullivan et al., 2001). At other times, however, athletes try to engage in thinking that allows them to take their mind off of, ignore, reinterpret, or cope with the pain (Deroche, Woodman, Stephan, Brewer, & LeScanff, 2011; Meyers, Bourgeois, Stewart, & LeUnes, 1992). Negative thought content in the form of pain catastrophizing is elevated among individuals with patellofemoral pain syndrome, a chronic pain condition frequently diagnosed at sports medicine clinics (Thomeé, Thomeé, & Karlsson, 2002). It is associated with a disinclination to play sport (Deroche et al., 2011) or engage in physical activity (Sullivan et al., 2002) while experiencing pain. Further, in a study of recreational athletes undergoing rehabilitation after ACL reconstruction surgery, pain castastrophizing was positively correlated with fear of reinjury and negatively correlated with confidence in returning from injury (Tripp, Stanish, Ebel-Lam, Brewer, & Birchard, 2007).

Cognitive content that can be more constructive includes preparatory information and goals. In accordance with the parallel processing model (Leventhal & Everhart, 1979), receiving information about the sensory properties of aversive stimuli can potentially occupy attention that might otherwise be directed at emotional responses to the stimuli; consequently, it may attenuate the experience of pain. Support for this idea was obtained through an experiment in which collegiate athletes immersed a foot in cold water (1 °C) for 21 minutes after either receiving no information about the sensations they were about to experience or being introduced to one of four groups of sensory terms pertaining to the cold-water immersion. Athletes who received the preparatory sensory information gave lower ratings of pain intensity than did those who were given no sensory information (Streator, Ingersoll, & Knight, 1995). Another study demonstrated the beneficial effect of goal cognition on pain tolerance in a rehabilitation-related activity. In this study, young athletes who were given a time goal for the cold pressor task immersed their hands in water just above 0 °C for a longer time than did those who were given no goal (Lord, Kozar, Whitfield, & Ferenz, 1994).

Emotional Factors

The parallel processing model posits detrimental effects of focusing attention on emotional aspects of potentially painful stimuli (Leventhal & Everhart, 1979), and research has found that some negative emotions are indeed associated with higher levels of pain in athletes with injury. For example, although one study of male amateur and professional soccer players (Otzekin, Boya, Ozcan, Zeren, & Pinar, 2008) found that depression was *not* related to pain either before ACL surgery or one week or three weeks after surgery, a study of males and females who varied in age and sport involvement (Brewer et al., 2007) found that high levels of daily negative mood *were* associated with higher daily ratings of pain during the first six weeks of rehabilitation after ACL surgery. In addition, a study of male and female recreational athletes (Tripp, Stanish, Coady, & Reardon, 2004) found that anxiety was positively correlated with pain 24 hours after ACL surgery.

Social and Environmental Factors

Whereas demographic and individual-difference variables, as well as cognitive and emotional factors, reside primarily within the person, social and environmental factors exist outside of the person and highlight the extent to which pain is an interactive phenomenon. Environmental influence on sport-related pain is illustrated vividly in research showing that the setting in which pain is experienced affects responses to pain. Specifically, in a study of responses to pressure stimulation, bodybuilders, regular exercisers, and sedentary individuals reported higher pain thresholds in an exercise setting than they did in a neutral laboratory setting; body builders also displayed higher pain *tolerance* in the exercise setting (Bartholomew, Lewis, Linder, & Cook, 1993). It is possible, then, that merely being in an exercise setting invokes cues associated with the culture of risk (Nixon, 1992) and prompts people to minimize overt responses to painful stimulation.

Responses to pain can also be affected by the presence of people in a given environment. For example, young athletes (i.e., second- and third-grade students) have displayed greater pain tolerance on the cold pressor test when other people were close by in the laboratory during the test than when no other people were present (Lord & Kozar, 1989). The presence of coaches may be especially influential in athletes' responses to painful stimulation. In this vein, another study involving the cold pressor test (Coutu, 1995) found that high school athletes gave lower pain ratings and showed greater pain tolerance when their tests were observed by their coach than when no observer was present. In addition, when testing was observed only by a researcher, the athletes' pain tolerance was significantly greater than when they took the test alone but significantly lower than when the test was witnessed by their coach. (Pain ratings taken when the researcher was observing the test did not differ significantly from those obtained during the other two conditions.) Thus, by their mere presence, coaches may prompt athletes to endure more pain and report experiencing less pain than when they are not present.

Going beyond the mere presence of another person, pain responses in the context of sport and physical activity can also be affected by the behavior of other people and by one's interaction with them. A person's response to pain can be influenced by other individuals' actions through the process of observational learning, in which the other people serve as models whose behavior is imitated. Research has shown that being exposed by video to a same-sex model exhibiting signs of distress (e.g., facial grimaces, moans, tight muscles) during a physical exercise task can adversely affect the viewer's responses to subsequent performance of the task depicted in the video. For example, women riding a bicycle ergometer for 20 minutes at 80 percent of their predicted maximum aerobic capacity reported experiencing more negative affect before performing the task and greater perceived exertion during the task after watching an intolerant model than after watching a tolerant model (Rejeski & Sanford, 1984). Similarly, men performing an isometric-sitting (i.e., wall-sit) task showed greater pain endurance and reported a higher pain threshold, as well as a slower increase in pain during the activity, after watching a tolerant model than after watching an intolerant model (Symbaluk, Heth, Cameron, & Pierce, 1997). These findings suggest that in clinical rehabilitation settings where multiple athletes are undergoing rehabilitation simultaneously, it is important to be aware of the messages that athletes send to each other (perhaps inadvertently) through their degree of tolerance of activities that may involve pain or discomfort.

In the sport environment, of course, competition is a highly engaging form of social interaction that can produce a form of stress-induced analgesia (SIA) in which the release of endogenous opiate neurotransmitters and other mechanisms attenuate responses to pain; the other mechanisms include top-down processes that can "close the gate," such as distraction and relaxation (Sternberg, 2007). For example, a study of collegiate athletes from various sports showed that sensitivity to thermal stimulation was significantly lower immediately after a competition than it was either two days before or two days after competition (Sternberg, Bailin, Grant, & Gracely, 1998). This reduced sensitivity to pain may increase athletes' vulnerability to injury during competition as they push themselves beyond their physical limits; it may also, however, enable sport health care providers to cautiously and judiciously introduce a competitive element into potentially (and benignly) painful activities performed for preventive or rehabilitative purposes.

Interpreting and Acting on Sport-Related Pain

Because pain technically does not exist until it is detected, the initial step in the process of interpreting and acting on sport-related pain is simply to notice the symptoms. Noticing symptoms may occur during the heat of training or competition, immediately after a training or competitive event, or at any subsequent point in time before the next training or competition. As suggested by both gate control theory (Melzack & Wall, 1965) and the parallel processing model (Leventhal & Everhart, 1979), top-down processes (e.g., attentional diversion) can at least temporarily prevent symptoms from reaching conscious awareness. At some point, however, if symptoms are of sufficient magnitude and duration, they will likely be detected. Once detected, symptoms undergo primary and secondary appraisal processes and are subjected to the influence of a multitude of biological, psychological, and social factors. Athletes are thus presented with critical questions regarding the nature of their symptoms and how to continue, contingent on the appraisals they make.

Distinguishing Between Pain and Injury

At the heart of the appraisal process lies the distinction between symptoms that "merely" hurt and those that introduce a degree of harm. Various contrasting terms have been used to label this distinction, such as "routine pain" versus "injury pain" (Heil, 1993b), "performance pain" versus "injury pain" (J. Taylor & Taylor, 1997), and "threatening" pain versus "nonthreatening" pain (Addison & Kremer, 1997; Addison et al., 1998). Regardless of the terms used, unless athletes have experienced the specific symptoms before and can relate them to a corresponding medical condition, it can be a challenge to distinguish between pain and injury. This difficulty is increased by the diverse types of sport-related pain (Addison & Kremer, 1997; Addison et al., 1998), the wide array of body parts in which sport-related pain can be located, and the dearth of research on the subject. Nevertheless, as noted earlier, it has been suggested that pain is benign when it "is dull, does not persist after activity, and is not accompanied by swelling or increased tenderness" (Heil, 1993b, p. 163). Conversely, pain associated with injury is thought to be sharp; localized to a particular area; present both during and after sport participation; persistent; accompanied by swelling and tenderness; and perceived as negative, uncontrollable, and dangerous (Heil, 1993b; J. Taylor & Taylor, 1997).

Playing With Pain

The appraisal of pain as either benign or indicative of injury may influence, but not determine, the course of action taken by an athlete. In other areas of health care, pain is among the symptoms most likely to signal people to seek medical treatment (Safer, Tharps, Jackson, & Leventhal, 1979), and this is probably the case with sport injury as well. In the culture of risk (Nixon, 1992), however, and in accordance with the sport ethic (Hughes & Coakley, 1991), athletes may receive encouragement from coaches, teammates, family members, the media, and even their own internalized beliefs to hide their pain and delay seeking medical attention (Heil & Podlog, 2012). Although delaying evaluation by medical professionals may expose athletes to the risk of more extensive damage and thus hamper their eventual recovery from injury, some athletes decide that the potential rewards are worth the risks and choose to play with pain.

Despite the influence of social forces and other external factors, electing to play through pain is typically a personal decision that may be affected by psychological factors. Athletes may decide to play with pain because playing

- is a normal, expected part of sport involvement (Hibberd & Myers, 2013),

- aligns with their self-identity as athletes (Ritter-Taylor, 1998; Weinberg, Vernau, & Horn, 2013),

- allows them to pursue deeply held performance goals,

- affirms the sheer importance of sport in their lives, and

- helps them avoid any negative emotions associated with *not* competing.

Alternatively, athletes may elect to play with pain simply because they do not perceive the injury or pain-producing condition as severe enough to warrant not participating (Shaffer, 1996). Decisions about whether to play through pain may also be affected by the strategies that athletes use to cope with pain. Although athletes' inclination to play through pain does not seem to be affected by a pain-coping strategy when pain intensity is *low*, athletes who report attempting to control *high* levels of pain by ignoring it are more inclined to play through pain than are those who report not ignoring it (Deroche et al., 2011).

Little is known about the consequences of deciding to play through pain. It is likely to increase the risk of exacerbating the physical condition producing the pain, but this effect has not been substantiated empirically. In terms of how the choice to play through pain affects sport performance, sport history is replete with examples of athletes who, through tremendous powers of concentration and sheer force of will, have triumphed over severe pain and achieved remarkable feats. Laboratory studies have shed some light on this phenomenon, suggesting that the type of motor task involved may moderate the effects

of pain on sport performance. The results of investigations in which participants performed motor tasks under conditions of experimentally induced pain (e.g., DOMS, electrical stimulation, ischemic pain, pressure pain) suggest that pain exerts an especially adverse effect on performance of fine-grained motor tasks such as golf putting but not on less complex motor tasks such as lifting weights or pumping a rubber bulb (Brewer, Van Raalte, & Linder, 1990; F.J. Evans & McGlashan, 1967; J. Walker, 1971). Even so, pain can impair performance of even relatively simple motor tasks (Sullivan et al., 2002); it can also adversely affect attention and executive function (Boselie, Vancleef, Smeets, & Peters, 2014; Moore, Keogh, & Eccleston, 2012), both of which can play vital roles in sport performance.

Managing Pain

As noted at the beginning of the chapter, much of the pain that occurs in association with sport in general and sport injury in particular can be prevented, avoided, escaped, or reduced simply by ceasing sport participation on a temporary or permanent basis. Nevertheless, even athletes who heed their body's signals and curtail sport involvement may encounter circumstances that result in their experiencing substantial pain, such as in the immediate aftermath of an acute injury or a surgical procedure, during rigorous rehabilitation activities, or after a painful condition has become chronic. For these athletes—as well as those inhabitants of the culture of risk who persist in sport involvement despite experiencing pain that is exacerbated by sport participation—managing pain is an important issue.

Athletes may initiate pain management efforts either informally, on their own, or more formally, through consultation with sport health care professionals. When an athlete pursues the latter option, key aspects of the athlete's pain (e.g., intensity, location, source, type) are typically identified in the initial evaluation through assessment. Taking this information into account, sport health care professionals can formulate plans for pain management based on the athlete's specific needs and coping styles. It is common for pain management efforts to involve the concurrent use of multiple treatment approaches (Kolt, 2004) and, sometimes, multiple professionals (in different disciplines).` Among the pain management approaches available are pharmacological treatments, physical therapies, and psychological methods.

Pharmacological Treatments

Analgesics, which are medications that reduce pain, are routinely administered for management of pain associated with sport injury. The analgesics used most widely by athletes include aspirin, ibuprofen, naproxen, paracetamol (acetaminophen), and, to a lesser extent, codeine (Garnham, 2007). Aspirin and ibuprofen are examples of nonsteroidal anti-inflammatory drugs (NSAIDs), which reduce pain and inflammation without sedation. NSAIDs are typically used for a brief period of time during the early stages of the postinjury inflammatory response (Kolt, 2007), an hour or more after injury occurrence and the initiation of treatment so as not to interfere with blood clotting at the injury site. Gastrointestinal side effects (e.g., stomach pain, indigestion, nausea, diarrhea) are fairly common with NSAIDs, but more serious complications are considered rare. Paracetamol and codeine can provide pain relief but do not reduce inflammation (Garnham, 2007).

Although aspirin, ibuprofen, and paracetamol are available over the counter in the United States, codeine requires a prescription because it is an opioid (a form of narcotic). For noncancer pain, opioids tend to raise concerns about tolerance and dependence (DiMatteo & Martin, 2000); even so, they are sometimes prescribed for sport-related postsurgical pain, but their use diminishes rapidly in the immediate aftermath of surgery (Tripp, Sullivan, Stanish, Reardon, & Coady, 2001). Despite the potential dangers of opioids, a survey of retired professional American football players suggests that misuse of these potent pain relievers is widespread in the sport and that former players misuse opioids at a rate three times higher than that of the general public (Cottler et al., 2011).

When considering pharmacological treatments for pain associated with sport injury, athletes and sport health care professionals must take into account not only the potential side effects but also the status of a medication in the eyes of any pertinent sport governing bodies (Heil & Podlog, 2012). These issues are vividly illustrated by the case of corticosteroids, which exert a potent anti-inflammatory effect and are often prescribed to athletes for severe injury-related pain. With regard to side effects, there is some concern that corticosteroids, particularly those administered through local injection, may impair healing and increase vulnerability to subsequent injury (Garnham, 2007; Kolt, 2007). Moreover, some sport organizations require notification or even approval of corticosteroid treatment prior to competition (Garnham, 2007). Another issue not unique to corticosteroids involves the risk of using pharmacological treatment to mask pain, thus allowing an athlete to do further damage by enabling him or her to engage in short-term sport activity without pain (Heil & Podlog, 2012).

Physical Therapies

Various physical therapies are widely used in the treatment of sport-related pain. Some of the therapies are designed to address the source of the pain (Kolt, 2007), whereas others are based on the principle of *counterirritation*, in which pain is relieved by creating competing or counteracting sensations in a nearby area (Straub, 2012). Among the more commonly applied physical therapies for pain are electrophysical agents, manual techniques, and exercise. Empirical support for these strategies is varied.

Electrophysical Agents Electrophysical agents use electrical stimulation to produce analgesic effects. Examples that are widely used to treat pain associated with sport injury include transcutaneous electrical nerve stimulation (TENS), interferential electrical stimulation, and ultrasound (Kolt, 2007). As conventionally implemented, TENS involves application of high-frequency electric current to the skin. This treatment produces comfortable tingling sensations that can reduce pain presumably by closing the neurological gate. TENS can also be applied with strong, *low*-frequency current in an acupuncture-like fashion; when used in this way, it produces less pleasant sensations and reduces pain by triggering the release of endogenous opiates (e.g., endorphins) in the brain (Snyder-Mackler, Schmitt, Rudolph, & Farquhar, 2007).

Like TENS, interferential stimulation involves applying electric current to the skin. For this treatment, however, two alternating medium-frequency currents are applied through electrodes positioned so that the currents intersect in the painful area. As with conventional TENS, interferential stimulation is essentially a counterirritation approach that closes the neurological gate by stimulating the large-diameter A-beta nerve fibers (Kolt, 2007). In contrast, ultrasound treatment applies high-frequency *sound* waves to the skin. When administered in a continuous (as opposed to pulsed) manner, ultrasound can provide warmth and potentially pain relief to deep tissues. Electrophysical agents can also be used to deliver anti-inflammatory and analgesic medications; for example, iontophoresis uses electrical means and phonophoresis uses ultrasound to introduce the medications (Snyder-Mackler et al., 2007).

Manual Techniques   In implementing manual techniques, sport health care professionals facilitate pain reduction by using combinations of massage, mobilization, and manipulation of soft tissue (e.g., muscles, ligaments) or joints (Kolt, 2007). Therapeutic massage, for example, is a form of counterirritation using one of a variety of specific methods of rubbing or kneading soft tissue in order to relax the muscles involved in painful conditions (J. Taylor & Taylor, 1997). Pain relief is thought to occur as the muscles relax, chemicals associated with nociception dissipate from the injured area, and large-diameter nerve fibers are stimulated (Kolt, 1997; Prentice, 2011). Manual techniques are readily combined with other

physical therapies and cognitive-behavioral methods (J. Taylor & Taylor, 1997).

Exercise   Just as physical activity is typically involved in the creation of painful conditions experienced by athletes, it can also play an important role in remediating those conditions. In fact, exercise is a central element of physical therapy for the rehabilitation of sport injuries and the concomitant reduction of injury-related pain. More specifically, sport health care professionals may prescribe targeted exercises to improve muscular strength, flexibility, endurance, coordination, and balance in order to correct movement dysfunctions that are associated with injury occurrence or that stand in the way of recovery. Therapeutic regimens aimed at rehabilitation include various types of exercise, such as stretching, resistance, and proprioceptive training; in this process, pain relief may be either a primary or secondary aim.

In addition to reducing pain by correcting movement dysfunctions, exercise can help athletes with pain management through several other routes. For example, it has the potential to distract athletes from stressful events in their lives, facilitate relaxation, boost self-efficacy (Kolt, 2007), improve mood, and provide a context for social support—all of which are incompatible with the experience of pain. Even if athletes are restricted from engaging in certain forms of exercise, engaging in physical activities that do not exacerbate their pain or risk further damage to the injured body part may both enhance their fitness and provide psychological benefits (including pain relief). Aerobic exercise, for instance, whether in the form of regular training or a single session, can produce an analgesic response to noxious stimulation (e.g., Anshel & Russell, 1994; Gurevich, Kohn, & Davis, 1994).

Other Physical Therapies   Several other physical therapies for pain management warrant mention, namely cold and heat treatments, surgery, and acupuncture. Cold and heat are among the most commonly used treatments for sport-related pain. Cryotherapy is part of the RICE formula (rest, ice, compression, elevation) for treatment during the inflammatory phase in the immediate aftermath of sport injury; it is also used after other events that produce inflammation, such as surgery and rehabilitation exercises. In addition to ice (in the form of ice bags and ice massage), cold can be applied to the painful area through cold gels, cold packs, cooling cuffs, and immersion in cold water (Snyder-Mackler et al., 2007). Cryotherapy is generally effective as a short-term analgesic for soft-tissue injury (Bleakley, McDonough, & MacAuley, 2004). Heat, in contrast, is generally not used in the treatment of sport injury until the inflammatory phase is completed, usually 48 hours or more after injury occurrence. It is commonly applied to the painful area by means of hot gels, moist hot packs, and warm water whirlpools (Snyder-Mackler et al., 2007) and can provide pain relief for sport-related musculoskeletal conditions (Petering & Webb, 2011).

Although surgery is sometimes used as a treatment of last resort for chronic painful conditions (Straub, 2012), it is rarely used to treat pain in association with sport injury. Surgery for sport-related conditions is typically performed not specifically to relieve pain but to repair damage to the body and restore functional capabilities. Acupuncture, on the other hand, is a complementary therapy that is used increasingly both to treat pain and to facilitate recovery from sport injury. Treatment with acupuncture generally involves inserting needles into the skin at strategic locations (acupuncture points). The needles are sometimes stimulated with heat, touch, or electricity to strengthen the treatment effect. The mechanisms by which acupuncture relieves pain are not well understood, but it does represent a potentially viable and safe option for athletes with painful conditions (Wadsworth, 2006).

Psychological Methods

The use of psychological techniques to help manage sport-related pain accords with the tenets of gate control theory (Melzack & Wall, 1965) regarding the role of top-down processes in pain perception. It also provides ways to engage the abundance of demographic, individual-difference, cognitive, emotional, and social-learning variables associated with pain in sport. In this context, psychological techniques possess several desirable characteristics; in particular, they are safe, nonpharmacological, portable, versatile, and flexible (for more on the safety of psychological techniques, see this chapter's Focus on Application box). Lacking apparent harmful side effects, psychological techniques also appeal to athletes who seek pain management approaches other than medication, which can compromise healing and reduce perceptions of control and confidence (J. Taylor & Taylor, 1997). Furthermore, athletes are more likely than nonathletes to use psychological techniques to cope with acute pain—and to do so adeptly (Manning et al., 1997).

Psychological approaches to pain management can be differentiated on the basis of what they are designed to change:

- Cognitive content
- Cognitive coping
- Behavior (Jensen, 2011)

Most psychological techniques require no special equipment. They can also be readily applied to a variety of pain types in multiple situational contexts and can be deployed to help athletes cope with pain experienced before, during, or after involvement in sport and rehabilitation activities. For example, a technique such as imagery can be used to help athletes alleviate pain or discomfort associated with a prospective treatment (e.g., the initial portion of cryotherapy), postinjury activities of daily living (e.g., climbing stairs), and challenging sport tasks (e.g., competing in a bicycle race).

Given the ubiquity of pain in sport, and especially in sport injury, surprisingly little research has been done on the efficacy of psychological techniques of pain management in sport. Numerous cognitive and behavioral techniques drawn from the clinical pain literature have been recommended as potential treatments for sport-related pain, including attentional focusing, biofeedback, deep breathing, hypnosis, imagery, information, operant conditioning, pain reconceptualization, and

Dissociation Not a Risk Factor for Endurance Sport Injury Occurrence

Safety is a primary consideration when choosing pain management strategies. With pharmacological treatments, for example, potential threats to safety (e.g., dependence, overdose, drug interaction) are taken into account when prescribing medications. In contrast, psychological pain management techniques are generally considered to be safe and free of harmful side effects. Nevertheless, Morgan (1978) expressed concern about the safety of endurance athletes who overuse the attentional focusing strategy known as dissociation, in which athletes attempt to distract themselves from pain by focusing their attention on external stimuli. Specifically, he proposed that athletes who dissociate excessively are at elevated risk for injury because, with their attention cut off from their bodily sensations, they may fail to notice physical warning signs of injury.

Although the potential exists for misuse of any pain management strategy, Morgan's concerns about the use of dissociation appear to be unwarranted. No evidence of a relationship between the use of dissociation and injury occurrence was obtained in five studies that collected data about attentional focusing and injury (for a summary, see Brewer & Buman, 2006). It has even been suggested that focusing attention on bodily symptoms during the performance of endurance activities, as is done in the strategy known as *association*, may not protect athletes from injury. Association is not inherently problematic, but athletes who use it tend to be more competitive, push themselves harder, and, consequently, incur more injuries than those who use dissociation (Masters & Ogles, 1998; Masters, Ogles, & Jolton, 1993).

Attentional focusing involves directing attention intentionally to internal or external stimuli. Attention directed externally, away from pain, is labeled *distraction* (or *avoidance*), whereas attention directed internally, toward the sensory aspects but not the emotional aspects of pain, is called *redefinition* (or *attention*). Both distraction and redefinition have been found effective as compared with control conditions in coping with acute pain. Some evidence suggests that distraction is more effective than redefinition for pain of short duration or low intensity and that redefinition is more effective than distraction for pain of longer duration or greater intensity (for reviews, see McCaul & Malott [1984] and Suls & Fletcher [1985]).

Attentional focusing has been examined extensively as a means of coping with discomfort and enhancing performance in endurance sports with heavy exertional demands (e.g., running, swimming). Instead of redefinition and distraction, the terms *association* and *dissociation* (popularized by Morgan, 1978) have been used to refer, respectively, to internally focused attention and externally focused attention. Both association and dissociation are effective for facilitating endurance performance, although association seems to be effective primarily for experienced competitors (for a review, see Brewer & Buman, 2006). Presumably, experienced competitors are better than inexperienced competitors at interpreting the bodily sensations encountered during rigorous physical activity in an unemotional manner.

One of the challenges of coping with sport-related pain is that it often occurs in the context of sport or rehabilitation task performance, where the goals often go beyond merely tolerating discomfort or making the experience less aversive. As noted by both Heil (1993b) and Stevinson and Biddle (1998), a simple internal–external dichotomy does not adequately characterize the attentional dynamics of much sport-related pain, in which diverting attention from the sport or rehabilitation task can exert an adverse effect on performance. For example, directing attention externally to cues that are relevant to the sport or rehabilitation task

relaxation (Kolt, 2004, 2007; Singer & Johnson, 1987; J. Taylor & Taylor, 1997). Only a few of these techniques, however, have been found effective for pain management purposes in controlled experimental evaluations in the context of sport—namely, attentional focusing, information, and multimodal interventions.

might facilitate both task performance and pain control, whereas attention directed externally toward cues that are irrelevant to the task might maximize pain control at the expense of task performance. Similarly, the effects of internally focused attention may differ depending on whether attention is directed toward or away from body parts and sensations involved in task performance. When task performance is not an issue, such as when an athlete experiences pain while trying to sleep or receiving a passive therapeutic modality, attentional focusing strategies can be selected solely on the basis of effectiveness for coping with pain. However, when pain occurs in the context of task performance (and involvement in the task has been deemed safe), task demands need to be considered when selecting an appropriate attentional focusing strategy.

As for information and multimodal interventions, only a few studies have provided experimental evidence of efficacy. Support for the use of information in pain management was obtained in the Streator et al. (1995) study described earlier in this chapter. In its broadest sense, giving athletes information involves furnishing them with anatomical, physiological, and sensory details specific to their pain and injury situation (Kolt, 2004). Provision of this sort of information can instill a sense of control in athletes and direct their attention toward informational aspects rather than emotional aspects of painful stimuli, both of which can help minimize the experience of pain. Even the minimal amount of sensory information given by Streator et al. was sufficient to decrease the amount of pain reported by athletes participating in the foot-and-ankle immersion in cold water.

Multimodal interventions have been effective in reducing sport-related pain in two studies. In the first, athletes who received training in multiple psychological pain management techniques—self-monitoring of pain and distress, deep breathing, relaxation, imagery, positive self-talk, and self-reinforcement—reported less pain after knee-cartilage surgery than did those who received no training (Ross & Berger, 1996). In the second study, athletes who received an intervention combining relaxation and guided imagery (using healing, coping, and motivational images) reported less pain six months after ACL surgery than did athletes who received placebo treatment or no treatment (Cupal & Brewer, 2001). The multimodal nature of the interventions in these two studies makes it impossible to determine the degree to which the individual components of the interventions contributed to pain reduction. Nevertheless, the findings for multimodal interventions suggest that the component parts, used individually or in combination, offer promise in the treatment of sport-related pain with psychological techniques. Because the multimodal interventions affect treatment outcomes beyond pain, they are discussed in greater detail in chapter 8.

Biopsychosocial Analysis

Pain is the epitome of a biopsychosocial phenomenon; indeed, contemporary definitions, models, assessments, and treatments of pain all involve biological, psychological, and social features. These factors figure in the onset, experience, expression, management, and reduction of pain. The biological processes of physical stimulation, nociception, and sensation often initiate a pain episode, but the psychological and social processes of attention, cognition, expectation, and socialization can add to, subtract from, or neutralize the biological processes.

The cases of Veronica, Luis, Kijuan, Roberta, and Scott presented at the beginning of the chapter illustrate a broad cross-section of the kinds of pain experienced in association with sport participation. With the exception of Kijuan, these cases reflect the typically acute nature of sport-related pain. Although the responses to pain vary considerably across the cases—as do the sources, intensity, quality, and interpretations of pain—these scenarios collectively highlight the widespread nature and accompanying normalcy of pain in sport. Indeed, athletes both expect and accept pain as part of the sport experience, and it is improbable that pain will disappear from the sport landscape anytime soon. However, full consideration of the complex array of contributors to sport-related pain offers the potential to enhance the prevention and management of long-term pain such as that encountered by Kijuan.

Summary

As a central theme in both sport and physical injury, pain is the quintessential example of a biopsychosocial phenomenon of relevance to sport injury. Pain is commonly described as an unpleasant experience that includes sensory and emotional components and relates to either real or possible tissue damage. It can be useful to draw general distinctions between types of pain based on duration (i.e., acute pain versus chronic pain) and symptom attributes (e.g., causalgia, phantom-limb pain, referred pain), but classifications of pain that are specific to sport (e.g., performance pain versus injury pain) may hold greater utility for understanding the experience of sport injury.

Pain can be considered in terms of both quality and intensity. Quality relates to how the pain is described, whereas intensity corresponds to the strength of the pain stimulation. With regard to intensity, pain threshold is the amount of stimulation needed for a stimulus to be perceived as painful; pain tolerance, on the other hand, is the amount of stimulation that one can withstand before refusing additional stimulation. Pain is difficult to assess but can be measured through psychophysiological, behavioral, and self-report methods, each of which is characterized by both strengths and weaknesses.

Various models and theories of pain have been proposed, successively taking into account advances in the knowledge of pain and evolving from a sensory conceptualization (which considered pain as a direct, bottom-up response to tissue damage) to perspectives that incorporate top-down attentional and neurological influences on pain perception. According to contemporary views of pain, the experience of pain in sport is associated with a variety of factors, including demographic, individual-difference, cognitive, emotional, social, and environmental elements. For example, in terms of the demographic and individual-difference factors of gender and athlete status, athletes have demonstrated higher pain tolerance than nonathletes, whereas men and women have shown similar levels of pain perception. The main cognitive factors linked to sport-related pain are attention and cognitive content. When distraction from pain is not possible or desirable, attention directed toward pain can be effective as a means of coping with sport-related pain to the extent that it focuses on sensory aspects of the stimulus rather than its emotional aspects.

Negative thought content, particularly in the form of pain catastrophizing, can be counterproductive, whereas more positive thoughts (e.g., goal setting, focus on preparatory information) are associated with adaptive responses to pain. Similarly, negative emotions are positively related to levels of sport-related pain. In terms of social and environmental factors, both noticing and tolerating sport-related pain are associated with the physical environment (e.g., exercise setting versus laboratory setting) and with the presence of and interaction with other people (including in competition).

Issues involved in interpreting and acting on sport-related pain include distinguishing between pain and injury, playing with pain, and managing pain. Options available to athletes for managing sport-related pain include pharmacological treatments (e.g., aspirin, ibuprofen, paracetamol), physical therapies (e.g., TENS, massage, exercise, cryotherapy, heat, acupuncture), and psychological techniques (e.g., distraction, multimodal interventions).

Discussion Questions

1. What is the difference between pain and nociception?
2. What is the difference between pain tolerance and pain threshold?
3. What are some strengths and weaknesses of the various methods of assessing pain?
4. How does the phenomenon of athletes playing through pain relate to the sport ethic, and what social and cultural factors might encourage athletes to conceal injuries?

Rehabilitation of Sport Injury

The chapters in part III focus on psychological aspects of sport injury rehabilitation. More specifically, they provide in-depth examination of adherence to rehabilitative (and preventive) interventions. They also explore pathways through which psychological factors may influence sport injury rehabilitation outcomes. In addition, they consider the potential utility of implementing psychological interventions to bring about desired clinical outcomes in rehabilitation.

Chapter 6

Adherence to Sport Injury Prevention and Rehabilitation Programs

Chapter Objectives

1. To examine the measurement, theories, predictors, and enhancement of adherence to interventions designed to prevent or rehabilitate sport injury

2. To explore the dose–response relationship between treatment adherence and sport health care outcomes

On his drive home after working late to close an important account, Carlos reflected on his meteoric rise up the corporate ladder. All his hard work in college had paid off; getting good grades had played a key role in being selected for an interview with his current company. His gift for social interaction had done the rest. It didn't hurt that he had played D-I baseball—his boss was as competitive as anyone he knew, in both business and corporate recreation. Officially, the work group played in a "recreational" softball league, but this was no beer-and-cigarettes outfit. Carlos knew that major battles were fought on the softball field, and he did his best to help the cause. Even though shoulder problems had ended what little hope he had harbored of a professional baseball career, he was still a force both at the plate and in the field, even as compared with his surprisingly fit corporate colleagues. Carlos had managed to avoid shoulder surgery after assuring his doctor that he would complete daily stretching and strengthening exercises on an indefinite basis. A physical therapist had shown him how to do the exercises, and Carlos had been reasonably dedicated to following the program. Tonight, however, he was tired and just didn't feel like doing his exercises. Besides, his shoulder had been feeling fine lately, despite the abuse he had been giving it in softball. Carlos fixed himself some dinner, turned on the television, and, a little while later, drifted off to sleep.

Tammy and Teena are both 16 years old and have much more in common than their age. Although they have never met, both are standouts in their respective sports—Tammy in volleyball, Teena in basketball—and the suburbs in which they live are separated by less than 10 miles. In addition, they both had ACL reconstructive surgery with the same surgeon (two days apart) and did their rehabilitation at the same clinic (Tammy on Mondays and Wednesdays, Teena on Tuesdays and Thursdays) with the same physical therapist. Despite these similarities, these two young women had dramatically different rehabilitation experiences. Teena, the more extroverted of the two, experienced little swelling or pain after surgery, attended most (but not all) of her scheduled rehabilitation appointments, and did about one-quarter of the home rehabilitation exercises prescribed by the therapist, preferring instead to "hang out" with her friends and do things that she normally did not have time to do. Her recovery was remarkable: She hit her six-month benchmarks just four months after surgery and returned to training with her club team without missing a beat. In contrast, Tammy, a quiet, serious young woman, experienced major swelling and substantial pain for nearly a month after surgery. She followed her physical therapy program religiously, faithfully attending every scheduled rehabilitation session and diligently completing all of her prescribed home exercises. Her progress through rehabilitation was slow, and nine months after surgery she had yet to achieve her six-month benchmarks.

A wide variety of innovative methods have been developed in athletic training, medicine, physical therapy, psychology, public health, and other fields to help prevent and treat sport injuries and their sequelae. Many of the methods engage athletes in certain behaviors intended either to reduce the likelihood of injury occurrence or to facilitate recovery from injury. These interventions are underlain by the fundamental assumption that their success depends on the athlete's completion of the prescribed behaviors.

As illustrated in the cases of Carlos and Teena, athletes sometimes have difficulty carrying out these behaviors in injury prevention and rehabilitation programs. In other words, they have problems with treatment *adherence*—the extent to which an athlete completes the prescribed behaviors in a treatment regimen designed to prevent injury or facilitate recovery from it (Granquist & Brewer, 2013). The term *adherence* is often used interchangeably with *compliance*. However, whereas *compliance* connotes a relatively passive role for the athlete in obediently following instructions given by sport health care professionals, *adherence* connotes "active, voluntary, collaborative involvement of the patient in a mutually acceptable course of behavior to produce a desired preventative or therapeutic result" (Meichenbaum & Turk, 1987, p. 20). Given the potentially far-reaching effects of adherence on the occurrence and treatment of sport injury, this chapter examines the measurement, theories, predictors, and enhancement of adherence to

preventive and rehabilitative interventions. The chapter also explores the dose–response relationship between adherence and outcome in sport health care.

Adherence to Sport Injury Prevention Programs

As discussed in chapter 3, recent years have brought a surge in attempts to prevent the occurrence of sport injuries. This surge has been accompanied by growing recognition of the vital importance of adherence both in preventing sport injuries and in documenting the effectiveness of preventive interventions (C.F. Finch & Donaldson, 2010; Van Tiggelen, Wickes, Stevens, Roosen, & Witvrouw, 2008). C.F. Finch (2006) asserted that in order to "prevent injuries, sports injury prevention measures need to be acceptable, adopted, and complied with by the athletes and sports bodies they are targeted at" (p. 5). Unfortunately, the extent of adoption and adherence by targeted groups and individuals has not routinely been considered in research studies (C.F. Finch, 2011). When adherence rates *have* been assessed, they have been found to vary considerably—ranging from not at all (Duymus & Gungor, 2009) to 100 percent (Heidt, Sweeterman, Carlonas, Traub, & Tekulve, 2000)—depending on the population under consideration and on how adherence was measured.

Although preventive efforts can involve administrators, legislators, and sport health care professionals, this part of the chapter focuses on adoption of preventive behaviors by athletes. Preventive behaviors that athletes may be encouraged to adopt include completing physical exercises (e.g., warm-up, stretching, strengthening, agility, jumping, balance), hydrating, wearing protective equipment, and doing stress management activities (e.g., Emery & Meeuwisse, 2010; Gissane, White, Kerr, & Jennings, 2001; Perna et al., 2003). The following sections address adherence to sport injury prevention programs in terms of measurement, theories, predictors, and enhancement of adherence.

Measurement

It is not possible to evaluate the effectiveness of sport injury prevention programs without knowing how well athletes adhere to the behavioral aspects of those programs. For example, if a program is found to be ineffective but the athletes did not adhere to it, then one cannot determine whether the program simply does not work or whether it would work if athletes adhered to it. Knowledge of adherence can be obtained only by operationally defining and measuring the construct. Consequently, both practitioners and researchers have a stake in measuring adherence.

Sport injury prevention activities can be implemented in both team and individual settings. The most common method of measuring adherence to sport injury prevention programs in team settings has been for coaches to keep a record of training sessions in which the prevention program was implemented and, in some cases, which athletes attended each session. These data can be used to calculate adherence indexes, such as the percentage of team training sessions in which the prevention program was implemented, the percentage of players on the team who completed a requisite number of training sessions that included the program, and a composite that accounts for both team and individual completion of prevention program sessions (e.g., Junge et al., 2011; Keats, Emery, & Finch, 2012; Soligard et al., 2008; Soligard, Nilstad, et al,. 2010; Sugimoto et al., 2012; van Beijsterveldt, Krist, van de Port, &

Backx, 2011a, 2011c). Adherence to preventive activities completed on an individual basis— away from the team environment—has been assessed with self-report questionnaires (Chan & Hagger, 2012a; Emery, Rose, McAllister, & Meeuwisse, 2007).

Adherence reports from both coaches and athletes are subject to the usual potential limitations of self-report assessment—for example, forgetting, inaccuracy, and socially desirable responses. However, in at least one investigation of the effectiveness of an injury-prevention training program, coach reports were verified and validated through monitoring by independent observers (van Beijsterveldt, Krist, van de Port, & Backx, 2011a). Independent observers have also been used to monitor and record athletes' use of protective equipment, such as headgear and mouth guards (Braham & Finch, 2004). On the whole, measurement of adherence to sport injury prevention programs is still in the early stages. More sophisticated measures are needed in order to capture aspects of adherence that are not typically examined (e.g., intensity of effort and use of proper technique during neuromuscular training) and to assess adherence more objectively (Chan & Hagger, 2012a).

Theoretical Perspectives

Theory helps us understand the processes by which athletes adopt preventive behaviors; it also guides the implementation of preventive interventions.

Until recently, the examination of adherence to sport injury prevention programs had been a largely *atheoretical* enterprise. Adherence had been assessed in epidemiological studies examining the prevalence of various preventive behaviors and in trials evaluating the effectiveness of prevention programs, but few researchers had made theory-guided attempts to understand why athletes adhere or do not adhere to the preventive activities. Indeed, a review (McGlashan & Finch, 2010) of 100 studies identified as investigating safety behaviors in association with sport injury prevention—the vast majority of which addressed the wearing of protective equipment—found that only 11 studies deployed theories or models from the behavioral and social sciences.

The only theoretical perspective used in more than two studies involved the theory of reasoned action (TRA; Ajzen & Fishbein, 1980; Fishbein & Ajzen, 1975), including its extension, the theory of planned behavior (TPB; Ajzen, 1991). When the TRA is adapted to behavior designed to prevent sport injury, it holds that the likelihood of engaging in preventive behavior is influenced directly by the *intention* to engage in such behavior. Intention, in turn, is affected by an athlete's attitudes toward the preventive behavior, as well as the opinions held by others in the athlete's social environment (i.e., subjective norms). In TPB, Ajzen (1991) added a third contributor to the athlete's intention to complete the preventive behavior—namely, the athlete's beliefs about personal control over the behavior. Therefore, from the perspective of TPB, adherence to sport injury prevention programs would be highest when

- athletes and their associates value the preventive behavior and its potential beneficial outcomes;
- athletes perceive themselves as having control over the preventive behavior; and
- as a direct consequence of the preceding two items, athletes intend to engage in the preventive behavior.

Noting the widespread support for TPB in the physical activity domain, Keats et al. (2012) advocated integrating it with self-determination theory (SDT; R.M. Ryan & Deci, 2000), a perspective thought to aid understanding of why athletes develop certain attitudes, beliefs, and intentions about behaviors designed to prevent sport injury. Specifically, athletes would be expected to value, perceive the support of others for, perceive control over, and intend to engage in preventive behavior when they experience satisfaction of basic psychological needs for autonomy, competence, and relatedness. Athletes experience autonomy when their decisions to complete preventive behavior are self-determined—that is, motivated by intrinsic factors (within the self) as

opposed to extrinsic factors (outside the self). In addition, to the extent that the athletes perceive preventive behavior as being linked to sport success and favorable interpersonal relationships with important others (e.g., coaches, teammates), their needs for competence and relatedness are satisfied and TPB components conducive to adherence are elicited (Chan & Hagger, 2012b; Keats et al., 2012).

Figure 6.1 presents a graphic depiction of the model integrating TPB and SDT. Preliminary support has been found for SDT tenets in predicting athletes' motivation to engage in behaviors that reduce their risk of sport injury (Chan & Hagger, 2012a). With this in mind, an integrated approach such as that proposed by Keats et al. (2012) shows considerable promise as a means of understanding adherence to sport injury prevention programs and guiding the implementation of such programs.

Predictors

The general lack of theory-based research on factors associated with adherence to sport injury prevention programs has resulted in a hodgepodge of predictors of preventive behavior that lacks organizing themes. For the sake of discussion, the predictors can be divided into intrinsic factors and extrinsic factors, depending on whether they reside inside or outside of the individual. Intrinsic factors include injury history, personal characteristics, and cognitive variables. Athletes with a previous injury in a part of the body that can be protected by a particular kind of equipment (e.g., lower extremity, eyes, mouth) have been found more likely than those without such an injury to wear protective gear during sport participation (Cornwell, Messer, & Speed, 2003; Eime, Finch, Sherman, & Garnham, 2002; Yang et al., 2005). With respect to personal characteristics, some evidence suggests that athletes who are older (Cornwell et al., 2003; Eime et al., 2002; Yang et al., 2005) or more experienced (Eime et al., 2002) use protective equipment to a greater extent than do their younger, less experienced counterparts—and that female athletes are more likely than male athletes to wear protec-

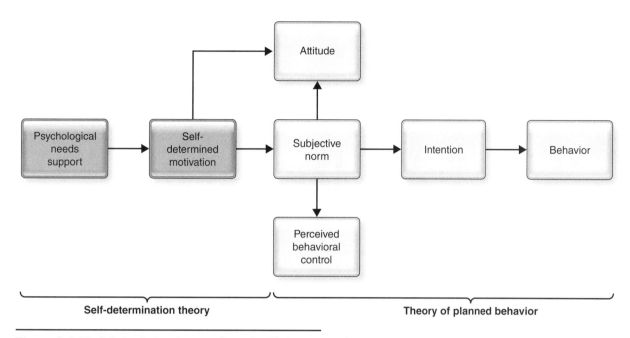

Figure 6.1 Model depicting integration of self-determination theory and the theory of planned behavior.
Sports Medicine, "Theoretical integration and the psychology of sport injury prevention, 42: 725-732, 2012, D.K. Chan and M.S. Hagger, Adis ©2012 Springer International Publishing AG. With permission of Springer.

tive gear (Yang et al., 2005). For neuromuscular training, however, experience was inversely related to adherence for both coaches and athletes (McKay, Steffen, Romiti, Finch, & Emery, 2014).

The cognitive factors found to predict adherence to sport injury prevention programs include the intention to adhere, self-efficacy expectations, knowledge of injury risk, and a host of theoretically derived attitudes and beliefs. Athletes have been found to be more likely to wear protective gear when they are confident in their ability to wear the gear, intend to wear it (De Nooijer, De Wit, & Steenhuis, 2004), possess knowledge of injury risk (Eime et al., 2002), perceive fewer barriers to wearing gear, perceive themselves as susceptible to injury without gear, perceive injuries incurred without gear to be severe, and perceive more benefits to wearing gear (R.M. Williams-Avery & MacKinnon, 1996).

In the most extensive examination of adherence to sport injury prevention activities— which involved a sample of elite athletes in a variety of sports—Chan and Hagger (2012b) documented positive associations between a wide array of cognitive factors and a composite of behaviors considered to be protective against sport injury (e.g., warming-up, stretching, resting adequately, icing, taking supplements). Consistent with self-determination theory (R.M. Ryan & Deci, 2000), the study also found that greater self-reported adoption of protective behaviors was related to high levels of general factors such as satisfaction of basic psychological needs, self-determination for sport, and self-determination for injury prevention. Adherence was also positively correlated with several highly specific attitudes and beliefs. Some of the correlations were consistent with what would be expected, such as those involving beliefs about commitment to safety, worry about sport injury, and prioritization of injury prevention activities. Other correlations were the opposite of what would be anticipated, such as those involving attitude toward safety violations (i.e., viewing safety violations as sometimes necessary in pursuit of sport performance) and fatalism about injury prevention (i.e., viewing sport injury as unavoidable). Additional research is needed to clarify the nature of the relations between these specific attitudes and adherence to sport injury prevention activities.

Extrinsic factors associated with adherence to sport injury prevention programs include social influences and program and implementation features. In terms of social influences, athletes have demonstrated greater adherence to preventive behaviors when a large proportion of their teammates or friends are adhering (De Nooijer et al., 2004; Yang et al., 2005), when they perceive a high degree of support for autonomy (Chan & Hagger, 2012a), and when they report experiencing pressure from their parents to adhere (De Nooijer et al., 2004). Program and implementation features involve characteristics of prevention programs and the ways and contexts in which they are implemented with athletes. For example, athletes attending small high schools with low player-to-coach ratios have been found to wear protective equipment to a greater extent than do athletes at larger schools with higher ratios (Yang et al., 2005). Similarly, Australian squash players were more likely to wear protective eyewear when posters and stickers reminded them to do so and when the eyewear was readily available (Eime, Finch, Wolfe, Owen, & McCarty, 2005).

In the case of neuromuscular training programs designed to prevent musculoskeletal injuries, adherence is associated with the following program and implementation features: The program focuses on performance enhancement rather than injury prevention (Alentorn-Geli et al., 2009; Hewett, Ford, & Myer, 2006); it is not perceived by coaches as being too time consuming (Soligard, Nilstad, et al., 2010); and it is implemented by coaches (Hewett et al., 2006), especially those who have previously used prevention practices and perceive the athletes as highly motivated (Soligard, Nilstad, et al., 2010). Thus, athletes' level of adherence to preventive interventions is likely influenced not only by factors within the athletes themselves but also by other people and by characteristics of the interventions and their implementation.

Barriers to adoption of preventive measures, though not technically predictive of adherence to sport injury prevention programs, are directly relevant to adherence. To put it simply, when athletes perceive barriers to adherence, they may be less likely to adhere.

In studies of the use of protective equipment (e.g., eyewear, headgear, mouth guards) during sport participation, athletes have identified a number of reasons for not wearing protective gear. Examples include cost (Chatterjee & Hilton, 2007; Pettersen, 2002), difficulty breathing (P.J. Chapman, 1985), difficulty communicating (C.F. Finch, McIntosh, & McCrory, 2001), dislike (Braham et al., 2004), restricted vision (Eime et al., 2002), transportation difficulties (Chatterjee & Hilton, 2007; Pettersen, 2002), and discomfort (Braham, Finch, McIntosh, & McCrory, 2004; C.F. Finch et al., 2001; Pettersen, 2002; Schuller, Dankle, Martin, & Strauss, 1989; Upson, 1982).

Enhancement

Although adherence is becoming increasingly recognized as vital to the success of sport injury prevention programs, only limited attempts have been made to improve the potency of preventive interventions by enhancing adherence. One important step toward boosting adherence is that of incorporating behavioral theory into the design and implementation of sport injury prevention programs (McGlashan & Finch, 2010). Consistent with the recommendations of C.F. Finch (2006), more rigorous, systematic, experimental, theory-based exploration of factors associated with adherence can inform the development and evaluation of *meta-interventions* (i.e., interventions for interventions)—that is, procedures intended to facilitate adoption of and adherence to preventive interventions. For example, we can systematically manipulate key components of the model integrating TPB and SDT (described earlier in this chapter) and various predictors of adherence (identified in the preceding section) to determine features of prevention programs that optimize adherence to—and, ultimately, the preventive impact of—the interventions.

Adherence to Sport Injury Rehabilitation Programs

Athletes who seek treatment for injury from a sport health care professional are often given a prescribed program or regimen to facilitate their return to health by alleviating symptoms, repairing damaged body tissues and structures, restoring function, and returning the athlete to sport participation. Although the behavioral requirements of rehabilitation programs vary considerably depending on the injury being treated, adherence tends to involve some common behaviors. Examples include "attending and actively participating in clinic-based rehabilitation appointments, avoiding potentially harmful activities, wearing therapeutic devices (e.g., orthotics), consuming medications appropriately, and completing home rehabilitation activities (e.g., exercises, therapeutic modalities)" (Brewer, 2004; pp. 39–40). In some rehabilitation programs, adherence behaviors may occur predominantly away from the clinical setting and outside the purview of sport health care professionals. The following sections address measurement, theories, predictors, and enhancement of adherence to sport injury rehabilitation programs.

Measurement

As with prevention programs, practitioners and researchers alike have an interest in measuring adherence to sport injury rehabilitation programs. Due to the diverse array of behaviors involved in rehabilitation programs, an abundance of measures of adherence have been developed. Some of these measures target adherence to rehabilitation behaviors that occur in the clinical setting, whereas others target adherence to behaviors that occur away from the clinical setting, most typically at home.

Clinic-Based Measures

Adhering to the clinic-based portion of a sport injury rehabilitation program typically involves engaging in behaviors such as showing up for scheduled rehabilitation appointments, following instructions given by sport health care professionals, completing rehabilitation exercises, and receiving therapeutic modalities. Measurement of adherence to clinic-based activities commonly focuses on the first of these behaviors—attendance at rehabilitation sessions. Attendance scores are typically calculated simply by dividing the

number of rehabilitation appointments attended by the number of appointments scheduled. They provide a simple, straightforward, and objective assessment of adherence, and this information is unquestionably valuable, because athletes cannot adhere to the rehabilitation program if they do not attend rehabilitation sessions. Most athletes do, however, show up for the vast majority of their rehabilitation sessions; therefore, attendance scores are mainly useful only for detecting gross nonadherence. Furthermore, they reveal nothing about what athletes do during the sessions. Although sport health care professionals are adept at getting athletes to "buy in" and complete rehabilitation programs, some athletes pursue clinic-based rehabilitation activities with less effort and enthusiasm than others.

To assess what athletes actually do during rehabilitation sessions, one must observe their behavior and record one's observations in a standardized way so that the behavior can be compared across athletes and within a given athlete over time. The most comprehensive tool for observing and recording athletes' behavior during rehabilitation sessions is the Sports Medicine Observation Code (SMOC; Crossman & Roch, 1991). The SMOC consists of 13 behavior categories—active rehabilitation, initial treatment, attending-related, attending-unrelated, interaction-related, interaction-unrelated, waiting, initial diagnosis, preventive treatment, maintenance, nonactivity, unrelated activity, and exclusion. For several categories, it also indicates whether the behavior is related or unrelated to treatment of the athlete's injury.

To apply the SMOC, trained observers monitor an athlete's rehabilitation sessions and record which of the 13 categories best describes the behavior in which the athlete is engaged either during or at the end of each of a series of brief (e.g., 10-second, 20-second) intervals over the course of the sessions being observed. The main strength of the SMOC is that it yields a high volume of richly detailed information about athletes' behaviors during clinic-based rehabilitation sessions. However, the practicality of this coding system is limited by its time-, labor-, and cost-intensiveness; indeed, most clinical and research groups simply do not have the human and financial resources to use the SMOC on a widespread basis. Moreover, because it was not designed to measure adherence, the SMOC does not take into account what athletes are *supposed* to be doing during rehabilitation sessions.

To address some of the SMOC's limitations and create more user-friendly indexes of adherence to clinic-based sport injury rehabilitation, researchers have developed brief scales on which sport health care professionals rate the athletes' adherence. Instead of the SMOC approach of observing athletes' behavior during rehabilitation sessions and recording their observations, sport health care professionals observe athletes' behavior during rehabilitation and then assign ratings based on their observations. Rating scales sacrifice the breadth and volume of information obtained through the SMOC but offer the benefits of brevity and direct relevance to adherence. Two rating scales have been subjected to empirical validation—the Sport Injury Rehabilitation Adherence Scale (SIRAS; Brewer Van Raalte, Petitpas, et al., 2000) and the Rehabilitation Adherence Measure for Athletic Training (RAdMAT; Granquist, Gill, & Appaneal, 2010).

The SIRAS contains a mere three items, on which sport health care professionals rate the intensity of effort displayed by athletes and the degree to which they follow instructions or advice and are receptive to changes in the rehabilitation program during sessions. Research has shown the SIRAS to be a reliable and valid instrument that can distinguish between athletes exhibiting low, moderate, and high levels of adherence (Brewer, Avondoglio, et al., 2002; Brewer, Van Raalte, Petitpas, et al., 2000; Granquist et al., 2010; Kolt, Brewer, Pizzari, Schoo, & Garrett, 2007). Although the SIRAS can be used in a single administration to assess athletes' general adherence tendencies, it was designed for repeated use over the course of rehabilitation. The brevity of the SIRAS enables sport health care professionals to document session-to-session variation in adherence in just a few seconds at the end of each appointment.

With 16 items, the RAdMAT is much longer than the SIRAS, but what it lacks in brevity it makes up for in breadth and depth. Worded to reflect athletes' behavior in rehabilitation sessions in general, rather than in a single session, the RAdMAT includes subscales that measure attitude and effort, attendance and participation, and communication in the clinical setting. As with the SIRAS, the RAdMAT is an internally consistent questionnaire that can discriminate between low, moderate, and high levels of adherence. In addition, its three subscales and larger number of items allow for a more fine-grained analysis of athletes' adherence to clinic-based activities than does the SIRAS. In addition, the RAdMAT may help identify appropriate adherence-enhancement interventions for athletes having difficulty with their clinic-based rehabilitation program (Granquist & Brewer, 2013).

Home-Based Measures

Completion of home rehabilitation activities is considered vital to the success of some sport injury rehabilitation programs. Just as teachers need to know how much of the homework they assign is completed by their students in order to facilitate their lesson planning, sport health care professionals need to know what rehabilitation activities their athletes are doing at home in order to guide their planning of clinic-based rehabilitation. It can be difficult, however, to assess adherence to home-based aspects of sport injury rehabilitation because it occurs away from the clinic. Short of arranging a cost-prohibitive, privacy-invading, round-the-clock video feed from an athlete's home, sport health care professionals and researchers cannot directly observe home-based rehabilitation activities.

It may be tempting to draw conclusions about athletes' adherence to home rehabilitation activities on the basis of their recovery progress—that is, assuming stronger adherence by athletes who recover better or more quickly. Such inferences, however, are inappropriate because adherence is a rehabilitation *process*, whereas recovery progress is a rehabilitation *outcome* (Brewer, 1999b). As suggested by the biopsychosocial model (Brewer, Andersen, & Van Raalte, 2002), adherence does contribute to rehabilitation outcomes, but those outcomes are also influenced by other factors, such as heredity and clinic-based treatment. As a result, complete adherence to a rehabilitation program does not necessarily result in a favorable rehabilitation outcome—a reality that is illustrated by the case of Tammy at the start of this chapter and addressed by research discussed later in the chapter (in the section on the adherence–outcome relationship). Thus, any conclusions about athletes' adherence to home rehabilitation activities should be based *not* on how quickly or how well they recover but on assessment of their adherence.

An especially challenging aspect of measuring adherence to home-based rehabilitation programs involves the sheer diversity of activities that athletes may be asked to perform. Such programs may include, for example, doing exercises, applying therapeutic modalities (e.g., ice), taking medications, avoiding potentially harmful physical activities, and using or wearing therapeutic or protective devices (e.g., splints).

Assessment of adherence to home-based rehabilitation programs has focused on two approaches: self-report and objective measurement. Each is addressed in detail in the following sections.

Self-Report Measures   The most direct, convenient, and versatile approach to measuring what athletes do at home with respect to their rehabilitation programs is simply to ask them. Self-report goes straight to the source of the home rehabilitation behavior—athletes—and can be readily adapted to the array of home-based activities to which athletes may be asked to adhere. The home-based activity for which adherence has been assessed most frequently is that of performing rehabilitation exercises, and the most common way of assessing home-exercise completion has been self-report, typically in the form of a single retrospective self-report (Brewer, 1999b).

Despite the clear advantages of self-report for measuring adherence to home-based rehabilitation programs, most self-report measures in this domain lack established validity (Bol-

len, Dean, Siegert, Howe, & Goodwin, 2014; Hall et al., 2015). Moreover, adherence information obtained through self-report is not always accurate. For example, when athletes are asked to recall their home rehabilitation behavior over a long period of time, self-reports can be inaccurate because athletes may not remember the details of what they have done. In addition, athletes who wish to present themselves in a positive light, or who wish *not* to disappoint their sport health care professionals, may exaggerate their adherence (Brewer, 1999b). In support of these arguments, even self-reports taken on a daily basis tend to overestimate the degree of adherence (Brewer, Cornelius, Van Raalte, Brickner, Sklar, et al., 2004); see this chapter's Focus on Research box for more information.

Objective Measures   In assessing adherence to home rehabilitation activities, the limitations of self-report can be avoided when objective measures of adherence are available. For example, here are some objective methods for assessing athletes' adherence to a prescribed medication regimen:

- Measuring the athletes' medication (e.g., counting their pills)

- Reviewing their pharmacy data (e.g., prescription, quantity of medication dispensed, refill dates)

- Electronically monitoring the use of their medication container

- Analyzing their biochemistry (e.g., blood and urine assays)

- Directly observing their rehabilitation (Rand & Weeks, 1998)

Although only the last method—direct observation—assesses medication-taking behavior, each of the methods offers a potentially unbiased means of validating athletes' self-reports and identifying athletes who may not be taking their medication.

The aspect of home rehabilitation programs that has been measured objectively most often is completion of rehabilitation exercises. As shown in table 6.1, electronic monitoring has made it possible to determine

TABLE 6.1   Examples of Devices Used for Electronic Monitoring of Home-Exercise Completion

Study	Device
Belanger & Noel (1991)	Motion sensor embedded in ankle exerciser
Levitt, Deisinger, Wall, Ford, & Cassisi (1995)	EMG biofeedback unit used for knee exercises
Petrosenko, Vandervoort, Chesworth, Porter, & Campbell (1996)	Counter mounted on ankle exerciser
Olivier, Neudeck, Assenmacher, & Schmit-Neuerburg (1997)	Step counter hidden in orthotics
Dobbe et al. (1999)	Counter attached to finger splint
Schlenk et al. (2000)	Accelerometer
Brewer et al. (2004)	Counter embedded in videocassette used to convey exercise instructions
Rathleff, Bandholm, Ahrendt, Olesen, & Thorborg (2014); Rathleff et al. (2015)	Stretch sensor attached to elastic exercise band

the extent to which athletes complete rehabilitation exercises using certain pieces of equipment. Although the monitoring devices have typically been used in rehabilitation with clinical populations other than athletes, they can readily be applied to rehabilitation of sport injury. With the exception of the accelerometer and the EMG biofeedback unit, the devices listed in the table are custom made and are specific to the pieces of exercise equipment they monitor. Therefore, they illustrate not standard practices but what is possible for objective assessment of adherence to home exercise prescriptions. Furthermore, objective measures are not readily available for adherence to home application of therapeutic modalities, avoidance of potentially harmful activities, and use of most protective devices. Consequently, using objective means to measure adherence to home rehabilitation programs generally requires extra initiative, innovation, time, effort, and expense. Overall, then, objective measures of adherence can yield valuable information, but it is not always practical, cost-effective, or even necessary to develop and implement them.

Theoretical Perspectives

The issues associated with adhering to sport injury rehabilitation programs are substantially similar to those associated with adhering to other medical regimens. Fundamentally, regardless of the particular medical condition, adherence to treatment involves engaging in behavior intended to restore health. As a result, attempts to explain why athletes adhere or fail to adhere to their rehabilitation programs have borrowed heavily from theories developed for other health behaviors. As shown in table 6.2, the theoretical perspectives that have been applied to adherence to sport injury rehabilitation programs include the adapted planned behavior model (Levy, Polman, & Clough, 2008), the integrated model of psychological response to sport injury (Wiese-Bjornstal, Smith, Shaffer, & Morrey, 1998), personal investment theory (Maehr & Braskamp, 1986), protection motivation theory (Prentice-Dunn & Rogers, 1986), self-determination theory (R.M. Ryan & Deci, 2000), and the transtheoretical model (Prochaska & DiClemente, 1983).

Are Athletes' Reports of Adherence to Home Rehabilitation Activities Trustworthy?

Sport health care professionals educate athletes about their home rehabilitation programs and do their best to facilitate adherence, but they also know that athletes who leave the clinical environment with a set of instructions for home rehabilitation may not carry out those instructions as written. They are also aware that some athletes, when not under the watchful eyes of sport health care professionals, do less of their home program than recommended and that other, highly motivated athletes "overadhere" by doing more rehabilitation activity than instructed (Granquist, Podlog, Engel, & Newland, 2014; Niven, 2007; Podlog, Gao et al., 2013). Thus concern about adherence to home rehabilitation programs is justified. In addition, Webborn, Carbon, and Miller (1997) found that the vast majority (77 percent) of athletes receiving treatment at a sport injury clinic had less than a full understanding of the components of their rehabilitation program. If athletes cannot accurately report what they are supposed to be doing, it is highly unlikely that they are adhering to the program! Furthermore, if self-reports of home adherence behavior are also subject to the limitations of forgetting and biased recall (Brewer, 1999b), can sport health professionals really trust the information they receive from athletes about what they are doing at home?

It appears that the answer is a qualified yes. As part of a larger study of rehabilitation following ACL surgery, Brewer, Cornelius, Van Raalte, Brickner, Sklar, et al. (2004) examined the correspondence and concordance between self-reported home-exercise completion and objectively assessed home-exercise completion. Here, the term *correspondence* refers to how strongly the two measures of adherence are related, whereas *concordance* refers to the discrepancy between the two measures of adherence. The study monitored participants' adherence to a home rehabilitation exercise program for the first 42 days of rehabilitation after ACL surgery. Instructions for and demonstrations of the home exercise prescription were given in the form of a videocassette that was modified as participants progressed through the program. Participants were asked to record how many times they completed their assigned set of exercises each day with and without the videocassette, then forward their self-reports to the researchers on a daily basis through postal mail.

Unbeknownst to the participants, each videocassette was equipped with an electronic counting device that logged each time the videocassette was played at regular speed (not fast forward or rewind) for at least five minutes. The positive correlation ($r = .58$) obtained between the self-report and the electronic-counter completion values provided a degree of corroboration of the self-reports. Despite this correspondence, however, participants tended to over-report the extent to which they completed their home exercises by 0.41 sets per day. Overall, then, it appears that under certain circumstances, self-reports of adherence to home rehabilitation can be trusted with the understanding that they may be slightly exaggerated.

Several features of this study may have enhanced the accuracy of the self-reports. First, the chance of forgetting the number of sets completed was minimized by obtaining self-reports on a daily basis. Second, the demand for socially desirable responses was reduced by having participants send their self-reports to the researchers rather than to the sport health care professionals overseeing their rehabilitation. Third, the quality of the self-reports may have been boosted by the fact that participants received compensation for completing and returning them (the amount of compensation was not contingent on the content of the self-reports). These features are not typically present in most clinical settings, but there are steps that sport health care professionals can take to make it more likely that athletes will furnish them with accurate self-reports of adherence to their home programs. Specifically, they can request self-reports on a frequent basis, remind athletes of the contents of their home rehabilitation programs, and emphasize that accurate self-reports regarding adherence are vital to tailoring the rehabilitation protocol to each athlete's particular needs (Finney, Putnam, & Boyd, 1998).

Focus on Research

TABLE 6.2   Theoretical Perspectives Applied to Adherence to Sport Injury Rehabilitation Programs

Theoretical perspective	Key constructs hypothesized to contribute to adherence
Adapted planned behavior model	Perceived severity, perceived susceptibility, self-efficacy, self-motivation, goal orientation, attitude, behavioral intention, coping ability, treatment efficacy, social support, intention to adhere
Integrated model of psychological response to sport injury	Cognitive appraisals, emotional responses, behavioral responses, personal factors, situational factors
Personal investment theory	Personal incentives, sense-of-self beliefs, perceived options
Protection motivation theory	Perceived severity, perceived susceptibility, belief in treatment efficacy, self-efficacy
Self-determination theory	Satisfaction of basic psychological needs for autonomy, competence, and relatedness
Transtheoretical model	Stages of readiness for change, experiential and behavioral processes of change, self-efficacy, decisional balance

Inspection of table 6.2 reveals that each of these theoretical perspectives fits squarely within a biopsychosocial framework. The perspectives posit a variety of psychological factors (particularly cognitive factors) and a pair of social or contextual factors (i.e., social support, relatedness) as contributors to adherence to sport injury rehabilitation programs (adherence would be considered a behavioral factor in a biopsychosocial approach). As the table makes evident, these perspectives are not conceptually independent, as the key concepts overlap substantially. For example, multiple perspectives feature self-efficacy, treatment efficacy, and various cognitive appraisals. Furthermore, because the perspectives have not been compared directly in research investigations, there is currently no empirical justification for selecting one perspective over the others. Examination of common features across the perspectives suggests that athletes can be expected to adhere to their rehabilitation programs when they

- are motivated to adhere,
- believe in their ability to adhere,
- believe in the efficacy of their treatment,
- perceive rehabilitation as necessary and important,
- intend to adhere, and
- are supported by others in adhering.

As shown in the next section, research has documented these features as being predictive of adherence to sport injury rehabilitation.

Predictors

Guided to a large extent by the theoretical perspectives discussed in the preceding section, researchers have conducted numerous investigations with the intent of identifying predictors of adherence to sport injury rehabilitation programs. As in the general health care literature, which has identified more than 200 variables associated with treatment adherence (Meichenbaum & Turk, 1987), studies have also documented many factors predictive of adherence to sport injury rehabilitation. With only a few exceptions (described later, in the section on adherence enhancement), these studies have featured correlational research designs. Because causation cannot be inferred from these studies, the term *predictors* is used instead of *determinants*, *causes*, or *contributors*.

Early studies of adherence to sport injury rehabilitation tended to be retrospective or cross-sectional, meaning that they assessed prospective predictors of adherence either after adherence (i.e., a retrospective approach) or at the same time as adherence (i.e., a cross-sectional approach). More recent studies have been prospective; that is, prospective predictors were assessed before measuring adherence. Although still correlational, prospective research designs enhance the plausibility of

arguments that predictors may exert a causal influence on adherence.

Predictors of adherence can be grouped within categories of the biopsychosocial approach to sport injury rehabilitation depicted in figure 6.2. Adherence is considered to be a behavioral factor in the psychological factors category; therefore, it can be subject to the influence of variables in all of the categories shown in the figure. Illustrating the diversity of predictors of adherence to sport injury

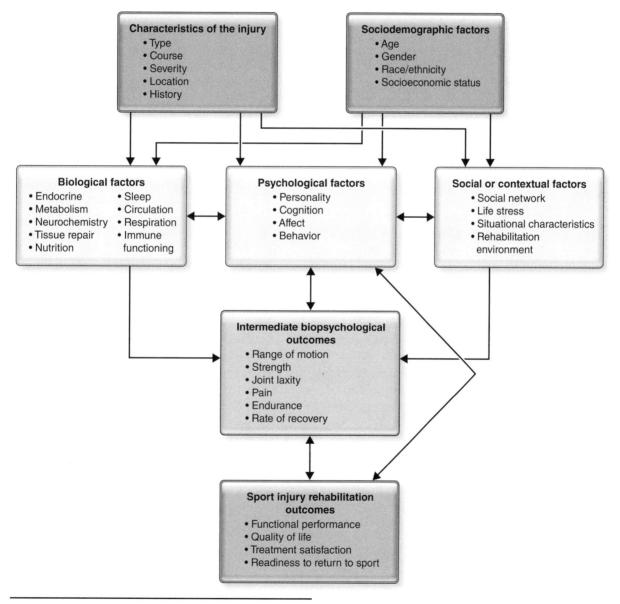

Figure 6.2 A biopsychosocial approach to sport injury rehabilitation.

rehabilitation, associations with adherence have been documented for at least one variable in all of the categories except biological factors.

Characteristics of the Injury

Few attempts have been made to link characteristics of sport injuries to rehabilitation adherence. Nevertheless, a positive association has been observed between rehabilitation adherence and injury severity (A.H. Taylor & May, 1996). Notwithstanding the limitations of the concept of injury severity (outlined in chapter 1), it is possible that severe injuries prompt athletes to adhere to their rehabilitation programs by underscoring the magnitude of the threat that the injuries pose to their health, well-being, and sport performance. Because Taylor and May used a self-report measure to assess injury severity, it cannot be determined whether it is the perception of injury severity or the actual injury severity that is related to adherence. Results from two other studies, however, suggest that actual injury severity, filtered through the perceptions of athletes, plays a role in adherence to rehabilitation. In a study in which injury severity was held constant (i.e., all participants had the same injury), *perceived* injury severity was *not* a significant predictor of adherence (Brewer, Cornelius, Van Raalte, Petitpas, et al., 2003a). On the other hand, in a study of physical therapy patients with a wide variety of injuries (Grindley, Zizzi, & Nasypany, 2008), perceived injury severity *was* a significant predictor of adherence (i.e., sticking with or dropping out of rehabilitation). Thus, perceived injury severity alone does not appear to account for the reported positive associations between injury severity and rehabilitation adherence (Grindley et al., 2008; A.H. Taylor & May, 1996).

Sociodemographic Factors

Among the sociodemographic factors listed in figure 6.2, only age has emerged as being predictive of sport injury rehabilitation adherence. In a sample of competitive and recreational athletes with various injuries, young athletes adhered to their rehabilitation programs significantly better than did older athletes (Levy,

Polman, & Borkoles, 2008; Levy, Polman, & Clough, 2008). In addition to this finding of a direct relationship between age and adherence, age has also been found to moderate associations between adherence and several other psychosocial variables. For example, in a study of rehabilitation after ACL surgery (Brewer, Cornelius, Van Raalte, Petitpas, et al., 2003b), athletic identity was positively correlated with adherence for younger participants but unrelated to adherence for older participants. In this same study, self-motivation and social support were positively correlated with adherence for older participants but unrelated to adherence for younger participants. Consistent with the findings of Brewer and colleagues (Brewer, Cornelius, Van Raalte, Petitpas, et al., 2003b) for social support, Levy, Polman, and Borkoles (2008) found that perceived autonomy support was positively associated with adherence for older athletes but unrelated to adherence for young athletes. Age, therefore, appears to be an important sociodemographic variable to consider when examining adherence to sport injury rehabilitation programs.

Social and Contextual Factors

Sport injury rehabilitation does not occur in a vacuum; rather, it takes place in social and environmental contexts that influence (and are influenced by) athletes' behavior. For example, the rehabilitation programs that guide athletes' postinjury behavior are typically created and supervised by sport health care professionals, and they often take place in specialized physical environments (e.g., clinics) populated with other athletes who are also engaged in rehabilitation. Unsurprisingly, then, associations have been found between adherence to rehabilitation and both social and environmental variables.

From a social standpoint, athletes tend to adhere better to their rehabilitation programs when they perceive that sport health care professionals expect them to adhere (A.H. Taylor & May, 1995) and that other people support their rehabilitation (Byerly, Worrell, Gahimer, & Domholdt, 1994; Duda, Smart, & Tappe, 1989; Fisher, Domm, & Wuest, 1988; Johnston & Carroll, 2000; Levy, Polman, & Borkoles, 2008; Levy, Polman, & Clough, 2008). Similarly, when athletes perceive that the sport health care professionals supervising their rehabilitation support their autonomy, they report experiencing greater autonomous treatment motivation, which is positively correlated with adherence to rehabilitation (Chan, Lonsdale, Ho, Yung, & Chan, 2009). From an environmental standpoint, perceptions of a comfortable clinic setting and convenient appointment scheduling are positively associated with adherence to sport injury rehabilitation programs (J. Fields, Murphey, Horodyski, & Stopka, 1995; Fisher et al., 1988). Thus, support, comfort, and convenience are potential contributors to sport injury rehabilitation adherence.

Psychological Factors

Given that adherence is a behavior, the vast majority of identified predictors of adherence to sport injury rehabilitation are psychological factors. Consistent with the psychological factors listed in figure 6.2, research has found that adherence is predicted by a wide variety of personal, cognitive, emotional, and behavioral variables.

Personal Factors   As best illustrated by personality characteristics, personal factors are stable, enduring aspects of a person that can be used both to describe that person and to differentiate him or her from others. Personal attributes associated with sport injury rehabilitation adherence include athletic identity, internal health locus of control, mental toughness, pain tolerance, self-motivation, task involvement, agreeableness, conscientiousness, and openness to experience. Specifically, athletes who adhere well to their rehabilitation programs tend to be

- strongly identified with the athlete role (Brewer, Cornelius, Van Raalte, Petitpas, Sklar, et al., 2003b; Brewer, Cornelius, Van Raalte, Tennen, & Armeli, 2013);
- consistent in their belief across situations that how they behave can influence their health status (Murphy, Foreman, Simpson, Molloy, & Molloy, 1999);
- tolerant of pain (Byerly et al., 1994; J. Fields et al., 1995; Fisher et al., 1988);
- self-motivated (Brewer, Daly, Van Raalte, Petitpas, & Sklar, 1999; Brewer, Van Raalte,

Cornelius, et al., 2000; Duda et al., 1989; J. Fields et al., 1995; Fisher et al., 1988; Levy, Polman, & Clough, 2008; Noyes, Matthews, Mooar, & Grood, 1983);

- motivated more by self-improvement than by defeating others (Duda et al., 1989); and
- high in the personality characteristics of agreeableness, conscientiousness, and openness to experience (Hilliard, Brewer, Cornelius, & Van Raalte, 2014).

The relationship between mental toughness and adherence is less clear because both positive and negative correlations have been reported (Levy, Polman, Clough, Marchant, & Earle, 2006; Wittig & Schurr, 1994).

Cognitive Factors   Of the many cognitive variables found to predict adherence to sport injury rehabilitation programs, most involve thoughts or beliefs about rehabilitation and recovery. As compared with athletes who adhere poorly to rehabilitation, those who adhere well tend to

- believe to a greater extent in the effectiveness of their rehabilitation program (Brewer, Cornelius, Van Raalte, Petitpas, Sklar, et al., 2003a; Duda et al., 1989; Noyes et al., 1983; A.H. Taylor & May, 1996),
- value their rehabilitation more highly (A.H. Taylor & May, 1996),
- report a higher level of perceived exertion during rehabilitation activities (Fisher et al., 1988),
- consider themselves more motivated by self-determination (Chan et al., 2009),
- identify stabwle and personally controllable factors as responsible for their recovery (Laubach, Brewer, Van Raalte, & Petitpas, 1996),
- indicate a stronger intention to adhere to their rehabilitation program (Bassett & Prapavessis, 2011; Levy, Polman, & Clough, 2008), and
- express more confidence in their ability to cope with their injuries (Daly, Brewer, Van Raalte, Petitpas, & Sklar, 1995; Levy, Polman, & Clough, 2008) and finish their rehabilitation program (Brewer, Cornelius, Van Raalte, Petitpas, Sklar, et al., 2003a; Levy, Polman, & Clough, 2008; Milne, Hall,

& Forwell, 2005; A.H. Taylor & May, 1996; Wesch et al., 2012).

More generally, better adherence is associated with reporting fewer threats to self-esteem (Lampton, Lambert, & Yost, 1993) and greater use of the cognitive strategies of goal setting, positive self-talk (Scherzer et al., 2001), and imagery (Scherzer et al., 2001; Wesch et al., 2012). In addition, two experimental studies (L. Evans & Hardy, 2002a; Penpraze & Mutrie, 1999) found evidence of a facilitative causal relationship between adherence and goal setting.

Emotional and Behavioral Factors   One emotional factor (mood disturbance) and one behavioral factor (instrumental coping) have been found to predict adherence to sport injury rehabilitation programs. Because mood disturbance encompasses a wide array of emotions (e.g., anger, anxiety, confusion, depression, fatigue), it is less a single emotional factor than a composite of emotional aspects and a general indicator of psychological distress. Athletes experiencing mood disturbance tend to adhere less well to their rehabilitation programs than athletes not experiencing mood disturbance (Alzate et al., 2004; Daly et al., 1995; Kingen, Shapiro, Katz, & Mullan, 2013). For example, being angry, anxious, or depressed may interfere with an athlete's ability to engage in goal-directed behavior and complete prescribed rehabilitation activities. In contrast, reaching a state of psychological acceptance may facilitate adherence (Tatsumi, 2013).

As with mood disturbance, instrumental coping is a composite of multiple behaviors in which athletes take action to cope with their injuries—for example, seeking information about what they can do to facilitate their rehabilitation. Athletes who report using instrumental coping to a large extent tend to adhere better to their rehabilitation than do athletes who report using it to a lesser extent (Udry, 1997). Thus it may be possible that, at least for some athletes, adhering to rehabilitation is part of a broader, potentially adaptive orientation toward instrumental action when dealing with challenging circumstances.

Outcomes

Associations have been documented between adherence to sport injury rehabilitation programs and the two outcome types depicted in figure 6.2—that is, intermediate biopsychosocial outcomes and sport injury rehabilitation outcomes. However, because adherence is generally considered predictive of outcome, rather than the other way around, these relations are discussed later in this chapter in the section addressing consequences of adherence.

Enhancement

The abundance of identified predictors for rehabilitation adherence provides a wealth of potential targets for interventions designed to enhance adherence. However, despite the potential implications of adherence for improving rehabilitation outcomes, few empirical studies have reported on efforts to enhance adherence. To date, in fact, goal setting is the only method that has been found effective relative to a control group in enhancing adherence to *sport* injury rehabilitation programs (L. Evans & Hardy, 2002a; Penpraze & Mutrie, 1999). Presumably, helping athletes set appropriate goals for their rehabilitation activities boosts their perceived control over and responsibility for their recovery, as well as their attention to rehabilitation tasks, their self-efficacy (or confidence) for completing rehabilitation, and their motivation to adhere (L. Evans & Hardy, 2002b)—all of which have been identified as predictors of adherence (see the preceding section of this chapter). Experimental support for goal setting is augmented by correlational research that indicates a positive association between adherence to postoperative treatment and self-reported use of goal setting (and positive self-talk) during ACL rehabilitation. Overall, it is currently unknown whether the dearth of research on the effectiveness of interventions designed to enhance adherence results from a lack of studies being conducted or from an absence of supporting results.

Interventions for enhancing adherence, particularly those involving an educational approach, have attracted greater interest in research on the rehabilitation of conditions outside the realm of sport injury. For example, patient education (i.e., "back school") for low-back pain was shown to have a positive effect on adherence in a meta-analysis of 19 prospective randomized controlled trials (DiFabio, 1995). In addition to *what* is taught in rehabilitation programs, instructional aspects of *how* educational content is presented appear to play an important role in rehabilitation adherence. For example, patients adhere to home rehabilitation programs better when they are supervised than when they are unsupervised (Bentsen, Lindgarde, & Manthrope, 1997; Hidding et al., 1994); they also adhere better when program content is presented to them through instructional media such as audio recordings (Gallo & Staskin, 1997) and specifically tailored written and illustrated materials (L.D. Jackson, 1994; Schneiders, Zusman, & Singer, 1998).

In addition to patient education, multimodal intervention has shown promise as a means of enhancing adherence to rehabilitation programs outside the domain of sport injury (McLean, Burton, Bradley, & Littlewood, 2010). Multimodal interventions combine multiple potentially beneficial procedures. In one study, for example, a multimodal intervention—which combined components such as behavioral contracting, education, goal setting, homework, mental practice facilitation, modeling, and program reminders—enhanced rehabilitation adherence among persons with rheumatoid arthritis (Hammond & Freeman, 2001). One occasional component of multimodal interventions—reinforcement—has also demonstrated a facilitative effect on rehabilitation adherence independent of other modalities. For example, reinforcement of desired rehabilitation behaviors has been associated with higher levels of adherence to therapeutic exercises in people with hemophilia (Greenan-Fowler, Powell, & Varni, 1987) and people with severe burns (Hegel, Ayllon, VanderPlate, & Spiro-Hawkins, 1986).

As with patient education, research has yet to determine the effectiveness of multimodal interventions and reinforcement in enhancing adherence to *sport* injury rehabilitation programs. There is no reason to believe, however,

that such approaches could not be adapted, with suitable tailoring, to improve the athletes' adherence to rehabilitation. In the relative absence of research specific to sport injury on methods of enhancing rehabilitation adherence, Granquist and Brewer (2015) have advocated a broad-based approach in which sport health care professionals obtain pertinent biopsychosocial information about athletes at the beginning of rehabilitation, identify potential barriers to adherence to the rehabilitation protocol, and implement strategies to reduce the adherence-compromising effects of the barriers. The theories and empirical findings discussed earlier in this section can be useful in identifying potential targets for intervention.

Consequences of Adherence to Sport Injury Prevention and Rehabilitation Programs

As noted at the beginning of the chapter, the importance placed on adherence to sport injury prevention and rehabilitation programs rests on the implicit assumption that athletes who adhere achieve better outcomes than those who do not adhere. In other words, it is assumed that fully completing preventive and rehabilitative regimens is associated with fewer injuries, less time lost due to injury, and faster and better recovery from injury. However, support for these assumptions is less robust than one might expect. With that in mind, this section examines sport injury prevention and rehabilitation in terms of adherence–outcome and dose–response relationships.

Adherence–Outcome Relationships

The lore of sports medicine is rife with heroic tales of athletes who recovered miraculously from injury and returned successfully to sport after religiously completing all aspects of their rehabilitation programs. That lore is also replete with cautionary tales of misery involving athletes who disregarded or failed to complete their rehabilitation programs and therefore experienced poor outcomes, such as delayed recovery or even reinjury. Fewer such stories are told about sport injury *prevention*, perhaps because prevention programs have only recently been initiated systematically on a widespread basis—or, more likely, because a prevented injury is a nonevent and accounts of nonevents are not terribly compelling or captivating. Lost among the anecdotal reports of athletes experiencing favorable (or unfavorable) rehabilitation outcomes due to adherence (or nonadherence) are the undoubtedly numerous but unnoticed cases of athletes who recovered remarkably even though they adhered poorly or who failed to recover quickly or well despite adhering perfectly.

As underscored in chapters 2 and 7, a multitude of factors contribute to the occurrence of, and recovery from, sport injury. Therefore, prevention and rehabilitation programs—and the extent to which they are followed—constitute but two of the many factors that influence whether an athlete sustains an injury and how well or quickly he or she recovers.

Theoretically, three kinds of relationship are possible between adherence and outcome: positive correlation, negative correlation, and no correlation. A positive correlation indicates that the more athletes adhere to the prevention or rehabilitation protocol, the better their outcome is likely to be. The simplest interpretation of a positive correlation is that the protocol is effective and that athletes gain from the program what they put into it. It is also possible, however, that staying free of injury or recovering quickly from injury encourages athletes to adhere, or that some other factor (e.g., fitness) facilitates both adherence and favorable prevention and rehabilitation outcomes.

A negative correlation indicates that the more athletes adhere to the prevention or rehabilitation protocol, the *worse* their outcome is likely to be. One interpretation of a negative correlation carries profound implications for professional practice: that the protocol is counterproductive and that adhering to it is detrimental to favorable prevention or rehabilitation outcomes (see this chapter's Focus on Application for a possible response to observing a negative correlation). In a possible alternative interpretation, resilient athletes who are rarely injured or who recover quickly may

choose not to adhere to preventive or rehabilitative activities because they do not perceive a need to do so.

No correlation signifies a lack of association between adherence and outcome, thus indicating that, across many people, adhering to a given program is related to no better and no worse outcomes than not adhering. Adherence-outcome correlations of zero or near zero can be difficult to interpret, because although sometimes they reflect a true lack of association, the adherence–outcome relationship can be attenuated by measurement error (Brewer, 2004; DiMatteo, Giordani, Lepper, & Croghan, 2002) and by situations in which negative adherence–outcome associations in some athletes cancel out positive adherence–outcome associations in other athletes.

All three kinds of adherence–outcome relationship have been documented in research investigations. In the general medical literature, across a wide variety of medical conditions and treatment regimens, patients with high treatment adherence have been found to experience 26 percent better outcomes than patients with low treatment adherence (DiMatteo et al., 2002). Such effects are far from uniform, however, as illustrated vividly in a study by Hays et al. (1994) in which only 11 of 132 comparisons of adherent and nonadherent patients revealed significant outcome differences favoring adherent patients. Trends toward positive adherence–outcome correlations are evident in the realm of sport injury prevention and rehabilitation. For sport injury prevention, research suggests that better adherence to neuromuscular training programs is related to reduced risk for injuries to the ACL (Sugimoto et al., 2012), ankle (Verhagen, Hupperets, Finch, & van Mechelen, 2011), hamstring (Goode et al., 2015), and leg in general (Pasanen et al., 2008).

The findings regarding adherence in sport injury rehabilitation mirror the findings of research on rehabilitation of conditions other than sport injury, in that positive correlations between adherence and outcome have been the general trend (for reviews, see Brewer [2004] and Mendonza, Patel, & Bassett, 2007). Despite this tendency, the complexity of the adherence–outcome relationship in sport injury rehabilitation is evidenced by three separate studies that documented the full complement of possible relations between adherence and outcome—that is, positive correlation, negative correlation, and no correlation (Brewer, Cornelius, Van Raalte, Brickner, Sklar, et al., 2004; Pizzari, Taylor, McBurney, & Feller, 2005; Quinn, 1996). How is it possible for adherence to be positively associated, negatively associated, and unassociated with outcome in a single study? Both adherence and outcome are multifaceted constructs which are typically assessed with multiple indicators that are often only weakly related to each other (Brewer, Cornelius, Van Raalte, Brickner, Sklar, et al., 2004); therefore, a variety of potential relations can occur between adherence and outcome.

In the study by Pizzari et al. (2005), for example, adherence to a regimen of home rehabilitation exercises after ACL surgery was positively associated with several outcomes as assessed by questionnaire for athletes under 30 years of age, negatively associated with outcomes assessed by questionnaire for athletes 30 years of age or older, and unrelated to outcomes assessed through clinical evaluation and performance on functional tests. None of the clinic-based indexes of adherence used by Pizzari et al. were associated with any of the assessed rehabilitation outcomes. Thus, adherence to different aspects of a sport injury rehabilitation program may be differentially related to different outcomes of the program.

Dose–Response Relationships

Adherence–outcome relationships in sport injury prevention and rehabilitation are underlain by relationships between the "dose" of preventive or rehabilitative activities received by athletes and the responses of the athletes to those activities. In this context, adherence is the *percentage* of the recommended dose of the treatment received, whereas the dose is the actual *amount* of treatment received. Dose–response relationships are established most effectively in clinical or laboratory settings in which the dose can be carefully controlled. In contrast, adherence–outcome relationships are established in settings in which athletes engage in the preventive

When Poor Adherence Sparked a Revolution in ACL Rehabilitation

After performing literally hundreds of ACL reconstructions, orthopedic surgeon Donald Shelbourne observed a negative correlation between adherence to the postsurgical rehabilitation program that he prescribed and the outcomes that his patients experienced. Reflecting the conventional wisdom at the time, the rehabilitation protocol was a conservative one in which athletes were immobilized without weight bearing for an extended period of time, were prevented from gaining full extension, and were generally brought along slowly in order to protect the integrity of the surgical graft. Shelbourne noticed, however, that athletes who adhered poorly to the rehabilitation program achieved better outcomes than athletes who adhered well (Shelbourne & Wilckens, 1990).

Interpreting the negative correlation as a sign that the customary approach to postsurgical ACL rehabilitation was in error, Shelbourne developed an "accelerated" rehabilitation protocol that, in addition to including a component of preoperative rehabilitation activities (which have become known as "prehab"), focuses on healing wounds rapidly, acquiring full extension, minimizing swelling, and regaining control of the affected leg. After implementing the new protocol, Shelbourne and Wilckens (1990) "documented improved stability, decreased complications, increased predictability, and improved patient acceptance when using the same surgical procedure and changing only the rehabilitation program" (Shelbourne & Wilckens). The revised program turned postsurgical ACL rehabilitation on its ear and changed the standard practices in the orthopedic sports medicine community—all because Shelbourne identified a negative adherence-outcome relationship.

Focus on Application

or rehabilitative activities. These settings are often located away from the clinic environment, thereby making it more difficult to determine the exact dose applied.

The distinction between adherence and dose is illustrated by the following example:

Two athletes, Janel and Tracy, are prescribed the same group of home exercises to complete as part of their injury rehabilitation programs. Janel is prescribed two sets of the exercises per day but completes only one set per day, whereas Tracy is asked to complete one set per day and faithfully does so. Therefore, Janel's *adherence* rate for the home program is only half that of Tracy's (50 percent versus 100 percent), but their *dose* of home exercise is identical (one set per day).

Adherence enhancement efforts should be informed by answers to the following critical questions regarding dose–response relationship:

1. What is the minimum dose of treatment needed in order to produce the desired preventive or rehabilitative effect?

2. What dose of treatment produces the optimal preventive or rehabilitative effect?

3. At what point, if any, does increasing the dose become counterproductive, either by diminishing the preventive or rehabilitative effect or by producing harm?

4. What factors moderate the dose–response relationship for a given prevention or rehabilitation program?

Unfortunately, answers to these questions are unavailable for all but a few treatments in sport health care; however, pockets of information do exist that bear on dose–response relationships. Arguably the most extensive evaluation of dose–response relationships involves stretching, a common component of both prevention and rehabilitation programs. For example, Boyce and Brosky (2008) demonstrated that the optimal number of 15-second passive hamstring stretches for increasing hamstring length was four. Each repetition through the first four produced significant gains in knee-extension range of motion (ROM), an indirect measure of hamstring length; additional repetitions, however, failed to produce significant gains. Similarly, E.D. Ryan et al. (2009) showed that at least two 30-second constant-torque passive stretches of the lower leg were needed to produce a significant reduction in the musculoskeletal stiffness of the plantar flexor muscles. In an example not involving

stretching, Snyder-Mackler, Delitto, Stralka, and Bailey (1994) presented empirically derived dose–response curves for neuromuscular electrical stimulation for muscle strengthening after ACL surgery. More dose–response research is needed across the full range of sport injury prevention and rehabilitation activities in order to inform treatment planning, establish meaningful targets for adherence, and determine the points above which additional rehabilitation activities (i.e., overadherence) are detrimental.

Biopsychosocial Analysis

As with many concepts addressed in this book, adherence to sport injury prevention and rehabilitation programs is readily understood as a biopsychosocial phenomenon. Subject to the influence of a wide range of biological, psychological, and social factors, adherence is a behavior that can itself affect a slew of biological, psychological, and social factors. Some of these influences are vividly illustrated in the cases presented at the beginning of the chapter. Carlos, for example, skipped his home stretching and strengthening exercises because of fatigue, an apparent lack of motivation, and an absence of physical symptoms. Social distractions, on the other hand, seemed to stand between Teena and her home rehabilitation, whereas Tammy's personality appeared conducive to single-minded dedication to her program.

As emphasized throughout this chapter, many of the most efficacious, scientifically validated interventions for prevention and rehabilitation are not effective unless athletes adhere to them. In other words, the success of procedures that remediate or prevent the occurrence of damage to biological structures (i.e., physical anatomy) can be contingent on adherence, a behavior that is subject to psychological and social influences. As suggested by the cases of Tammy and Teena, however, the link between adherence and clinical outcomes is not always straightforward. Despite Tammy's staunch adherence to her rehabilitation program, she did not experience favorable clinical outcomes; in contrast, Teena adhered poorly but enjoyed a remarkable recovery.

These complications notwithstanding, understanding of adherence offers the possibility of valuable insights into the prevention and rehabilitation of sport injury.

Summary

The effectiveness of sport injury prevention and rehabilitation programs presumably depends on the extent to which athletes adhere to their prescribed regimens. Such adherence, which is sometimes labeled "compliance," involves completing program activities designed to prevent or rehabilitate sport injuries. To adhere to sport injury rehabilitation programs, athletes are asked to adopt behaviors such as completing physical exercises, hydrating, wearing protective gear, and doing stress management activities.

Estimates of athlete adherence to sport injury prevention programs vary from 0 percent to 100 percent and are typically obtained by observing team or athlete behavior and obtaining coach or athlete self-reports. Although most research on adherence to sport injury prevention has been *atheoretical*, the theory of planned behavior has shown some promise as a means of explaining why athletes adhere or do not adhere. This theory holds that athletes are more likely to adhere to injury prevention activities when they intend to do so, value injury prevention, have associates who also value injury prevention, and perceive themselves as having control over their completion of the activities.

Predictors of adherence to prevention programs can be classified as either intrinsic or extrinsic. Intrinsic factors include history of previous injury, personal characteristics, and cognitive variables. Athletes with previous injuries, experienced athletes, and female athletes have been found to be more likely to wear protective equipment than are athletes without injuries, inexperienced athletes, and male athletes. Athletes are also more likely to adhere to preventive activities when they have knowledge of the risks of injury and favorable perceptions of the activities and their ability to engage in them. Extrinsic factors include social influences and program or implementation features. Athletes tend to adhere better to preventive activities when many of their friends or teammates are also adhering and when they perceive others as supporting their adherence. Program and implementation characteristics that are associated with high levels of adherence include low player-to-coach ratios, visual reminders to adhere, and program implementation by coaches. Barriers to adhering to protective-equipment interventions include cost, as well as discomfort or difficulty with breathing, communicating, or seeing while wearing the equipment.

Sport injury rehabilitation programs feature both clinic- and home-based activities designed to facilitate recovery. Adherence to clinic-based activities—such as showing up for rehabilitation appointments, following practitioner instructions, completing exercises, and receiving therapeutic modalities—can be measured by recording athletes' attendance at rehabilitation sessions and observing or rating their behavior during rehabilitation sessions. Adherence to home-based activities—such as doing exercises, wearing therapeutic or protective devices, and taking prescribed medications—can be assessed through athletes' self-reports of their home rehabilitation behavior and through objective measures (e.g., electronic monitoring, biochemical analysis).

Various overlapping theories have been used to explain why athletes either do or do not adhere to sport injury rehabilitation programs. Common elements across the theories include motivation and intent to adhere, support from others to adhere, and belief in the efficacy of treatment and in one's ability to adhere. Numerous predictors of adherence to sport injury rehabilitation have been identified, including one injury characteristic (severity), one sociodemographic factor (age), and an abundance of psychological factors. Psychological predictors of adherence include personal factors (e.g., athletic identity, internal health locus of control, mental toughness, pain tolerance, self-motivation, conscientiousness), cognitive factors (e.g., belief in rehabilitation effectiveness, valuing of rehabilitation, intention to adhere), emotional factors (e.g., mood disturbance, psychological acceptance of injury), and one behavioral factor (instrumental coping). Goal setting is the only intervention demonstrated experimentally to enhance adherence to sport injury rehabilitation. However, a variety of interventions have been found effective in enhancing adherence to the rehabilitation of conditions other than sport injury, including patient education, reinforcement, and multimodal approaches.

The importance placed on adherence to sport injury prevention and rehabilitation programs rests on the assumption that athletes who adhere achieve better prevention and rehabilitation outcomes than those who do not adhere. However, because preventive and rehabilitative activities are but two of many factors that influence injury occurrence and recovery, better adherence is not always associated with better outcomes. Nevertheless, a lack of correspondence between adherence and outcomes may signify the need to revise the injury prevention or rehabilitation program.

Discussion Questions

1. What methods can be used to assess adherence to sport injury prevention and rehabilitation interventions, and what are the advantages and disadvantages of those methods?

2. What intrinsic and extrinsic factors are related to adherence to sport injury prevention interventions?

3. What are the key ideas of the main theories and models that have been proposed to explain adherence to sport injury rehabilitation?

4. What can be learned from examining the relationship between treatment outcomes and adherence to sport injury prevention and rehabilitation interventions?

Chapter 7
Psychological Factors in Sport Injury Rehabilitation

Chapter Objectives

1. To review theoretical and empirical support for pathways by which psychological factors may affect sport injury rehabilitation outcomes

2. To explore the concept of psychological readiness to return to sport after injury

Sam, a leading middle-distance runner at a small college, had recently qualified for the national championships in the 800-meter run. While warming up for his next race at an unimportant triangular meet, he noticed that he did not feel like his "normal self" and that his legs felt "tight and heavy." He tried to brush his worries aside but could not escape the thought that something might be wrong. Sure enough, his concern was borne out when he found himself barely able to walk after a substandard performance in the race—nearly four seconds off his qualifying time.

Hobbled by the condition of his leg, Sam skipped the customary cool-down and instead limped directly to the athletic training room, where he was promptly diagnosed with a mild hamstring strain and given instructions to refrain from vigorous physical activity, practice the RICE method (i.e., rest, ice, compression, and elevation), and take ibuprofen. In about four days, the trainer explained, Sam would likely be able to begin a program of stretching and strengthening that would enable him to transition back into his sport. Sam could hardly believe what he was hearing. Four days might as well be a lifetime with the national championships coming up. Sam nodded his head in apparent agreement, all the while thinking that although it might take most athletes four days or more to recover from this type of injury, he would be back at it in a couple of days at the most.

The next two days were the longest 48 hours of Sam's life. He found himself consumed with worry about how quickly he would lose his conditioning, when he would be able to return to training, whether he would be sufficiently prepared for the national championships, and how he would feel if he let down himself and his coach, family, and friends with a poor performance at the nationals. The worries interfered with his sleep and left him with an unsettled stomach that inhibited his appetite. No longer able to contain himself, and having decided that enough time had elapsed for his hamstring to have healed, Sam discreetly made his way to an unoccupied intramural-recreation field far away from the track-and-field facility and went for a brief jog with a few short sprints to "test" his hamstring. He felt fine at first, but his hamstring began to howl shortly thereafter, and he limped back to the locker room dejected and nearly in tears.

Thinking he was alone, Sam bemoaned his fate aloud, muttered an expletive, and slammed his locker door. Unbeknownst to Sam, his tirade was overheard by Erik, a free-spirited high jumper whom Sam respected for his dedicated, if unconventional, approach to sport. "You've got to chill, dude," said Erik, "and have a more positive attitude. You can still run nationals, but there's no way your body is going to heal with all that negative energy." Beaten down by his ordeal and desperate for a solution, Sam set aside his typical defensive response and wondered if Erik might be onto something. Were all of his worries and pessimistic thoughts about his injury and its potential consequences interfering with his recovery?

As shown in chapter 4, athletes exhibit a wide range of psychological responses to sport injury. Sam's question about whether these responses exert a causal influence on sport injury rehabilitation outcomes has intrigued the sport health care community for decades. The primary purposes of this chapter are to identify pathways by which psychological factors may affect the results of sport injury rehabilitation, review theoretical and empirical support for those pathways, and examine the concept of psychological readiness to return to sport. First, however, in order to clarify its focus, the chapter addresses the nature of sport injury rehabilitation outcomes.

Sport Injury Rehabilitation Outcomes

The emphasis on evidence-based practice (EBP) in sport health care has drawn attention to the end results of clinical practice (T.A. Evans & Lam, 2011). The empirical foundation on which EBP rests is provided by assessment of rehabilitation outcomes (Sackett, Rosenberg, Gray, Haynes, & Richardson, 1996). Although "recovery outcomes" were considered to be a unitary construct in early models of psychological response to sport injury (Gordon, 1986; Weiss & Troxel, 1986; Wiese & Weiss, 1987), a more complex, multidimensional conceptualization of treatment outcomes has emerged in light of evidence showing that common indexes of sport injury rehabilitation outcomes are only weakly related to

each other (Neeb, Aufdemkampe, Wagener, & Mastenbroek, 1997).

For the purposes of this chapter, the term *rehabilitation outcomes* refers to both the intermediate biopsychological outcomes (e.g., range of motion, strength, joint laxity, pain, endurance, rate of recovery) and the sport injury rehabilitation outcomes (e.g., functional performance, quality of life, treatment satisfaction, readiness to return to sport) depicted in figure 6.2. As acceptance of the concept of EBP has grown in the sport health care community, an early emphasis on clinician-rated outcomes has expanded to include and value patient-rated outcomes. Whereas the former typically focus on impairment (i.e., reduced physiological capacity) and are commonly assessed through clinical evaluations, the latter usually focus on disability (i.e., inability to perform functional tasks or fulfill societal roles) and are assessed by asking athletes how well they have achieved the desired outcomes (Jette, 1995).

Another way to classify sport injury rehabilitation outcomes corresponds with the three interrelated domains of functioning in which the outcomes reside: cognitive-affective (e.g., quality of life, reinjury anxiety, subjective symptom reports), behavioral (e.g., avoidance, bracing, functional performance, return to sport), and physical (e.g., bone healing, joint laxity, range of motion). Inevitably, this scheme overlaps heavily with the methods by which outcomes are assessed. More specifically, cognitive-affective outcomes are often assessed via self-report, behavioral outcomes are measured through observation, and physical outcomes are determined through indicators of physiological processes or anatomical structures. Although the scheme provides a logical, intuitive way to describe types of sport injury rehabilitation outcome, it has not been validated empirically; in addition, it clusters factors within a category that may be only weakly related to each other, and it does not account for outcomes such as pain, which may include elements of all three categories (i.e., cognition and affect, behavior, and physical stimulation). Despite these limitations, the scheme offers a means of introducing potential pathways through which psychological factors may influence sport injury rehabilitation outcomes.

Charting a Course From Psychological Factors to Sport Injury Rehabilitation Outcomes

The potential influence of psychological factors on sport injury rehabilitation outcomes has long been suspected and has become the subject of a growing body of scientific inquiry. Development of a theoretical rationale for *why* psychological factors might be expected to affect the results of sport injury rehabilitation has not kept pace with the proliferation of research on the topic. However, progress has been made in developing a theoretical basis for psychological influence on sport injury rehabilitation outcomes.

In a report on what may well have been the first investigation into the role of psychological factors in sport injury rehabilitation outcomes (Wise, Jackson, & Rocchio, 1979), no a priori explanation is provided for why personality (as measured by the Minnesota Multiphasic Personality Inventory) might predict subjective evaluations of symptoms and functioning after knee surgery other than to note that such a relationship was documented for people who had undergone back surgery. Less than a decade later, early models of psychological response to sport injury (Gordon, 1986; Weiss & Troxel, 1986; Wiese & Weiss, 1987) posited

that cognitive appraisals, emotional responses, and behavioral responses to injury affected recovery outcomes; these models did not specify the mechanisms of effect. Elaborations of these early models (Wiese-Bjornstal & Smith, 1993; Wiese-Bjornstal, Smith, & LaMott, 1995), however, suggested that the predicted effects of cognitions and emotions on sport injury rehabilitation outcomes were mediated by behaviors such as adhering to rehabilitation, using social support, taking risks, and expending effort in rehabilitation. In other words, these elaborations proposed that cognition and emotion influence athletes' behavioral responses to injury, which, in turn, contribute to rehabilitation outcomes.

The range of possible paths by which psychological factors could affect sport injury rehabilitation outcomes was expanded considerably by the biopsychosocial model (Brewer, Andersen, & Van Raalte, 2002). As shown in figure 6.2, psychological factors (i.e., personality, cognition, affect, and behavior) are thought to influence rehabilitation outcomes both directly and through their relations with biological and social-contextual factors, as well as other outcomes. These paths, along with the behavioral route specified in models of psychological response to sport injury (e.g., Wiese-Bjornstal & Smith, 1993; Wiese-Bjornstal et al., 1995), provide a preliminary basis for charting a course from psychological factors to sport injury rehabilitation outcomes.

Given the diverse array of potential psychological variables and rehabilitation outcomes involved, it is not surprising that multiple routes can be taken to reach the destination. A diagram mapping key pathways is presented in figure 7.1. The diagram does not account for the origins of the psychological factors (many of which are addressed in chapter 4) or the likelihood of a feedback loop in which, over time, the outcomes depicted exert an effect on psychological factors (which then exert further influence on outcomes). Instead, the diagram focuses on "west to east" travel from psychological factors to rehabilitation outcomes through four pathways, which are labeled A through D. The following sections of the chapter describe these pathways and summarize the available empirical support for each.

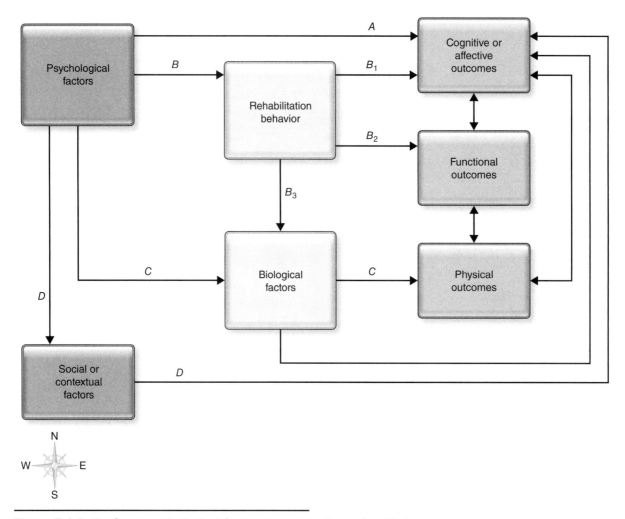

Figure 7.1 Paths from psychological factors to sport injury rehabilitation outcomes.

"The role of psychological factors in sport injury rehabilitation outcomes," B.W. Brewer, *International Review of Sport and Exercise Psychology*, 3, 40-61, 2010, Taylor and Francis, reprinted by permission of the publisher (Taylor & Francis Ltd, http://www.tandfonline.com)

Path A (the Northern Route)

The most direct route from psychological factors to sport injury rehabilitation outcomes is path A, in which psychological factors are thought to influence cognitive-affective outcomes. Of course, cognition and affect are themselves psychological factors, and a pathway leading from certain psychological factors to certain other psychological factors is not surprising; in fact, it would probably be more surprising if the Northern Route did *not* exist. Path A has a strong theoretical basis in that all of the many theories in which psychological factors are thought to influence thoughts or feelings are potentially applicable here. For example, the cogni-

tive appraisal process (Lazarus & Folkman, 1984), which is discussed in great detail in chapter 4, could explain how athletes' interpretations of their ability to cope with their injuries (a psychological factor) could affect their perceived well-being and quality of life (rehabilitation outcomes).

From an empirical standpoint, path A has the largest volume of research support of all of the pathways shown in figure 7.1. In a review of the literature, Brewer (2010) identified 12 (mostly retrospective or concurrent) correlational studies and 5 experimental studies that documented relations between a psychological factor and a cognitive-affective outcome (see this chapter's Focus on Research box for information on evaluat-

In Search of Psychological Cause and Effect in Sport Injury Rehabilitation

Strong evidence is required to back up a direct causal statement such as "psychological factors influence sport injury rehabilitation outcomes." Although they can be compelling, anecdotal reports of athletes who attribute their miraculous recoveries from injury to their "positive mental attitude" do not constitute the sort of evidence needed to infer a causal influence of psychological factors on rehabilitation outcomes. Similarly, causality cannot be inferred from retrospective or concurrent correlational studies in which psychological factors are measured after or at the same time as rehabilitation outcomes. More specifically, when using retrospective and concurrent correlational designs, it cannot be determined whether

- psychological factors caused the rehabilitation outcomes to occur,
- rehabilitation outcomes contributed to the occurrence of the psychological factors, or
- some other factor or factors affected both psychological factors and rehabilitation outcomes.

Even prospective studies, in which purported causes (i.e., psychological factors) are measured before their proposed effects (i.e., rehabilitation outcomes), do not permit causal inferences to be drawn when associations are found between psychological factors and subsequent rehabilitation outcomes. Consider, for example, a hypothetical study in which athletes demonstrating high levels of "recovery confidence" at the beginning of rehabilitation are shown to recover faster or better than their less confident peers. The favorable rehabilitation outcome achieved by athletes who were high in recovery confidence *might* be due to their confidence, but it might also be attributable to a potential source of their confidence, such as a history of rapid recovery from sport injury.

As in most scientific disciplines, the strongest evidence in support of the contention that psychological factors influence sport injury rehabilitation outcomes derives from experimental studies in which researchers manipulate psychological factors and measure the effects on rehabilitation outcomes. Unfortunately, relatively little experimental research has been conducted on the effects of psychological factors on sport injury rehabilitation outcomes. Unlike the quest to determine whether psychological factors contribute to the *occurrence* of sport injury, where ethical considerations restrict researchers' ability to engage in experimentation (see the Focus on Research box in chapter 2), the main factors limiting experimental investigation of psychological influences on sport injury *rehabilitation* outcomes appear to involve pragmatic concerns. For one thing, in order to ensure adequate statistical power and "apples to apples" comparisons across conditions, one needs large samples that are homogeneous with respect to injury type. In addition, in order to detect psychological influences on rehabilitation outcomes, one must examine injuries for which recovery is not fully explained by biological factors and regarding which there is room for psychological factors to play a role. Furthermore, in order to assess *change* in outcome parameters as a function of psychological manipulations, one must conduct multiple assessments of psychological factors and sport injury rehabilitation outcomes. Because injury rehabilitation is a process that unfolds over time, studies may extend for weeks, months, or even years.

These time-, labor-, and cost-intensive requirements of conducting experimental investigations may be more than most researchers are willing to tolerate. As a consequence, the experimental literature pertaining to the role of psychological factors in sport injury rehabilitation outcomes remains small. Therefore, we need a new cadre of dedicated, persistent investigators who will overcome the pragmatic barriers to conducting the required experimental research to further support the strong causal assertion that psychological factors influence sport injury rehabilitation outcomes.

Focus on Research

ing research support for associations between psychological factors and sport injury rehabilitation outcomes). Since that review, path A has gained support from 13 additional correlational studies representing at least nine different datasets (Chmielewski et al., 2008; Chmielewski et al., 2011; George, Lentz, Zeppieri, Lee, & Chmielewski, 2012; Lentz et al., 2009; Lu & Hsu, 2013; Parr et al., 2014; Podlog, Lochbaum, & Stevens, 2010; Prugh, Zeppieri, & George, 2012; Swirtun & Renström, 2008; Thomeé et al., 2007b; Thomeé et al.,

2008; Van Wilgen, Kaptein, & Brink, 2010; Wadey et al., 2014).

The most common cognitive-affective outcomes for which associations with psychological factors have been demonstrated are subjective ratings of physical symptoms and functioning. These outcomes are followed distantly by reports of pain, recovery rate, self-efficacy and self-confidence, and a smattering of variables reflecting how athletes think and feel about their physical and mental status (e.g., return-to-sport concerns, fear and anxiety, satisfaction, quality of life, well-being, vitality). One might assume that subjective ratings of physical symptoms and functioning belong, respectively, in the physical and behavioral outcomes categories of figure 7.1. However, the ratings are *subjective* and therefore reflect athletes' symptoms and functionality as filtered through their attention, emotions, memories, and motives; therefore, they are most appropriately considered as cognitive-affective outcomes. This argument gains further support from the weak correspondence between subjective and objective indexes of symptoms and functioning (Neeb et al., 1997).

The most common psychological factors for which associations with cognitive-affective outcomes have been documented are self-confidence and self-efficacy, attributions for recovery and health locus of control, coping, injury representations, personality, and self-reported use of imagery and goal setting. Thus, the preponderance of evidence supporting path A is correlational and involves associations between cognitive and affective variables both as psychological factors *and* as cognitive and affective outcomes. The strongest form of evidence—experimental support—has been obtained in the form of reductions of pain and (reinjury) anxiety and increases in performance satisfaction, rehabilitation attitude, readiness for physical activity, and self-efficacy when using psychological interventions such as stress inoculation training, goal setting, stress management, relaxation and guided imagery, and

modeling (Brewer, 2010; see chapter 8 for more details).

Path B (the Central, Behaviorally Mediated Routes)

In figure 7.1, path B includes a set of routes through the center of the diagram in which rehabilitation behavior mediates the relationship between psychological factors and sport injury rehabilitation outcomes. The initial portion of path B links psychological factors to rehabilitation behavior, at which point one branch leads to cognitive and affective outcomes, another leads to functional outcomes, and a third heads toward physical outcomes through its effect on biological factors. If these proposed relationships sound eerily familiar, that is because they were examined in depth in chapter 6, with adherence to sport injury rehabilitation programs corresponding to the rehabilitation behavior box in figure 7.1.

With respect to the first stage of the journey along path B, numerous psychological factors have been found to predict adherence to sport injury rehabilitation programs. As discussed in chapter 6, the psychological predictors of rehabilitation behavior can be grouped into the categories of personal, cognitive, emotional, and behavioral variables. The personal factors related to rehabilitation adherence include athletic identity, internal health locus of control, mental toughness, pain tolerance, self-motivation, and task involvement. These factors indicate a general disposition to behave in a particular way across situations. For example, athletes who are generally more self-motivated display a tendency to be more self-motivated in rehabilitation situations, and this tendency is reflected in higher levels of adherence to rehabilitation. As noted in chapter 6, the types of cognition found to predict rehabilitation behavior are predominantly positive, rehabilitation-related thoughts, beliefs, and images that express confidence, self-investment, and engagement in the rehabilitation program. They also reflect motivation to adhere and the perception that desired rehabilitation outcomes can be controlled and achieved. As for emotional and behavioral variables, athletes are more likely to adhere to rehabilitation when they are not experiencing mood disturbance (Alzate, Ramírez, & Artaza, 2004; Daly, Brewer, Van Raalte, Petitpas, & Sklar, 1995) and when they are engaging in instrumental coping by taking an active role in the process (Udry, 1997).

After reaching rehabilitation behavior, the journey proceeds along separate paths to each of the three types of sport injury rehabilitation outcome. Path B1, which goes from rehabilitation behavior to cognitive and affective outcomes, is supported by research in which adherence to rehabilitation was positively associated with subjective ratings of physical symptoms and functioning (Brewer, Cornelius, Van Raalte, Brickner, Sklar, et al., 2004; Pizzari, Taylor, McBurney, & Feller, 2005; Treacy, Barron, Brunet, & Barrack, 1997). Path B2 is a straight shot from rehabilitation behavior to functional outcomes because injury rehabilitation programs typically include components in which, over time and through training, athletes reacquire capabilities reflected in behavioral outcomes. Positive associations between adherence to sport injury rehabilitation and behavioral outcomes have been documented in several studies (Alzate et al., 2004; Brewer, Van Raalte, Cornelius et al., 2000; Derscheid & Feiring, 1987).

Path B3 travels from rehabilitation behavior to physical outcomes via biological factors. By adhering to sport injury rehabilitation programs—for example, completing exercises, partaking in therapeutic modalities, avoiding potentially hazardous activities, taking prescribed medication—athletes presumably effect changes in biological factors that, in turn, produce physical outcomes. The proposed mediation by biological factors of the relationship between rehabilitation adherence and physical outcomes has not been demonstrated in a research investigation, although an unexpected negative correlation has been reported between rehabilitation adherence and knee laxity (Brewer, Van Raalte, Cornelius et al., 2000).

Path C (the Mysterious, Biologically Mediated South-Central Route)

If path A is an express route from psychological factors to sport injury rehabilitation outcomes and path B is a less direct but still clearly delineated route, path C is where the map gets blurry. Definitive evidence in support of path C has not been obtained, but the path is widely assumed to exist because it provides an economical explanation for the beneficial effects of psychological interventions (e.g., imagery, relaxation; see chapter 8) on physical outcomes. The influence of psychological factors on biological factors has been demonstrated, and the influence of biological factors on physical outcomes has been documented, but actual mediation of the effects of psychological factors on physical outcomes by biological factors has not been shown. It is as if the trail from psychological factors to physical outcomes grows cold as it enters the impenetrable jungle of biological factors, then heats up again as it leaves the jungle on the final stretch of the journey.

One of the difficulties in picking up the trail lies in the fact that psychological factors and biological factors have been measured separately but not together in most research investigations examining physical outcomes. For example, in a prospective study of patients undergoing rehabilitation after ACL reconstruction surgery (Brewer, Van Raalte, Cornelius, et al., 2000), associations were reported between two psychological factors (athletic identity and psychological distress) and a physical outcome (knee laxity), but potential biological mediators of the associations were not assessed. Consequently, while the correlational research design did not permit causal inferences to be drawn about the relationship between psychological factors and physical outcomes, it was difficult even to speculate about which causal path(s), if any, the psychological factors *might* have followed to the physical outcome. The pattern of nonsignificant associations between the psychological factors and both rehabilitation adherence and subjective ratings of physical symptoms suggested that paths A and B were not viable and, possibly, that path C was involved. However, because no biological parameters were measured, no direct support was obtained, for example, for the inference that psychological distress contributed indirectly to knee laxity through its effect on biological factors.

In the absence of a clearly marked route, it is worth considering some of the means by which psychological factors may influence physical outcomes via path C. Referring to figure 6.2, it is apparent that numerous biological factors could conceivably mediate relations between psychological factors and physical outcomes. Based on the available research, however, the range of promising candidates can be narrowed by focusing the discussion on biological responses to stress-related and emotion-related psychological factors—for example, stress, depression, anxiety, and worry—each of which can exert adverse effects on healing via multiple pathways in the immune and neuroendocrine systems (for a review, see Christian, Graham, Padgett, Glaser, & Kiecolt-Glaser, 2006).

Inflammatory processes are of particular relevance to sport injury. As noted in chapter 1, interactions between various chemicals in the body initiate an inflammatory response during the first phase of recovery. One of those types of chemical, pro-inflammatory cytokines, plays a critical role by helping prevent infection, preparing injured tissue to be repaired, and recruiting phagocytes to the injured area (Lowry, 1993). The inflammatory-response phase involves psychological factors insofar as psychological (and physical) stress—which can be present in abundance following sport injury (Evans, Wadey, Hanton, & Mitchell, 2012)—can lead to the dysregulation of pro-inflammatory cytokines. Specifically, evidence shows that, in some cases, stressors can inhibit the production of pro-inflammatory cytokines, thereby compromising the first stage of the healing process (for a review, see Christian et al., 2006). In other cases, however, although inflammation is a necessary and desirable part of recovery, stress and negative emotions (e.g.,

depression, anxiety) can lead to *overproduction* of pro-inflammatory cytokines, thereby contributing to chronic inflammation and interfering with recovery (for a review, see Kiecolt-Glaser, McGuire, Robles, & Glaser, 2002).

Negative psychological states can impair healing in other ways as well. In the endocrine system, for example, stress, depression, and anxiety can produce increases of cortisol, a hormone associated with slow wound healing (Kiecolt-Glaser et al., 2002), as well as glucocorticoids, hormones that suppress the production of pro-inflammatory cytokines and impede wound repair (Christian et al., 2006). An unfavorable endocrine-mediated influence on healing can also be exerted by problems with sleep, which is a health behavior that is affected adversely by stress, depression, anxiety, and worry. Specifically, poor sleep habits can result in elevated cortisol levels, diminished production of pro-inflammatory cytokines, and decreased secretion of growth hormone—all of which may impede the healing process (Christian et al., 2006; Kiecolt-Glaser et al., 2002).

Lest one think that only negative psychological states promote travel along path C, some evidence shows that positive psychological states can contribute to the occurrence of biological events that facilitate healing. In particular, positive affect (PA) has been linked to favorable biological states for circumstances as diverse as a "tape-stripping" procedure in the forearms (Robles, Brooks, & Pressman, 2009), radiation treatment for cancer (Sepah & Bower, 2009), and a period of daily living in the community (Kok et al., 2013). In the first of these studies, participants completed a measure of trait positive affect (PA) and negative affect (NA) and underwent a "tape-stripping" procedure on their forearms under conditions of either stress or no stress. The study found that PA buffered the effects of stress on skin-barrier recovery. More specifically, recovery (i.e., healing) was significantly faster in the stress condition for people who were high in PA than for those who were low in PA, whereas no difference was found in recovery of the two groups in the no-stress condition. The buffering effect was attributed to the possible influence of PA on various immune and inflammatory processes in the skin (Robles et al., 2009).

Positive emotions may also play a role in adaptive immune responses to radiation treatment for cancer. In a study in which people completed a measure of PA before undergoing radiation treatment for breast cancer or prostate cancer (Sepah & Bower, 2009), individuals who were high in PA showed significantly higher levels of the pro-inflammatory cytokines IL-1 beta and IL-6 during treatment than did those with low levels of pretreatment PA. Causation cannot be inferred from the correlational research design, but, as with the skin-barrier findings, the results are consistent with an interpretation of PA exerting a facilitative effect on inflammatory and tissue-repair processes.

Additional support for the potentially beneficial effects of positive emotions on healing was obtained in a field experiment in which half of the participants were instructed to self-generate positive emotions through a meditation procedure and the other half received no such instructions. Participants in the positive-emotions group had significantly higher cardiac vagal tone at the conclusion of the monitoring period (Kok et al., 2013). Vagal tone is a key aspect of the parasympathetic nervous system and is inversely related to inflammation (Thayer & Sternberg, 2006). The effect of positive emotions on vagal tone was mediated by perceptions of positive social connections with others. In other words, the meditation procedure induced positive emotions that led to greater perceived social connections and ultimately resulted in elevated vagal tone (Kok et al., 2013). On the surface, vagal tone, like skin-barrier recovery and immune responses to radiation treatment, may seem to have little relevance to sport injury. However, the inflammatory and tissue-repair processes involved in these instances are essentially similar to those at work in healing sport injuries. For that reason, they merit inclusion in a discussion of the influence of psychological factors on sport injury rehabilitation outcomes.

Path D (the Unexplored Southern Route)

Just as the famous Southern shipping routes around the Cape of Good Hope and Cape Horn were at one time uncharted and unexplored, little is known about the path at the bottom of figure 7.1. This route, labeled path D, is identified in the biopsychosocial model as a potential route from psychological factors to cognitive and affective outcomes via social-contextual factors (see figure 6.2). In path D, athletes effect changes in the social or physical environment; in turn, these changes affect how athletes think and feel about their injury situation.

A plausible example of how travel along path D might proceed involves athletes enlisting (or neglecting to enlist) social support and having that support (or lack thereof) influence their cognitive and affective outcomes. Although social support is relevant across the full spectrum of topics in the psychology of sport injury—antecedents of sport injury, injury prevention, psychological consequences of sport injury, pain and sport injury, and adherence to sport injury prevention and rehabilitation programs—the first leg of the journey, from psychological factors to social support, is the least charted portion of the route. Beyond several investigations of athletes' intentions to seek support in association with injury-related concerns (e.g., Hoar & Flint, 2008; Nixon, 1994b; Stadden & Gill, 2008), little is known about the process by which athletes obtain support from others. For the most part, researchers have yet to answer most questions about what athletes with injuries do (both intentionally and unintentionally) to attract support from others and about the efficacy of various help-seeking strategies.

In contrast to the speculative nature of the initial portion of travel along path D, the next leg of the journey is more clearly delineated and better supported empirically in the context of sport injury rehabilitation. Continuing with the example of social support as the social-contextual factor in question, there is reason to believe that the presence or absence of social support can affect cognitive-affective outcomes. As noted in chapter 4, athletes with injury who report low levels of (or low satisfaction with) social support are more likely to report low levels of emotional adjustment to sport injury (Brewer, Linder, & Phelps, 1995; S.L. Green & Weinberg, 2001; Malinauskas, 2010; Manuel et al., 2002; Rees, Mitchell, Evans, & Hardy, 2010). If emotional adjustment is considered a cognitive-affective outcome, then the route from psychological factors through social-contextual factors to cognitive-affective outcomes is viable.

The social support variables used in the studies cited in chapter 4 were all measured with questionnaires addressing athletes' *perceptions* of social support rather than more objective assessments of activity in the social environment. Consequently, what is viewed in this example as travel from social-contextual factors to cognitive and affective outcomes may simply be yet another illustration of a psychological variable (i.e., perceptions of social support) predicting a cognitive-affective outcome. As with the Cape shipping routes discovered centuries ago, extensive exploration is needed in order to affirm the existence, and develop a description, of path D.

Inter-Outcome Associations

The relationships between various sport injury rehabilitation outcomes are weak enough to dispel the notion that outcome is a unitary construct (Neeb et al., 1997); nevertheless, associations do exist between cognitive-affective, behavioral, and physical outcomes that indicate the possibility of additional psychological influences on rehabilitation outcomes. In keeping with the nautical theme of the previous section, the inter-outcome associations depicted in figure 7.1 resemble the reciprocal influences that proximally located island cultures can exert on each other.

The most abundant source of evidence of inter-outcome associations is provided by research on factors associated with returning to sport after ACL reconstruction. Both literature reviews (e.g., Bauer, Feeley, Wawrzyniak, Pinkowsky, & Gallo, 2014; Czuppon, Racette,

Klein, & Harris-Hayes, 2014; te Wierike, van der Sluis, van den Akker-Scheek, Elferink-Gemser, & Visscher, 2013) and a steady stream of subsequent investigations (e.g., Ardern, Taylor, Feller, Whitehead, &Webster, 2015; Gignac et al., 2015; Lentz et al., 2015) have documented relationships between cognitive-affective outcomes (particularly fear of reinjury, or kinesiophobia) and behavioral (i.e., return-to-sport) outcomes. It is not possible to discern causality with respect to the inter-outcome associations because of the research designs used in the studies, but plausible arguments can be advanced to explain how psychological factors could exert an ongoing influence on outcomes throughout rehabilitation. For example, certain physical sensations could prompt athletes to experience fear of reinjury that prevents them from returning to sport at their previous level of performance.

Psychological Readiness to Return to Sport

Sport injury rehabilitation outcomes are not all valued equally. Of course, for most athletes and coaches, one outcome stands above all others: return to sport. According to a sample of elite athletes, a successful return to sport (and, effectively, an end to rehabilitation) occurs when athletes return to their preinjury performance levels, achieve preinjury goals, stay on their preinjury path of performance, possess realistic expectations for their postinjury performance, and remain free of injury (Podlog & Eklund, 2009). Before attaining these aspirations, however, athletes are commonly required to demonstrate a state of readiness for return as recognized by a sport health care professional in the form of a "clearance" that permits resumption of sport activity. Determining readiness to return to sport can be as simple as deciding whether an athlete is physically able to play (Clover & Wall, 2010) or as complex as weighing multiple competing—and possibly conflicting—factors that bear on the decision (Creighton, Shrier, Shultz, Meeuwisse, & Matheson, 2010; Herring et al., 2002).

To help guide sport health care professionals through the process of deciding about an athlete's return to sport, Creighton et al. (2010) developed a three-step model that involves the following considerations:

1. Athlete's health status

2. Risks associated with sport participation

3. Situational factors that may modify the return-to-sport decision

In assessing an athlete's health status, a justifiable emphasis is placed on physical parameters. The medical factors evaluated in this first step include the athlete's demographic characteristics (e.g., age, sex), physical symptoms, medical history, physical signs (revealed through examination), laboratory test data, functional test data, injury seriousness, and, of particular relevance to the current chapter, psychological state. Although no definitive criteria or absolute standards exist for judging physical readiness to return to sport, general guidelines suggest that an athlete can be allowed to return when she or he is

- at or near preinjury levels, or symmetrical with the uninjured side, in muscular strength, joint range of motion, proprioception, endurance, and sport-specific functional performance; and

- free of pain, tenderness, swelling, inflammation, effusion, joint instability, and kinematic abnormality.

In the second step of the model, the health status of athletes is considered in light of their likely exposure to risk during sport participation. Factors taken into account in evaluating this degree of risk include the type of sport (e.g., collision, contact, noncontact), influence of limb dominance on typical sport activities, sport position played, level of competition, and ability to protect the injured part of the body. The model's third step, the return-to-sport decision, can be modified by situational factors, such as the portion of the sport season (e.g., playoffs), pressure from athletes or other individuals (e.g., coaches, administrators), the athlete's ability to mask symptoms, con-

flicts of interest for sport health care professionals (e.g., conflicting obligations to athlete and employer), and fear of litigation (due, for example, to premature clearance or prolonged restriction). Inclusion of these potential decision modifiers highlights the fact that return-to-sport decisions involve consideration of both the risks *and* the benefits of returning to sport; in this way, the model reflects the real-world context in which such decisions are made (Creighton et al., 2010). Even with a model to guide their return-to-sport decision making, sport health care professionals vary widely in how they weight the potential modifiers (Shultz et al., 2013).

Although "psychological state" is included in the model as a medical factor to be considered in assessing the health status of athletes with injury, Creighton et al. (2010) provided no information about what psychological state would preclude a return to sport. Similarly, in a consensus statement on return-to-sport issues ("The team physician," 2012), a panel of experts from six major sports medicine organizations identified "psychosocial readiness" as one of eight essential criteria for clearing athletes to return to sport but did not define the concept. This lack of definitional clarity regarding psychological readiness raises important questions: What does it mean to be psychologically ready to return to sport, and what happens when an athlete returns to sport without being psychologically ready to do so? Preliminary answers to these questions can be developed by examining the proposed characteristics of psychological readiness and the consequences of a lack of such readiness.

Characteristics

Despite growing interest in the topic from athletes, coaches, sport health care professionals, and sport psychology researchers, no widely accepted definition exists of psychological readiness to return to sport. In general, however, athletes can be considered psychologically ready when they possess (or have access to) psychological resources that facilitate a safe, productive, and enjoyable return to sport—and are free of psychological attributes or states that impede such a return. Among the main prospective characteristics of psychological readiness identified in a literature review (Ardern, Taylor, Feller, & Webster, 2013), one is the absence (or only low levels) of potential impediments (fear and anxiety) and two are potential facilitating resources (confidence and motivation).

Absence or Low Levels of Fear and Anxiety

Fear and anxiety are ubiquitous following sport injury. As discussed in chapter 4, they are common short-term responses to sport injury; they are also salient among athletes who are completing rehabilitation and making the transition back into sport involvement, particularly those with ACL tears and other severe injuries (Carson & Polman, 2012; Heijne, Axelsson, Werner, & Biguet, 2008; Kvist, Ek, Sporrstedt, & Good, 2005; Podlog, Dimmock, & Miller, 2011; Podlog & Eklund, 2006). During the return to sport, the main source of fear and anxiety is concern about reinjury (Podlog et al., 2011; Podlog & Eklund, 2006; N. Walker, Thatcher, & Lavallee, 2010), but concerns about performance and appearance may also be apparent (Podlog et al., 2011; Podlog & Eklund, 2006). The primary evidence supporting the contention that fear and anxiety indicate a lack of psychological readiness to return to sport lies in the fact that among athletes who have completed rehabilitation following ACL surgery, fear of reinjury is one of the most commonly cited reasons that they have not returned to sport, either at all (Ardern, Webster, Taylor, & Feller, 2011) or at their preinjury level (Ardern, Taylor, Feller, & Webster, 2012; Flanigan, Everhart, Pedroza, Smith, & Kaeding, 2013; McCullough et al., 2012). No information is available, however, regarding *how much* fear or anxiety is needed in order to render an athlete not psychologically ready to return to sport.

Confidence and Self-Efficacy

One key task of sport injury rehabilitation is that of regaining confidence—in the injured body part, in one's ability to perform physically, and in one's ability to avoid reinjury (Carson & Polman, 2012). Unsurprisingly, confi-

dence and the related construct of self-efficacy tend to increase over the course of rehabilitation (Chmielewski et al., 2011; Thomeé et al., 2007a). Moreover, they are inversely related to fear of sport injury occurrence (Cartoni, Minganti, & Zelli, 2005; Reuter & Short, 2005), which suggests that athletes' confidence and self-esteem rise as their fears of reinjury abate and vice versa. Given the consistent pattern of positive associations between confidence and self-efficacy and cognitive-affective outcomes (path A in figure 7.1), rehabilitation behavior (path B in figure 7.1), and behavioral outcomes (Thomeé et al., 2008), it is logical to consider confidence and self-efficacy as possible characteristics of psychological readiness to return to sport. As with fear and anxiety, however, research has yet to determine the levels of confidence and self-efficacy required for psychological readiness.

Motivation

Without a sufficient amount, or intensity, of motivation, athletes recovering from injury may simply elect not to return to sport, but amount (intensity) is not the only aspect of motivation to confer readiness on athletes. Readiness to return may also be affected by the type of motivation experienced by an athlete. In particular, intrinsic, self-determined motivation may be especially indicative of psychological readiness to return to sport following injury. In an extensive series of studies of athletes with injury, coaches, and parents of young athletes with injury, Podlog and colleagues obtained consistent evidence that the concerns expressed by athletes who are returning to sport after injury suggest that their basic needs for competence, relatedness, and autonomy are not being met (e.g., Podlog & Dionigi, 2010; Podlog & Eklund, 2005, 2006, 2010; Podlog et al., 2010; Podlog, Kleinert, Dimmock, Miller, & Shipherd, 2012).

During a return to sport, athletes may encounter numerous circumstances in which their attempts to meet these basic needs are thwarted. For example, competence issues may surface when athletes worry about living up to personal performance standards, experiencing reinjury, or appearing unfit. Relatedness issues may include concerns about letting coaches and teammates down, as well as feelings of isolation from coaches and teammates. Autonomy issues may include feeling pressured by others to return to sport and succumbing to the sport ethic by attempting to play through pain (Podlog & Eklund, 2007). When basic needs are not satisfied, self-determination theory (R.M. Ryan & Deci, 2000) posits that motivation becomes less intrinsic and self-determined and may, as a result, exert an adverse effect on emotional responses (Podlog & Eklund, 2010; Podlog et al., 2011). Research has yet to identify levels of need satisfaction below which psychological readiness is compromised.

Consequences

When athletes return to sport before they are *physically* ready to do so, they run an increased risk of reinjury. What are the risks to athletes when they return to sport before they are *psychologically* ready? What consequences might they encounter? In keeping with the definition of psychological readiness to return to sport as a state that facilitates (and does not impede) "a safe, productive, and enjoyable return to sport," making a return when one is not psychologically ready to do so could adversely affect one's safety, productivity, and enjoyment in sport. With respect to safety, reinjury (or a new injury to another body part) is distinctly possible to the extent that a lack of psychological readiness overlaps with the psychological vulnerability to injury outlined in chapter 2. Areas of overlap between lack of readiness and injury vulnerability include anxiety, fear of reinjury, and perceived lack of social support (i.e., lack of relatedness), which could contribute to (re)injury in athletes who resume sport participation after injury.

In terms of productivity, athletes who return to sport when they are not psychologically ready to do so could experience sport performance problems as a result. Although a degree of performance rust is expected of athletes returning to sport after injury rehabilitation, pro-

nounced performance decrements may occur when athletes don't have their "head in the game." In this vein, the fear, anxiety, low confidence, and low motivation that presumably characterize a lack of psychological readiness may be accompanied by features that compromise sport performance, such as tentativeness, restraint, distraction, and lack of preparation.

With respect to enjoyment, resuming sport participation before being psychologically ready to do so may reduce the pleasure that an athlete derives from sport involvement. For example, a lack of psychological readiness may be characterized by unpleasant states—such as fear, anxiety, lack of confidence, and extrinsic motivation—that may dampen athletes' enthusiasm for sport and even threaten their continued participation.

Given these potential effects of a lack of psychological readiness, it is imperative to identify when athletes are not psychologically ready to return to sport. Therefore, the assessment of psychological readiness is covered in this chapter's Focus on Application box.

Biopsychosocial Analysis

The end results of sport injury rehabilitation are marked by cognitive-affective, behavioral, and physical outcomes. In the case presented at the beginning of the chapter, Sam exhibits concern primarily about a behavioral outcome (performance in the national championships), but other concerns are also salient—specifically, concerns about cognitive-affective outcome (perceived pain) and physical outcome (muscle healing). Although Erik's suggestion that Sam's "negative energy" is getting in the way of his recovery cannot be verified, there is merit in Sam's resulting question about whether his worries and pessimistic thoughts are interfering with his healing. Given the interrelationships between the various types of sport injury rehabilitation outcome proposed in figure 7.1, Sam's thoughts could affect his recovery in multiple ways. Specifically, his worries and pessimism could influence the healing of his hamstring through their effects on

Assessing Psychological Readiness to Return to Sport After Injury

To help determine an athlete's *physical* readiness to return to sport, sport health care professionals can use a variety of clinical tools, tests, and procedures. For example, goniometers can be used to measure joint range of motion, and hop tests can be used to gauge functional ability. Options are considerably more limited, however, for assessing an athlete's *psychological* readiness to return to sport. Lack of an established definition of the concept notwithstanding, sport health care professionals are restricted to behavioral observation and self-reports as ways to obtain information about an athlete's psychological readiness. Furthermore, both approaches have drawbacks. Let's consider each one in more detail.

Behavioral observation involves watching an athlete engage in rehabilitation and sport tasks in order to detect any overt sign that he or she is not psychologically ready to return to sport. Although this approach is not yet empirically validated, when fully realized it will involve identifying behavioral manifestations of a lack of readiness that increase the likelihood of negative consequences. Logical targets for observation include behaviors reflective of fear and anxiety (e.g., bracing or hesitating when performing sport-related movements), lack of confidence (e.g., playing tentatively, going at half-speed in drills), and lack of self-determined motivation (e.g., failing to attend rehabilitation or training sessions, talking about feeling pressured to return to sport too quickly). Aside from the lack of empirical validation, the primary limitations of using behavioral observation to assess psychological readiness include the fact that athletes may modify their behavior when they know they are being watched (i.e., reactance may occur) and that some aspects of psychological readiness are not readily observable.

The most direct approach to assessing psychological readiness to return to sport is simply to ask athletes about their state of mind, both before and while the athletes resume sport participation. The rationale for using self-report is that the athletes are in the best position to identify their own thoughts and feelings about returning to sport. For example, athletes can describe their levels of fear, anxiety, confidence, and motivation during the transition back into sport.

As shown in table 7.1, several self-report questionnaires have been developed to assess characteristics of psychological readiness to return to sport. Preliminary research suggests that self-report instruments may have utility in helping identify athletes who are not psychologically ready. For example, low scores on the ACL Return to Sport after Injury (ACL-RSI) scale (Webster, Feller, & Lambros, 2008) in the first 4 to 6 months after ACL reconstruction surgery are associated with a decreased likelihood of having returned to sport at 12 months after surgery (Ardern, Taylor, Feller, Whitehead, & Webster, 2013; Langford, Webster, & Feller, 2009). However, self-report questionnaires for assessing aspects of psychological readiness have not been validated to an extent that enables determination of cutoff scores corresponding to high, moderate, and low levels of readiness. Nor have rates been ascertained for false positives (i.e., concluding that an athlete is psychologically ready when he or she actually is not) or false negatives (i.e., concluding that an athlete is not psychologically ready when she or he actually is).

Beyond the evolving state of the psychometric development of self-report measures of psychological readiness, the chief limitation of self-report methods of assessment in this context involves the fact that athletes may be less than completely truthful in their responses. Indeed, in some respects, using self-report to assess psychological readiness is like asking the fox to guard the proverbial henhouse. Athletes seeking a rapid return to sport may not accurately share

cognitive-affective outcomes (path A), rehabilitation behavior (path B), biological factors (path C), and social-contextual factors (path D). Sam's travel along path B is especially apparent, as his concerns have led him to prematurely try fast running and thus aggravate his hamstring condition. By virtue of his interactions with Erik, Sam has also taken path D. Specifically, Sam's overt distress prompted Erik to give him some advice, which, in turn, led Sam to contemplate adopting a new perspective on his rehabilitation. This reconsideration may alter his behavior and, ultimately, his physical recovery.

TABLE 7.1 Self-Report Measures of Psychological Readiness to Return to Sport After Injury

Measure	Readiness characteristics assessed
ACL Return to Sport after Injury (ACL-RSI) scale (Webster et al., 2008)	Fear, anxiety, confidence, risk appraisal
Attention Questionnaire of Rehabilitated Athletes Returning to Competition (AQ-RARC; Christakou, Zervas, Psychountaki, & Stavrou, 2012)	Functional attention and distraction when returning to sport competition following musculoskeletal injury
Causes of Re-Injury Worry Questionnaire (CR-IWQ; Christakou, Zervas, Stavrou, & Psychountaki, 2011)	Reinjury worries due to rehabilitation and opponent ability
Composite Return from Injury to Sport Scale (CRISS; Ankney, Jauhar, Schrank, & Shapiro, 2012)	Confidence, achievement, support, rehabilitation experience
Injury-Psychological Readiness to Return to Sport (I-PRRS) scale (Glazer, 2009)	Confidence
Need Satisfaction Scale (Gagné, Ryan, & Bargmann, 2003; adapted by Podlog et al., 2010)	Satisfaction of basic psychological needs (required for self-determined motivation)
Re-Injury Anxiety Inventory (RIAI; N. Walker et al., 2010)	Rehabilitation anxiety, return-to-competition anxiety
Sport Injury Trait Anxiety Scale (SITAS; Kleinert, 2002)	Concerns about injury
Tampa Scale of Kinesiophobia (TSK; Miller, Kori, & Todd, 1991)	Fear of movement

their thoughts and feelings due to fear of having their return delayed. Therefore, if questionnaires are to be used to assess psychological readiness, they may need to be less transparent than the current crop of available measures. For example, tests of implicit cognition (Greenwald, McGhee, & Schwartz, 1998) offer a potential avenue for measuring psychological readiness in a way that avoids some of the limitations of self-report. However, until such tests are available in the context of sport injury rehabilitation—and validated protocols have been developed for evaluating psychological readiness—it behooves sport health care professionals to form impressions of athletes' psychological readiness by observing their behavior, talking with them candidly about their state of mind regarding the prospect of returning to sport, and consulting any additional pertinent information that is available (e.g., coach reports, questionnaire responses).

Just as Sam is not physically ready to return to sport participation, he also appears not to be psychologically ready. He does not have a problem with fear of reinjury, but he does lack confidence in his hamstring and in his ability to perform physically; his self-determined motivation may also be compromised. Being sidelined by injury clearly thwarts Sam's need for competence, and his worries about letting others down may be getting in the way of satisfying his need for relatedness. Although Sam may become more psychologically ready to return to sport as his physical condition improves, it cannot be taken for granted that his performance-related concerns will dissipate, that his confidence will return, or that his self-determined motivation will be restored in time for the national championships.

Summary

In accordance with the emphasis placed on evidence-based practice in sport health care, increased attention has been paid to assessment of sport injury rehabilitation outcomes. Three general types of outcome can be examined: cognitive-affective, behavioral, and physical. It has long been assumed that psychological factors influence sport injury rehabilitation outcomes, but the emergence of a body of empirical evidence to support this assumption is a relatively recent development. Because most of the evidence is correlational, conclusions about causation remain largely tentative. Nevertheless, consistent with the biopsychosocial model, at least four pathways have been identified by which psychological factors could affect sport injury rehabilitation outcomes.

The most direct (and most empirically supported) route from psychological factors to sport injury rehabilitation outcomes is a path where factors such as self-confidence, self-efficacy, attributions for recovery, health locus of control, coping, injury representations, personality, and self-reported use of imagery and goal setting are related to cognitive-affective outcomes such as pain, recovery rate, and subjective ratings of physical symptoms or functioning. Another proposed pathway focuses on rehabilitation behavior (e.g., adherence) as a mediator of the relationship between psychological factors (e.g., self-efficacy, self-motivation) and sport injury rehabilitation outcomes. The third potential route, which is less direct than the first two and has little definitive empirical support, features biological mediators (e.g., cortisol production, inflammation) of the relationship between psychological factors (e.g., stress, negative emotions) and sport

injury rehabilitation outcomes (particularly physical outcomes, such as wound healing). A fourth pathway involves the proposed influence of social-contextual factors (e.g., social support) on cognitive-affective outcomes such as emotional adjustment.

Of the various rehabilitation outcomes, returning to sport participation is the one valued most highly by athletes and coaches. Although no universal criteria exist by which sport health care professionals can deem athletes ready to return to sport, athletes are generally given permission to resume sport participation when their strength, range of motion, proprioception, endurance, and functional sport performance levels approximate those achieved prior to injury (or by the uninjured side of the body) *and* when the athletes are free of symptoms such as pain, tenderness, swelling, inflammation, effusion, joint instability, and kinematic abnormality. In addition to the medical status of athletes, the process of judging athletes' readiness to return to sport may also consider factors such as likely exposure to risk upon returning to sport (which can be affected by the type of sport, sport position, level of competition, and use of protective gear) and situational influences (e.g., stage of the sport season, pressure from coaches or teammates, professional conflicts of interest, fear of litigation).

Although psychological readiness to return to sport is considered important, no consensus exists regarding how to define (or measure) the concept. Proposed characteristics of psychological readiness include absence (or low levels) of fear and anxiety (about reinjury, performance, and appearance), high levels of confidence (in the injured body part, in one's ability to perform physically, and in one's ability to avoid reinjury), and high levels of motivation (to return to sport of one's own accord). Consequences of returning to sport when not psychologically ready may include reinjury, poor sport performance, and lack of enjoyment.

Discussion Questions

1. What are some examples of cognitive-affective, behavioral, and physical outcomes of sport injury rehabilitation?

2. What pathways have been proposed to explain how psychological factors affect sport injury rehabilitation outcomes?

3. What factors are thought to indicate psychological readiness to return to sport after injury?

4. Based on what is currently known about the role of psychological factors in relation to sport injury rehabilitation outcomes, what are some logical targets of psychological intervention?

Chapter 8

Psychological Interventions in Sport Health Care

Chapter Objectives

1. To identify, describe, and discuss empirical support for psychological interventions in postinjury sport health care
2. To consider issues involved in decisions about who should implement psychological interventions with athletes with injury

It was just a broken leg, for goodness' sake! There was no alphabet soup of ligament damage: ACL, MCL, PCL, LCL. Why, then, was this rehabilitation taking so long? Kyle shared his frustrations with his sport psychology consultant, who, true to form, answered Kyle's question with another question. After listening to Kyle vent his pent-up feelings, the consultant suggested that Kyle try using imagery to boost his motivation and his spirits while progressing through the darkest days of rehabilitation. "You mean the same kind of imagery I used to do to get ready for my matches?" asked Kyle. "Exactly," responded the consultant, who then worked with Kyle to generate a set of visual, auditory, kinesthetic, olfactory, gustatory, and tactile images that Kyle could re-create in his mind to augment his rehabilitation and, he hoped, accelerate his recovery.

Marzuki's athletic trainer, Paula, explained that his tight hamstrings could be a factor in most of his lower-leg injuries and that, although dynamic stretching was currently in favor, he could benefit from a regular, brief regimen of static hamstring stretching. Marzuki was not completely convinced. He said that he had been trying to improve the flexibility of his hamstrings but had made little progress. Paula asked Marzuki to show her how he did his static hamstring stretches. Marzuki obliged, exclaiming, "You see, I get to about here . . . and then I can't go any farther." "Ah, but you can, my friend," assured Paula. "Next time, when you get to that brick wall, ease off on the stretch a bit for a few seconds, take a deep diaphragmatic breath—not up here in your chest, but down here in your belly. Then reapply pressure on the stretch as you exhale and you'll find yourself going a little farther than you did before."

In both of these case examples, a sport health care professional implemented a psychological intervention. Kyle received help with using imagery during rehabilitation of his broken leg, and Marzuki received help with relaxation during static hamstring stretching. Do these sorts of treatment actually work? Can psychological interventions help athletes recover from injury? There is ample reason to say that the answer is yes, based both on empirical findings and on theoretical models that address the relationship between psychological factors and sport injury rehabilitation outcomes (as presented in chapter 7). The primary purposes of this chapter are to identify, describe, and discuss the empirical support for psychological interventions in sport health care. Because interventions designed to decrease sport injury occurrence are addressed in detail in chapter 3, this current chapter focuses mainly on treatments applied *after* injury.

Psychological Interventions

As shown in table 8.1, numerous psychological interventions have been used to treat athletes with injury. The interventions have tar-

TABLE 8.1   Psychological Interventions in Sport Health Care

Intervention	Common targets	Potential pathways	Experimental support*
Biofeedback	Muscle activity, muscle strength, range of motion	Paths B, B2, B3, C	Yes
Counseling	Coping with injury	Paths A, B1, B2	No
Expressive writing	Emotional and physical health	Paths A, C	No
Goal setting	Lifestyle behavior, rehabilitation behavior, sport performance	Paths A, B, B1, B2, B3	Yes
Imagery	Confidence, healing, pain, rehabilitation activities, sport performance	Paths A, B, C	Yes
Modeling	Anxiety, confidence, distress, knowledge, motivation, rehabilitation behavior	Paths A, B, C	Yes
Multimodal interventions	Anxiety, confidence, healing, pain, rehabilitation adherence, rehabilitation attitude, self-efficacy	Paths A, B, C, D	Yes
Performance enhancement groups	Anxiety, emotional responses, knowledge, recovery rate, social support, stress	Paths A, B, C, D	No
Relaxation training	Anxiety, mood, muscle tension, pain, personal control, stress	Paths A, C	No
Self-talk	Behavior, cognition, emotion, motivation, physiological responses	Paths A, B, C, D	Yes
Social support	Confidence, emotional responses, motivation, practical tasks	Paths A, B, C, D	No

*This column refers to comparisons with a control or placebo condition in the context of sport injury rehabilitation.

Dealing With Expectations in Postinjury Psychological Intervention Studies

As discussed in the Focus on Research box in chapter 3, randomized controlled trials (RCTs) constitute the gold standard for evaluating investigations into the efficacy and effectiveness of interventions designed to *prevent* sport injury occurrence. They also set the standard for studies assessing the effects of psychological interventions on sport injury *rehabilitation* outcomes. Before concluding that a particular psychological intervention is efficacious or effective in facilitating a given rehabilitation outcome, researchers must rule out alternative explanations for the observed effects. For example, athletes may report experiencing less pain or less functional impairment after receiving a psychological intervention not because of any properties inherent in the intervention but because they *expect* to improve as a result of the treatment. This influence exerted by expectations is known, of course, as the *placebo effect*. To control for such effects, RCTs involving pharmaceutical interventions give some patients an inert substance instead of the experimental drug under study.

Although the use of placebo conditions is standard practice in studies evaluating the effects of oral medications on health outcomes, they have rarely been included in studies of psychological interventions for sport injury rehabilitation outcomes. In an exception to this prevailing trend in the literature, researchers devised a placebo condition to control for the nonspecific effects of psychological treatments (e.g., hope, expectations of healing, social support). As compared with participants who received the primary psychological intervention of interest—relaxation exercises and guided imagery—participants in the placebo condition had the same amounts of time designated for out-of-clinic rehabilitation activities and structured, face-to-face contact with the professional who delivered the intervention (Cupal & Brewer, 2001).

In contrast with the therapeutic effects of placebo, expectations can sometimes elicit harmful responses. Such adverse consequences are known as the *nocebo effect*, which, fortunately, appears not to have been documented in association with psychological interventions used in sport injury rehabilitation. In a research study, evidence of nocebo would be provided to the extent that a placebo condition produced deleterious effects. Although the benign nature of most psychological interventions makes the nocebo effect an unlikely occurrence in the context of sport injury rehabilitation, we must remain cognizant of the possibility that a given psychological intervention could be harmful to a given athlete.

geted a variety of cognitions, emotions, and behaviors that correspond closely to the pathways outlined in chapter 7 (and depicted in figure 7.1) through which psychological factors might affect sport injury rehabilitation outcomes. Relatively few (i.e., slightly more than half) of these interventions, however, have received experimental support, and fewer still have been compared with placebo conditions (for more on placebos, see this chapter's Focus on Research box). Nevertheless, research is providing a growing evidentiary basis for implementing psychological interventions in sport health care. Due to the substantial overlap among the various interventions' methods, goals, and levels of empirical support, the table presents the interventions in alphabetical order.

Biofeedback

In biofeedback, people receive information about one or more of their bodily processes. This technique is arguably the first psychological intervention to be applied and evaluated systematically in the context of sport health care. The particular type used most frequently in sport injury rehabilitation has been electromyographic (EMG) biofeedback, particularly as a component of both conservative and postoperative treatments for knee conditions (Brewer, 2010; Silkman & McKeon, 2010). In EMG biofeedback, athletes receive information about electrical activity in muscles on which electrodes are placed (e.g., quadriceps for knee rehabilitation) and use this information to enhance their participation in behaviors designed to increase the strength of those muscles (e.g., therapeutic exercises).

Although controlled experimental research has not been uniformly supportive of the efficacy of biofeedback, it has documented the beneficial effects of EMG biofeedback on both behavioral outcomes (e.g., strength, range of motion) and physical outcomes (e.g., EMG activity, recovery time) (Brewer, 2010; Silkman & McKeon, 2010). The research findings suggest that—in terms of the pathways shown in figure 7.1—it is likely that the flow of effects from psychological intervention to rehabilitation outcomes progresses along paths B, B2, B3, and C. Along with EMG biofeedback, some other forms—which provide information about activity in the brain (electroencephalographic [EEG] biofeedback), heart (electrocardiographic [ECG] biofeedback), and skin (electrodermographic [EDG] biofeedback)—can also be useful in managing stress and anxiety (Schafer, 1996), presumably by traveling down path A to cognitive-affective outcomes. These techniques, however, have not been evaluated in the specific context of sport injury rehabilitation.

Counseling

As defined by Shertzer and Stone (1966), counseling is "an interaction process which facilitates meaningful understanding of self and environment and results in the establishment and/or clarification of goals and values for future behavior" (p. 26). In the context of sport injury, the purpose of counseling is to help athletes identify and develop resources for coping with their injuries. Counseling athletes with injury most likely follows paths A, B1, and B2, and it generally involves the following elements:

- Building rapport and developing a working alliance with athletes

- Ensuring that athletes have accurate information about their injuries, treatments (and any side effects), and rehabilitation aims

- Collaborating with athletes to identify their existing coping resources and develop new ones

- Helping athletes set rehabilitation goals and anticipate barriers to goal attainment

- Facilitating interaction with members of athletes' support systems to coordinate a smooth rehabilitation process (A.J. Petitpas, 2002)

Although the efficacy of counseling has not been examined in controlled investigations in the specific context of sport injury rehabilitation, counseling has been found credible as an intervention for athletes with injuries (Brewer, Jeffers, Petitpas, & Van Raalte, 1994; Myers, Peyton, & Jensen, 2004). In addition, case study data suggest that counseling may be helpful to the well-being of athletes undergoing injury rehabilitation (Rock & Jones, 2002).

Expressive Writing

As noted in chapter 4, emotional disturbance is common among athletes with injury, especially shortly after an injury occurs. Consequently, negative emotion can be a topic of discussion during the course of counseling and other psychological interventions. Identification of negative emotions is most explicitly part of the treatment in expressive writing. In this approach, developed by Pennebaker (1997), participants write for 15 to 30 minutes per day over the course of three to five days about a traumatic experience or emotional issue that has affected their life. Expressive writing is thought to affect cognitive, emotional, and physiological parameters; therefore, paths A and C are presumably the most salient routes to sport injury rehabilitation outcomes. Expressive writing can also influence behavior, although Pennebaker noted that it does not seem to increase exercise; thus path B is less plausible.

A meta-analysis of early expressive-writing studies indicated that the intervention could improve both physical outcomes (e.g., immune functioning) and psychological outcomes (e.g., anxiety, depression, mood disturbance) (Smyth, 1998). In contrast, a more recent meta-analysis of randomized controlled trials concluded that expressive writing had no significant effect on physical and psychological health (Mogk, Otte, Reinhold-Hurley, & Kröner-Herwig, 2006). In the realm of sport injury rehabilitation, Mankad and her colleagues (Mankad & Gordon, 2010; Mankad, Gordon, & Wallman, 2009a, 2009b) explored the use of expressive writing with nine elite athletes with long-term injuries. The athletes completed measures of immune functioning, stress, mood disturbance, and psychological adjustment to injury three times before and three times after participating in three 20-minute sessions of expressive writing. Favorable changes were reported for each type of outcome assessed, and examination of the writing samples showed enhanced cognitive processing and disinhibition of negative (and positive) emotions. However, firm conclusions cannot be drawn about the efficacy of expressive writing for athletes with injury due to the absence of a control group and the likelihood of athletes demonstrating similar improvements with the passage of time in the absence of any intervention.

Goal Setting

Although athletes with injury may lack familiarity with biofeedback, counseling, and expressive writing, they are likely to be intimately acquainted with the intervention of goal setting. Indeed, athletes in both individual and team sports commonly implement the process of setting goals, developing plans to achieve them, implementing the plans, and revising the goals as necessary based on performance feedback (Arvinen-Barrow & Hemmings, 2013). Goal setting involves identifying an objective that one would like to accomplish within a particular period of time and working toward achievement of that aim (R.S. Weinberg, 2002). Although the concept of goal setting is simple, numerous variations exist in the qualities of the goals that athletes set.

Goals can vary in many ways, including difficulty, specificity, target domain, target type, temporal focus, and valence (J. Taylor & Taylor, 1997; R.S. Weinberg, 2002). In terms of difficulty, goals can range from the easily attainable to the seemingly impossible. Goals are considered specific when they correspond to clearly defined and measurable tasks (e.g.,

perform 10 heel slides), whereas general goals are vaguer and more difficult to assess (e.g., feel better). A goal's target domain consists of its particular content area; for example, some goals address completion of rehabilitation activities, whereas others pertain to sport-related tasks (e.g., reviewing game footage of future opponents) or lifestyle activities relevant to recovery (e.g., good nutrition and sleep).

A goal's target type, in contrast, corresponds to whether the goal is directed at outcomes or processes. Outcome goals involve achieving end results that may or may not be under the athlete's control (e.g., regaining full mobility of the left leg), whereas process goals involve completing tasks that facilitate goal achievement and generally do fall within the athlete's control (e.g., perform stretching exercises for 10 minutes per day). In terms of temporal focus, or time frame, goals range from short-term (e.g., within a particular rehabilitation session) to long-term (e.g., by end of rehabilitation or after a return to sport). Goal valence refers to the extent to which goals are positively stated (e.g., swing loosely at the shoulder) versus negatively stated (e.g., don't tighten your shoulder).

Extrapolating from research findings on the use of goal setting to enhance sport performance—and from applied experience with athletes undergoing injury rehabilitation—researchers have recommended that rehabilitation goals should

- be challenging, yet realistic and attainable;
- be specific and measurable;
- address multiple content domains (e.g., recovery, performance, lifestyle);
- target both processes and outcomes (with an emphasis on processes);
- cover both short-term and long-term activities; and
- be positively stated—that is, stated in terms not of what should be avoided but of what should be accomplished (Arvinen-Barrow & Hemmings, 2013; J. Taylor & Taylor, 1997).

In addition to recommendations about *what* kinds of goal to set, guidelines have also been provided for *how* to set goals. Sport health care professionals often possess advanced knowledge of what might constitute realistic goals over the course of rehabilitation for a variety of injuries, and they may take the lead in initiating goal setting with athletes. Nevertheless, it has been recommended that goal setting should be a collaborative venture between athletes and sport health care professionals and, when useful, should include input from coaches and other individuals. Including athletes in the process may help ensure that the goals are viewed as important and are clearly understood; it may also foster a sense of control in the athletes and facilitate their investment in attaining the goals (Arvinen-Barrow & Hemmings, 2013; Petitpas & Danish, 1995; J. Taylor & Taylor, 1997). Athletes can also help sport health care professionals identify potential roadblocks to goal attainment and develop strategies to overcome the barriers (Petitpas & Danish, 1995).

Once rehabilitation goals have been set, they should be written down or recorded in such a way that they can serve as an ongoing reminder of what the athlete hopes to accomplish in rehabilitation. J. Taylor and Taylor (1997) advocated the use of a written contract that explicitly outlines both the athlete's goals for rehabilitation and the strategies that he or she will implement in order to accomplish them. Such a document can be shared with others to enlist support and encouragement for the athlete's pursuit of rehabilitation goals. The success of goal interventions depends on monitoring athletes, furnishing regular feedback on their progress toward goal attainment, and supporting their efforts in pursuing their goals. In the likely event that athletes do not achieve all of their rehabilitation goals, research has suggested taking a flexible approach emphasizing the *degree* of goal completion (rather than absolute goal attainment) and revising goals as necessary (Arvinen-Barrow & Hemmings, 2013; J. Taylor & Taylor; Wadey & Evans, 2011).

Goal setting provides an informational frame of reference for rehabilitation accomplishments and encourages both effort and persistence. In these ways, it is thought to enhance psychological states associated with better adherence to rehabilitation (e.g., effort, motivation, persistence, self-efficacy, task focus). In turn, following path B and subsequent paths B1, B2, and B3 in figure 7.1, improved rehabilitation behavior can exert a favorable influence on cognitive-affective, behavioral, and physical outcomes (Arvinen-Barrow & Hemmings, 2013; Wadey & Evans, 2011). Furthermore, to the extent that the psychological states that facilitate adherence are deemed cognitive-affective outcomes, path A can also be considered a mechanism of effect for goal setting.

In contrast to other psychological interventions covered in this chapter, goal setting is considered important to rehabilitation by both athletes and sport health care professionals (e.g., Arvinen-Barrow, Hemmings, Becker, & Booth, 2008; Brewer, Jeffers, Petitpas, & Van Raalte, 1994; Francis, Andersen, & Maley, 2000; Hamson-Utley, Martin, & Walters, 2008; Lafferty, Kenyon, & Wright, 2008; Ninedek & Kolt, 2000). Consequently, sport health care professionals are likely to meet with less resistance from athletes when introducing goal setting than when introducing any other psychological intervention.

Despite this acceptance and the ubiquity of goal setting in sport injury rehabilitation settings (Arvinen-Barrow & Hemmings, 2013)—as well as the large volume of research on goal setting for enhancement of sport performance (for a review, see R.S. Weinberg, 2002)—the research base supporting the use of this technique in sport injury rehabilitation is surprisingly slender. However, evidence from controlled experimental studies does indicate that goal setting can enhance the rehabilitation behavior of adherence (L. Evans & Hardy, 2002a; Penpraze & Mutrie, 1999), the behavioral rehabilitation outcome of strength (Theodorakis, Beneca, Malliou, & Goudas, 1997; Theodorakis, Malliou, Papaioannou, Beneca, & Filactakidou, 1996), and the cognitive-affective rehabilitation outcome of performance satisfaction (Theodorakis, Beneca, Malliou, & Goudas, 1997). Because only one goal-setting condition was closely aligned with goal-setting guidelines in each of these experimental studies, no conclusions can be made about the relative merits of various types of goal or goal-setting practice in the context of sport injury rehabilitation. It is strongly suspected, for example, that goals focusing on rehabilitation processes are more effective than goals focusing on rehabilitation outcomes, but validation of that suspicion requires research in which the effectiveness of process goals and outcome goals are compared directly. In addition to these experimental studies supporting the use of goal setting in sport injury rehabilitation, athletes who report greater use of goal setting during injury rehabilitation have been found to recover more quickly (Ievleva & Orlick, 1991) and to adhere better to the rehabilitation program than those reporting less use of the technique (Scherzer et al., 2001).

Imagery

When athletes use imagery, they intentionally generate internal representations "that give rise to the experience of perception in the absence of appropriate sensory input" (Wraga & Kosslyn, 2002, p. 466). As with goal setting and several other psychological interventions used in injury rehabilitation, imagery can either be applied spontaneously by athletes or be implemented in a structured fashion with help from a sport health care professional. Research on spontaneous use of imagery by athletes suggests that imagery content generally pertains to themes of healing, pain management, rehabilitation processes, and sport performance. Healing images involve envisioning internal bodily processes taking place during rehabilitation. In pain management imagery, athletes create representations of themselves in a pain-free state. Rehabilitation images involve picturing oneself successfully completing rehabilitation activities and dealing with challenges encountered during rehabilitation. When using performance imagery, athletes mentally rehearse sport-specific skills (Walsh, 2005).

Although imagery can involve any or all of the senses, the spontaneous imagery used by athletes undergoing rehabilitation seems to be primarily visual and kinesthetic (Driedi-

ger, Hall, & Callow, 2006). This finding suggests that athletes both "see" and "feel" the content of their images. Athletes with injuries have reported spontaneous images to be predominantly facilitative (or positive) but occasionally debilitative (Driediger et al.; Monsma, Mensch, & Farroll, 2009).

The content of athletes' spontaneous imagery appears to be closely tied to the imagery's intended function (L. Evans, Hare, & Mullen, 2006). Four types of function have been identified for imagery used during injury rehabilitation: cognitive, motivational, healing, and pain management (Driediger et al., 2006; Sordoni, Hall, & Forwell, 2000, 2002). One example of a cognitive function involves the use of imagery to learn and properly perform rehabilitation exercises. Athletes use imagery for motivational purposes when they envision themselves achieving goals pertaining either to their sport or to their recovery from injury. They use imagery for healing purposes when they create positive images of internal physiological processes to facilitate recovery. Imagery is used for pain management purposes when athletes' images are designed to prepare them for potentially painful experiences, distract them from painful situations, or transform pain that they are experiencing (Driediger et al.). Of these four purposes, athletes with injury tend to report using imagery for cognitive, motivational, and pain management more than for healing (Milne, Hall, & Forwell, 2005; Sordoni et al., 2002; Wesch, Hall, Polgar, & Forwell, 2008).

Investigations of patterns in athletes' spontaneous use of imagery over the course of rehabilitation have provided evidence of both change and stability. For example, athletes interviewed by L. Evans et al. (2006) and those surveyed by Monsma et al. (2009) reported differences in their use of imagery over the course of rehabilitation. In contrast, Fox (2004) found that the functions of imagery did not differ across two assessments (one at injury occurrence and another just before the athlete's return to training), and Milne et al. (2005) found that imagery use was not associated with the length of time in rehabilitation.

For help in resolving the apparent discrepancy in the findings of L. Evans et al. (2006)

and Monsma et al. (2009) versus the findings of Fox (2004), we can consider the results of a case study conducted by Hare, Evans, and Callow (2008). The elite swimmer studied by Hare et al. displayed a general progression from imagery involving rehabilitation rehearsal to imagery involving sport performance, thus reflecting a transition from an athlete undergoing rehabilitation to one preparing to return to sport. Amid this trend toward greater use of performance imagery, the swimmer's use of imagery to increase confidence, facilitate relaxation, maintain a positive attitude, and enhance motivation remained remarkably consistent over the course of rehabilitation. Thus, although the general emphasis of spontaneous imagery may change as the focus of rehabilitation changes, the specific underlying reasons for using imagery may remain fairly constant.

Given the diverse array of imagery content and functions associated with sport injury rehabilitation, imagery has the potential to influence rehabilitation outcomes via multiple pathways. Paths A, B, and C in figure 7.1 seem particularly relevant. Imagery that reduces anxiety or enhances confidence and feelings of well-being traverses path A, whereas imagery that facilitates completion of rehabilitation exercises follows path B. The use of path C here is admittedly more speculative, but preliminary evidence suggests that imagery exerts a favorable effect on neurobiological factors of potential relevance to physical outcomes in athletes undergoing injury rehabilitation (Maddison et al., 2012).

Acceptance of imagery as an intervention for use during sport injury rehabilitation appears to be less than uniformly positive. In some studies, athletes have identified imagery as one of the more commonly used spontaneous strategies for coping with injury (Clement, Arvinen-Barrow, et al., 2012; DeFrancesco, Miller, Larson, & Robinson, 1994), and sport health care professionals have reported holding positive perceptions of the effectiveness of imagery for athletes undergoing rehabilitation (Hamson-Utley et al., 2008). In other studies, however, more modest (and even negative) opinions and expectations of imagery have

been expressed by both athletes (Francis et al., 2000) and sport health care professionals (Francis et al.; Ninedek & Kolt, 2000; Wiese, Weiss, & Yukelson, 1991). Athletes with injury who have been exposed to imagery interventions have tended to report favorable perceptions of imagery (e.g., Brewer et al., 1994; Handegard, Joyner, Burke, & Reimann, 2006), albeit less favorable than for goal setting (Brewer et al., 1994).

Empirical evaluations of imagery interventions and spontaneous imagery use suggest that imagery may exert beneficial effects on sport injury rehabilitation processes and outcomes. Case study data have provided vivid examples of athletes for whom imagery may have enhanced

- cognitive-affective outcomes such as confidence, relaxation, positive attitude, and motivation via path A (Hare et al., 2008);
- the quality and intensity of rehabilitation behavior via path B (Brewer & Helledy, 1998); and
- perceptions of change at the muscular level via path C (Handegard et al., 2006).

In addition, prospective correlational studies have documented positive associations between self-reported spontaneous use of imagery and adherence to rehabilitation (path B) (Scherzer et al., 2001; Wesch et al., 2012). In retrospective and concurrent correlational studies, high levels of self-reported spontaneous use of imagery have been associated with high levels of coping and task efficacy (path A; Milne et al., 2005) and shorter recovery times (multiple potential paths; Ievleva & Orlick, 1991).

The strongest evidence in support of the efficacy of imagery in sport injury rehabilitation comes from a handful of controlled experimental studies in which imagery interventions were applied to athletes with injury. Although one study (Christakou & Zervas, 2007) found that imagery produced no significant effects on sport injury rehabilitation outcomes (i.e., pain, edema, range of motion) for athletes with ankle injuries, four other investigations obtained favorable results along multiple pathways. Specifically, relative to control conditions, imagery interventions have

- produced greater knee strength and lower pain and reinjury anxiety following ACL reconstructive surgery (path A; Cupal & Brewer, 2001);

- enhanced wrist range of motion (flexion and extension) following a period of forearm immobilization (path C; Newsom, Knight, & Balnave, 2003);

- produced better muscular endurance for athletes with ankle sprains (paths B and B2; Christakou, Zervas, & Lavallee, 2007); and

- reduced knee laxity and the levels of two recovery-related neurotransmitters (noradrenaline and dopamine) after ACL reconstructive surgery (path C; Maddison et al., 2012).

In a related investigation of older adults (not athletes) undergoing rehabilitation following hip or knee surgery, Waters (2005) found that, as compared with a condition controlling for amount of relaxation induced and social support received, an imagery intervention was associated with higher levels of confidence (in the injured body part, in one's own body, and in the ability to perform upon returning to daily activities) and with lower levels of stiffness, fear of injury upon returning to regular activities, and difficulty in resuming regular activities. Thus, it appears that imagery may have utility as a means of influencing important processes and outcomes in the rehabilitation of sport-related and other orthopedic conditions.

Modeling

Modeling involves exposing the participant, usually through visual means, to one or more individuals who display behaviors, attitudes, thoughts, or values that are considered desirable for the participant to acquire. Also known as imitation, observational learning, and vicarious learning, modeling is used by athletes to learn or refine sport skills, sport strategies, and mental states that facilitate sport performance (McCullagh, Ste-Marie, & Law, 2014). It has also long been advocated for use in sport injury rehabilitation (Flint, 1991).

Modeling is a flexible intervention with many variations. For instance, it can be done with live (i.e., in-person) models, video models, or even audio models. Furthermore, models can either display mastery of the focal content of the intervention in order to create an aspirational standard or be shown grappling (coping) with the subject matter in order to highlight the importance of persistence through adversity and to convey a realistic impression of what it takes to meet the demands of the tasks at hand. Although other people (e.g., fellow athletes at more advanced stages of rehabilitation) commonly serve as models, athletes can also serve as models for themselves through the processes of self-observation and self-modeling. In the context of sport injury rehabilitation, self-observation might involve viewing unedited video replays of oneself performing rehabilitation exercises, whereas self-modeling might involve viewing video of oneself performing actions that one cannot currently perform in the injured state but could perform prior to injury (McCullagh et al., 2014). The type of information presented in modeling videos can be used both to decrease anxiety, pain, and sympathetic arousal (e.g., heart rate, blood pressure, muscle tone) and to increase knowledge, cooperation, and coping ability (Gagliano, 1988)—all of which can be helpful during sport injury rehabilitation.

The mechanisms by which modeling achieves beneficial effects in sport injury rehabilitation and other domains are not fully understood. Paths A, B, and C are, however, potential pathways along which modeling might influence sport injury rehabilitation processes and outcomes. With respect to path A, consistent with the proposals of Bandura (1997), learning information about rehabilitation procedures and observing oneself or similar others dealing successfully with the aftermath of sport injury can promote feelings of confidence in one's ability to complete rehabilitation tasks (Flint, 1991) and create realistic expectations for the sensations and events that may be encountered during rehabilitation (Maddison, Prapavessis, & Clatworthy, 2006). Modeling can also favorably affect the cognitive-affective outcomes of pain and anxiety (Gagliano, 1988). Path B, in turn, could provide a route for the beneficial effects of modeling on self-efficacy for rehabilitation activities (Flint, 1991), which can translate into improvements in adherence to rehabilitation (Brewer, Cornelius, et al., 2003a; Levy, Polman, & Clough, 2008; Milne et al., 2005; A.H. Taylor & May, 1996; Wesch et al., 2012). As for path C, although they have yet to be demonstrated in the context of sport injury rehabilitation, the calming effects of modeling on sympathetic arousal (Manderino & Bzdek, 1984; Melamed, Yurcheson, Fleece, Hutcherson, & Hawes, 1978) could represent progress on this path and contribute to desired rehabilitation outcomes.

As with most of the psychological interventions discussed in this chapter, the efficacy of modeling in the context of sport injury rehabilitation has been examined in relatively few controlled studies. In a seminal investigation, Flint (1991) found that an intervention featuring videotaped coping models increased self-efficacy (path A) after ACL reconstructive surgery to a greater extent than did a control condition. Favorable changes were also observed in functional outcomes, but the results did not reach statistical significance due to the small sample size (n = 10 per group). Weeks et al. (2002) demonstrated that, as compared with a control condition (i.e., instruction in rehabilitation exercises by static illustrations), video modeling of rehabilitation exercises produced higher-quality performance of rehabilitation exercises (path B) and superior motivation and confidence for completing rehabilitation exercises (path A). Maddison et al. (2006) reported that among individuals undergoing ACL reconstruction surgery, a modeling intervention produced lower preoperative expectations for postoperative pain (path A), greater postoperative self-efficacy for completing rehabilitation (path A), and better physician-evaluated knee function (paths B and C).

Overall, although modeling has shown clear signs of potential applicability in sport injury rehabilitation, more research is needed to determine how best to implement the intervention in terms of what type of model to use (e.g., mastery versus coping, self versus others) and what outcomes to target.

Multimodal Interventions

Multimodal interventions combine multiple interventions to provide a more comprehensive approach to treatment than that afforded by single interventions. As shown in table 8.2, the interventions are drawn almost without exception from the cognitive-behavioral tradition and are consistent with mental-skills training approaches used with athletes for performance enhancement. Goal setting, imagery, and relaxation training are staples of the multimodal interventions used in sport injury rehabilitation. Multimodal interventions offer athletes with injury variety and an opportunity to "connect" with a particular approach to treatment if the others in the package are not to their liking. Depending on the specific components of a given multimodal intervention, its mechanisms of effect could include any or all of the pathways depicted in figure 7.1. In general, research on multimodal interventions suggests that they are perceived favorably by athletes with injury (Appaneal & Granquist, 2007; Brewer et al., 1994; L. Evans, Hardy, & Fleming, 2000; Shapiro, 2009) and are effective in influencing sport injury rehabilitation processes and outcomes, such as adherence to rehabilitation, anxiety, attitude toward rehabilitation, competitive anxiety, escape behavior, extroversion, hedonic tone, pain, readiness for physical activity, recovery time, security, self-efficacy, social orientation, sport confidence, and tension (Elaziz, 2010; Johnson, 2000; Marcolli, Schilling, & Segesser, 2001; Ross & Berger, 1996).

One challenge associated with multimodal interventions lies in the fact that it is difficult to determine the extent to which the individual components of an intervention contribute to treatment outcomes. It is possible to conduct systematic component analyses of multimodal interventions, but the state of the science in evaluating the effects of psychological interventions on sport injury prevention and rehabilitation outcomes is not yet at that level. In the long run, determining the necessity and sufficiency of components of multimodal

TABLE 8.2   Examples of Multimodal Psychological Interventions for Sport Injury Rehabilitation

Study	Intervention components
Brewer et al. (1994)	Goal setting, counseling, imagery
Ross & Berger (1996)	Stress inoculation training (self-monitoring, relaxation, imagery, positive self-talk, self-reinforcement)
Johnson (2000)	Stress management and cognitive control, goal setting, relaxation and guided imagery
L. Evans et al. (2000)	Social support, goal setting, imagery, simulation training, verbal persuasion
Marcolli et al. (2001)	Goal setting, relaxation, imagery
Appaneal & Granquist (2007)	Relaxation, refocusing, imagery, self-monitoring
Shapiro (2009)	Goal setting, relaxation, imagery, self-talk (combinations of two of the preceding components)
Elaziz (2010)	Goal setting, relaxation, imagery, positive self-talk

interventions for achieving desired results is vital to the project of providing athletes with efficacious, time-efficient, evidence-based treatments. Until that is achieved, however, sport health care professionals can look to research on the individual components for guidance while taking care to ensure that athletes are not overloaded with different approaches.

Performance Enhancement Groups

For the most part, the interventions discussed in this chapter are delivered to athletes on an individual, one-to-one basis. It can be advantageous, however, to deliver psychological interventions in a group format. In addition to enabling professionals who deliver psychological interventions to use their time more efficiently and expand the reach of their services, group settings can facilitate social support among group members, allow group members who are coping well to serve as models for those who are experiencing difficulty, and provide a safe context in which athletes can disclose their thoughts and feelings to others. ·

Although group interventions for athletes with injury have long been advocated (Swenson & Dargan, 1994; Granito, Hogan, & Var-

num, 1995) and guidelines for developing and implementing such interventions have been established (Clement, Shannon, & Connole, 2012a, 2012b), little empirical support exists for the practice. Portenga, Sommer, and Statler (2001) presented a qualitative investigation of a psychological performance-enhancement group (SAFARI: Student Athletes for Active Rehabilitation of Injuries) that they conducted with six collegiate athletes with injuries. In the group, members gave support to and received support from their peers and were taught mental skills of potential utility for returning to sport rapidly and successfully. In the evaluation of SAFARI, members identified strengths and limitations of the program and made suggestions for improvement in the future.

The particular pathways (shown in figure 7.1) through which performance enhancement groups might influence sport injury rehabilitation processes and outcomes depend entirely on the content addressed during group meetings. The groups can vary widely with respect to content structure, ranging from support groups with no predetermined agenda to psychoeducational groups with a planned didactic component (Petrie, 2007). Therefore, any and all of the paths are potentially viable, and research is needed in order to determine what can and cannot be accomplished in performance enhancement groups for athletes with injury.

Along with their pragmatic advantages, performance enhancement groups are also subject to practical challenges that may limit their utility with athletes with injury. It can be difficult, for example, to coordinate the schedules of a sufficient number of athletes whose injuries are severe enough (i.e., season ending) and who are interested in attending performance-enhancement group sessions at the time a group is formed (Clement, Shannon, et al., 2012b).

Relaxation Training

One of the more ubiquitous psychological interventions in sport injury rehabilitation, relaxation training encompasses an array of techniques designed to reduce the stress response (Sherman & Poczwardowski, 2000). Relaxation produces physiological changes (e.g., decreased heart rate, respiration rate, and muscle tension) and psychological changes (e.g., decreased anxiety, improved decision making, increased confidence) that can be beneficial in sport injury rehabilitation (J. Taylor & Taylor, 1997; Sherman & Poczwardowski; R. Weinberg, 2010). Approaches to relaxation training can be loosely divided into those that are predominantly somatically oriented and those that are predominantly cognitively oriented (Payne, 2004).

Common relaxation techniques that are somatically oriented include progressive muscle relaxation and diaphragmatic (or abdominal) breathing. In progressive muscle relaxation, which was developed by Jacobson (1938), the athlete is instructed to alternately tense and relax major muscle groups and note the difference in muscle tension between contracted muscles and released muscles. The tensing component is decreased gradually as the athlete becomes more skilled in relaxing the muscles; eventually, it is ceased altogether. Diaphragmatic breathing involves learning to take deep, slow breaths in which air is drawn into the lower portions of the lungs (R. Weinberg, 2010). Initial sessions are typically done while lying on one's back, as illustrated in the following narrative:

> I am just going to sit here and talk you through a simple exercise. You can close your eyes or leave them open, but it might be easier with your eyes closed. Either bend your knees or let your legs go straight, whatever is most comfortable. I'd like you to put your right hand on your abdomen, right at your waist, and your left hand on your chest, right at your sternum. Just breathing normally, simply notice how you breathe. As you inhale, which hand moves the most—the hand on your chest or the hand on your abdomen? Continue breathing for a while. It looks like your abdomen hand is moving. I would like you to exhale as fully as possible now, getting all the air out of your lungs. Good. Now inhale with a deep-belly or abdominal breath. Good, just keep breathing like that, trying to keep your chest hand still while the abdomen hand rises. Good. How does that feel? (Sherman & Poczwardowski, 2000, p. 53)

With practice, an athlete can get to the point where he or she can achieve a relaxed state with a few deep, diaphragmatic breaths in any position (e.g., standing, sitting, lying down); therefore, the technique is feasible for use during rehabilitation activities (N. Walker & Heaney, 2013).

One example of a cognitively oriented relaxation technique is autogenic training, which is a form of self-hypnosis. It involves repeating a set of self-statements that suggest sensations of heaviness and warmth in the arms and legs (e.g., "my right arm is heavy," "my left leg is warm"), regulation of heart rate and breathing (e.g., "my breathing is calm"), and sensations of warmth in the abdomen and coolness in the forehead (e.g., "my forehead is cool"). By practicing autogenic training regularly over a period of months, an athlete can become proficient at creating the desired sensations and achieving a deepened state of relaxation (Payne, 2004; R. Weinberg, 2010).

Presumably, relaxation training acts on sport injury rehabilitation processes and outcomes through paths A and C (see figure 7.1). After doing relaxation training, for example, an athlete may feel less anxious and more confident, both as a direct result of completing the relaxation training activities (path A) and as an indirect consequence of training-induced reductions in muscle tension (path C), the latter of which may contribute directly to physical outcomes (N. Walker & Heaney, 2013). Relaxation training has been used frequently as a facilitator of imagery interventions (e.g., Christakou et al., 2007; Cupal & Brewer, 2001; Maddison et al., 2012) and as a component of other multimodal treatments (e.g., Johnson, 2000; Marcolli et al., 2001; Ross & Berger, 1996) that have been found to affect sport injury rehabilitation outcomes; however, it has not yet been validated as an effective stand-alone intervention in sport injury rehabilitation. Inconclusive findings were reported in two small studies that investigated the effects of relaxation training on sport injury rehabilitation outcomes (Castillo, Cremades, & Butcher, 2002; Naoi & Ostrow, 2008). On the other hand, research has provided consistent support for the utility of relaxation training in treating a wide range of physical and psychological conditions (Carlson & Hoyle, 1993; K.M. Kerr, 2000; Stetter & Kupper, 2002). Thus, it appears that relaxation training has considerable promise as an intervention for use during sport injury rehabilitation.

Self-Talk

Cognition is central to most of the psychological interventions used in sport injury rehabilitation, and that is the case with self-talk, which consists of "what athletes say to themselves out loud or internally and privately" (Van Raalte, 2010, p. 510). This self-directed cognitive content can vary in terms of both valence and function. Valence is determined by the affective tone of self-talk—that is, whether it is positive (e.g., praising, encouraging) or negative (e.g., criticizing, discouraging). In terms of function, self-talk can serve both instructional and motivational purposes. Instructional self-

talk provides specific direction regarding how to think, feel, or behave, whereas motivational self-talk encourages persistence and commitment to goal achievement (Tod, Hardy, & Oliver, 2011; Van Raalte).

Given the boundless reservoir of content from which an athlete's self-statements can be drawn, all four of the main paths depicted in figure 7.1—paths A, B, C, and D—are viable routes by which self-talk can influence sport injury rehabilitation outcomes. The versatility of self-talk as an intervention is highlighted by the various cognitive techniques designed to harness its power, such as thought replacement, positive affirmations, motivational self-talk, cue words, and self-instruction. In thought replacement, athletes are taught to identify inappropriate or counterproductive thoughts and replace them with more appropriate or productive thoughts (Van Raalte, 2010); this approach is indicative of path A. Also suggestive of path A is the use of positive affirmations (i.e., encouraging self-statements), which can be recited to boost confidence and mood (J. Taylor & Taylor, 1997). Motivational self-talk can prompt an athlete to engage vigorously in rehabilitation activities (path B), whereas cue words (e.g., "calm," "chill," "relax") can facilitate desired physiological changes (path C). Self-instruction can help an athlete learn technical aspects of rehabilitation activities (path B) or guide the athlete to interact with other people in ways that are potentially beneficial to rehabilitation (path D; Van Raalte; R. Weinberg, 2010).

Although self-talk is widely advocated for use in sport injury rehabilitation (N. Walker & Hudson, 2013), only limited research has examined the effects of self-talk on sport injury rehabilitation processes and outcomes. In the first and largest trial, athletes undergoing injury rehabilitation who received a self-talk intervention improved their quadriceps strength to a greater extent than those who did not receive the intervention (Theodorakis, Beneca, Malliou, Antoniou, et al., 1997). In a follow-up study with physically active individuals who had undergone a meniscectomy (arthroscopic knee surgery) six months earlier, Beneka et al. (2013) found that whereas instructional and motivational self-talk interventions produced improved performance on a balance task, the conditions of neutral self-talk and no self-talk yielded no improvement in balance-task performance. The findings of studies in which a self-talk technique was paired with a relaxation technique suggested that the interventions contributed to reductions in reinjury anxiety (N. Walker, 2006) and negative mood (Naoi & Ostrow, 2008). In addition to these intervention studies, correlational research has shown that the use of self-reported positive self-talk is positively associated with adherence to rehabilitation following ACL reconstruction (Scherzer et al., 2001); that the content of self-reported self-talk varies according to the phase of sport injury rehabilitation (i.e., early, middle, late); and that athletes report that their self-talk during rehabilitation enhances their focus, confidence, effort, drive, motivation, and encouragement (Hodge, Evans, Hanton, & Hardy, 2009).

Social Support

As suggested in chapter 1 and borne out in subsequent chapters, social support is associated with athletes' risk for incurring sport injury, their psychological responses to sport injury, and their recovery from sport injury. Although numerous definitions of social support have been proposed, there is no single, universally accepted way of defining the construct. The common theme across definitions is that social support pertains to "people acting as a provider of resources when needed" (Arvinen-Barrow & Pack, 2013). Embedded within that pithy description are the ideas that people are providers of social support and that social support provides people with resources that meet particular needs.

In the context of sport injury, Arvinen-Barrow & Pack (2013) loosely grouped potential providers of social support into the following (occasionally overlapping) categories: family and friends, sport team members (e.g., coaches, teammates), and sports medicine team members. These researchers also addressed the types of resources that can be provided to athletes. Specifically, they went beyond the emotional, informational, and tangible dimen-

sions of support identified by Hardy, Burke, and Crace (1999) to identify a wide variety of resource types, including those intended to bolster confidence (esteem support), convey a sense of being listened to (listening support), instill feelings of comfort and security during an emotionally trying period (emotional support), enhance motivation for completing rehabilitation activities (emotional-challenge support and motivational support), facilitate realistic appraisals of the injury situation (shared reality support), reinforce effort and accomplishment in rehabilitation (technical support), foster excitement about and creativity in rehabilitation (technical-challenge support), help solve problems or provide feedback in rehabilitation (personal-assistance support), and furnish practical or monetary assistance (material support).

The types of support that athletes seek, as well as the individuals from whom they seek it, vary over the course of rehabilitation (Johnston & Carroll, 1998; Peterson, 1997; Udry, 1997). For example, emotional support and material support may be especially valued in the immediate aftermath of injury, when athletes tend to be most distressed and their activities of daily living most disrupted. In contrast, athletes' need for technical support and technical-challenge support may be strongest during the heart of their rehabilitation programs. Similarly, certain providers may be more adept than others at delivering certain types of support. In one study, athletes reported greater satisfaction with the task-challenge support provided by their coaches than with that provided by their teammates, but they rated their teammates as more available than their coaches for provision of emotional support (Corbillon, Crossman, & Jamieson, 2008). In another study, athletes rated the listening support and task-appreciation support they received from their athletic trainers as contributing more to their well-being than that received from their head coaches and assistant coaches (Robbins & Rosenfeld, 2001).

Although athletes report that they are generally satisfied with the social support they receive while injured (T. Bianco, 2001; Judge, Harris, & Bell, 2009; Yang, Peek-Asa, Lowe, Heiden, & Foster, 2010), they do not uniformly rate potential providers as supportive (Abgarov, Jeffery-Tosoni, Baker, & Fraser-Thomas, 2012; Peterson, 1997; Rees, Smith, & Sparkes, 2003; Yang et al., 2010), and they may report having received less support than providers claim to have given (Beaton & Langdon, 2012). Even friends, family, and athletic trainers—providers who have routinely received high marks from athletes for their supportiveness (Clement & Shannon, 2011; Finnie, 1999; Peterson, 1997; Robbins & Rosenfeld, 2001; Yang et al., 2010)—are sometimes perceived as unsupportive (Abgarov et al., 2012; Peterson, 1997; Rees et al., 2003; Yang et al., 2010). Moreover, not all support given by providers, despite their best intentions, is considered by athletes with injury to be helpful or beneficial (Rees et al., 2003). Similarly, the commonly recommended practice of keeping athletes with injury involved with their teams in order to preserve their social support systems (among other reasons) is not inevitably valued by athletes as a source of social support (T.M. Bianco, 2007). The issue of who should implement social support (and other psychological) interventions is tackled in this chapter's Focus on Application box.

As shown in table 8.1, social support is yet another intervention that presumably can influence sport injury rehabilitation outcomes through all four of the main pathways specified in figure 7.1. If social support is defined as one's *perception* of the resources received from others (i.e., as a psychological factor), then research findings are consistent with a path A route in indicating that social support (and satisfaction with social support) buffers the effects of life stress on postinjury psychological adjustment (Malinauskas, 2010; Rees, Mitchell, Evans, & Hardy, 2010) and is inversely related to postinjury emotional distress (Brewer, Linder, & Phelps, 1995; S.L. Green & Weinberg, 2001; Malinauskas, 2010; Manuel et al., 2002; Rees et al., 2010). If, on the other hand, social support is construed as consisting of the *actual* resources received from others (i.e., as a social-contextual variable), then those same findings are aligned with a path D route. In terms of path B, social support may enhance injured athletes' motivation (T. Bianco, 2001) and is positively asso-

ciated with adherence to sport injury rehabilitation programs (Byerly, Worrell, Gahimer, & Domholdt, 1994; Duda, Smart, & Tappe, 1989; Fisher, Domm, & Wuest, 1988; Johnston & Carroll, 2000; Levy, Polman & Borkoles, 2008; Levy, Polman, & Clough, 2008). With respect to path C, although not pertaining directly to sport injury, perceived positive social connections with others may contribute to elevated vagal tone (Kok et al., 2013), a parameter that is inversely related to inflammation (Thayer & Sternberg, 2006).

Despite an abundance of research suggesting that social support plays an important role in the occurrence of sport injury, as well as in responses to and recovery from sport injury, there is a dearth of experimental studies assessing the effects of a social-support manipulation on sport injury rehabilitation outcomes (for an exception, see Horton, 2002). Inquiry into the topic may have been impeded by difficulty in defining and subsequently operationalizing social support in the form of a replicable intervention. Nevertheless, social support holds great potential as a means of enhancing sport injury rehabilitation outcomes and thus warrants further investigation.

Biopsychosocial Analysis

The interventions discussed in this chapter reflect conscious, direct attempts by athletes or sport health care professionals to enhance cognitive-affective, functional, and physical outcomes by psychological means. Presumably, psychological interventions initiate processes akin to those depicted in figure 7.1 which influence the biological, psychological, and social factors that contribute to rehabilitation outcomes. In the first case presented at the beginning of this chapter, a multisensory array of images was designed to influence cognitive-affective states (e.g., motivation, mood) that may contribute not only to Kyle's mental well-being but also to his rehabilitation behavior (i.e., adherence) and functional and physical outcomes (i.e., recovery rate). Similarly, the simple relaxation exercise that Paula implemented with Marzuki was intended to exert a direct effect on his biological functioning (i.e., hamstring flexibility).

Who Should Deliver Psychological Interventions in Postinjury Sport Health Care?

As evidence accrues of the potential benefits of psychological interventions for athletes with injury, the question of who should implement the interventions becomes increasingly salient. The answer to this seemingly simple question is actually quite complex and goes a long way toward explaining why psychological interventions are not used with greater frequency in sport health care settings. Determining which professionals should intervene psychologically with athletes who have incurred injury requires thoughtful consideration of issues pertaining to competence, access, availability, and interest.

With respect to competence, professionals affiliated with most of the disciplines involved in providing sport health care services are professionally, ethically, and perhaps even legally obligated to be competent in the services they provide (Loubert, 1999; Makarowski, 2007). Professionals typically achieve competence through a combination of knowledge acquisition and supervised experience. Assuming that the interventions are not being implemented for treatment of a mental health condition (e.g., depression, eating disorder, substance use disorder), most professionals credentialed in sport psychology (or another psychology-related field) are presumably capable of delivering a wide array of basic psychological interventions to athletes with in-

juries. Of course, for sport health care professionals who do *not* have formal psychological training, the range of psychological interventions that can be provided competently is considerably narrower. (The proficiency of sport health care professionals in delivering psychological interventions can, of course, be expanded through curricular changes in the training of sport health care professionals [Gordon, Potter, & Ford, 1998] and educational programs [Arvinen-Barrow et al., 2008; Heaney, 2013; Stiller-Ostrowski, Gould, & Covassin, 2009].)

It almost goes without saying that access to athletes with injuries is a prerequisite for implementing psychological interventions in association with sport injury. Such access is generally possible for sport health care professionals by virtue of their frequent contact with athletes with injury. On the other hand, it is rare for professionals who are *not* directly involved in providing sport health care services (e.g., sport psychology consultants) to have consistent, unfettered access to athletes with injuries. In addition, access alone is not tantamount to availability. For example, sport health care professionals who have near-daily access to athletes with injury may still be limited in their availability to implement anything more than minimal psychological interventions. Sport psychology consultants, in

Several (though not all) of the psychological interventions examined in this chapter—specifically, goal setting, imagery, relaxation training, and self-talk—involve the same sorts of techniques used with athletes for performance enhancement. Noting parallels between the challenges of preparing for sport performance and those of completing sport injury rehabilitation, Heil (1993b) advocated that athletes participate in psychological skills training not only to address issues associated with rehabilitation (e.g., anxiety, fear, motivation, pain) but also to maintain continuity with their sport; to enhance their performance in rehabilitation; and to facilitate control of cognitions, emotions, and psychomotor skills

relevant to both sport injury rehabilitation and sport performance. For athletes who are already involved in a regimen of psychological skills training for enhancement of sport performance, such an approach would be a logical extension of their preinjury involvement.

Summary

A variety of psychological interventions have been used to treat athletes with injury. Relatively few of these interventions have experimental support. Nevertheless, research is providing increasing evidentiary support for implementing psychological interventions in sport health care. Among the interventions contrast, may be more routinely available to implement psychological interventions systematically but may lack the needed access to do so.

Another issue to consider when determining who should implement psychological interventions in sport health care is the degree to which professionals are interested in and comfortable with intervening psychologically with athletes with injury (Ray, Terrell, & Hough, 1999). Regardless of their competence, access, and availability, professionals are unlikely to implement psychological interventions with athletes during injury rehabilitation unless they are interested in doing so. On this point, in summarizing the findings of a survey examining the psychosocial strategies implemented by athletic trainers, Clement, Granquist, and Arvinen-Barrow (2013) noted that athletic trainers "may be using psychosocial strategies they are more confident in using, instead of those that are most effective and appropriate" (p. 518).

Indeed, most psychological interventions that have been found effective in enhancing sport injury rehabilitation processes and outcomes are not implemented on a standard basis. More specifically, research suggests that goal setting and communication skills (which are addressed in chapter 9) are the only psychological interventions used with regularity across various populations of sport health care professionals (Clement et al., 2013; Francis et al., 2000; Lafferty et al., 2008; Ninedek & Kolt, 2000; Stiller-Ostrowski & Hamson-Utley, 2010). Moreover, sport psychology consultants are generally not in a position to narrow this gap between science and practice because they lack consistent access to athletes with injuries. This prevailing pattern in implementation is likely to change only if we address issues pertaining to the competence, access, availability, and interest of professionals with respect to administering psychological interventions to athletes with injuries.

It is a promising sign that although sport health care professionals have reported a lack of formal training in psychological aspects of sport injury (Kamphoff et al., 2010; S. Pero, Tracey, & O'Neil, 2000; Stiller-Ostrowski & Ostrowski, 2009), they have also expressed an interest in learning more about the use of psychological interventions (Arvinen-Barrow et al., 2008; Clement et al., 2013; Kamphoff et al., 2010; Larson, Starkey, & Zaichkowsky, 1996; Stiller-Ostrowski & Ostrowski, 2009). Nevertheless, a definitive answer cannot yet be given to the question of who should implement psychological interventions in sport injury rehabilitation.

that have been applied are biofeedback, counseling, expressive writing, goal setting, imagery, modeling, multimodal interventions, performance enhancement groups, relaxation training, self-talk, and social support.

In using biofeedback, athletes with injuries receive information about one or more of their bodily processes. In electromyographic (EMG) biofeedback, which is the type used most frequently in sport injury rehabilitation, athletes receive feedback about electrical activity of a muscle or muscle group. This information can be used to facilitate increases in strength and range of motion.

In the context of sport injury, counseling involves supporting athletes as they identify and develop resources for coping with their injuries. In counseling, sport health care professionals build rapport and working alliances with athletes in order to help them address the challenges of sport injury rehabilitation.

Expressive writing, which for injured athletes involves writing about their injuries, is thought to affect cognitive, emotional, and physiological parameters. Athletes who have used expressive writing during rehabilitation have been observed to experience favorable changes in immune responses, stress levels, mood disturbances, and psychological adjustment.

Goal setting is commonly used to enhance both sport performance and sport injury rehabilitation. It involves identifying objectives that one would like to accomplish within a set time period. Goals can vary in terms of difficulty, specificity, target type, target domain, and timing. Rehabilitation goals should be challenging but realistic, specific and measurable, process- and outcome-focused, positively stated, and written down. Goal setting has been shown to exert favorable effects on rehabilitation adherence, strength, and performance satisfaction.

In sport health care, imagery involves athletes in intentionally generating internal representations that give rise to constructive perceptions of the injury experience. Imagery can serve cognitive, motivational, healing, and pain management purposes and has been shown to exert beneficial effects on cognitive-affective, behavioral, and (perceived) physical rehabilitation outcomes.

In modeling (sometimes referred to as imitation, observational learning, or vicarious learning), injured athletes are exposed to other athletes with injuries who display behaviors, attitudes, thoughts, or values considered desirable for successful rehabilitation. Visual exposure to adaptive models can be done either in person or by video. Researchers have not yet developed a good understanding of the mechanisms by which modeling achieves beneficial effects on cognitive-affective, behavioral, and physical rehabilitation outcomes.

Multimodal interventions combine interventions such as goal setting, imagery, and relaxation training to provide a more comprehensive treatment approach than might be possible with single interventions. Featuring almost exclusively cognitive-behavioral components, multimodal interventions give athletes the opportunity to connect with interventions that are to their liking. They have been perceived favorably by athletes and have been found effective in influencing a wide variety of rehabilitation outcomes. One particular challenge with multimodal interventions is that of establishing how much the individual components contribute to treatment outcomes.

In performance enhancement groups, psychological interventions are delivered to athletes with injury in a group setting. These groups use time and resources effectively and have the potential to equip athletes with social support and coping models during rehabilitation. They involve challenges, however, with respect to scheduling and creating appropriate groupings of athletes with injury.

Relaxation training includes an array of interventions designed to decrease responses to stress. Relaxation produces changes in both physiological parameters (e.g., heart rate, respiration rate, muscle tension) and psychological parameters (e.g., anxiety, decision making, confidence). Progressive relaxation and diaphragmatic (or abdominal) breathing are common relaxation techniques that may help athletes feel less anxious and more confident in their rehabilitation and return to play.

Self-talk interventions in sport injury rehabilitation involve teaching athletes with injuries to make statements to themselves that serve productive ends, such as learning new rehabilitation tasks, boosting motivation to adhere to rehabilitation activities, and managing stress. A versatile intervention, self-talk can be used to modify thoughts, feelings, behaviors, and physiological responses.

Social support consists of the resources that people close to athletes with injury provide as needed. Common providers of social support to athletes with injuries include family and friends, teammates and coaches, and sport health care professionals. Types of resources include those that bolster confidence, convey a sense of being listened to, instill feelings of comfort and security, enhance motivation, help solve problems, and furnish practical assistance during rehabilitation.

Despite the growing body of evidence that psychological interventions can exert beneficial effects on sport injury rehabilitation outcomes, they are not implemented routinely in sport health care. Although it is unclear as to which sport health care professionals are best situated and equipped to intervene psychologically in the context of sport injury, key considerations include competence and interest in implementing psychological interventions, consistency of access to athletes with injuries, and availability to implement the interventions.

Discussion Questions

1. Which psychological interventions in postinjury sport health care have the strongest empirical support, and what are the potential mechanisms by which they are effective?

2. What are some key considerations in determining which professionals should deliver psychological interventions to athletes with injuries?

3. What can sport health care professionals do to enhance the potentially positive effects of goal setting in sport injury rehabilitation?

4. What factors may influence athletes' receptiveness to psychological interventions in sport health care?

PART IV

Communication in Sport Injury Management

Part IV focuses on the vital importance of communication in the practice of sport health care professionals. Specifically, these two chapters address sport health care professionals' communication with patients and with professionals in other fields. These chapters emphasize the value of acquiring basic counseling skills and proficiency in referring athletes for psychological services.

Chapter 9

Communicating With Patients

Chapter Objectives

1. To describe the context of communication between athletes and sport health care professionals
2. To discuss models of the patient–practitioner relationship in sport health care
3. To examine functions, modes, congruence, factors affecting, and means of enhancing patient–practitioner communication in sport health care

Judging from the amount of blood seeping through her softball pants and on the dirt near second base, Erica knew that her injury was serious. She had sustained it in a collision with the base runner—or, more precisely, the baserunner's cleats. What she couldn't quite figure out was why she wasn't more upset about it. Perhaps the blood loss and the accompanying dizziness had gone to her head. More likely, however, it was the calm demeanor of the team's athletic trainer, Danielle, that had kept her from panicking. Ordinarily, Erica was squeamish around blood, but a few encouraging words, a brief grasping of her hand as she was lifted onto the gurney, and a general display of grace under pressure by Danielle had proved tremendously reassuring. Before her collision at second base, Erica had experienced only minimal direct contact with Danielle because she had been injury free. Nevertheless, Danielle had been around the team all season and had earned the players' trust—a trust that carried over in Erica's response to her injury and its aftermath.

Allison's rotator cuff surgery was happening in five days, and she was terrified. She wasn't sure why she felt so afraid. She had never had surgery before and didn't even know much about the procedure she was about to undergo. She figured that as one of the country's top 10 distance swimmers at the last Olympic Trials, she knew how to deal with pain better than most surgery patients. So she chalked her anxiety up to a fear of the unknown. With that uncertainty on her mind and her knees practically buckling under the weight of her worries, Allison was ushered from her surgeon's waiting room to the treatment area, where she was introduced to Phil, the physician assistant who would be guiding her through the preoperative visit and standing at her surgeon's side. Phil explained what would happen on the night before the surgery (i.e., fasting after 7 p.m.), on the day of surgery, and in the days and weeks afterward. He had Allison read a pamphlet about the surgery and watch *a brief video about the postoperative rehabilitation program, after which he answered her questions about the procedure and helped her think through her options for anesthesia and immediate postoperative care. As she departed from the clinic, Allison realized that as far as her surgery was concerned, the unknown had just gotten a lot smaller.*

As illustrated by these case examples, communication plays a central and inescapable role in the relationships between sport health care professionals and the athletes with whom they work. In surveys, both athletes (DeFrancesco, Miller, Larson, & Robinson, 1994; Fisher & Hoisington, 1993) and sport health care professionals (Fisher, Mullins, & Frye, 1993; Gordon, Milios, & Grove, 1991; Larson, Starkey, & Zaichkowsky, 1996; Wiese, Weiss, & Yukelson, 1991) have ascribed a high level of importance to communication in sport injury rehabilitation. Although research on patient–practitioner communication in the context of sport injury has been limited, evidence from other areas of health care suggests that the consequences of poor patient–practitioner communication include confusion, patient dissatisfaction, nonadherence to treatment, reduced future use of medical services, antibiotic resistance, and malpractice litigation (S.E. Taylor, 2012). In contrast, positive patient–practitioner communication can help build a trusting relationship, foster rehabilitation adherence, and activate placebo effects (Bystad, Bystad, & Wynn, 2015; Wright, Galtieri, & Fell, 2014).

With mindfulness of the potential effects of patient–practitioner communication on a variety of important processes and outcomes associated with sport injury, this chapter examines models of the patient–practitioner relationship, as well as functions, modes, congruence, factors affecting, and means of enhancing patient–practitioner communication. First, however, it considers the context in which patient–practitioner communication occurs.

Context of Patient–Practitioner Communication

Although considerable variability exists across sport health care systems, disciplines, visit purposes, and practitioners, most encounters with sport health care professionals tend to follow the same general format. That format, which constitutes the context in which athletes and sport health care professionals communicate with each other, has four main components (DiMatteo & Martin, 2002; Stiles, Putnam, Wolf, & James, 1979):

1. History taking and interviewing
2. Physical examination and diagnostic tests
3. Treatment
4. Medical recommendations

History Taking and Interviewing

Sport health care encounters generally begin with history taking and interviewing, in which sport health care professionals ask questions and athletes provide responses. History taking and interviewing are typically used most extensively during the initial evaluation (or intake interview), during which sport health care professionals inquire about the athletes' medical history; their sport injury experiences; how the current injury was sustained; what symptoms the athletes have experienced; what makes the symptoms better or worse; what treatments have been tried; how successful those treatments have been; and other matters of potential relevance to the diagnosis, treatment, and general well-being of the athletes (Prentice, 2011). At subsequent meetings, this component of the encounter is typically shorter than during the initial evaluation (possibly as brief as a minute or two), and the questions tend to focus on treatment adherence, side effects, and any changes in injury status or symptoms.

In gathering information about athletes and taking a history, sport health care professionals ask three main types of question: open (or open-ended), closed (or closed-ended), and focused (DiMatteo & Martin, 2002). Open questions invite athletes to talk and to elaborate on their situation (e.g., "What sorts of difficulty have you been having with your arm?"). These questions are particularly useful in the early part of the interview and can help the professional build rapport with the athlete by conveying assurance that the athlete's input is both expected and valued (Petitpas & Cornelius, 2004). Closed questions, in contrast, can be answered in a few words (e.g., "Can you bend your elbow without pain?"). Because closed questions can restrict the athlete's input and involvement in the conversation, they are best used near the end of the interview in order to obtain detailed information and ensure that information given earlier in the interview is accurately understood. The third kind of question—focused—enables sport health care professionals to request specific information in a way that does not limit the athlete's responses. Focused questions are narrower than open questions, but broader than closed questions—for example, "What seems to make the pain in your elbow worse?" (DiMatteo & Martin, 2002).

Athletes generally participate in history taking and interviewing by responding (or by not responding) to the questions they are asked. Their responses usually take the form of concerted answers, but even nonresponses (e.g., ignoring or failing to respond) can provide sport health care professionals with valuable information about the athletes and their attitude toward treatment.

Physical Examination and Diagnostic Tests

Physical examination and diagnostic tests generally follow history taking and interviewing, but a portion of the physical examination—observation—may begin while the history is taken, as the sport health care professional notes any evident deformities, swelling, atrophy, movement difficulties, protrusions or lumps, postural malalignments, or other signs of injury (Prentice, 2011). For athletes with injury, physical examinations and diagnostic testing commonly include palpation (touch) of both injured and uninjured sites, range-of-joint motion assessment, muscle strength testing, functional-performance testing, postural ex-

amination, and anthropometric measurements (Prentice). Additional information, if needed, can be gleaned (typically at another venue) through means such as X-rays (and other radiological tests), blood tests, and urinalysis in subsequent medical encounters.

Of all of the components of typical sport health care encounters, the physical examination and diagnostic tests most clearly highlight the discrepancy in power between sport health care professionals and athletes. Specifically, the fully clothed professional is allowed to poke, prod, and palpate the often scantily clad athlete, but reciprocity is not permitted (H. Friedman, 2002). This power differential is an important characteristic of the context in which communication occurs between sport health care professionals and athletes.

Treatment

Although treatment is not customarily included in descriptions of the basic format of medical encounters (DiMatteo & Martin, 2002; Stiles et al., 1979), it is addressed here in this framework due to its centrality to sport health care. For many athletes with injury, the vast majority of their encounters with sport health care professionals focus on participating in interventions designed to rehabilitate injured parts of the body. Some of these treatment activities closely resemble those of the physical-examination and diagnostic-testing component insofar as they involve sport health care professionals in touching athletes or challenging their physical capabilities. There is, however, an important distinction. Whereas the activities of the physical-examination and diagnostic-testing component are geared toward finding out what is wrong with the athlete, the activities of the treatment component are aimed at helping the athlete get better. This distinction creates a dynamic with important ramifications for how sport health care professionals and athletes with injury communicate with each other.

Medical Recommendations

Whether focused on diagnosis or treatment, most sport health care encounters conclude with medical recommendations. During initial evaluations, common recommendations include prescriptions for medication or physical therapy, suggestions for home health behavior (e.g., lifestyle changes, rehabilitation exercises, use of therapeutic modalities), and referrals to other professionals for treatment or additional diagnostic testing. At the conclusion of treatment sessions, recommendations tend to emphasize what athletes should do away from the office or clinic between appointments. Although the medical-recommendations component is more likely than the other three components to involve "telling" rather than "asking," sport health care professionals can still benefit from listening carefully to any questions, comments, or concerns that athletes have about recommendations.

Models of the Patient–Practitioner Relationship

It has long been recognized that relationships between health care professionals and their patients can be characterized by several distinct styles of interaction. In a classic article, Szasz and Hollender (1956) identified three styles of doctor–patient interaction: activity–passivity, guidance–cooperation, and mutual participation. In the traditional activity-passivity pattern, practitioners take responsibility for the personal welfare of their patients because patients are unable to participate in their own care (due to factors such as medical condition and lack of knowledge). A slightly less paternalistic role is ascribed to practitioners in the guidance–cooperation style, in which practitioners still take the main responsibility for diagnosis and treatment but patients must cooperate by providing information to the practitioners and following their recommendations. In the mutual participation pattern, patients and practitioners share the responsibility of making decisions about all aspects of health care (e.g., diagnostic tests, treatments). Subsequent descriptions of relationship patterns between patients and practitioners (Ballard-Reisch, 1990; Roter & Hall, 1992) have included categories similar to those put forth by Szasz and Hollender, with the notable addition of a patient autonomy (or consumerist) style in

which patients wield the power and assume all responsibility for health care decisions.

In sport health care, the activity–passivity pattern may be especially likely to occur with athletes who have sustained severe injuries that require major medical intervention (e.g., emergency surgery), whereas the guidance–cooperation pattern may prevail with athletes who are undergoing a complex program of postinjury physical rehabilitation. If athletes are knowledgeable about their injuries and the available diagnostic and treatment options, they may be inclined to engage in the mutual participation style of interaction with sport health care professionals. If they learn of treatments used effectively with other athletes, they may adopt a patient autonomy approach and request those treatments from their own sport health care professionals.

Given that patient–practitioner relationships are by definition interactive, patterns of communication are likely to vary both across and within practitioners. In other words, a given practitioner may adopt typical ways of interacting with athletes that differ from the approaches taken by another practitioner; in addition, the first practitioner's interactions with athletes may vary widely among themselves, depending on each athlete's characteristics and behavior. For example, some athletic trainers exhibit a general tendency toward a guidance–cooperation approach but may support a patient autonomy style when faced with athletes who are highly educated about their injury and rehabilitation options and hold strong opinions about how rehabilitation should proceed.

Functions of Patient– Practitioner Communication

Communication between athletes with injury and sport health care professionals serves two broad functions: informational and socioemotional. In terms of the informational function, one primary function of communication in sport health care is to convey injury-related and treatment-related details and recommendations to athletes; such informational communication is predominant in rehabilitation settings (Hokanson, 1994; Owen & Goodge, 1981). Although microlevel analyses are not available for the information exchanged between athletes and their sport health care professionals, it has been suggested that professionals should clearly communicate the following types of information:

- The nature, severity, and likely course of the injury
- The prescribed rehabilitation program and the rationale for it
- Expectations about pain, symptoms, mobility, and recovery
- The necessity of injury management skills
- Willingness to listen to and address the athlete's injury-related concerns (Wiese & Weiss, 1987)

On a day-to-day basis, informational communication in sport health care tends to focus on changes in the athlete's injury status since the preceding office visit, as well as any modifications in the rehabilitation program.

Socioemotional communication is the means through which sport health care professionals convey that they are warm and empathic people who genuinely care about the physical and psychological well-being of athletes (O'Hair, O'Hair, Southward, & Krayer, 1987). Less common than its informational counterpart in rehabilitation settings (Hokanson, 1994; Owen & Goodge, 1981), socioemotional communication can play an important role in building working alliances between athletes and sport health care professionals (Petitpas & Cornelius, 2004). Examples of socioemotional communication include inquiring about how athletes feel or are dealing with activities of daily living, engaging in conversation about topics unrelated to injury, and using gestures that convey support (e.g., nodding one's head in agreement, giving a pat on the back).

Modes of Patient–Practitioner Communication

Sport health care professionals and athletes with injuries communicate with each other both verbally and nonverbally. Verbal interaction is used to fulfill most of the informational function of their communication, whereas the socioemotional function is performed both verbally and nonverbally. Both modes can be used to convey details of critical importance in treating injured athletes.

Verbal Communication

Verbal communication includes both spoken and written words. As noted earlier (in the section on history taking and interviewing), the wording of a question can affect the type, quantity, and quality of information obtained in response. Other aspects of verbal communication can also influence how effectively information is provided and received in sport health care. In particular, it has been suggested that sport health care professionals can enhance their verbal communication by attending to the vocabulary, organization, clarity, and length of the messages they communicate (Wiese-Bjornstal, Gardetto, & Shaffer, 1999). With respect to vocabulary, excessive use of medical jargon can hamper communication with athletes. When sport health care professionals use overly technical terms, athletes may not fully understand the information being offered, but—wishing not to appear unintelligent, uneducated, or inattentive—athletes may not inform the professionals of this lack of understanding. Sport health care professionals may use jargon more often than necessary for the following reasons:

- They are so familiar with technical language that they forget that athletes may not fully understand it.
- They want to present themselves as competent, educated practitioners.
- They don't want to take the time to communicate in simpler terms.
- They wish to keep an "emotional distance" from athletes' medical concerns.
- They want to disguise their lack of certainty about athletes' medical condition. (DiMatteo & Martin, 2002; Friedman, 2002)

Athletes are often more knowledgeable about their bodies than are the typical medical patient, but even basic medical knowledge cannot be assumed without taking the risk of going "over the head" of athletes.

Effective communication between sport health care professionals and athletes also requires good organization, clarity, and appropriate message length. To increase the likelihood that verbal messages get through to athletes as intended, professionals should organize their information logically, deliver it both clearly and concisely, and present the most important details both at the start and multiple times thereafter (Wiese-Bjornstal et al., 1999). Approaching verbal communication in this manner requires forethought and planning, but doing so reduces the potential for misunderstanding and other hazards of poor communication.

Verbal messages may also be more effective when they are phrased positively and when the amount of "noise" in the communication system is minimized. Positively phrased messages indicate not which behaviors athletes should avoid but which ones they should carry out. For example, a sport health care professional could specify which preventive or rehabilitative exercises athletes should perform and then offer reinforcement as the athletes make progress toward completing the exercise prescription (Wiese & Weiss, 1987). Noise, on the other hand, consists of factors that impede the successful transmission of messages from senders to receivers (R. Martens, 1987). As suggested by Wiese-Bjornstal et al. (1999), noise can contribute to miscommunication due to factors associated with the sport health care professional (e.g., past experiences, poorly composed messages, personal biases), factors associated with the athlete (e.g., emotional state, attention), and other factors (e.g., environmental distractions). Presumably, minimizing noise can enhance the extent to which verbal messages get through to athletes.

Nonverbal Communication

Nonverbal communication also plays a prominent role in interactions between sport health care professionals and athletes with injuries. Indeed, the nonverbal behavior of practitio-

ners conveys a great deal of information, both about the practitioners and about their perceptions of athletes. Athletes with injury often are experiencing an emotionally uncertain situation and may look to sport health care professionals for subtle clues about their medical condition and prognosis (Friedman, 2002). Attending to practitioners' nonverbal behavior can enable athletes to "read between the lines" of verbal communication, detect deception (e.g., minimizing an injury's effects in order to spare the athlete's emotions), and learn how to respond to the situation. Relative to practitioners, athletes with injury occupy a position of weakness and may seek nonverbal feedback regarding how they are doing as patients (DiMatteo & Martin, 2002). Consequently, it is important for sport health care professionals to become aware of their nonverbal behavior and how it can affect athletes.

Just as patients can learn by examining practitioners' nonverbal behavior, sport health care professionals can attend to athletes' nonverbal behavior in order to gain a better understanding of them. For example, athletes who are reluctant to disclose injury-related fears or depressed mood in words may instead reveal their emotional state nonverbally. Therefore, ignoring patients' nonverbal communication can cut practitioners off from a potentially valuable source of information that may be hard to access through verbal assessment. Furthermore, patients tend to be more satisfied and cooperative with practitioners who are adept at reading their nonverbal cues (DiMatteo, Hays, & Prince, 1986; DiMatteo, Taranta, Friedman, & Prince, 1980).

A framework proposed by R. Martens (1987) and adapted to the context of sport health care by Wiese-Bjornstal et al. (1999) posits three dimensions of nonverbal communication: kinesics, proxemics, and paralanguage. As displayed in table 9.1, the nonverbal behaviors associated with each dimension may convey a specific, culturally relative message; that is, the messages conveyed by certain nonverbal behaviors may vary both across cultures and across individuals within a culture. The broadest of the three dimensions, kinesics, covers a wide range of nonverbal behaviors,

TABLE 9.1 Nonverbal Communication

Kinesics	
Nonverbal communication	**Possible message(s) conveyed**
Attention to personal appearance (e.g., manner of dress, grooming, fitness level)	Professionalism
Punctuality	Respect (Caveat: some cultures view a certain amount of tardiness as respectful.)
Upright, purposeful posture and gait	Enthusiasm, confidence
Gestures such as rubbing hands together	Anticipation, enthusiasm
Gestures such as extending arms out in front with palms up	Sincerity, openness
Firm, positive handshake	Confidence
Holding the other person's hands in yours just in front of your chest	Calming, reassurance
Lightly touching the speaker's arm	Desire to interrupt (politely)
Looking directly into each other's eyes (known as *line of regard*) for a long time	Conflict, anger
Facial expressions such as smiles and "smiling eyes"	Happiness, relaxation
Facial expressions such as a glazed or unfocused look in the eyes	Boredom, distraction, fatigue
Facial expressions such as a furrowed brow	Puzzlement, deep thought, concentration
Smells (e.g., overpowering cologne or perfume)	May be intolerable to patients
Proxemics*	
Communication through use of space	**Important considerations**
Moving into the *intimate zone* (0-1.5 ft., or 0-0.5 m, apart), which is necessary for physical examinations and therapeutic interventions	Be sensitive to the fact that the athlete may feel threatened or embarrassed because this space is usually reserved for lovers and very close friends.
Moving into the *personal zone* (1.5-4 ft., or 0.5-1.2 m, apart), as in a one-on-one meeting with an athlete	Realize that this zone is typically reserved for friends and acquaintances; thus there may be some discomfort with having to share at so personal a level. Allow athletes to back off slightly if they seem more comfortable that way.
Interactions in the *social zone* (4-12 ft., or 1.2-3.7 m, apart), which is the distance for most professional interactions with athletes, coaches, and sports medicine colleagues	This seems to be a safe distance from which to conduct most professional business with people from different cultures.
Interactions in the *public zone* (more than 20 ft., or 6 m, apart), as when conducting group education sessions or teaching classes	This distance conveys a more impersonal presence, which may or may not be desired, depending on the purpose of the communication.

(continued)

TABLE 9.1   *(continued)*

Paralanguage	
Vocal components of speech	**Possible message(s) conveyed**
Lowering of vocal pitch	Fatigue, calmness, depression
Rising of vocal pitch	Joy, fear, anger
Thin resonance	Insecurity, weakness, indecisiveness
Rich resonance	Firmness, self-assurance, strength
Articulation slightly slurred; drawl	Atmosphere of comfort or intimacy
Articulation crisp and clear	Decisiveness, confidence
Fast tempo	Excitement, persuasion (but may also suggest insecurity or make the listener nervous)
Slower tempo	Sincerity, thoughtfulness
Louder voice	Confidence, enthusiasm (but may also suggest aggressiveness or arrogance)
Softer voice	Trustworthiness, caring, understanding (but may also suggest lack of confidence)

*Distances given are generally relevant for cultures in North America; they may vary for other cultures.
Adapted from Martens 1987.

including physical appearance, body language (e.g., gestures, posture, gait), facial expressions, touch, and smell. Body language is the most difficult nonverbal medium to control, and it conveys information about emotional states (DiMatteo & Martin, 2002) and attempts at deception (H.S. Friedman, Hall, & Harris, 1985; Riggio & Friedman, 1983). For example, fidgeting may suggest nervousness or anxiety, a slumped posture may indicate dejection or depression, and a vigorous stride may correspond to optimism or confidence (DiMatteo & Martin).

Like body language, facial expressions convey an abundance of information about psychological states, such as the six basic emotions (anger, disgust, fear, happiness, sadness, and surprise) and pain (Friedman, 2002). Unlike body language, however, facial expressions are controllable (Ekman & Friesen, 1974), and practitioners can use their facial expressions to communicate sympathy, understanding, and a positive outlook to their patients (Friedman, 2002). Practitioners can also enhance commu-

nication by attending to their patients' facial expressions. As is the case with nonverbal communication in general, practitioners who are skilled at reading their patients' emotions from their facial expressions tend to elicit favorable evaluations and cooperative behavior from patients (DiMatteo, Taranta, et al., 1980; DiMatteo, Hays, & Prince, 1986). Particularly important to facial expressions are the eyes, sometimes characterized as "windows to the soul," which contribute substantially to the power of nonverbal communication. Eye contact can intensify prevailing emotions (whether for better or for worse) and can signify that the practitioner is attending to and interested in hearing what the patient has to say. Patients generally seek more eye contact than they receive from practitioners, whose focus is often directed at medical charts or at body parts other than the patient's face (DiMatteo & Martin, 2002; Petitpas & Cornelius, 2004).

Touch is a nonverbal medium of particular relevance to sport health care; indeed, in some branches (e.g., athletic training, massage therapy, physical therapy), touch can be an essential part of the service delivered to athletes. Examples include palpation, deep tissue massage, and joint mobilization, which of course cannot be applied without the practitioner touching the patient (Kolt, 2000). As noted earlier, touch between practitioners and patients is not reciprocal. Nevertheless, it can imbue relationships between sport health care professionals and the athletes they are treating with a (high) level of closeness not typically present in patient–practitioner interactions. Some athletes find the amount of touch involved in sport health care to be discomforting and reflective of the power differential between patients and practitioners, whereas others interpret touch as a sign of caring and thus experience it as relaxing and facilitative of emotional release (Kolt, 2000; Nathan, 1999).

The final category is smell. Athletes and sport health care professionals alike (as well as their apparel) may acquire distinctive odors by virtue of the physical exertion that characterizes both sport and rehabilitation activities and the provision of sport health care services. These odors render smell a nonverbal medium of potential relevance in sport health care. Strong, unpleasant smells—regardless of whether they are due to body odor, liniment, or perfume or cologne—can repel an individual and thus may alter the facial expression of one who inhales them (Friedman, 2002). If athletes or practitioners retreat from such a smell, or express displeasure facially, this behavior is unlikely to facilitate either effective treatment or a positive patient–practitioner relationship.

Proxemics

Pertaining solely to communication through the occupation of space (R. Martens, 1987), proxemics is the narrowest of the three dimensions of nonverbal communication. In sport health care, one especially meaningful aspect of proxemics involves the distance between patients and practitioners. As already noted, depending on the particular diagnostic or therapeutic services being provided, sport health care professionals and athletes with injuries may interact in close quarters—so close, in fact, that they may touch. When touching or in

very close proximity, patients and practitioners are interacting in what has been characterized as an intimate distance (E.T. Hall, 1966). Such closeness may cause patients to feel uncomfortable, especially if they do not know what practitioners are doing or why it is being done. To address such concern, some physicians explain why they are putting a cold stethoscope on a patient's chest and warn the patient when the touch is coming. Similarly, an athletic trainer can, for example, indicate which parts of an athlete's body will be touched before helping the athlete with certain stretches.

Beyond the intimate zone, in order of outward progression, lie the personal, social, and public zones (E.T. Hall, 1966). Like most aspects of nonverbal communication, the specific distances corresponding to each zone are culturally relative. Therefore, a distance that feels like an invasion of personal space to athletes from one culture may seem completely appropriate to athletes from another culture. Approximations of the four zones for North America are depicted in table 9.1. The potential for a patient to experience discomfort due to the practitioner's proximity is generally greatest at the intimate and personal distances. However, difficulties can also arise if a patient perceives the practitioner as reluctant to touch or get close to the athlete or if the practitioner discusses personal or private matters at a social or public distance that might allow others to overhear (DiMatteo & Martin, 2002).

Paralanguage

The third dimension of nonverbal communication—paralanguage—can influence how verbal messages that are delivered orally (i.e., through spoken words) are interpreted. Paralanguage involves vocal characteristics (e.g., articulation, pitch, resonance, tempo, volume) that communicate information about patients and practitioners over and above what is communicated by their words. For example, depending on the context, a high-pitched voice might convey joy, fear, or anger (Wiese-Bjornstal et al., 1999). One particular form of paralanguage that athletes with injuries may largely escape is that of "baby talk," in which practitioners use simplified vocabulary uttered in a high-pitched tone. Although baby talk is evident among practitioners serving other patient populations (Friedman, 2002), the emphasis on stoicism in the sport ethic (see chapter 1) may militate against its use in sport health care settings, where a "gruff," no-nonsense presentation of verbal information may operate in its place. It behooves sport health care professionals to develop adequate paralanguage skills, because research has shown that practitioners with better voice control tend to be better liked by their patients than those with less voice control (Friedman, DiMatteo, & Taranta, 1980).

Congruence of Patient and Practitioner Perceptions

Given the importance of communication in sport health care, it is vital for patients and practitioners to be "on the same page" with respect to injury-related issues. Often, however, this is not the case, according to a small body of literature addressing the congruence between perceptions held by sport health care professionals and those held by athletes with injuries. This research has examined the correspondence between patients' and practitioners' perceptions of rehabilitation regimens, recovery progress, and psychological states.

Rehabilitation Regimens

Rehabilitation regimens constitute a key aspect of sport health care because they provide objective blueprints for athletes' recovery from injury. It is surprising, therefore, that patients and practitioners are less than wholly congruent in their views of what is expected of athletes undergoing rehabilitation. For example, Kahanov and Fairchild (1994) investigated discrepancies between athletes and their athletic trainers regarding what transpired during the initial evaluation. The study found significant patient–practitioner disagreement regarding whether the athlete understood the rehabilitation program (disagreement for 52 percent of athlete–athletic trainer pairs), whether the goal of returning to activity was discussed (48 per-

cent disagreement), whether weekly objectives were discussed (62 percent disagreement), and whether a written rehabilitation protocol was given to the athlete (54 percent disagreement). These levels of disagreement are astonishing when one considers that the perceptions were assessed within 24 hours for all participants and within 3 hours for the majority! Presumably, the discrepancies would have been even larger with the passage of more time.

Similar findings were obtained in studies by May and Taylor (1994) and Webborn, Carbon, and Miller (1997). May and Taylor compared athletes' estimates of the time required to do their home rehabilitation exercises with estimates from the physiotherapists who had prescribed them. On average, the athletes' estimates were 42 percent lower than those of the physiotherapists. In the Webborn et al. study, sport injury patients at a clinic were questioned immediately after a rehabilitation session in which they had been prescribed an exercise program. Specifically, they were asked to identify the site (i.e., body location), frequency, number of repetitions, and purpose of their prescribed exercise(s). Despite the short interval of time between prescription and inquiry, the athletes' retention of the information was poor; indeed, 77 percent responded incorrectly regarding at least one aspect of the exercise program. Thus, in terms of perceptions of a rehabilitation program, it appears that a general lack of congruence exists between the perceptions of athletes with injuries and their sport health care professionals.

Recovery Progress

As the central focus of sport injury rehabilitation, patient progress is a matter in which patients and practitioners are mutually interested and invested. Research on perceptions of recovery progress has yielded evidence of both congruence and discrepancy between the perceptions of athletes with injury and those of sport health care professionals. In the first study on this topic, Crossman and Jamieson (1985) documented moderate positive correlations between athlete and athletic-trainer ratings of the seriousness and disruptiveness of patients' injuries. Nevertheless, the athletes' ratings were significantly higher than those of the athletic trainers for injury severity and significantly lower than those of the athletic trainers for injury disruptiveness. In the absence of objective outcome data, it is unclear how accurate the athletes and athletic trainers were in their ratings. The important point is that discrepancies appeared between patients and practitioners in their perceptions of important parameters in sport injury rehabilitation. The disruptiveness finding of Crossman and Jamieson was replicated by Crossman, Jamieson, and Hume (1990), who reported that athletes rated their injuries as having significantly more of a disruptive effect than did sport health care professionals.

These findings by Crossman and her colleagues (Crossman & Jamieson, 1985; Crossman et al., 1990) have been bolstered by additional research documenting significant positive associations between the recovery-progress perceptions of athletes with injury and those of sport health care professionals. Specifically, athletes' views of their progress in sport injury rehabilitation were found congruent with those of athletic trainers (Van Raalte, Brewer, & Petitpas, 1992), sports medicine physicians (Brewer, Linder, & Phelps, 1995), and a mixed group of physical therapists and athletic trainers (Brewer, Van Raalte, Petitpas, Sklar, & Ditmar, 1995). Thus, although athletes may sometimes paint a more optimistic picture of their rehabilitation status than their sport health care professionals do (e.g., Brewer, Van Raalte, et al., 1995; Van Raalte, Brewer, & Petitpas, 1992), there is also evidence of a "shared reality" between patients and practitioners in sport health care—a state that may reflect the quality of communication between the two constituencies.

Psychological States

It is reasonable to expect congruence between patient and practitioner perceptions of something as objectively verifiable as a rehabilitation regimen and possibly even something as overtly manifested as rehabilitation progress. It is decidedly more ambitious, however, to expect sport health care practitioners' perceptions of patients' psychological states to match the patients' perceptions of those states. In order for practitioners to obtain knowledge of a patients' states, it is necessary for

a. the patients to exhibit evidence of the psychological states through their behavior;
b. the patients to disclose their psychological states to the practitioners;
c. the practitioners to administer diagnostic tests designed to identify the psychological states; or
d. some combination of options a, b, and c to occur.

Because assessment of psychological states is *not* standard practice in most sport health care settings, practitioners generally must rely on their observations of and conversations with patients in order to infer what patients might be experiencing psychologically.

Of the many psychological states that athletes may experience, one of the most important is psychological distress. Not only is psychological distress discomforting in its own right, but also, as noted earlier, emotional disturbance is inversely related to both rehabilitation adherence (chapter 6) and rehabilitation outcomes (chapter 7). Unsurprisingly, however, for the reasons identified in the preceding paragraph, one study (Brewer, Petitpas, Van Raalte, Sklar, & Ditmar, 1995) found that practitioners' ratings of athlete behaviors suggestive of psychological distress were not correlated with athletes' reports of their own psychological distress. In a second study (S.D. Maniar, Perna, Newcomer, Roh, & Stilger, 1999), athletic trainers' ratings of depression in athletes with injuries *were* positively correlated with the athletes' self-reported depression but were *not* associated with ratings of depression based on a clinical interview.

Lack of correspondence has also been found between athletes' self-reports and practitioners' perceptions of those athletes for another psychological state—motivation. In this study (Kahanov & Fairchild, 1994), athletic trainers rated the athletes with injuries as being more motivated than was indicated by the athletes' ratings of themselves. These findings highlight the need for sport health care professionals to work purposefully to be attuned to the psychological states of the athletes they treat.

Factors Affecting Patient–Practitioner Communication

Communication between athletes with injuries and sport health care professionals is clearly a two-way street. As a result, it can be influenced by the attitudes and behaviors of both practitioners and patients, as well as by factors reflecting the interaction between the two parties. Although there is a dearth of research examining factors that affect patient–practitioner communication in the specific setting of sport health care, inferences can be drawn from pertinent investigations in other areas of health care.

Practitioner Attitudes and Behaviors

Some of the difficulties that sport health care professionals and athletes with injuries encounter in communicating with each other can be attributed to attitudes and behaviors exhibited by the sport health care professional. Examples include failing to listen, treating patients as objects, maintaining stereotypes of patients, spending too little time with patients, and using medical jargon (Straub, 2012). When practitioners fail to listen adequately to their patients, they essentially block one path of the bidirectional flow of information that constitutes communication. Failure to listen is rarely intentional; instead, it usually occurs as a consequence of frequently interrupting patients or monopolizing conversations with them (Beckman & Frankel, 1984). One unfortunate consequence of failing to listen is that it can prevent patients from explaining their concerns and asking important questions.

When practitioners treat patients as objects rather than as people, they engage in a process known as depersonalization. This process may allow practitioners to focus on the medical problem at hand and offer them a defense against becoming emotionally overinvolved; for patients, however, it can be extremely dis-

tressing (S.E. Taylor, 2012). In sport health care, practitioners sometimes treat athletes as objects by referring to them not by name but by the injured body part (e.g., "Where's the Knee? I've got the Hip coming in at 3:30."). Referring to patients by name can, of course, help patients feel that they are being treated as people rather than objects—and as active partners in the rehabilitation process rather than passive recipients of treatment (Petitpas & Cornelius, 2004).

Practitioners can also adversely affect patient–practitioner communication by maintaining stereotypes of patients (Straub, 2012). Whereas some negative attitudes are directed toward patients with certain demographic characteristics (e.g., age, gender, race, ethnicity, or sexual orientation), others target sport-specific characteristics (e.g., position, sport). For example, viewing athletes in a particular sport as "wealthy, overprivileged, marijuana-smoking dirtbags with a strong sense of entitlement" could of course impede a practitioner's effective communication with athletes who participate in that sport.

Spending too little time with a patient can also hinder effective patient–practitioner communication because it can limit both the quality and the quantity of information that the practitioner presents to the patient; it can also undercut the practitioner's ability to listen to the patient. In sport health care, the amount of time that practitioners have available to spend with athletes can vary considerably, ranging from a few minutes (e.g., office appointment with a busy orthopedic surgeon, prepractice visit to a frenetic university athletic training room) to an hour or more (e.g., consultation with a professional who travels with the team). When time is short, it behooves practitioners to—at a minimum—greet their patients (ideally by name), inquire about how they are doing, and allow them to identify any issues or concerns they may have.

As noted earlier (in the section on verbal communication), effective communication is also compromised when practitioners overuse medical jargon. When only one of the parties in the patient–practitioner dyad fully understands the language being used, the potential for miscommunication increases dramatically. Therefore, it is generally appropriate for sport health care professionals to use lay terminology and explanations when interacting with athletes—unless, of course, they are sure that a given athlete is familiar with more technical language.

Patient Attitudes and Behaviors

As a partner in the patient–practitioner dyad, the patient also bears some responsibility for the communication that takes place between the two parties. In fact, the way in which a patient reports and responds to health-related information can be particularly influential on patient–practitioner communication. For instance, patients who are high in neuroticism (a personality characteristic) tend to portray their symptoms in an exaggerated manner (Ellington & Wiebe, 1999), which makes it difficult for practitioners to accurately assess what these patients are experiencing. In another example, anxiety can occur in sport health care environments when athletes are unsure about the nature of their injury and its ramifications for sport participation; this anxiety can impair athletes' ability to attend to, process, and recall information (Graugaard & Finset, 2000). Patients can also hamper communication in the following ways: focusing on symptoms to the exclusion of the underlying causes of injury, failing to provide key details about their medical history, neglecting to ask questions when they are unclear about what a practitioner has said, or minimizing potentially important symptoms (S.E. Taylor, 2012). This latter behavior is particularly salient in sport health care settings due to the sport ethic (discussed in chapter 1) and to athletes' legitimate concerns that full disclosure of their symptoms may result in restriction of their sport participation.

Interactive Factors

The third group of influences on patient–practitioner communication resides neither in patients nor in practitioners; instead, it is a product of the interaction between the two parties. In some respects, *all* influences on pa-tient–practitioner communication—including the practitioner and patient factors described in the preceding paragraphs—can be considered interactive factors. Communication is a process in which the participants exert a mutual influence on each other. For example, although there are certainly some sport health care professionals who do not allow time for athletes to ask questions, there are also athletes who lack the assertiveness to ensure that their questions are answered (DiMatteo & Martin, 2002).

Because some practitioners are so rushed that even the most assertive patients will be unable to ask questions and some athletes are so unassertive that they won't ask questions of even the most solicitous practitioners, however, some influences can be considered *more* interactive than the ones just mentioned. One such influence involves the extent to which athletes with injuries and sport health care professionals differ from each other on important demographic characteristics. That is, misunderstandings are more likely to occur between patients and practitioners when the two parties differ in age, gender, race, ethnicity, religion, or sport background. Of course, such differences do not inevitably doom patient–practitioner communication, and effective dialogue can be facilitated by either individual, or both, through active efforts to bridge the gap as necessary.

Another interactive influence on patient–practitioner communication involves the process by which sport health care professionals receive (or, more accurately, do not receive) feedback about their behavior from patients. For example, when athletes with injury regularly attend rehabilitation sessions over an extended period of time, practitioners can reasonably infer that the things they are saying and doing are, at a minimum, not chasing the athletes away and may actually be contributing to the athletes' recovery. So far, so good. But what about when athletes do *not* return for further treatment? In this situation, sport health care professionals rarely receive direct feedback about their communication with the athletes either before or after the athletes' departure.

As a result, practitioners are left with questions: Did the athletes not return because they are healed and completely satisfied? Because they are not at all recovered and are grossly dissatisfied? Because the athletes moved out of town and switched to a new practitioner? Much of the time, practitioners cannot answer such questions because they do not receive feedback about their behavior. Even when athletes *do* return for ongoing treatment, sport health care professionals may not receive feedback about their relationship with the athlete or the extent to which the athlete is adhering to treatment recommendations away from the rehabilitation facility. Given the lack of feedback about communication with patients, it would be surprising if practitioners were inclined to change the way they interact with them (S.E. Taylor, 2012).

Enhancing Patient– Practitioner Communication

As the preceding sections indicate, important outcomes are associated with the quality of patient–practitioner communication, which serves key informational and socioemotional functions in sport health care. However, significant discrepancies have been documented between the perceptions reported by patients and those reported by practitioners; therefore, we have much to gain by enhancing communication between the two parties. This goal has been pursued by means of two main approaches—interventions with practitioners and interventions with patients.

Interventions With Practitioners

Having recognized the advantages of physicians being attuned to the needs of their patients, medical schools have developed training programs to help doctors communicate more effectively with patients. These programs typically target common interpersonal courtesies (e.g., greeting patients by name, explaining procedures, saying goodbye), discussion of sensitive or difficult health topics, delivery of bad news, patient education, and how to help patients ask questions and remember key in-

formation. To help doctors develop such communication skills, training programs use video feedback and role-play exercises (Straub, 2012; S.E. Taylor, 2012). Similar coursework has been implemented with physical therapists and found effective in improving their communication skills (Ladyshewsky & Gotjamanos, 1997; Levin & Riley, 1984).

Although communication skills are recognized as vital to the practice of sport health care (Ray, Terrell, & Hough, 1999), relevant training for sport health care professionals has not reached the level of that found in medical schools on a consistent basis. With an eye toward addressing this gap, Gordon, Potter, and Ford (1998) proposed an extensive psychoeducational curriculum for sport health care professionals that prominently featured both lecture and applied experiences devoted to building communication skills in the context of sport health care. However, this curriculum has remained in prototype form and has not been implemented on a widespread basis. Even so, many sport health care professionals do receive some training in relevant communication skills through coursework in counseling. Basic counseling skills overlap heavily with the communication skills used in sport health care and therefore can help sport health care professionals build effective working alliances with patients.

In the context of sport health care, working alliances are relationships in which professionals and athletes collaborate to help athletes manage their injuries. A working alliance is designed to create an environment of trust and unified purpose, thus forging an emotional bond between the sport health care professional and the athlete and ensuring that the two parties are in agreement with respect to the goals and methods of treatment (Petitpas & Cornelius, 2004). Based on the influential work of Carl Rogers (1957), Petitpas and Cornelius suggested that an effective working alliance with an athlete depends on the practitioner's ability to communicate genuineness, acceptance, and empathy. Practitioners exhibit genuineness when they are true to themselves, aware of and open to appropriately sharing their feelings, and able to display nonverbal communication that is consistent with their verbal communication. Practitioners convey acceptance when they demonstrate unconditional positive regard for athletes and show respect for them regardless of what they do, think, or feel. Finally, practitioners display empathy when they show understanding of athletes' feelings and experiences from the athletes' perspectives. By communicating genuineness, acceptance, and empathy to athletes with injuries, sport health care professionals can facilitate the creation of an atmosphere of trust, caring, and understanding in which a working alliance can grow and thrive (Petitpas & Cornelius, 2004).

So, how exactly do sport health care professionals go about communicating genuineness, acceptance, and empathy? Learning and implementing basic counseling skills may help practitioners not only accomplish this goal but also help them put into practice their knowledge about patient–practitioner communication (e.g., informational and socioemotional functions, verbal and nonverbal modes). Basic counseling skills can be organized and described according to multiple models (e.g., Culley & Bond, 2007; Egan, 2014; Ivey, Ivey, & Zalaquett, 2013; Kottler, 2003; M.E. Young, 2012). These frameworks vary with respect to terminology and skill categorization but feature substantially similar behaviors. Specifically, in the context of sport health care, basic counseling skills can be divided into three groups based on their main function: *attending* to athletes and their concerns, *exploring* athletes' current concerns, and *influencing* athletes' thoughts or behaviors pertaining to their current concerns. These three types of skill are neither discrete nor mutually exclusive; rather, the boundaries between the categories are permeable—for example, there is no clear line at which exploring ends and influencing begins—and some skills (e.g., listening) overlap more than one category. Still, for the purpose of understanding, it is useful to examine each type individually.

Attending Skills

Also known as "invitational skills" (M.E. Young, 2012), attending skills involve verbal and non-verbal behaviors that convey the practitioner's interest in "tuning in" (Egan, 2014) or listening to what athletes with injury have to say. As the term implies, attending involves paying attention to athletes, which can be communicated nonverbally by maintaining direct eye contact (as appropriate, without staring), displaying receptive body language (e.g., encouraging gestures and facial expressions, relaxed posture, slight forward lean facing athletes at a socially appropriate conversational distance), and using appropriately varied vocal tones (Culley & Bond, 2007; Ivey et al., 2013; Kottler, 2003; M.E. Young). Verbal indicators, on the other hand, include inviting athletes to speak and staying on the topics that they bring up (Ivey et al.; M.E. Young). When practitioners give their attention to athletes and show their willingness to listen, they communicate genuineness and acceptance right from the start (Waumsley & Katz, 2013).

Exploring Skills

Through the process of exploration, sport health care professionals and athletes alike can learn more about the athletes' current concerns. Exploring typically begins when the practitioner asks questions. As discussed earlier in this chapter, the various types of question—closed, open, and focused—can generate different sorts of response from athletes. After the use of questioning gets the conversation started, the professional can help continue it by restating a few key words or phrases uttered by the athlete (e.g., "skiing career went kaput," "trained too hard") or by using brief statements that nudge athletes gently without intruding on their ideas (e.g., "tell me more," "uh huh," "and . . ."). Such encouragement not only stimulates conversation but also serves as an important form of active listening to the athlete's responses. Whereas passive listening involves merely hearing what another person says, active listening involves making a conscious effort to understand what the person is saying and communicating that effort back to the person, along with any understanding gained (Culley & Bond, 2007; Kottler, 2003).

Other forms of active listening include paraphrasing, reflecting feeling, and summarizing

(Culley & Bond, 2007; Egan, 2014; Ivey et al., 2013; Kottler, 2003; M.E. Young, 2012). Paraphrasing involves repeating back to athletes key portions of their statements in an abbreviated form that uses at least some of their own words (e.g., "so the 'swelling has gone down' but your knee is 'even wobblier than it was before'"). Reflecting feeling involves identifying the athletes' emotions based on their verbal or nonverbal communication (e.g., "sounds like you're feeling pretty angry about how your surgery has turned out so far"). Whereas paraphrasing deals with thought content, reflecting feeling addresses emotional content; essentially, it involves paraphrasing athletes' expression of emotion. When sport health care professionals engage in summarizing, they offer athletes a pithy, organized account of the thoughts, feelings, behaviors, and meanings the athletes have conveyed in the interview.

The active listening skills of encouraging, paraphrasing, reflecting feeling, and summarizing serve multiple purposes in the process of exploration. Using these skills can be instrumental in helping sport health care professionals convey empathy to athletes and further demonstrate that the professionals are attending to the athletes (i.e., are interested in and willing to hear what they have to say). Practitioners can also use athletes' responses to these techniques to confirm or correct their understanding of what the athletes have been telling them.

Influencing Skills

For most sport health care professionals, the acquisition of attending skills and exploring skills provides a sufficient foundation for enhancing their ability to communicate with athletes. These skills enable practitioners to listen to patients, gain understanding of what they are experiencing, build rapport, express empathy, and solidify a working alliance. Although these skills are clearly nondirective, they are generally highly effective for collecting information and connecting with patients. Nevertheless, proficiency in the use of influencing skills can also be advantageous in the practice of sport health care. As implied by the term, influencing skills involve a more directive ap-proach in which practitioners try to foster alternative ways for patients to think, feel, and act regarding their interactions in the world. There are three main clusters of influencing skills that vary in terms of whether they attempt to alter patients' cognitive processes, furnish patients with information, or prompt patients to act in some clearly defined way.

Two related influencing skills aimed at affecting patients' cognitive processes are reframing and focus analysis. Reframing, which is sometimes referred to as interpretation, involves encouraging athletes to think about a situation from a different, potentially more adaptive point of view (e.g., "So, you've told me a lot of ways that your injury has been problematic for you. What's on the other side of the ledger? What positive things have you experienced as a result of your injury?"). In a similar vein, focus analysis asks athletes to consider multiple aspects of a problem or situation. As shown in table 9.2, athletes can be asked to consider their injury using a patient (athlete) focus; an "other" focus; a family focus; a problem or main-theme focus; a practitioner focus; a patient–practitioner ("we") focus; or a cultural, environmental, or context focus. The locus (or type) of focus varies as deemed appropriate to facilitate understanding of the problems or situations experienced by the athlete. Although this type of analysis typically emphasizes helping athletes understand themselves and their concerns from their own perspective, it is sometimes valuable to broaden the focus in order to gain a fuller, more complete understanding of the pertinent issues and—when the "we" focus is involved—a better sense of what is happening in the patient–practitioner relationship (Ivey et al., 2013).

Another group of influencing skills involves providing patients with information designed to affect their thoughts or behaviors. Examples include providing advice or other information, self-disclosure, feedback, logical consequences, instruction or psychoeducation, and confrontation. Giving advice, a technique that is best used sparingly, involves recommending a course of action for the patient to take or furnishing the patient with new information that might be useful. Self-disclosure

TABLE 9.2   Examples of Focus Analysis

Focus	Sample practitioner statement or question
Athlete	"This injury seems to have hit you pretty hard."
Other	"What effect has your injury had on your teammates?"
Family	"How has your family reacted to the injury?"
Problem or main theme	"It sounds like not knowing exactly what is wrong with your shoulder is the main thing you are struggling with right now, more than the pain and more than not being able to play. It might make sense to see what options there are for getting you in to see a specialist sooner than the insurance person told you was possible."
Practitioner	"I've been there—not with my shoulder, but with my knee. It took me a couple of months to receive an accurate diagnosis, and I was really frustrated."
Patient-practitioner ("We")	"We don't seem to be making much progress in deciding what to work on next."
Cultural, environmental, or contextual	"In some sports, such as the one you participate in, injury seems to be almost an inevitability."

involves sharing current or past personal experiences with the patient (e.g., "Yeah, I know what you mean. I had to do rehab after ankle surgery a while back. It was pretty frustrating to see a lack of progress from day to day, but I guess I wanted it and stuck with it anyway."). Although self-disclosure can help build trust between patients and practitioners, the practitioner should be cognizant of whose needs are being served by disclosing the personal information.

Another skill in this group—feedback—involves letting patients know how their behavior is perceived by the practitioner and other people (e.g., "From what I've seen of your interactions with our staff, I have the impression that you've been quite angry these past few weeks"). A related skill—the use of logical consequences—involves informing patients about likely outcomes of their behavior (e.g., "As you might suspect, skipping your rehabilitation exercises may come back to bite you down the road in terms of a restricted range of motion and increased risk for injury in the future."). In using instruction, or psychoeducation, practitioners explicitly teach patients skills that may enhance their psychological state. Although instruction of some type accounts for a large part of what many sport

health care professionals do, the skills they teach are often physical or technical in nature (as discussed later in this chapter). Psychoeducational content, of course, is most likely to be taught by sport health care professionals whose work with athletes is geared primarily toward effecting changes in psychological factors (e.g., cognition, emotion, behavior)—for example, sport psychology consultants and mental health specialists.

A third cluster of influencing skills includes techniques that issue a call to action—rather than providing information—intended to affect the patient's cognitions, emotions, behavior, or a combination thereof. Skills in this category include the use of confrontation, directives, goal setting, problem solving, stress management, reinforcement, and therapeutic lifestyle changes. In confrontation, which is far less adversarial than the term implies, practitioners note and bring to the patient's attention discrepancies in how the patient is thinking, feeling, and behaving. For example, if an athlete has repeatedly missed supervised rehabilitation sessions, the practitioner might say, "Throughout your rehabilitation, you've talked about how important it is for you to return to your sport as quickly as you can. Your actions, however, don't seem to match your stated goal. You're missing a lot of your appointments and seem to be going through the motions when you're here. What do you think is going on?" The next technique—using directives—is similar to giving advice or information in that it involves asking (rather than recommending or suggesting) that the patient take a particular course of action (e.g., "Today, I would like for you to do three sets of 15 reps at each station"). Because directives have the potential to undermine the patient's autonomy, they (like the sharing of advice, information, and self-disclosure) should be used with discretion.

The next three skills—goal setting (discussed in detail in chapter 8), problem solving, and stress management—are pragmatic influencing skills with which practitioners can help patients achieve clearly defined ends. In goal setting, for example, practitioners help patients set and pursue goals and evaluate their attainment of those goals. Similarly, in problem solving, practitioners guide patients through the process of defining problems, developing plans to address those problems, selecting the best plans, implementing the chosen plans, and evaluating the effectiveness of the chosen course of action (i.e., whether the plan worked). In stress management, practitioners help patients identify stressors and devise, implement, and evaluate plans to manage them.

The final two skills are reinforcement and therapeutic lifestyle changes. Reinforcement is a widely applicable skill that involves providing support and encouragement for patient behaviors deemed desirable (e.g., completing rehabilitation exercises, asking questions about rehabilitation). The practitioner can also help patients implement therapeutic lifestyle changes (e.g., regarding diet, smoking, exercise) to enhance both their general health and their injury-related health (Egan, 2014; Ivey et al., 2013; Kottler, 2003).

Issues in Enhancing Patient–Practitioner Communication Through Training in Counseling

When using training in counseling to enhance patient–practitioner communication in sport health care, one must address issues related to theory and sociocultural context. First, as one progresses from using attending skills to implementing exploring skills and, later, to applying influencing skills, the role of theory expands dramatically. When practitioners are listening to patients and attempting to understand what they are thinking, feeling, and behaving, theory may play a relatively minor part in the process. It becomes more important, however, in guiding practitioners as they choose which influencing skills to use and how, when, and why to use them. Therefore, sport health care professionals should obtain training and supervision in the use of influencing skills before implementing them on a widespread basis. This chapter's Focus on Application box features general suggestions for enhancing the working alliance between practitioner and patient that are relevant to the incorporation of influencing skills in sport health care.

Second, it is absolutely essential to take into account the sociocultural context—which includes, among other things, the age, disability status, gender, race, ethnicity, and sexual orientation of the practitioner and the patient—when implementing counseling skills in sport health care. As with theory, sociocultural context may influence the process through which counseling skills are applied. With this reality in mind, sport health care professionals can become more culturally competent communicators by examining the cultures of groups other than their own, learning about key personal and interpersonal aspects of the cultures, identifying specific skills and strategies that may be helpful in interacting with individuals of a given cultural group, and testing those skills and strategies in practice (Ivey et al., 2013).

The importance of the practitioner's cultural competence in rehabilitation settings is evidenced by preliminary research suggesting that cultural competence training may have a favorable effect on patient adherence (May & Potia, 2013). At the same time, practitioners must avoid falling prey to stereotypes and remember to listen to the individual athletes sitting or standing before them, who may or may not conform to expectations regarding their sociocultural group. In the sport environment, stereotypes can extend beyond demographic characteristics to include beliefs about athletes who participate in particular

Littlefoot Guidelines for Counseling Athletes

Through decades of experience in counseling athletes and supervising trainees who were learning to do so, A.J. Petitpas (2000) developed what he referred to as the Littlefoot approach to athletic counseling, which provides guidelines not so much for *what* to do when working with athletes but more for *how* to work with them. The guidelines were originally developed with psychology-focused professionals in mind, but adhering to the guidelines may help strengthen working alliances between patients and practitioners of all specialties in sport health care settings. Here are the key aspects of the Littlefoot approach:

a. *Understand the problem before you try to fix it.* One must know how athletes perceive their own problems and what they want from treatment before attempting to help them find solutions.

b. *Be inquisitive and avoid mind reading.* The best way to learn about athletes and how they perceive their situations is to ask them questions and check to ensure that their responses are understood correctly.

c. *Pace before you lead.* Practitioners should attend to athletes' immediate concerns and feelings before intervening.

d. *Encourage but avoid discounting.* Sport health care professionals should wait until they have built rapport with athletes before offering encouragement, and even then they should not minimize the amount of work required to deal with the athletes' problems.

e. *Listen for the "but."* Athletes' doubts about treatment and concerns about recovery can sometimes be identified by noticing when athletes discount the potential benefits of a prescribed course of action—or diminish the progress they have made in rehabilitation—through use of the word *but.* Here are some examples: "That stretching routine may work with some athletes, but I don't think my muscles will respond like everyone else's." "The swelling has gone down, but I'm not so sure I'll be back to training anytime soon."

f. *Put doubts in the doubts.* When athletes express doubts, either by using the word *but* or in another way, sport health care professionals can erode their lack of confidence (i.e., build their confidence) by gently challenging their doubts on logical or factual grounds (e.g., "What does it usually mean when swelling subsides?").

g. *Athlete-clients will bring you back where they believe they need to be.* If sport health care professionals follow the lead of athletes with injuries and listen (for the "buts") long enough, the athletes are likely to make their concerns known.

h. *Acknowledge the difficulty of the change process.* Doing rehabilitation and acquiring the skills to deal effectively with injury can be challenging for some athletes; acknowledging that difficulty can help athletes set realistic expectations for the recovery process.

i. *Plan for plateaus and setbacks.* Practitioners can also help athletes establish realistic expectations for recovery by accounting for the likelihood of periods of little progress (and even reversals of progress) and helping athletes develop skills to cope effectively with such difficult periods.

j. *Train for generalization.* Sport health care professionals should help ensure that athletes with injuries are able to use their newly acquired coping skills in settings beyond the one in which they learned them.

sports (e.g., lacrosse, figure skating) and even to athletes who play specific positions within a particular sport (e.g., quarterbacks versus line players versus placekickers in American football; sprinters versus distance runners versus throwers in track and field). Here again, the solution is to listen to individual athletes rather than stereotypes.

Interventions With Patients

Given that practitioners interact with many patients on a regular basis, it makes obvious sense to implement interventions focused on enhancing practitioners' communication skills. Patients, in contrast, see only a relative few practitioners, yet compelling reasons exist to improve patients' communication skills as well. Specifically, patients possess unique insights into their own bodies and—even as compared with the most competent, compassionate, and empathic practitioners—are particularly invested in their own health care outcomes. Interventions designed to improve patients' communication skills have primarily targeted patients' levels of participation in health care encounters and their knowledge about their medical condition (Straub, 2012; S.E. Taylor, 2012).

As a result of the stress inherent in sport health care encounters—and the power differential between patients and practitioners—even the most assertive patients sometimes neglect to ask important questions or share key details with their practitioners. In other areas of health care, interventions have been conducted in which patients are instructed to write down in advance the questions that they would like to ask their practitioners. They have also been encouraged by practitioners to ask questions at their next appointment and coached in how to be (appropriately) more assertive in their interactions with health care professionals. These interventions have been found effective in increasing the amount of information that patients obtain from practitioners, enhancing patients' perceived control, increasing their satisfaction with their office visits, and helping them achieve better health care outcomes (Greenfield, Kaplan, Ware, Yano, & Frank, 1998; Straub, 2012; Thompson, Nanni, & Schwankovsky, 1990). Interventions designed to help patients take a more active role in their health care have not been implemented or investigated systematically in association with sport injury, but the promise they have shown in other branches of health care suggest that they may be useful in helping athletes communicate more effectively with sport health care professionals.

Although eliciting more information from practitioners is one potential benefit for patients who take a more active role in their health care encounters, not all information is of equal value. Presumably, some kinds of information—and some modes of disseminating information—are more useful than others. Ideally, the information that patients receive addresses their questions in a user-friendly manner. Is it necessary, though, for practitioners to wait for patients to seek information before they provide it? Can practitioners anticipate patients' questions and give patients useful information proactively? These issues are tackled in this chapter's Focus on Research box.

Biopsychosocial Analysis

Communication is inherently a social process, thereby shifting the emphasis of this chapter more clearly toward the social dimension of *biopsychosocial* than is the case in any of the preceding chapters. The biological and psychological dimensions are not ignored, however, because they figure prominently in the communication that takes place between sport health care professionals and the athlete-patients they serve. Biological aspects occupy a central role in terms of the content of patient–practitioner communication. When patients and practitioners communicate with each other, the topics covered often pertain to prognosis, symptoms, and treatments, all of which include biological aspects. Psychological factors also play an important role in patient–practitioner communication, influencing what messages are sent, how they are sent, and what responses they elicit.

Biological, psychological, and social elements can be identified for each of the two cases presented at the beginning of the chapter. The blood surrounding Erica at second base served as an ample reminder of the biological trauma she had incurred. Still cognitively alert, she was able to reflect on why she wasn't more distressed psychologically, and she concluded that the support provided by Danielle, the athletic trainer, enabled her to experience the injury and its aftermath so calmly. Due to the urgent nature of Erica's situation, her encounter with Danielle did not fit the typical sport health care encounter (i.e., history taking and interviewing, physical examination and diagnostic tests, treatment, medical recommendations).

Interventions in which patients are given health-related information are based, at least in part, on the premise that "knowledge is power" and that information relevant to patients' medical conditions can enhance not only the patient–practitioner communication but also other important sport injury rehabilitation processes, as well as outcomes. Although the potential of educational interventions has not been thoroughly examined in association with sport injury, informational approaches have proven useful in a variety of other health care contexts (e.g., Gagliano, 1988; Mahler & Kulik, 1998). In addition, preliminary research suggests that the means by which patients partaking in rehabilitation are furnished with pertinent information may influence the effects of providing that information. Specifically, effects of various information-delivery methods have been examined for completion of rehabilitation exercises and for preparation for ACL surgery.

Regarding the completion of rehabilitation exercises, it is obvious that patients need some information and instruction regarding how to do their exercises properly when they are first prescribed. Not surprisingly, among patients given an illustrated brochure of rehabilitation exercises to complete, those who received direct supervision from a physical therapist performed their exercises more correctly than did those who received no supervision (Friedrich, Cermak, & Maderbacher, 1996). Similarly, patients who learned a set of rehabilitation exercises through video instruction exhibited higher-quality exercise performance and experienced higher levels of motivation and confidence than did patients who learned the exercises solely through an illustrated brochure (Weeks et al., 2002). Thus, essentially the same factual information can exert different influences on patients depending on how it is presented.

Although providing patients with procedural and sensory information about their upcoming surgery has long been an effective part of the patient education process (Suls & Wan, 1989), only relatively recently has it been applied in the sport injury domain. Building on findings in other areas of surgery (e.g., Sechrest & Henry, 1996; Webber & Rinehart, 1992), researchers have used interactive multimedia technology to facilitate patient education for individuals undergoing ACL reconstruction surgery. One study evaluated the effectiveness of an interactive CD-ROM containing written and video information on a broad array of topics pertaining to ACL surgery and rehabilitation (e.g., knee anatomy, procedural details, anesthesia, medications, preoperative restrictions, postoperative symptoms and limitations, pain, effect on daily living, potential side effects). Patients who received the CD-ROM before surgery reported feeling more confident in their ability to cope with their surgery and the subsequent rehabilitation than did patients who received a commercially available pamphlet with standardized written and illustrated information designed specifically for patient education purposes (Brewer, Cornelius, & Van Raalte, 2010). Approximately six months after surgery, patients who had received the CD-ROM reported having been more prepared for surgery and having consulted their patient education materials more frequently than did patients who had received the pamphlet (Van Raalte, Brewer, & Cornelius, 2012). It appears, therefore, that presenting patient education information in a dynamic, interactive format may provide some advantages over a standard print format in preparing patients for surgery.

Focus on Research

Furthermore, although Erica and Danielle had had few previous direct interactions with each other, the urgency of the situation may have prompted them into more of an activity–passivity dynamic than they would otherwise have adopted. The communication depicted between Erica and Danielle was largely socioemotional and illustrated the potentially powerful effect of touch and proxemics. Displaying excellent attending and listening skills, Danielle recognized Erica's mounting distress, and

Erica responded favorably to Danielle's displays of support.

As with Erica, Allison's appointment with Phil did not follow the typical format for sport health care encounters because it was a preoperative visit, scheduled immediately prior to rotator cuff surgery. Due to the highly technical nature of Allison's pending surgical procedure, her relationship with Phil appeared to fall into the guidance–cooperation category, with elements of mutual participation manifested in the shared decision making regarding anesthesia and postoperative care. In contrast to the communication between Erica and Danielle, the communication between Allison and Phil was predominantly informational and verbal. Allison dealt with her distress by asking Phil questions when given the opportunity to do so. Her anxieties were eased by the information she received from Phil and from the multimedia materials she viewed.

Summary

Effective communication is widely recognized as a crucial aspect of the relationship between athletes and sport health care professionals because it may affect key processes and outcomes in sport injury rehabilitation. Patient–practitioner communication in sport health care generally occurs during encounters that involve four main components. In the initial component, history taking and interviewing, information about the injury is gathered and documented. The next component, physical examination and diagnostic tests, involves the use of methods such as observation, palpation, range-of-motion assessment, strength testing, and anthropometric measurement to gain a more thorough understanding of the athlete's injury situation. The third component, treatment, features activities designed to facilitate the athlete's recovery. In the final component, consisting of medical recommendations, the sport health care professional suggests a course of action for the athlete to follow.

Interactions between sport health care professionals and athletes with injuries vary in terms of the level of responsibility that each party assumes for making decisions about diagnosis and treatment. Patient–practitioner communication in sport health care serves both informational and socioemotional functions. Information communicated by practitioners to athletes may include the nature and severity of the injury, the expected course of recovery, and the components and expectations of the rehabilitation program. In socioemotional communication, sport health care professionals demonstrate to athletes that they are warm, empathic, and concerned about all aspects of athletes' well-being. Socioemotional communication can play an important role in developing an effective alliance between the practitioner and the athlete in order to facilitate desired rehabilitation outcomes.

Communication between sport health care professionals and athletes with injuries occurs through both verbal and nonverbal modes. Verbal communication by a sport health care professional is enhanced when the vocabulary, organization, clarity, and length of a message (whether spoken or written) are appropriate for the athlete to whom the message is addressed. Messages may also be more effective when they are logical and positively phrased. Communication can be hampered if the practitioner makes extensive use of medical terminology.

Nonverbal communication also plays an important role in the patient–practitioner relationship. Athletes with injuries look to the nonverbal communication of sport health care professionals for information about their progress. At the same time, sport health care professionals can learn about the emotional states of the athletes they treat by attending to the athletes' nonverbal behavior. Three dimensions of nonverbal communication have been proposed: kinesics, proxemics, and paralanguage. Kinesics includes physical appearance, body language, facial expression, touch, and smell. Proxemics, which involves communication through the occupation of space, includes the positioning of and distance between athletes with injuries and sport health care professionals. Paralanguage includes characteristics of voice, such as pitch, tone, tempo, and volume; it can influence how verbal communication is interpreted.

Reflecting the need for improved patient–practitioner communication, discrepancies can emerge between the perceptions of sport health care professionals and those of athletes with injuries on matters as important as the content of the rehabilitation program and athletes' psychological states. Factors that can adversely affect patient–practitioner communication include attitudes and behaviors of sport health care professionals (e.g., failing to listen, depersonalizing, maintaining stereotypes), attitudes and behaviors of athletes (e.g., omitting medical details, neglecting to ask questions, minimizing symptoms), and interactive aspects (e.g., demographic differences between patient and practitioner, lack of patient feedback about practitioner communication).

Patient–practitioner communication in sport health care can be enhanced through interventions with both practitioners and athletes. Practitioner-focused interventions typically provide training in interpersonal courtesies, basic counseling skills (e.g., attending, exploring, influencing), and cultural competence. Patient-focused interventions are generally designed to increase athletes' participation and knowledge in sport health care encounters.

Discussion Questions

1. What events are included in a typical sport health care encounter during which patient–practitioner communication occurs?

2. What are the main differences between the activity–passivity, guidance–cooperation, and mutual participation styles of patient–practitioner communication?

3. What are some examples of informational, socioemotional, verbal, and nonverbal communication in sport health care?

4. How can a lack of congruence in patient–practitioner communication be problematic in sport health care?

5. What can patients and practitioners do to enhance communication in sport health care?

Chapter 10
Referring Athletes for Psychological Services

Chapter Objectives

1. To define, provide a rationale for, and describe the context of referral of athletes by sport health care professionals for psychological services
2. To identify common circumstances warranting referral for psychological services in sport health care
3. To present practical guidelines for making referrals and setting up referral networks

Kelley, a licensed athletic trainer, had been providing treatment to Hillary, an elite figure skater, for a stubborn groin injury for three weeks when Kelley noticed some strange scars on the back of Hillary's left hand. Given what Hillary had said repeatedly in the past about not wanting to "pile on the pounds" during her rehabilitation, Kelley felt a sneaking suspicion that Hillary might have an eating disorder—specifically, bulimia nervosa. Although Kelley thought it might be a good idea for Hillary to see a mental health professional, she did not feel comfortable asking Hillary directly about her eating behavior, and the topic just never seemed to come up in conversation. After a while, Kelley figured that she would know it if Hillary had a serious problem and told herself that the scars must have been caused by something other than Hillary's teeth during self-induced vomiting episodes.

Coming back after two consecutive season-ending knee injuries—both of which had led to surgery and a lengthy rehabilitation period—Aaron was understandably tentative on the basketball court. He had been medically cleared to play, but he seemed to be unable to commit to his cuts and explode to the hoop. Aaron shared his doubts with his athletic trainer, Jacquelyn, who acknowledged Aaron's concerns and asked him if he might be interested in working with a sport psychology consultant to boost his confidence, reduce his worries, and enhance his performance. She explained what meeting with a sport psychology consultant typically involves. Without hesitation, Aaron said, "Count me in!" Jacquelyn offered to make an introductory phone call to the sport psychology consultant and help Aaron schedule an initial appointment.

"Thanks, but no thanks, dude," said Blair, an elite junior skier living away from home at an alpine academy. "I appreciate the thought," he went on, "but I'm good. I don't have a problem." Blair was clearly balking at the suggestion made by John, the academy's physical therapist, that he talk with someone about his alcohol use. Blair had sustained a concussion several weeks earlier in a mishap on the slopes, and his comment a few hours afterward that "the hangover hurts way worse than the concussion" had raised a red flag for John. That flag was raised even higher two days later when a pair of Blair's fellow residents had come to John to express their concern that Blair's drinking and recreational drug use were putting his health and safety at risk. Now, with Blair having refused John's attempt at a referral, John asked Blair if it would be okay to follow up with him about his drinking and substance use at a later time. "Sure, dude," replied Blair. "No problem, but I'm still fine . . ."

To put it in the kindest terms, Karla was a study in contrasts. As a collegiate tennis player, she had great strokes but couldn't win a match against outside competition to save her soul. She sought feedback from her coaches and told them she would do anything to improve, but when they gave her the requested information she argued with them and told them she was playing "great." Meanwhile, though she was often effusively friendly to her teammates, she was also downright angry and mean on many other occasions. Now, both her coaches and her teammates were sick of it. Something had to change—and soon. It simply was not a pleasant or productive team environment, and all but Karla's closest friends on the team referred to her as "PB," which was short not for "peanut butter" but for a more derogatory colloquial moniker in which the P corresponds to "psycho." The head coach asked the team's athletic trainer, Renee, if anything could be done about the situation. Renee, who taped Karla's ankles on a regular basis and had largely been spared Karla's wrath, told the coach that the matter lay outside of her area of expertise but that she would try to set something up for Karla. Almost as if by plan, Karla was in tears the next time she was being taped before practice. This gave Renee the entry point she needed to tell Karla that she often seemed to be upset and ask her if she might be interested in having a counselor come to meet with both of them (together) privately to find out how to help her feel better. To Renee's surprise, Karla agreed.

As discussed in chapter 9, communication is vital to the relationships between sport health care professionals and the athletes with whom they work. Communication is also a critical aspect of the relationships among the various health care professionals who treat athletes, especially when those relationships involve professionals across multiple settings and disciplines. The communication skills of even the most experienced professionals can be challenged when referring athletes for psychological services. Referrals are commonplace in medical settings, often in the form of seeing a specialist for evaluation, treatment, or diagnostic testing. Although referral of athletes from one professional to another can function seamlessly in sport health care settings, referral of athletes for psychological services in particular can be a complex, delicate process that requires effective communication both interprofessionally (i.e., between professionals) and between patient and practitioner.

Discomfort about discussing psychological issues in sport health care settings can come to a head when an athlete requires referral for psychological services. To address that challenge, this chapter pursues the following aims: define, present a rationale for, and contextualize referral for psychological services by sport health care professionals; identify common circumstances warranting referral; and provide practical information about how to make referrals and set up referral networks. Along the way, this chapter addresses issues pertaining to collaboration, networking, documentation, legal and ethical obligations, and clinical decision making.

Definition of and Rationale for Referral

According to Lemberger (2008), "Psychosocial referral is a dynamic helping process in which one human service provider connects a patient to a resource that can better assist in the patient's life functioning" (p. 70). This definition contains a large clue as to why sport health care professionals refer athletes for psychological services: above all other reasons, referrals are made to help athletes function better. Not coincidentally, this is also the same reason for which sport health care professionals refer athletes to specialists in disciplines other than those in the psychosocial realm. As with those referrals, connecting athletes with resources (i.e., professionals) to address their psychosocial needs helps sport health care professionals practice within their own scope of competence and, in so doing, fulfills an important professional, ethical, and, potentially, legal obligation (Brewer, Petitpas, & Van Raalte, 1999). Therefore, proficiency in recognizing mental health issues and directing individuals with such issues to appropriate practitioners has long been formally expected of athletic trainers (Mensch, 2008) and considered essential for team physicians (Herring et al., 2006).

Socioclinical Context of Referral

Precise estimates are not available regarding how often sport health care professionals refer athletes for psychological assistance (for more on this topic, see this chapter's Focus on Research box), but research suggests that such referrals are not routine (B.J. Mann, Grana, Indelicato, O'Neill, & George, 2007; Roh & Perna, 2000). Given that referrals for psychological services have been deemed an important area of competence for sport health care professionals (Herring et al., 2006; Mensch, 2008), why are such referrals not more common? Clearly, this pattern does not derive from a lack of need for psychological assistance among athletes with injuries. In addition to the mental health reasons discussed in this chapter, an abundance of common and appropriate reasons for psychological referral have been identified in other chapters, including dysfunctional psychological responses to sport injury (chapter 4), pain (chapter 5), nonadherence to

rehabilitation (chapter 6), and injury recovery (chapter 8).

One potential explanation for the infrequency of psychological-service referrals by sport health care professionals lies in the perceived or actual unavailability of qualified sport psychology consultants or mental health practitioners (Clement & Shannon, 2009; Mann et al., 2007; Moulton et al., 2007; Roh & Perna, 2000). A study in the early 1990s revealed that only a small percentage of physical therapy clinics employed or engaged the services of a sport psychology consultant (Cerny, Patton, Whieldon, & Roehrig, 1992), and there is no evidence that the employment status of psychology professionals in sport injury rehabilitation settings has changed appreciably since then.

Another possible contributor to the infrequency of referrals involves discomfort about discussing psychological issues. In support of this idea, a survey by Misasi et al. (1996) revealed that athletic trainers considered themselves better trained for and more active in counseling athletes about injury rehabilitation, injury prevention, and nutrition than in counseling them about suicide, family matters, and issues involving finances, race, relationships, sexuality, and alcohol and drug use and abuse. Furthermore, Boots (2010) found that undergraduate athletic-training students reported lower levels of comfort associated with asking athletes questions pertaining to the psychosocial-intervention and referral domain of competence than for several other domains (e.g., acute care of injury and illness, conditioning and rehabilitative exercise, nutrition, orthopedic clinical exam and diagnosis, risk management and injury prevention, and therapeutic modalities). Discomfort with psychological issues may be attributable, at least in part, to a lack of familiarity with the subject, since the participants in Boots' study rated their knowledge of and experience with asking questions in the psychosocial-intervention and referral domain as significantly lower than in the other domains.

Knowledge of psychological aspects of sport injury alone, however, may not be sufficient to prompt sport health care professionals

Improving Estimates of Psychological Referral Frequency in Sport Health Care

How often do sport health care professionals refer athletes for psychological assistance? Knowing the frequency of such referrals can help us determine how well the sport health care system meets the psychosocial needs of athletes with injuries. However, close inspection of the studies examining this issue (e.g., Brewer, Van Raalte, & Linder, 1991; Clement, Granquist, & Arvinen-Barrow, 2013; Jevon & Johnston, 2003; Larson, Starkey, & Zaichkowsky, 1996; B.J. Mann et al., 2007; Misasi, Davis, Morin, & Stockman, 1996; Moulton, Molstad, & Turner, 1997; Pantano, 2009) yields an estimate of referral frequency no more precise than "not very often."

Most empirical studies of the referral practices of sport health care professionals have involved the use of surveys, although qualitative methods have also been used (Jevon & Johnston, 2003). Although surveys might be expected to enable numerical estimates of practitioners' referral behavior, such is not the case, because the survey questions have been asked in ways that are not conducive to generating precise interpretations of referral frequency. For example, ratings of past or likely referral frequency on Likert or Likert-type scales (e.g., B.J. Mann et al., 2007; Pantano, 2009) are imprecise because connotations of response options such as "rarely" may vary widely across respondents; furthermore, even endorsement of such seemingly precise terms as "never" and "always" fails to indicate the denominator in the referral estimate (i.e., how many athletes have never or always been referred). Similarly, even for surveys on which a specific number of referred athletes was requested (e.g., Larson et al., 1996; Moulton et al., 1997), the number of athletes who could potentially have been referred was not ascertained.

To close this gap, at least three methodological approaches could be used to obtain estimates of referral frequency. The simplest approach would be to request information about how many athletes the practitioner did, and did *not*, refer over a given period of time. Though simple, however, this approach is the least desirable of the three because it relies on retrospection and therefore is susceptible to both forgetting and recall bias. A second possible approach would be to conduct a review of medical records at sport health care facilities. The success of this archival route depends on full documentation of referrals for psychological assistance. A third approach, and arguably the best, would be to collect referral data over a particular period of time in order to derive a precise account of referral frequency. Although this approach would likely require more time and resources than the other two, it could also be used to gather data about the use of psychological techniques by sport health care professionals—another area where the data are far less precise than they could be.

to make psychological referrals. In athletic training, for example, competence in addressing psychosocial issues and making appropriate referrals has been an important part of the profession (in various forms) for more than 50 years (Mensch, 2008). Similarly, along with pharmacological, nutritional, conditioning, and training issues, psychological issues have long been an "integral part of . . . training programs" (Lombardo & Wilkerson, 1996, p.77) in clinical sports medicine. Educational programs responsible for preparing students for professional practice in athletic training and sports medicine have used a variety of pedagogical methods (including workshops and academic courses devoted exclusively to the psychology of sport injury) to increase students' exposure to and knowledge of psychological issues. Such programs have been found effective in modifying sport health care professionals' attitudes toward, perceptions of, and use of psychological applications with athletes in the context of sport injury (Clement & Shannon, 2009; Harris, Demb, & Pastore, 2004; S.F. Pero, 1995); they have not, however, increased the number of referrals for psychological services (Clement & Shannon, 2009).

Another potential contributor to practitioners' discomfort with psychosocial issues and psychological-service referral can be found in culturally based attitudes about experiencing and seeking treatment for mental health problems. Athletes are often highly visible and seemingly invulnerable people who are celebrated for their individualism, independence, and self-reliance (Begel, 1994; Etzel, Zizzi, Newcomer-Appaneal, Ferrante, & Perna, 2007). This context can make it difficult for an athlete to accept (and for a sport health care professional to give) a psychological referral, because doing so may be seen as admitting weakness or acknowledging psychopathology—both of which contradict societal stereotypes of athletes. Facing the possibility of derogation (Linder, Brewer, Van Raalte, & DeLange, 1991; Linder, Pillow, & Reno, 1989) and stigmatization (Schwenk, 2000), athletes may not even entertain psychological referral as a viable option.

All is not lost, however, with respect to referral of athletes for psychological assistance. Despite the sociocultural forces that conspire against sport health care professionals being comfortable with making psychological referrals—and athletes being comfortable with accepting them—several reasons suggest that practitioners can refer athletes for psychological assistance competently, effectively, and with greater frequency than has generally been done in the past. First, as noted by Heil (1993c), the stigma associated with seeking psychological help is not as pronounced as it once was, particularly when consultation is sought for a sport-related purpose (Van Raalte, Brewer, Brewer, & Linder, 1992). Toward this end, referral can be presented as a means of enhancing an athlete's performance—in sport, in rehabilitation, and in life (Heil, 1993b; J. Taylor & Taylor, 1997).

Second, although conversations with athletes about psychological referral are often awkward or uncomfortable, athletes with injury have expressed a preference for discussing psychosocial issues with sport health care professionals to a greater degree than with physicians, counselors, psychologists, and sport psychology consultants (S. Maniar, Perna, Newcomer, Roh, & Stilger, 1999; S.D. Maniar, Perna, Newcomer, Roh, & Stilger, 2000). Thus, even if sport health care professionals may not be athletes' final destination for addressing psychological issues, the trust they build with athletes can help initiate conversations about

referral. Third, athletes with injuries tend to be receptive to psychological interventions (e.g., Appaneal & Granquist, 2007; Brewer, Jeffers, Petitpas, & Van Raalte, 1994; L. Evans, Hardy, & Fleming, 2000; Handegard, Joyner, Burke, & Reimann, 2006; Myers, Peyton, & Jensen, 2004; Shapiro, 2009), thereby increasing the likelihood that they will find the treatments resulting from referrals to be acceptable and will participate actively in the process.

Reasons for Referral

In the spirit of helping athletes function better, sport health care professionals should refer athletes for psychological assistance for a variety of reasons. Although athletes sometimes explicitly request psychological referrals, the reasons for referral generally involve practitioners encountering "circumstances that exceed their training, competence, or comfort or represent a conflict between the interests of the athletic organization and those of the injured athlete" (Brewer, Petitpas, & Van Raalte, 1999, p. 129). Reasons for referral can be divided into two broad categories: prevention and remediation (Lemberger, 2008).

Prevention, of course, is proactive, and preventive referrals are made before the emergence of psychological difficulties. One example would be to routinely refer athletes to a sport psychology consultant in order to help them learn psychological skills that can reduce injury risk or facilitate rehabilitation and return to sport. Another example would be to make a referral for supportive psychological assistance for athletes experiencing significant life changes (either in or away from sport) and those whose rehabilitation is especially complicated (Heil, 1993c; Lemberger, 2008). In contrast, remediation is reactive, and rehabilitative referrals are made in response to "evident psychological difficulties" (Heil, 1993c) manifested by athletes when they experience rehabilitation-related behavioral or adjustment problems, display adjustment difficulties in personal and social functioning, or exhibit (or report) signs or symptoms of psychopathology (Brewer, Petitpas, & Van Raalte, 1999).

Preventive applications of training in psychological skills are addressed in chapters 3 and 8. Rehabilitation-related behavioral or adjustment problems—specifically, pain and poor adherence to rehabilitation—are examined in depth in chapters 5 and 6, respectively. Difficulties in adjusting to injury, either personally or socially, can involve problems in interacting with others or functioning in academic or occupational settings. Psychopathology displayed by athletes with injury can pertain to a wide variety of disorders, ranging from extreme forms of psychological distress in response to injury (as discussed in chapter 4) to a wide array of conditions that occur independent of (and may or may not be exacerbated by) injury. The remainder of this section of the chapter is devoted to recognizing forms of psychopathology that sport health care professionals may encounter in their contact with athletes who have sustained injuries.

Means of Recognizing Psychopathology in Athletes With Injuries

Sport health care professionals have at their disposal several means of recognizing psychopathology experienced by athletes with injuries. As noted by Granquist and Kenow (2015), information about the psychological status of an athlete with an injury can be gleaned through athlete self-reports (i.e., what athletes say about their thoughts, feelings, and behaviors), other reports (i.e., what other people [e.g., teammates, coaches, friends, family members] say about the athlete's thoughts, feelings, and, especially, behaviors), and observations of the athlete's behavior (i.e., what the athletes does). Athlete self-reports and other reports can be obtained through interviews or conversations. To help sport health professionals identify athlete behaviors indicative of psychological distress, several observational tools have been developed.

Examples include the Sports Medicine Injury Checklist (Heil, 1993d), the Psychological Distress Checklist (J. Taylor & Taylor, 1997), and the list of warning signs of poor adjust-

ment to sport injury offered by Petitpas and Danish (1995). Drawn from both clinical experience and the research literature, these overlapping checklists include behaviors that, when manifested overtly, are presumably indicative of a condition for which psychological referral may be desirable or even necessary. For example, the Sports Medicine Injury Checklist (Heil, 1993d) includes behaviors pertaining to rehabilitation processes, pain, psychological functioning, life circumstances, and coping resources. Although these checklists were rationally constructed, they have not yet been empirically validated. Given the low correspondence found in one study (Brewer, Petitpas, Van Raalte, Sklar, & Ditmar, 1995) between sport health care professionals' ratings of athlete behaviors suggestive of psychological distress and athletes' reports of their own psychological distress, further development of the checklist approach is needed before it can be recommended on a widespread basis.

Forms of Psychopathology Potentially Warranting Referral

Since 1952, the American Psychiatric Association has published the *Diagnostic and Statistical Manual of Mental Disorders* (*DSM*), which serves as a guide for identifying psychopathology across the lifespan. Now in its fifth edition (i.e., *DSM-5*; American Psychiatric Association, 2013), the manual includes more than 300 mental-disorder diagnoses in 22 categories over nearly 1,000 pages. For each mental disorder listed in the *DSM*, a description of the disorder is typically provided, along with specific diagnostic criteria and the following types of information:

- Prevalence, development, and course
- Risk and prognostic factors
- Gender- and culture-related diagnostic issues
- Functional consequences
- Differential diagnosis and comorbidity

The frequent contact that sport health care professionals often have with athletes over an extended period of time leaves them well positioned to identify a wide range of conditions listed in the *DSM-5* that warrant referral. As noted earlier, some of the conditions may arise in reaction to the stresses of sustaining a sport injury, whereas others may be preexisting and perhaps chronic conditions for which an athlete may or may not be receiving care from a mental health professional.

One of the challenges in discussing psychopathology in relation to sport injury lies in the fact that few epidemiological studies have examined the prevalence of mental disorders (other than eating disorders and substance-related disorders) in athletes, and fewer still have done so in athletes with injuries (Reardon & Factor, 2010). Without knowing how common various disorders are in the population of interest, it can difficult for sport health care professionals to know what to expect when attempting to identify psychopathology in the athletes with whom they work. It may, therefore, be useful to provide a context for grouping and thinking about mental disorders and how they may present in athletes with injuries. For the purposes of this discussion, we can delineate three general categories of mental disorder:

1. Those involving reactions or responses to sport injury and its effects

2. Those pertaining to the body and medical treatment

3. Conditions (chronic or acute) that can exist independent of the circumstances in the first two categories

These categories are not mutually exclusive; therefore, a given disorder may apply to multiple categories across athletes. For example, a condition that involves a reaction to injury occurrence in one athlete (e.g., major depressive disorder, substance use disorder) may be an ongoing condition that predates injury occurrence in another athlete. Disorders corresponding to each of the three categories are outlined in table 10.1 and discussed in the sections that follow. For the vast majority of the disorders identified, the diagnostic criteria include stipulations that the psychological disturbance cannot be better explained by a different mental disorder and cannot be attributed to the effects of a substance or medical condition (except, of course, for disorders that include substance use or medical conditions as symptoms). To eliminate redundancy and enhance readability, these stipulations are not listed again in the table or in the following discussion.

Disorders Involving Reactions or Responses to Sport Injuries and Their Effects

Several disorders appear to be precipitated by the occurrence or aftermath of sport injury. One involves reactions to injury itself (neurocognitive disorder), whereas others involve responses either to the events during which injury is sustained (e.g., acute stress disorder, posttraumatic stress disorder, adjustment disorders) or to events or circumstances that have occurred as a result of the injury (e.g., adjustment disorders, major depressive disorder).

Neurocognitive Disorder   The most obvious example of a *DSM-5* disorder involving reaction to sport injury is major or mild neurocognitive disorder (NCD) due to traumatic brain injury. Typically sustained (in the context of sport) when an athlete experiences a blow to the head (i.e., concussion), the diagnosis of major or mild NCD requires that the athlete experience "cognitive decline from a previous level of performance" (American Psychiatric Association, pp. 602–603), either "immediately after the occurrence of the traumatic brain injury or immediately after recovery of consciousness," and that it persist "past the acute post-injury period" (p. 624). NCD can vary in severity. Major NCD is diagnosed when cognitive deficits interfere with the athlete's ability to engage independently in everyday activities, whereas minor NCD involves no such interference. Fortunately, cases of NCD due to traumatic brain injury in sport are increasingly likely to be identified, monitored, and addressed through application of the post-concussion protocols discussed in chapter 4.

Acute Stress Disorder and Posttraumatic Stress Disorder   Another condition that can be traced directly to the occurrence of sport injury is acute stress disorder, which is diagnosed

COVERAGE OF MATERIAL RELEVANT TO THE "PSYCHOSOCIAL STRATEGIES AND REFERRAL" CONTENT AREA OF THE *ATHLETIC TRAINING EDUCATION COMPETENCIES* DOCUMENT

TABLE 10.1 *DSM-5* Diagnoses of Potential Relevance to Sport Injury

Disorder	DSM-5 category	Salient features and symptoms
Disorders involving reactions or responses to sport injury and its effects		
Major or mild neurocognitive disorder	Neurocognitive disorders	Decline in cognitive functioning
Acute stress disorder	Trauma- and stressor-related disorders	≥9 symptoms of intrusion, negative mood, dissociation, avoidance, and arousal for 3 days to 1 month
Posttraumatic stress disorder	Trauma- and stressor-related disorders	Symptoms of intrusion, avoidance, and alteration in cognition or mood and in arousal or reactivity lasting >1 month following exposure to a traumatic event
Adjustment disorders	Trauma- and stressor-related disorders	Emotional or behavioral symptoms (e.g., anxiety, depressed mood) within 3 months of stressor onset
Major depressive disorder	Depressive disorders	Depressed mood, loss of interest or pleasure, weight loss or gain, sleep disturbance, fatigue, cognitive impairment, thoughts of death
Disorders pertaining to the body and medical treatment		
Body dysmorphic disorder	Obsessive-compulsive and related disorders	Preoccupation with perceived appearance deficit(s) and associated repetitive behaviors or mental acts
Somatic symptom disorder	Somatic-symptom and related disorders	Excessive thoughts, feelings, or behaviors related to distressing or disruptive somatic symptoms
Illness anxiety disorder	Somatic-symptom and related disorders	Preoccupation for ≥6 months regarding having or acquiring a serious illness; health anxiety; excessive health-related behaviors or avoidance
Conversion disorder (functional neurological symptom disorder)	Somatic-symptom and related disorder	Altered voluntary motor or sensory functioning incompatible with neurological and medical conditions
Psychological factors affecting other medical conditions	Somatic-symptom and other related disorders	Psychological or behavioral factors adversely affecting course, treatment, risk, or pathophysiology of a medical condition
Factitious disorder	Somatic-symptom and other related disorders	Presenting as ill, impaired, or injured with false or induced signs or symptoms
Anorexia nervosa	Feeding and eating disorders	Restricted energy intake, low body weight, fear of weight gain or behavior that interferes with weight gain, body image disturbance, undue influence of body weight or shape on self-evaluation
Bulimia nervosa	Feeding and eating disorders	Recurrent binge eating and inappropriate compensatory behavior once per week for 3 months; undue influence of body weight or shape on self-evaluation
Binge-eating disorder	Feeding and eating disorders	Recurrent binge eating once per week for 3 months; distress related to binge eating
Insomnia disorder	Sleep–wake disorders	Disturbance in quantity or quality of sleep ≥3 times per week for ≥3 months

Disorder	DSM-5 category	Salient features and symptoms
Disorders involving reactions or responses to sport injury and its effects		
Other chronic and acute conditions		
Attention-deficit or hyperactivity disorder	Neurodevelopmental disorders	Inattention, hyperactivity, impulsivity
Brief psychotic disorder	Schizophrenia-spectrum and other psychotic disorders	Delusions, hallucinations, disorganized speech, or disorganized or catatonic behavior for <1 month
Bipolar I disorder	Bipolar and related disorders	Major depressive and hypomanic episodes
Bipolar II disorder	Bipolar and related disorders	Manic episode
Cyclothymic disorder	Bipolar and related disorders	Hypomanic and depressive symptoms for ≥2 years
Persistent depressive disorder	Depressive disorders	Depressive symptoms for ≥2 years
Generalized anxiety disorder	Anxiety disorders	Excessive anxiety and worry for >6 months and 3 of 6 other symptoms (restlessness, fatigue, concentration difficulties, irritability, muscle tension, sleep disturbance)
Panic disorder	Anxiety disorders	Recurrent unexpected panic attacks
Obsessive-compulsive disorder	Obsessive-compulsive and related disorders	Time-consuming, distress-producing, or impairment-causing obsessions or compulsions
Substance intoxication	Substance-related and addictive disorders	Temporary psychological or behavioral symptoms due to physiological effects of a substance
Substance withdrawal	Substance-related and addictive disorders	Behavioral, physiological, or cognitive symptoms due to decreased consumption of a substance
Substance use disorder	Substance-related and addictive disorders	Pathological patterns of substance abuse behavior
Antisocial personality disorder	Personality disorders	Age ≥18 years, disregard for or violation of others' rights beginning before age 15
Avoidant personality disorder	Personality disorders	Social inhibition; low self-esteem; hypersensitivity to shame, ridicule, criticism, or rejection
Borderline personality disorder	Personality disorders	Instability in relationships, self-image, and affect; impulsivity
Dependent personality disorder	Personality disorders	Excessive reliance on others to be cared for; submissive or clinging behavior; fear of separation or abandonment
Histrionic personality disorder	Personality disorders	Excessive emotionality and attention seeking
Narcissistic personality disorder	Personality disorders	Grandiosity, need for admiration, lack of empathy
Obsessive-compulsive personality disorder	Personality disorders	Preoccupation with order, perfection, control; lack of flexibility, openness, efficiency
Paranoid personality disorder	Personality disorders	Persistent suspiciousness or distrust of others
Schizoid personality disorder	Personality disorders	Detachment from social relationships, restricted emotional expression
Schizotypal personality disorder	Personality disorders	Social or interpersonal deficits; discomfort with or reduced capacity for close relationships; odd thoughts, perceptions, speech

Adapted from American Psychiatric Association 2013.

when athletes incur (or witness in person) a traumatic injury and subsequently experience, for a duration of three days to one month, at least 9 of 14 symptoms involving intrusion (e.g., recurrent, distressing memories, dreams, flashbacks), negative mood, dissociation (e.g., loss of memory of injury occurrence), avoidance (e.g., efforts to avoid distressing thoughts or reminders of the injury), and arousal (e.g., sleep or concentration difficulties). The symptoms produce significant distress or substantially impair the athlete's performance of social, occupational, or other tasks of importance. When the symptoms persist for longer than one month, the diagnosis given is posttraumatic stress disorder (PTSD). As discussed in chapter 4, symptoms of acute stress disorder and PTSD have been documented in athletes following injury (Appaneal, Perna, & Larkin, 2007; McArdle, 2010; Newcomer & Perna, 2003; Shuer & Dietrich, 1997; Vergeer, 2006).

Adjustment Disorders   Much of the psychological distress described in chapter 4 as a reaction to sport injury and its consequences likely falls within the realm of adjustment disorders, in which the athlete experiences levels of distress that are disproportionate to the severity or intensity of the injury or that impair performance in social, occupational, or other key domains. As noted in *DSM-5*, "Adjustment disorders . . . may be the major psychological response to a medical disorder" (American Psychiatric Association, 2013, p. 289). In injury-related adjustment disorders, emotional symptoms (e.g., anxiety, depression), behavioral symptoms (e.g., disturbed conduct), or both emerge within three months of injury occurrence or of the onset of postinjury stress and persist no longer than six months after injury occurrence or after the dissipation of postinjury stress.

Major Depressive Disorder   Although much of what has been labeled "depression" in athletes with injuries is probably an adjustment disorder, at least some cases are likely to be major depressive disorder (MDD). Well beyond a period of feeling "down" or acting "mopey," MDD involves a marked departure from normal functioning in social, occupation-

al, and other key life domains. A diagnosis of MDD requires that the athlete manifest, over a two-week period, at least five of nine of the following symptoms (and definitely at least one of the first two):

1. Depressed mood (indicated by feelings of sadness, emptiness, hopelessness, and the like) most of the time almost every day

2. Anhedonia (i.e., lack of interest or pleasure in activities that were once enjoyable) almost every day

3. Substantial loss or gain of appetite, weight, or both

4. Lack of sleep or excessive sleep almost every day

5. Psychomotor agitation (e.g., hand wringing, difficulty sitting still) or psychomotor retardation (e.g., slowed body movement, thought, speech)

6. Fatigue almost every day

7. Feeling worthless or excessively or inappropriately guilty

8. Difficulty almost every day in thinking, concentrating, or making decisions

9. Suicidal thoughts or images, a plan to commit suicide, or an attempted suicide

Both the breadth and pervasiveness of MDD symptoms and the associated increase in risk for suicidal behavior make this disorder worthy of particular attention in the process of observing and treating athletes after they incur injury.

Disorders Pertaining to the Body and Medical Treatment

Sport injury is an assault on the body that often requires medical attention; as a result, it can intersect with several disorders involving concerns related to the body and medical treatment. Disorders in this heterogeneous group of conditions can precede and potentially contribute to psychological responses to sport injury, but they can also be exacerbated by the occurrence of sport injury and its physical and psychological effects. This group of disorders includes body dysmorphic disorder, somatic symptom disorder, illness anxiety disorder, conversion disorder, psychological factors affecting other medical conditions, factitious disorder, eating disorders, and insomnia disorder.

Body Dysmorphic Disorder Listed in the *DSM-5* section for obsessive-compulsive and related disorders, body dysmorphic disorder occurs when an individual is preoccupied with a perceived deficit in physical appearance that prompts him or her to engage in repetitive behavior or mental events or both and to experience "clinically significant distress or impairment in social, occupational, or other important areas of functioning" (American Psychiatric Association, 2013, p. 242). The form of body dysmorphic disorder that is most relevant to athletes, and potentially athletes with injuries, is muscle dysmorphia. Experienced primarily by men, it is characterized by preoccupation with a perceived deficit in leanness or muscularity and involves repetitive behaviors and mental events such as dieting, lifting weights, compulsively checking one's physique in the mirror, and comparing one's physique to others (Pope, Gruber, Choi, Olivardia, & Phillips, 1997). Although this has not been documented empirically, it is possible that male athletes are at increased risk for muscle dysmorphia as they lose muscle mass or become deconditioned after sustaining an injury.

Somatic Symptom Disorder Addressed in the *DSM-5* section bearing its name, somatic-symptom disorder involves the experience of at least one bodily symptom that produces distress or disrupts daily living, as well as "excessive thoughts, feelings, or behaviors related to the somatic symptoms or related health concerns" (American Psychiatric Association, 2013, p. 311). Individuals with this disorder think disproportionately and persistently about how serious their symptoms are, experience high levels of anxiety regarding their health or symptoms, or devote excessive amounts of time and energy to their symptoms or health issues. The symptoms of somatic symptom disorder can include pain and are labeled "persistent" if they are severe, produce marked impairment, and last more than six months. Little is known about somatic symptom disorder in relation to sport injury, but it

is easy to see how it might produce difficulties for athletes undergoing an extended period of rehabilitation and a return to sport.

Illness Anxiety Disorder Along with somatic symptom disorder, illness anxiety disorder is a new diagnosis to *DSM-5* that evolved from the condition known as hypochondriasis in earlier editions of the manual. A diagnosis of illness anxiety disorder requires individuals to

- be preoccupied (for at least 6 months) with the idea that they have acquired or may acquire a dreaded disease;
- experience a high degree of anxiety regarding their health;
- perform health-related behaviors excessively or avoid medical treatment; and
- have physical symptoms of not more than mild intensity (American Psychiatric Association, 2013).

Given the characteristic sensitivity of persons with illness anxiety to physical sensations and symptoms, intensive sport involvement is an unlikely choice for such individuals. Nevertheless, in circumstances where sport injury and illness anxiety disorder do intersect, complications may occur in the interpretation of the many subtle (and not-so-subtle) physical cues experienced during recovery from injury.

Conversion Disorder Also known as functional neurological symptom disorder, conversion disorder occurs when voluntary sensory or motor functioning is altered in at least one way that is incompatible with currently recognized medical and neurological conditions; cannot better be explained by such conditions; and produces distress or impaired functioning in social, occupational, or other key life domains. Essentially, people with conversion disorder have actual sensory disability (e.g., visual or hearing impairment) or motor disability (e.g., weakness, paralysis) that lacks an apparent medical basis and may contradict neurological principles. The onset of conversion disorder is sometimes associated with stress and can be met with an indifference not typically shown in response to incurring a disabling sensory or motor condition (American Psychiatric

Association, 2013). Pargman (1996) documented a conversion reaction in an athlete whose loss of vision in one eye was ultimately attributed not to the collision that appeared to precipitate it but to internal conflict associated with the athlete's unacceptable (to himself) wish to disengage from participating in American football.

Psychological Factors Affecting Other Medical Conditions Given the abundance of psychosocial variables that are predictive of sport injury occurrence and recovery from it (as discussed in detail in chapters 2 and 7, respectively), sport injury can be considered as one of the medical conditions in the diagnosis of "psychological factors affecting other medical conditions" (Brewer & Petrie, 2014). The diagnosis can be applied to athletes with an injury whose onset, treatment, or rehabilitation has been influenced by psychological factors (American Psychiatric Association, 2013). In addressing the ways in which psychological factors affect sport injury, viable approaches include the psychosocial interventions found effective for preventing sport injury (see chapter 3) and for facilitating sport injury rehabilitation outcomes (see chapter 8).

Factitious Disorder Athletes generally seek to return to play as quickly as possible following injury; indeed, as discussed in chapter 1, many athletes elect to play through pain and injury. A small minority, however, feign symptoms of injury (or illness). When athletes present themselves falsely to others as injured, ill, or otherwise impaired in the absence of any obvious external rewards for doing so—and when their behavior cannot be attributed to another mental disorder—they can be diagnosed with factitious disorder imposed on self. Athletes who intentionally injure themselves (or make themselves sick) under the same conditions can also receive a diagnosis of factitious disorder.

Factitious disorder can be distinguished from malingering, in which athletes fake physical or psychological symptoms for personal gain (American Psychiatric Association, 2013). As shown in the following list, athletes may engage in malingering for numerous reasons (Rotella, Ogilvie, & Perrin, 1993); in factitious disorder, however, these reasons are, by definition, absent.

Eating Disorders Under ordinary circumstances, the prevalence of eating disorders—such as anorexia nervosa, bulimia nervosa, and binge eating disorder—among athletes is comparable to or slightly higher than that in the general population. However, female athletes are especially vulnerable to eating concerns, and this is especially true for athletes in sports emphasizing appearance, weight, body shape, or body size (Brewer & Petrie, 2014). A diagnosis of anorexia nervosa is given to individuals who

- experience "a significantly low body weight" due to restricting their energy intake relative to their body's requirements;
- maintain an "intense fear of gaining weight or of becoming fat" or consistently behave in ways that prevent them from gaining weight; and
- experience disturbance regarding their body weight or shape, evaluate themselves unduly based on their body weight or shape, or fail to recognize the seriousness of maintaining a low body weight (American Psychological Association, 2013).

Anorexia nervosa has two types: restricting and binge eating/purging. Individuals with the restricting type typically diet, fast, or exercise excessively in order to lose weight, whereas those with the binge-eating/purging type have recurrent episodes in which they binge-eat or purge themselves of calories they have consumed by intentionally vomiting or misusing laxatives, diuretics, or enemas (American Psychological Association, 2013).

Sharing some of the symptoms of anorexia nervosa, bulimia nervosa is a diagnosis given to individuals whose evaluation of themselves is disproportionately influenced by the shape and weight of their body; who do not meet the criteria for anorexia nervosa; and who, on average, at least once per week over a three-month period have an eating binge over which they feel a lack of control and engage in inappropriate restricting or purging behavior. Individuals with binge eating disorder average at least one distress-inducing eating binge per week over a three-month period without engaging in any

Reasons for Malingering in Sport

· Using an insignificant injury to rationalize loss of starting status, reduction of playing time, or poor competitive performance

· Using injury-related disability to prevent loss of athletic scholarship

· Using injury to account for apparent decrease or change in motivation for participation

· Using injury to offset the personal realization of insufficient ability (talent) to compete successfully

· Using injury to attract needed or desired attention from others that has not been forthcoming elsewhere

· Using injury to demonstrate personal courage by "playing hurt"

· Using injury to offset expectations of coaches, teammates, and parents

· Using injury as a reason to desist from performing, thereby not contributing skill, talent, and ability to the team's effort, and thus expressing hostility or anger toward coaches, teammates, or parents

· Using injury to avoid the rigors of practice but still be able to compete since the coach may need the athlete's services on game day (i.e., athlete wishing not to "waste" his or her body)

· Using minor injury as a reason not to play in order to save one's body for collegiate or professional competition where the material rewards are greater than those at the present level

· Using injury as a way to disengage from a dimension of life that heretofore has proven to be undesirable but unavoidable (e.g., football traditionally played by all males in the family)

Reprinted, by permission, R. J. Rotella, B. C. Ogilvie, and D. H. Perrin, 1993, The malingering athlete: Psychological considerations. In *Psychological bases of sport injuries*, edited by D. Pargman (Morgantown, WV: Fitness Information Technology), 87.

inappropriate restricting or purging behavior (American Psychological Association, 2013).

Eating disorders may be connected to sport injury in at least two ways. First, the onset of thoughts and behaviors associated with disordered eating may be triggered by sport injury and ensuing increases in body mass index and percentage of body fat (Myer et al., 2014) that can serve as potential threats to self-identity,

body image, or both (Busanich, McGannon, & Schinke, 2014; Podlog, Reel, & Greviskes, 2014). Second, as part of the "female athlete triad" (recently relabeled "relative energy deficiency in sport"), disordered eating may leave athletes at increased risk of incurring bone-stress injuries (Mountjoy et al., 2014). Thus, it is possible that sport injury may be both a contributor to and an effect of an eating disorder.

Insomnia Disorder   As with eating, an athlete's quantity and quality of sleep can have important connections with sport injury. Sleep has restorative properties that may help protect athletes from sustaining injuries and contribute to the healing of sport injuries. In addition, both sleep and sport injury can be affected by stress. Specifically, stress can adversely affect sleep in terms of both quantity and quality, and (as discussed in chapter 2) it can make athletes more vulnerable to injury. In addition, as a stressor in its own right, injury (and concomitant pain, mood disturbance, and modifications in activity level) can also adversely affect sleep. An athlete can receive a diagnosis of insomnia disorder when the quantity or quality of sleep is disturbed to the extent that the athlete has difficulty initiating or maintaining sleep on a minimum of least three nights per week for a minimum of three months and experiences distress or impaired functioning in domains of importance (e.g., social, occupational, educational). Diagnoses of insomnia disorder are given only to individuals who have ample opportunity to sleep and whose symptoms cannot be better explained by another sleep–wake disorder, by the physiological effects of a substance, or by a different mental disorder or medical condition (American Psychiatric Association, 2013).

Other Chronic and Acute Conditions

The vast majority of disorders presented in *DSM-5* pertain to matters other than the body or medical treatment and are, in most cases, unlikely to be precipitated by incurring a sport injury. On the other hand, as stressors to the individuals who experience them, the disorders may act as factors in injury occurrence. They may also add to the cognitive, emotional, and behavioral effects of sport injury and, ultimately, influence sport injury rehabilitation outcomes. Although sport injury is itself a stressor and therefore can exacerbate these disorders, their onset is likely to predate the injury.

Referral may not be necessary, of course, for preexisting conditions for which athletes are already receiving treatment. In this circumstance, however, the athletes still need coordination of care between the professionals overseeing their treatment, along with frank discussion (with the athlete) about potential interactions between the various forms of treatment that they are receiving. Chronic and acute conditions that manifest in athletes with injuries reside in a wide range of diagnostic categories, including the following:

- Neurodevelopmental disorders
- Schizophrenia-spectrum and other psychotic disorders
- Bipolar and related disorders
- Depressive disorders
- Anxiety disorders
- Obsessive-compulsive and related disorders
- Substance-related and addictive disorders
- Personality disorders

Neurodevelopmental Disorders　The neurodevelopmental disorders category in *DSM-5* contains several well-known diagnoses, such as autism spectrum disorder, intellectual developmental disorder (formerly "mental retardation"), and tic disorders (e.g., Tourette's disorder). However, another well-known condition—attention-deficit/hyperactivity disorder (ADHD)—may be most relevant to sport injury. ADHD involves displaying an array of behaviors indicative of inattention, or of hyperactivity and impulsivity, or of both—at least some of which began prior to age 12, are present in multiple settings, and adversely affect functioning in the social, academic, or occupational domain (American Psychiatric Association, 2013).

Consistent with the suggestion by Burton (2000) that people with ADHD are drawn to physical activity and use sport as a means of coping with their disorder, the 7.3 percent

prevalence rate of ADHD in high school athletes reported by Heil, Hartman, Robinson, and Teegarden (2002) is higher than the 2.5 percent and 5 percent prevalence estimates listed in *DSM-5* for adults and children, respectively (American Psychiatric Association, 2013). Although inattention and impulsivity can conceivably place athletes at elevated risk for injury, evidence suggests that physical activity can enhance executive function and reduce symptoms of inattention and hyperactivity in children with ADHD (Gapin & Etnier, 2010a, 2010b). When athletes with ADHD experience injury, their physical activity levels can be diminished, which may in turn affect their symptoms and consequently their ability to adhere to a structured rehabilitation program.

Schizophrenia-Spectrum and Other Psychotic Disorders　Psychotic disorders involve a loss of contact with reality and include symptoms such as hallucinations, delusions, disorganized thinking and speech, and disorganized or abnormal motor behavior. Given these symptoms and the rigorous demands of participating in competitive sport, it is likely that the prevalence of schizophrenia-spectrum and other psychotic disorders among athletes is very low. Still, a potential connection between this diagnostic category and sport injury exists in the rare instances in which the stress and emotional turbulence experienced in response to sport injury triggers "brief reactive psychosis," a condition manifested in the form of brief psychotic disorder. A diagnosis of brief psychotic disorder is applied when an individual exhibits delusions, hallucinations, or disorganized speech for at least one day (but less than one month) and returns fully to their prepsychotic level of functioning. When symptoms persist beyond one month, diagnoses of schizophreniform disorder and schizophrenia become possible (American Psychiatric Association, 2013).

Bipolar and Related Disorders　Although several prominent athletes have discussed their experiences with bipolar disorder publicly (e.g., Berger, 2010; Visser, 2010), little is known about the occurrence and manifestations of bipolar and related disorders in sport populations. This diagnostic category consists of conditions (e.g., bipolar I disorder, bipolar II disorder, cyclothymic disorder) involving various combinations of manic (or hypomanic) and depressive symptoms. Symptoms of mania and hypomania include elevated, expansive, or irritable mood; increased energy; decreased need for sleep; inflated self-esteem; talkativeness; and racing thoughts. In contrast, symptoms of depression include depressed mood, diminished interest or pleasure in most activities, pronounced change in weight or appetite, insomnia or hypersomnia, and fatigue (American Psychiatric Association, 2013). The chief sport injury concerns associated with bipolar and related disorders are that people with bipolar disorder are at dramatically elevated risk for suicide (American Psychiatric Association, 2013) and that sport injury (musculoskeletal or brain) may confer additional risk for suicide on athletes with bipolar disorder (Baum, 2013).

Depressive Disorders   As noted earlier, depressive responses to sport injury can be manifested in adjustment disorder (with depressed mood) and MDD. Depression that predates (and potentially contributes to) the occurrence of sport injury may also linger and affect an athlete's life during injury rehabilitation. Another condition involving depression that may exert an ongoing influence on an athlete's behavior after injury occurrence is persistent depressive disorder (dysthymia). This diagnosis is given to adults who exhibit depressed mood for two years or longer, experience distress or impairment in important areas of functioning, and have at least two of the following symptoms: "poor appetite or overeating . . . insomnia or hypersomnia . . . low energy or fatigue . . . low self-esteem . . . poor concentration or difficulty making decisions . . . feelings of hopelessness" (American Psychiatric Association, 2013, p. 158). For children and adolescents, the duration requirement is one year and the mood can be either depressed or irritable. In order for the diagnosis of persistent depressive disorder (dysthymia) to apply, the individual must not have had a manic or hypomanic episode and may satisfy some, but not all, of the criteria for MDD (American Psychiatric Association, 2013). When athletes with

persistent depressive disorder (dysthymia) sustain an injury, their depression is more of an ongoing concern or chronic condition than an emotional reaction to the injury.

Anxiety Disorders   Just as not all depression that manifests after sport injury constitutes a reaction to the occurrence of injury, anxiety exhibited by an athlete following injury is not exclusively a phenomenon of reaction to a traumatic event (as discussed earlier in terms of acute stress disorder, PTSD, and adjustment disorder with anxiety) or to an anticipated stressor (as in the case of reinjury anxiety, which is described in chapter 7). Generalized anxiety disorder (GAD) and panic disorder are conditions involving anxiety that, like persistent depressive disorder (dysthymia), may predate and continue after the occurrence of sport injury. A diagnosis of GAD requires the following components: (a) the presence of excessive anxiety and worry that are difficult to control and pertain to multiple issues for six months or longer; (b) at least three (one for children) of a list of symptoms that includes restlessness, fatigue, concentration difficulties, irritability, muscle tension, and sleep problems; and (c) distress or impairment in important areas of functioning (American Psychiatric Association, 2013). With a prevalence rate of 6 percent, GAD was the most common recent or ongoing disorder reported among a large sample of French elite athletes (Schaal et al., 2011). When athletes with GAD are injured, any anxiety they exhibit may have more to do with their GAD than with anything specific about their injury.

Hallmarks of panic disorder include recurrent unexpected panic attacks that produce persistent worry about experiencing additional panic attacks (or their effects) or result in maladaptive behavior changes, or both. Panic attacks are episodes of intense dread in which at least 4 of a list of 13 symptoms surge abruptly to a peak in a matter of minutes; the symptoms include, among others, heart palpitation, sweating, shaking, smothering sensations, choking sensations, chest pain, nausea, dizziness, faintness, fear of dying. Although the 12-month prevalence rate for panic disorder is estimated at 2 to 3 percent, approximately 11 percent of the (adult) population experiences a panic attack over the course of a year. Although unpredictable, panic attacks are more likely to occur during or after periods of elevated stress, which could include experiences associated with sport injury occurrence (American Psychiatric Association, 2013). Nevertheless, when athletes with injury experience a panic attack, it cannot be assumed that the attack is injury related.

Obsessive-Compulsive and Related Disorders
The relevance to sport injury of one disorder in this category—body dysmorphic disorder—was described earlier in this chapter. The acronym for another condition in this category—obsessive-compulsive disorder (OCD)—has entered colloquial language as an adjective rather than the noun that it is and thus may cause confusion among those who are unaware of the characteristics of the disorder. OCD involves more than merely engaging in superstitious rituals confined to the sport context (Kamm, 2005; Reardon & Factor, 2010) or displaying a tendency toward tidiness and order. Rather, it is a disorder characterized by obsessions, compulsions, or both and considered to have genetic and neurological bases.

Obsessions are intrusive, unwanted, anxiety-producing thoughts, urges, or images that are experienced on a recurrent, persistent basis and that result in efforts to ignore, suppress, or neutralize them through thoughts or behaviors (e.g., compulsions). Compulsions are repetitive behaviors or mental acts in which an individual engages in order to decrease or eliminate the anxiety associated with obsessions or to prevent a feared event or situation from occurring. The compulsive behaviors or mental acts are either clearly excessive (as in repetitive hand washing) or not realistically tied to the circumstances they are intended to prevent. To be eligible for a diagnosis of OCD, a person must experience obsessions or compulsions that consume more than 60 minutes per day or produce distress or impairment in important domains of functioning (American Psychiatric Association, 2013). Thus, for athletes with injuries, *having* OCD may differ dramatically from "being OCD" in the colloquial sense.

Substance-Related and Addictive Disorders
Despite the common perception of athletes as following a clean, healthy lifestyle, evidence indicates that young athletes in the United States use alcohol, anabolic steroids, and smokeless tobacco to a greater extent than do their nonathlete peers. Although athletes may have lower levels of cigarette smoking and illegal drug use than nonathletes (Lisha & Sussman, 2010; Terry-McElrath, O'Malley, & Johnston, 2011), they are nevertheless susceptible to substance-related and addictive disorders. In *DSM-5*, substance-related and addictive disorders can be divided into two main categories—substance-induced disorders and substance use disorders—across 10 classes of drugs (i.e., alcohol; caffeine; cannabis; hallucinogens; inhalants; opioids; sedatives, hypnotics, or anxiolytics; stimulants; tobacco; and other or unknown). Substance-induced disorders include intoxication, withdrawal, and various mental disorders produced by psychoactive substances. Intoxication is a temporary maladaptive experience of psychological or behavioral symptoms due to accumulation of a substance in the body, whereas withdrawal refers to problematic psychological or behavioral symptoms that emerge in response to decreased consumption of a substance after an extended period of heavy use (American Psychiatric Association, 2013). As one might expect, substance intoxication is one of "easiest" diagnoses to achieve in *DSM-5*.

Coming closest to what was referred to as "psychoactive substance dependence" in previous editions of the *DSM*, substance use disorders involve a problematic pattern of substance use over a 12-month-period in which a person manifests at least 2 of the following 11 criteria:

1. Using the substance to a greater extent than intended

2. Persistently desiring or attempting to curb use of the substance

3. Spending a lot of time engaging in activities associated with obtaining, taking, or recovering from having taken the substance

4. Craving the substance

5. Failing to fulfill important occupational, academic, or family obligations as a result of recurrent substance use

6. Continuing to use the substance despite experiencing persistent or recurrent substance-related difficulties in social or interpersonal functioning

7. Forsaking important activities in the social, occupational, or recreational domains due to substance use

8. Using the substance in physically hazardous situations

9. Continuing to use the substance despite the presence of a physical or psychological problem attributable to or aggravated by the substance

10. Needing more of the substance to achieve the desired effect or experiencing a diminished effect with the same amount of the substance (i.e., tolerance)

11. Experiencing withdrawal (or using the substance to avoid experiencing withdrawal symptoms)

The diagnostic criteria apply to each of the various classes of substance except for caffeine, for which substance use disorder does not yet apply (American Psychiatric Association, 2013).

Among athletes, the substances used most frequently are alcohol and cannabis (i.e., marijuana) (Green, Uryasz, Petr, & Bray, 2001). Athletes use substances for both recreational and performance-enhancing purposes, some of which may be especially salient following injury. For example, athletes may use substances to facilitate injury recovery, relieve pain, or deal with the stress and frustration of being injured (M.P. Martens, Dams-O'Connor, & Kilmer, 2007). Furthermore, the cognitive, behavioral, and physiological effects of some substances may place athletes at increased risk for injury, and mild traumatic brain injury (e.g., concussion) can increase one's sensitivity to (or the effects of) certain substances (Morse, 2013). Key signs and symptoms of using common substances are shown in table 10.2.

TABLE 10.2   Signs and Symptoms of Substance Use

Substance	Signs and symptoms of use
Alcohol	Talkativeness, euphoria, bright mood, depressed mood, social withdrawal, cognitive impairment, impaired attention or memory, slurred speech, motor coordination problems, unsteady gait, rapid involuntary eye movements, smell of alcohol on breath
Cannabis	Euphoria, inappropriate laughter; sedation; lethargy; amotivation; anxiety; impaired short-term memory, motor coordination, or judgment; red (bloodshot) eyes; cannabis odor on clothing; yellowed finger tips; heightened craving for specific foods
Stimulants	Euphoria, confidence, dramatic behavioral changes, aggression, talkativeness, rambling speech, elevated pulse or blood pressure, decreased appetite, insomnia, pupil dilation, hyperactivity, restlessness, hypervigilance, anxiety, tension, anger, impaired social functioning

Personality Disorders In contrast to the vast majority of conditions discussed in this chapter—in which problem behaviors reflect a marked departure from the individual's normal mode of functioning—personality disorders involve behaviors that are representative of the individual's typical way of acting. Specifically, personality disorders refer to inflexible, maladaptive patterns of perception, thought, and behavior that endure over time, deviate from cultural expectations, cause impairment or distress in important areas of functioning, and are manifested in at least two of four symptom types: cognition, affectivity, interpersonal functioning, and impulse control. *DSM-5* lists personality disorders including antisocial, avoidant, borderline, dependent, histrionic, narcissistic, obsessive-compulsive, paranoid, schizoid, and schizotypal.

Each personality disorder corresponds to a distinctly different set of behaviors and inner experiences that can affect athletes and those with whom they interact across settings (American Psychiatric Association, 2013). For example, some individuals with antisocial personality disorder are characterized by reckless disregard for safety of self or others, and athletes who possess this characteristic may be at increased risk of injury. In another example, the symptoms of histrionic personality disorder can include excessive and overly dramatic displays of emotion, which can be disruptive and misleading in the context of sport injury rehabilitation. Research on the prevalence of personality disorders among athletes is limited, although there is some suggestion that obsessive-compulsive, borderline, and narcissistic personality disorders may be especially common in sport populations (Hendawy & Awad, 2013). In short, personality disorders can produce a challenging series of interpersonal interactions that may be understood better and addressed more effectively when the parties involved are aware of the issues and their possible influences on the situation.

Referral Process

Referral of athletes with injuries for psychological assistance is not simply an event that occurs; rather, it is a complex, delicate process that typically unfolds over time and involves multiple judgments and decisions on the part of sport health care professionals. In fact, Heil (1993c) described referral as "a psychological process in itself" (Heil, 1993c, p. 253). Similarly, Lemberger (2008) noted that referral is an ecological process that is affected by dynamic elements such as the athlete, the sport health care professional, the mental health professional, and the desired psychosocial outcome of the referral—all of which operate in and are influenced by a larger social context. This section of the chapter addresses key aspects of the referral process—namely, when to make referrals, how to make them, and to whom they should be made. Although the focus is primarily on

referral of athletes to mental health professionals, the process is essentially the same for referring athletes to sport psychology consultants in order to address issues pertaining more to sport performance than to psychopathology. Consequently, "sport psychology consultant" can be inserted in place of "mental health professional" in the material that follows.

When to Refer

There is no single "perfect time" to refer athletes for psychological assistance (Brewer, Van Raalte, & Petitpas, 2007); instead, in determining when to make a referral, the following factors should be taken into account (also see figure 10.1):

- Severity of the athlete's psychological symptoms
- Coping resources available to the athlete
- The sport health care professional's training and skills
- The relationship between the sport health care professional and the athlete
- The relationship between the sport health care professional and the mental health professional
- Characteristics of the immediate environment and situation (Brewer, Petitpas, et al., 1999)

Severity of the Athlete's Psychological Symptoms

As noted by Heil (1993c), a general rule of thumb for the timing of referrals holds that the more severe the athlete's psychological symptoms, the sooner a referral should be made. Referral is urgent when the symptoms signify a risk to the health and safety of the athlete or other people, as is the case, for example, with "highly agitated manner, disruptive and aggressive behavior, loss of contact with reality, suicidal or homicidal discussion, and impulsivity" (Lemberger, 2008, p. 91). Symptoms need not be life-, health-, or safety-threatening to warrant a swift referral; to the contrary, immediate attention may also be required for symptoms that are especially distressing to the

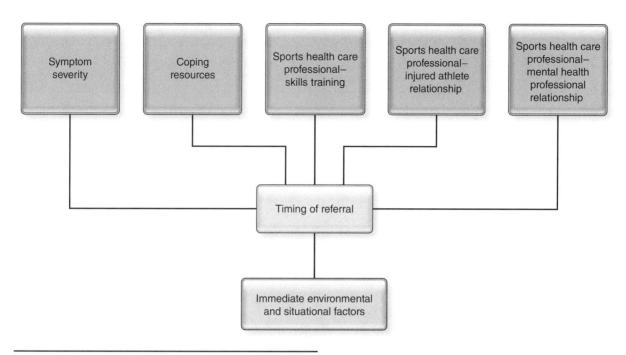

Figure 10.1 Factors affecting the timing of athlete referrals for psychological assistance.

athlete or that greatly impair the athlete's ability to perform tasks of daily living.

Coping Resources Available to the Athlete

In general, the stronger the coping resources available to the athlete, the less urgent it is to refer the athlete for psychological assistance (Brewer, Petitpas, et al., 1999). Coping resources include both internal assets and external assets. Internal assets pertain to the personal attitudes, beliefs, characteristics, and coping skills that the athlete possesses and that enable her or him to deal effectively with adversity. External assets, in contrast, refer to resources available to athletes through their social support system (Petitpas & Danish, 1995); dimensions, providers, and functions of social support are discussed in chapter 1.

The Sport Health Care Professional's Training and Skills

The timing of a sport health care professional's referrals for psychological assistance can be influenced by the practitioner's degree of training and by the extent to which the practitioner is proficient both in using the basic counseling skills described in chapter 9 (i.e., attending to

athletes, exploring their concerns, and influencing their thoughts and actions pertaining to those concerns) and in recognizing conditions and situations that warrant referral. Professionals who possess more extensive training and greater skill may make some referrals sooner than those with less background or capability because they are more adept at building rapport with athletes, identifying psychopathology, and initiating the referral process (Brewer, Petitpas, et al., 1999). On the other hand, trained and skillful professionals may sometimes delay referral longer than their less trained and less skillful counterparts would because they are more comfortable dealing with an athlete's psychological issues and do not feel pressed to make an urgent referral, preferring instead to wait a little longer while the situation "plays out."

The Relationship Between the Sport Health Care Professional and the Athlete

Given the sensitive nature of the referral process, the relationship between the sport health care professional and the athlete is vitally important to the timing of referral for psychological assistance. Building rapport with an athlete can enable the sport health care professional to gain the athlete's trust, access more easily the types of personal detail that may indicate a need for referral, and speak more comfortably with the athlete about the prospects of referral. Referring an athlete before rapport has been developed may adversely affect both the outcome of the referral and the relationship between the sport health care professional and the athlete. Therefore, unless the severity of the athlete's symptoms mandates an immediate referral, it behooves the sport health care professional to wait until a trusting relationship with the athlete has been established before making a referral for psychological assistance (Brewer, Petitpas, et al., 1999).

The Relationship Between the Sport Health Care Professional and the Mental Health Professional

Under optimal circumstances, sport health care professionals are acquainted with specific mental health professionals, what they can do, and how they work before referring athletes to see them. Maintaining established relationships with mental health professionals, particularly in the context of membership on the same treatment team, may make it easier for sport health care professionals to consult mental health professionals for advice and make prompt referrals as the need arises (Brewer, Petitpas, et al., 1999). As noted in the upcoming section on referral networks, proactive efforts on the part of sport health care professionals to reach out to and build relationships with mental health professionals can be richly rewarded when the time for referral comes.

Characteristics of the Immediate Environment and Situation

With the exception of the severity of the athlete's psychological symptoms, which can signal the need for immediate referral if they exceed a certain threshold, the other factors discussed in this section offer general guidance about the timing of referrals for psychological assistance but do not indicate exactly when sport health care professionals should initiate the referral process. In contrast, taking the characteristics of the immediate environ-

ment and situation into account may be useful in determining precisely when to make (or not to make) a referral. For example, some factors—such as the athlete's current mood and life stressors and the amount of privacy available in the sport health care setting—may prompt a practitioner to delay referral until a more private location in the clinical environment can be identified, until the athlete's mood is more conducive to receiving a referral, or until the abatement of immediate life stressors that might preclude the athlete from following up on a referral. Therefore, considering the characteristics of the immediate environment and situation can tip the scales in the practitioner's favor and increase the likelihood of making an effective referral (Brewer, Petitpas, et al., 1999).

How to Refer

Several similar models have been proposed for the referral process (Brewer, Petitpas, et al., 1999; Heil, 1993c; Lemberger, 2008; J. Taylor, Stone, Mullin, Ellenbecker, & Walgenbach, 2003; J. Taylor & Taylor, 1997). In each of these models, the referral itself is only one part—albeit an extremely important one—of a multistep process. Any discussion of how to make referrals must, therefore, consider what happens not only during the referral per se but also what needs to be done in the steps that come before and after it. The model of referral depicted in figure 10.2 features five phases: assessment, consultation, trial intervention, referral, and follow-up.

Assessment

The first phase of the referral process is assessment, during which the sport health care professional determines the athlete's psychological status by using the methods outlined earlier (in the section on recognizing psychopathology in athletes): listening to the athlete's self-reports, attending to other people's reports about the athlete, and observing the athlete's behavior (Brewer, Petitpas, et al., 1999; Granquist & Kenow, 2015). The assessment phase involves monitoring not only the athlete's cognitions, emotions, and behavior but also the

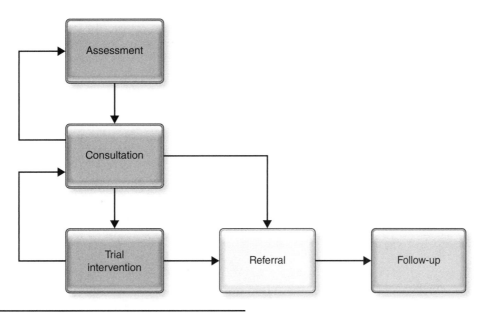

Figure 10.2 A model for referral of athletes with injury for psychological assistance.

composition and state of the athlete's support systems, the potential environmental and situational influences on the athlete's psychological functioning, and the effects of the athlete's behavior both on the athlete and on other people (Lemberger, 2008).

Consultation

The second phase of the referral process—consultation—enables the sport health care professional to tap into the expertise of mental health professionals before making a referral. Once the sport health care professional has identified a potential reason to refer an athlete for psychological assistance, the sport health care professional can contact an appropriate mental health professional, describe the athlete's circumstances in general terms, and receive guidance on how to proceed. This kind of interprofessional interaction is easily facilitated either formally or informally on a face-to-face basis when both professionals are members of a treatment team that meets regularly to discuss its patients (Brewer, Petitpas, et al., 1999). More often, however, the two professionals are not housed in the same facility; in this situation, the sport health care professional will need to initiate a telephone conversation (J. Taylor & Taylor, 1997). The

mental health professional is likely to provide the sport health care professional with a recommendation to either refer the athlete right away (in an urgent situation), conduct further assessment, or implement a trial intervention (Brewer, Petitpas, et al., 1999).

Trial Intervention

As illustrated in figure 10.2, the third phase of the referral process—trial intervention—does not inevitably follow consultation. For instance, it can be immediately skipped when the consultation yields a recommendation for immediate referral, and it may be delayed and potentially avoided altogether if the mental health professional advises an extension of the assessment phase. When recommended by the mental health professional, the trial intervention typically involves a simple procedure that falls within the bounds of the sport health care professional's competence and is easy for her or him to implement and for the athlete to follow (Brewer, Petitpas, et al., 1999).

The intervention is generally designed to give athletes an alternative way of coping with their situation (Heil, 1993c). For example, if the sport health care professional is having difficulty determining whether an athlete who keeps "forgetting" to do prescribed home rehabilitation is lazy, unmotivated, mildly depressed, overscheduled, or merely forgetful, the trial intervention advised by the mental health professional might involve teaching the athlete a few strategies for enhancing home rehabilitation-exercise adherence (see chapter 6). Once the trial intervention has been completed, the sport health care professional can evaluate the effects and determine whether additional consultation or referral is needed. Even if the intervention is successful, it is appropriate to let the mental health professional know that the issue has been resolved.

Referral

All phases of the referral process are important, but the fourth phase—referral—is clearly the "main event." After taking into account the outcomes of the assessment, consultation, and trial intervention phases, along with the factors affecting the timing of referral (see table 10.2), the next task facing the sport health care professional is to make the referral. As with asking a prospective romantic partner out on a date for the first time, merely broaching the subject of referral may be the most difficult part of the whole process for the sport health care professional. When introducing athletes to the idea of a referral for psychological assistance, practitioners can help put the athletes at ease by doing the following: explaining the reason(s) for referral; describing what it is like to work with the prospective referral target (i.e., the mental health professional); and reassuring the athletes that they are not being abandoned, disrespected, or doubted in any way (Brewer, Petitpas, et al., 1999; Heil, 1993c; J. Taylor & Taylor, 1997).

In bringing up the topic of referral with an athlete, it can be useful to tie an expression of concern for the athlete in with a mention of the behaviors that are the source of that concern (e.g., "Sal, I just wanted to let you know that I'm worried about you. From what I've seen here in rehab, it appears that you've been feeling pretty down lately."). Such an approach is both honest and direct, and it conveys that the sport practitioner cares about the athlete's well-being. Rather than focusing

on pathology, practitioners can present referral as a means of helping athletes accomplish their goals, both in and out of sport (J. Taylor & Taylor, 1997). In turn, the symptoms and behaviors that constitute the reason for the referral can be conceptualized as barriers to attaining the athlete's goals (e.g., "With such low energy, it's hard to bring the intensity that rehab requires.") or, if appropriate, to simply experiencing well-being (e.g., "That's a heavy burden for one person to carry for so long, feeling the way you do.") and meeting the demands of daily living (e.g., "It sounds like you're not getting much sleep and are falling behind in your work, too.").

Referral to a mental health professional offers athletes a way to address the psychosocial challenges that they are facing and can be presented as such with optimism (e.g., "There's a doctor affiliated with the clinic who has helped a lot of our athletes deal with issues like the ones you're having."). By describing what it is like to work with a given mental health professional, sport health care professionals can help athletes become more comfortable with the idea of referral (Heil, 1993c; J. Taylor & Taylor, 1997). For example, information about the frequency, nature, content, and cost of treatment can help alleviate concerns that athletes may have about accepting the referral (e.g., "With this doctor, there are usually weekly appointments lasting for an hour where you will likely talk about your injury and life situations and come up with strategies to help you feel and perform better. The doctor has a sliding fee scale, which means that you won't have to pay more than you can afford, and everything you say will be held in confidence.").

Even under the best of circumstances—such as when the sport health care professional has built a strong relationship with the athlete to whom the referral is being recommended—the process of referral can prompt feelings of embarrassment, abandonment, disrespect, and doubt in the athlete. Therefore, the sport health care professional should be sensitive to the athlete's emotions and reassure him or her that referrals to mental health professionals are appropriate, ethical, standard, and born out of concern for the athlete's well-being. Doing so can help preserve the athlete's dignity, prevent any negative feelings from escalating, and enhance the viability of the referral (Brewer, Petitpas, et al., 1999; Heil, 1993c; J. Taylor & Taylor, 1997; Van Raalte & Andersen, 2014). In situations where an athlete's feelings of abandonment are particularly salient and resistance to referral is strong, one possible alternative is that of "referring in" (M.B. Andersen, 1992), wherein the mental health professional comes to the sport health care facility to meet simultaneously with the athlete and the sport health care professional (at least until the athlete feels comfortable meeting individually with the mental health professional).

When an athlete accepts a referral for psychological assistance, the sport health care professional can help "seal the deal" by encouraging (and perhaps even helping) the athlete to schedule an appointment right away (Heil, 1993c; Lemberger, 2008; J. Taylor & Taylor, 1997). When, on the other hand, an athlete declines a referral altogether, the referral process is not necessarily over. Bearing in mind that it may take some time for the athlete to "buy in" to the rationale for referral, the sport health care professional can reintroduce the idea at a later date as deemed appropriate or necessary (Van Raalte & Andersen, 2014).

Follow-Up

Once an athlete has been referred for psychological assistance, the next—and final—phase of the referral process is the follow-up, during which the sport health care professional communicates with the athlete and perhaps also with the mental health professional. Of course, the athlete chooses whether and how much to share with the sport health care professional about the athlete's work with the mental health professional. If the athlete does not mention what has transpired as a result of the referral, it is not inappropriate for the sport health care professional to ask how things are going with the mental health professional. If the athlete still does not wish to discuss the subject, the sport health care professional can make an indirect assessment of the effects of the referral by observing the extent to which the factors that precipitated the referral have changed (Brewer, Petitpas, et al., 1999).

Mental health professionals can also serve as an important source of information about how the athletes have fared as a result of being referred and how the athletes' psychological state may affect their involvement in sport health care. When a mental health professional receives a referral from a health care professional, it is customary to send the health care professional a letter of acknowledgement and perhaps gratitude. If the athlete signs a waiver of confidentiality authorizing the release of information about the treatment to the sport health care professional, then the mental health professional may also provide the sport health care professional with updates regarding the athlete's progress. These updates may take the form of written consultation reports or less formal communications; the latter option is more typical when the referral is made within a clearly defined treatment team at a single location (Brewer, Petitpas, et al., 1999; Meyer, Fink, & Carey, 1988; Strein & Hershenson, 1991). When authorized by the athlete, such information is shared with the sport health care professional at the discretion of the mental health professional, with an emphasis on details of potential relevance to the provision of sport health care services (e.g., "Charles expressed anger at authority figures in sport, noting that he tends to work with others most effectively when they seek out and consider his input in the decision-making process.").

The athlete may also sign a waiver of confidentiality authorizing the sport health care professional to share pertinent details of the athlete's injury status and treatment with the mental health professional, thereby enabling two-way, interprofessional communication. As discussed in this chapter's Focus on Application box, when a sport health care professional confers with a mental health professional regarding an athlete under their mutual care, the sport health care professional should appropriately document the consultation on the athlete's medical chart (Brewer, Petitpas, et al., 1999).

Focus on Application

When circumstances warrant the referral of an athlete for psychological assistance, the issues precipitating the referral (e.g., mental disorder) can be sensitive and difficult for the athlete to discuss openly until the athlete trusts that the professionals involved will not share the information with other people. At the same time, however, as noted by Heil (1993c), clear communication between the professionals involved in the athlete's care is vital to the success of a team approach to sport health care. How can these potentially conflicting needs—for maintenance of a trusting relationship with the athlete and for clarity in interprofessional communication—be satisfied by professionals in sport health care and mental health care?

For starters, Heil (1993c) recommended clarifying "in the early phases of the treatment process . . . what kind of information will be shared and with whom" and then conscientiously following those rules (p. 252). In addition, Ray (1999) offered compelling reasons for sport health care professionals to document their counseling interactions with athletes (of which referral for psychological assistance is definitely one) and noted that documentation

· provides sport health care professionals with legal protection,

· helps sport health care professionals remember what transpired during their interactions with athletes,

· enables sport health care professionals to adhere to ethical and professional standards,

· improves communication with mental health professionals,

· helps satisfy the requirements of insurance companies, and

· contributes to improved care of athletes with injuries.

Although documentation of counseling interactions fulfills a number of essential functions of sport health care professionals, it also has potential pitfalls. As suggested by Ray (1999), documenting interactions can be problematic when it interferes with the practitioner's ability to listen actively to the athlete. For example, the simple act of taking notes can prevent the practitioner from noticing and responding appropriately to nonverbal cues from the athletes. And even though the motives for creating documentation are typically benevolent, information contained in reports and notes can be potentially damaging to an athlete's reputation. Therefore, in deciding what information to document from the psychosocial domain, the practitioner must weigh the potential utility of the information to an athlete's well-being against the potential harm it could cause to the athlete if it were accessed by people outside of the sport health care system—for example, employees of an insurance company (Ray, 1999).

Ray (1999) recommended that in addition to documenting data obtained through physical examination and treatment, sport health care professionals may also find it appropriate to record details pertaining to patient education, verbal orders (e.g., treatment prescriptions), telephone advice, and referrals that they initiate, as well as information about the athlete's mental status (e.g., appearance, behavior, cognition, emotion, memory, orientation) and any suicidal or violent behavior. Although thorough documentation of interactions with athletes is generally recommended, certain information may not be appropriate to include on a medical chart. For example, Soisson, Vande-Creek, and Knapp (1987) advocated the exclusion of statements based on emotion or personal opinion (e.g., hunches, value judgments) and noted that "information about illegal behavior, sexual practices, or other sensitive information that may embarrass or harm the client or others is rarely appropriate for the record" (p. 500).

Referral Networks

The array of mental health professionals to whom sport health care professionals refer athletes for psychological assistance constitutes a referral network. Even in the rare cases where mental health practitioners are full-fledged members of the sport health care treatment team, it is useful for sport health care professionals to cultivate a list of mental health professionals who can provide assistance in best meeting the varied needs of the athletes they serve. Although the composition of a given referral network is likely to vary depending on the size and characteristics (e.g., age, gender, race, ethnicity, typical psychological concerns) of the athlete population served by the sport health care professional, referral net-

TABLE 10.3   Typical Degrees and Domains of Practice of Various Mental Health Professionals

Title	Degree(s)	Domains of practice
Psychiatrist	MD or DO	Diagnosis and treatment of mental disorders; medication prescription
Psychologist	PhD, PsyD, or EdD	Assessment, diagnosis, and treatment of mental disorders and adjustment problems
Social worker	MSW	Broad-based mental health services
Counselor	MA, MS, or MEd	Broad-based services in mental health counseling, substance abuse counseling, marriage and family therapy, career counseling, athletic counseling, and other specialty areas

Adapted, by permission, from B. W. Brewer, A. J. Petitpas, and J. L. Van Raalte, 1999, Referral of injured athletes for counseling and psychotherapy. In *Counseling in sports medicine*, edited by R. Ray and D. M. Wiese-Bjornstal (Champaign, IL: Human Kinetics), 136.

works commonly include the following types of mental health professional: psychiatrists, clinical and counseling psychologists, clinical social workers, and counselors. Typical degrees and domains of practice of these professionals are displayed in table 10.3. Each type of professional offers a distinct blend of skills, techniques, and experiences that can be useful in meeting athletes' mental health needs. Sport health care professionals are encouraged to assemble a group of mental health professionals who are experienced in working with athletes (or at least willing to do so) and are diverse with respect to gender, race, ethnicity, cost, professional title, and theoretical orientation (Brewer, Petitpas, et al., 1999; Lemberger, 2008; J. Taylor & Taylor, 1997; Van Raalte & Andersen, 2014).

To develop a referral network, a sport health care professional can begin by identifying and contacting qualified and appropriately credentialed mental health professionals in the local area who may be appropriate referral targets. The sport health care professional can then seek to build working relationships with the mental health professionals identified. Specifically, the sport health care professional should seek to learn about the mental health professionals' areas of expertise, population served, preferred referral procedures, hours of operation, rates and methods of payment, insurance coverage policies, therapeutic approaches, and theoretical orientations. This information helps the sport health care profes-

sional direct athletes who need psychological assistance to the appropriate practitioners, manage the referral process smoothly, and convey an understanding of what athletes are likely to experience when working with practitioners in the network.

For example, knowing the mental health professionals' therapeutic approaches and theoretical orientations enables the sport health care professional to inform athletes about the extent to which treatment is likely to involve a focus on current thoughts and feelings, overt behaviors, or unconscious processes. Once a referral network is established, the sport health care professional should regularly update it, evaluate its efficiency and effectiveness, and modify it as needed (Brewer, Petitpas, et al., 1999; J. Taylor & Taylor, 1997; Van Raalte & Andersen, 2014; Wooten, 2008). Establishing and maintaining a referral network requires an initial and ongoing outlay of time and effort, but the investment helps the sport health care professional best meet the needs of athletes who require psychological assistance.

Biopsychosocial Analysis

As with chapter 9, the material covered in this chapter is firmly grounded in the psychosocial realm. Referral of athletes with injuries for psychological services is unquestionably a social process, but it takes place against a largely biological backdrop. The juxtaposition of the psychological reasons for referral with the prevailing biological (or, more accurately, biomedical) context—that is, the treatment of physical injury—is one of the things that may make both athletes and sport health care professionals uncomfortable with the referral process. In the case examples provided at the beginning of this chapter, discomfort associated with referral was evident in both Kelley (an athletic trainer) and Blair (an athlete). The referral process was initiated with Blair (and with Karla) for issues pertaining to (likely) psychopathology, whereas Aaron's referral to a sport psychology consultant was made for what seemed to be primarily a performance issue, and his receptiveness to the idea of referral, as compared with Blair's resistance, may have been facilitated by the fact that the reason for his referral carried less potential for stigma.

The biological context and psychological content notwithstanding, referral is still a distinctly social process, in which communication and relationships are paramount. For example, the quality of the relationship between Blair and his physical therapist, John, was readily apparent both in Blair's comfort with refusing John's offer of a referral while electing to continue working with John and in John's willingness to reintroduce the possibility of referral at a later date. Similarly, the relationships that Renee, an athletic trainer, had forged with Karla and with the counselor to whom Karla was referred were likely contributors to the effective communication between them. Specifically, it enabled Renee to get close enough to Karla to listen to her concerns, yet to stay outside of Karla's "firing zone" of angry behavior; it also enabled Renee to engage the counselor in being "referred in" to meet with Karla and Renee together in the clinical setting that was familiar to Karla.

Similarly, the strength of Aaron's relationship with his athletic trainer, Jacquelyn, was likely a key factor in his choice to share his concerns about returning to sport with her. In turn, her skillful communication regarding referral to a sport psychology consultant allowed her to "seal the deal" with Aaron. In contrast, Kelley's relationship with Hillary had not developed to the point where Kelley could even bring herself to ask Hillary about her eat-

ing behavior. It appears, therefore, that paying attention to a full complement of biological, psychological, and social factors can help to optimize the outcomes experienced by athletes with injuries.

Summary

Generally considered more challenging than typical referrals to medical specialists, referrals of athletes with injuries for psychological assistance involve both patient–practitioner communication and communication between health care professionals. Psychological referrals help athletes meet their psychosocial needs and enable sport health care professionals practice within their scope of competence and fulfill important professional, ethical, and legal obligations. Nevertheless, such referrals occur infrequently, perhaps because of perceived unavailability of qualified sport psychology or mental health professionals and because of discomfort about discussing psychological issues.

The main reasons for referral of athletes for psychological assistance are prevention and remediation of psychological difficulties. Psychopathology in athletes can be recognized through athlete self-reports, observation of athlete behavior, and reports from others (e.g., coaches, teammates, parents). Few epidemiological data have been obtained regarding the prevalence of mental disorders in athlete populations other than those for eating disorders and substance-related disorders. Three broad categories of mental disorder that are potentially relevant to athletes with injury have been identified. The first category—disorders that involve reactions or responses to sport injury and its effects—includes neurocognitive disorder, acute stress disorder, posttraumatic stress disorder, adjustment disorder, and major depressive disorder. The second category—disorders pertaining to the body and medical treatment—includes body dysmorphic disorder, somatic symptom disorder, illness anxiety disorder, conversion disorder, psychological factors affecting other medical conditions, factitious disorder, eating disorders, and insomnia disorder. The third category—other chronic and acute conditions—includes neurodevelopmental disorders, schizophrenia-spectrum and other psychotic disorders, bipolar and related disorders, depressive disorders, anxiety disorders, obsessive-compulsive and related disorders, substance-related and addictive disorders, and personality disorders.

Referral of athletes with injuries for psychological assistance is a complex, delicate process. Factors that should be considered in determining the timing of a referral include the severity of the athlete's psychological symptoms, the coping resources available to the athlete, the sport health care professional's training and skills, the relationship between the sport health care professional and the athlete, the relationship between the sport health care professional and the mental health professional, and the characteristics of the immediate environment and situation. Several highly similar models of the referral process have been proposed, one of which features phases that involve assessment of athletes and their situations, consultation with mental health professionals, a trial intervention recommended by mental health professionals, referral, and follow-up with athletes and mental health professionals. Establishing a diverse network of mental health professionals can help facilitate the referral of athletes with injuries for psychological assistance.

Discussion Questions

1. Why are referrals of athletes for psychological services by sport health care professionals not made more frequently?

2. What is the rationale for sport health care professionals referring athletes for psychological services?

3. What are some forms of psychopathology for which sport health care professionals might refer athletes for psychological services?

4. What is the process by which sport health care professionals can go about making psychological referrals, and what mental health professionals should sport health care professionals include in their referral network?

References

Aaltonen, S., Karjalainen, H., Heinonen, A., Parkkari, J., & Kujala, U.M. (2007). Prevention of sports injuries: Systematic review of randomized controlled trials. *Archives of Internal Medicine, 167,* 1585–1592. doi:10.1001/archinte.167.15.1585

Abenza, L., Olmedilla, A., & Ortega, E. (2010). Efectos de las lesiónes sobre las variables psicológicas en fubolistas juveniles [Effect of injuries on psychological variables among under-19 soccer players.]. *Revista Latinoamericana de Psicología, 42,* 265–277.

Abernethy, L., & Bleakley, C. (2007). Strategies to prevent injury in adolescent sport: A systematic review. *British Journal of Sports Medicine, 41,* 627–638. doi:10.1136/bjsm.2007.035691

Abgarov, A., Jeffery-Tosoni, S., Baker, J., & Fraser-Thomas, J. (2012). Understanding social support throughout the injury process among interuniversity swimmers. *Journal of Intercollegiate Sport, 5,* 213–229.

Addison, T., & Kremer, J. (1997). Towards a process model of the experience of pain in sport. In R. Lidor & M. Bar-Eli (Eds.), *Innovations in sport psychology: Linking theory and practice* (Part I, pp. 59–61). Netanya, Israel: International Society of Sport Psychology.

Addison, T., Kremer, J., & Bell, R. (1998). Understanding the psychology of pain in sport. *Irish Journal of Psychology, 19,* 486–503.

Ajzen, I. (1991). The theory of planned behavior. *Organizational Behavior and Human Decision Processes, 50,* 179–211. doi:0.1016/0749-5978(91)90020-T

Ajzen, I., & Fishbein, M. (1980). *Understanding attitudes and predicting social behavior.* Englewood Cliffs, NJ: Prentice-Hall.

Akehurst, S., & Oliver, E.J. (2014). Obsessive passion: A dependency associated with injury-related risky behaviour in dancers. *Journal of Sports Sciences, 32,* 259–267. doi: 10.1080/02640414.2013.823223

Alabas, O.A., Tashani, O.A., Tasabam, G., & Johnson, M.I. (2012). Gender role affects experimental pain responses: A systematic review with meta-analysis. *European Journal of Pain, 16,* 1211–1223. doi:10.1002/j.1532-2149.2012.00121.x

Albinson, C.B., & Petrie, T. (2003). Cognitive appraisals, stress, and coping: Preinjury and postinjury factors influencing psychological adjustment to athletic injury. *Journal of Sport Rehabilitation, 12,* 306–322.

Alentorn-Geli, E., Myer, G.D., Silvers, H.J., Samitier, G., Romero, D., Lázaro-Haro, C., & Cugat, R. (2009). Prevention of non-contact anterior cruciate ligament injuries in soccer players. Part 2: A review of prevention programs aimed to modify risk factors and to reduce injury rates. *Knee Surgery, Sports Traumatology, Arthroscopy, 17,* 159–179.

Almeida, P.L., Luciano, R., Lameiras, J., & Buceta, J.M. (2014). Beneficios percibidos de las lesiónes deportivas: Estudio cualitativo en futbolistas profesionales y semiprofesionales. *Revista de Psicología del Deporte, 23,* 457–464.

Alzate, R., Ramírez, A., & Artaza, J.L. (2004). The effect of psychological response on recovery of sport injury. *Research in Sports Medicine, 12,* 15–31. doi:10.1080/15438620490280567

American Psychiatric Association. (2013). *Diagnostic and statistical manual of mental disorders* (5th ed.). Washington, DC: Author.

Andersen, M.B. (1992). Sport psychology and procrustean categories: An appeal for synthesis and expansion of service. *Association for the Advancement of Applied Sport Psychology Newsletter, 7*(3), 8–9.

Andersen, M.B., & Stoové, M.A. (1998). The sanctity of p < .05 obfuscates good stuff: A comment on Kerr and Goss. *Journal of Applied Sport Psychology, 10,* 168–173. doi:10.1080/10413209808406384

Andersen, M.B., & Williams, J.M. (1988). A model of stress and athletic injury: Prediction and prevention. *Journal of Sport & Exercise Psychology, 10,* 294–306.

Andersen, M.B., & Williams, J.M. (1999). Athletic injury, psychosocial factors, and perceptual changes during stress. *Journal of Sports Sciences, 17,* 735–741. doi:10.1080/026404199365597

Andersen, T.E., Floerenes, T.W., Arnason, A., & Bahr, R. (2004). Video analysis of the mechanisms of ankle injuries in football. *The American*

Journal of Sports Medicine, 32, 69S–79S. doi:10.1177/0363546503262023

Andersen, T.E., Larsen, O., Tenga, A., Engebretsen, L., & Bahr, R. (2003). Football incident analysis: A new video-based method to describe injury mechanisms in professional football. *British Journal of Sports Medicine, 37,* 226–232. doi:10.1136/bjsm.37.3.226

Ankney, I., Jauhar, E., Schrank, L., & Shapiro, J. (2012). Factors that affect psychological readiness to return to sport following injury. In *Association for Applied Sport Psychology—2012 conference proceedings & program* (p. 86). Indianapolis: Association for Applied Sport Psychology.

Anshel, M.H., & Russell, K.G. (1994). Effect of aerobic and strength training on pain tolerance, pain appraisal, and mood of unfit males as a function of pain location. *Journal of Sports Sciences, 12,* 535–547. doi: 10.1080/02640419408732204

Appaneal, R.N., & Granquist, M.D. (2007). Shades of grey: A sport psychology consultation with an athlete with injury. In D. Pargman (Ed.), *Psychological bases of sport injury* (3rd ed., pp. 335–350). Morgantown, WV: Fitness Information Technology.

Appaneal, R.N., Levine, B.R., Perna, F.M., & Roh, J.L. (2009). Measuring postinjury depression among male and female competitive athletes. *Journal of Sport & Exercise Psychology, 31,* 60–76.

Appaneal, R.N., Perna, F.M., & Larkin, K.T. (2007). Psychophysiological response to severe sport injury among competitive male athletes: A preliminary investigation. *Journal of Clinical Sport Psychology, 1,* 68–88.

Arnason, A., Engebretsen, L., & Bahr, R. (2005). No effect of a video-based awareness program on the rate of soccer injuries. *The American Journal of Sports Medicine, 33,* 77–84. doi:10.1177/0363546503262688.

Ardern, C.L., Taylor, N.F., Feller, J.A., & Webster, K.E. (2012). Fear of re-injury in people who have returned to sport following anterior cruciate ligament reconstruction surgery. *Journal of Science & Medicine in Sport, 15,* 488–495. doi:10.1016/j.jsams.2012.03.015

Ardern, C.L., Taylor, N.F., Feller, J.A., & Webster, K.E. (2013). A systematic review of the psychological factors associated with returning to sport following injury. *British Journal of Sports Medicine, 47,* 1120–1126. doi:10.1136/bjsports-2012-091203

Ardern, C.L., Taylor, N.F., Feller, J.A., Whitehead, T.S., & Webster, K.E. (2013). Psychological responses matter in returning to preinjury level of sport after anterior cruciate ligament reconstruction surgery. *The American Journal of Sports Medicine,* 41, 1549–1558. doi:10.1080/02640419408732204

Ardern, C.L., Taylor, N.F., Feller, J.A., Whitehead, T.S., & Webster, K.E. (2015). Sports participation 2 years after anterior cruciate ligament reconstruction in athletes who had not returned to sport at 1 year: A prospective follow-up of physical function and psychological factors in 122 athletes. *The American Journal of Sports Medicine, 43,* 848–856. doi:10.1177/0363546514563282

Ardern, C.L., Webster, K.E., Taylor, N.F., & Feller, J.A. (2011). Return to sport following anterior cruciate ligament reconstruction surgery: A systematic review and meta-analysis of the state of play. *British Journal of Sports Medicine, 45,* 596–606. doi:10.1136/bjsm.2010.076364

Arvinen-Barrow, M., & Hemmings, B. (2013). Goal setting in sport injury rehabilitation. In M. Arvinen-Barrow & N. Walker (Eds.), *The psychology of sport injury and rehabilitation* (pp. 56–70). London: Routledge.

Arvinen-Barrow, M., Hemmings, B., Becker, C.A., & Booth, L. (2008). Sport psychology education: A preliminary survey on chartered physiotherapists' preferred methods of training delivery. *Journal of Sport Rehabilitation, 17,* 399–412.

Arvinen-Barrow, M., & Pack, S. (2013). Social support in sport injury rehabilitation. In M. Arvinen-Barrow & N. Walker (Eds.), *The psychology of sport injury and rehabilitation* (pp. 117–131). London: Routledge.

Astle, S.J. (1986). The experience of loss in athletes. *Journal of Sports Medicine and Physical Fitness, 26,* 279–284.

Bahr, R. (2004). Acute ankle injuries. In R. Bahr & S. Mæhlum (Eds.), *Clinical guide to sports injuries: An illustrated guide to the management of injuries in physical activity* (pp. 393–407). Champaign, IL: Human Kinetics.

Bahr, R., & Krosshaug, T. (2005). Understanding injury mechanisms: A key component of preventing injuries in sport. *British Journal of Sports Medicine, 39,* 324–329. doi:10.1136/bjsm.2005.018341

Bahr, R., & Lian, O. (1997). A two-fold reduction in the incidence of acute ankle sprains in volleyball. *Scandinavian Journal of Medicine & Science in Sports, 7,* 172–177. doi: 10.1111/j.1600-0838.1997.tb00135.x

Ballard-Reisch, D. (1990). A model of participative decision making for physician-patient interaction. *Health Communication, 2,* 91–104.

Bandura, A. (1977). Self-efficacy: Toward a unifying theory of behavior change. *Psychological Review, 84,* 191–215. doi:0.1037/0033-295X.84.2.191

Bandura, A. (1982). Self-efficacy mechanism in human agency. *American Psychologist, 37,* 122–147. doi:10.1037/0003-066X.37.2.122

Bandura, A. (1997). *Self-efficacy: The exercise of control.* New York: Freeman.

Baranoff, J., Hanrahan, S.J., & Connor, J.P. (2015). The roles of acceptance and catastrophizing in rehabilitation following anterior cruciate ligament reconstruction. *Journal of Science and Medicine in Sport, 18,* 250–254. doi:10.1016/j.jsams.2014.04.002

Bartholomew, J.B., Lewis, B.P., Linder, D.E., & Cook, D.B. (1993). *Exercise associated conditioned analgesia.* Unpublished manuscript, Arizona State University, Tempe.

Bassett, S.F., & Prapavessis, H. (2011). A test of an adherence-enhancing adjunct to physiotherapy steeped in the protection motivation theory. *Physiotherapy Theory and Practice, 27,* 360–372. doi:10.3109/09593985.2010.507238

Bauer, M., Feeley, B.T., Wawrzyniak, J.R., Pinkowsky, G., & Gallo, R.A. (2014). Factors affecting return to play after anterior cruciate ligament reconstruction: A review of the current literature. *The Physician and Sportsmedicine, 42*(4), 71–79. doi:10.3810/psm.2014.11.2093

Baum, A.L. (2013). Suicide in athletes. In D.A. Baron, C.L. Reardon, & S.H. Baron (Eds.), *Clinical sports psychiatry: An international perspective* (pp. 79–88). Chichester, UK: Wiley-Blackwell.

Beaton, J., & Langdon, S. (2012). Discrepancies between injured athletes' and coaches' perceptions of social support [Abstract]. In *Association for Applied Sport Psychology—2012 conference proceedings & program* (p. 86). Indianapolis: Association for Applied Sport Psychology.

Beckman, H.B., & Frankel, R.M. (1984). The effect of physician behavior on the collection of data. *Annals of Internal Medicine, 101,* 692–696. doi:10.7326/0003-4819-101-5-692

Beecher, H.K. (1959). *Measurement of subjective response.* New York: Oxford University Press.

Begel, D. (1994). Occupational, psychopathologic, and therapeutic aspects of sport psychiatry. *Direct Psychiatry, 14*(11), 108.

Belanger, A.Y., & Noel, G. (1991). Compliance to and effects of a home strengthening exercise program for adult dystrophic patients: A pilot study. *Physiotherapy Canada, 43,* 24–30.

Beneka, A., Malliou, P., Gioftsidou, A., Kofotolis, N., Rokka, S., Mavromoustakos, S., & Godolias, G. (2013). Effects of instructional and motivational self-talk on balance performance in knee injured. *European Journal of Physiotherapy, 15,* 56–63. doi:10.3109/21679169.2013.776109

Bentsen, H. Lindgarde, F., & Manthrope, R. (1997). The effects of dynamic strength back exercise and/ or a home training program in 57-year-old women with chronic low back pain. *Spine, 22,* 1494–1500.

Berger, K. (2010, November 22). West deals with bipolar disorder, gets back on track. CBS Sports. Retrieved from www.cbssports.com

Bianco, T. (2001). Social support and recovery from sport injury: Elite skiers share their experiences. *Research Quarterly for Exercise and Sport, 70,* 376–88.

Bianco, T., Malo, S., & Orlick, T. (1999). Sport injury and illness: Elite skiers describe their experiences. *Research Quarterly for Exercise and Sport, 70,* 157–169.

Bianco, T.M. (2007). Sport injury and the need for coach support. In D. Pargman (Ed.), *Psychological bases of sport injury* (3rd ed., pp. 237–266). Morgantown, WV: Fitness Information Technology.

Bleakley, C., McDonough, S., & MacAuley, D. (2004). The use of ice in the treatment of acute soft tissue injury: A systematic review of the literature. *The American Journal of Sports Medicine, 32,* 251–261. doi:10.1177/0363546503260757

Bollen, J.C., Dean, S.G., Siegert, R.J., Howe, T.E., & Goodwin, V.A. (2014). A systematic review of measures of self-reported adherence to unsupervised home-based rehabilitation exercise programmes, and their psychometric properties. *BMJ Open, 4,* e005044. doi:10.1136/bmjopen-2014-005044

Booth, W. (1987). Arthritis Institute tackles sports. *Science, 237,* 846–847.

Boots, L.M. (2010). *Dealing with the psychological aspects of athletes: How prepared are athletic training students* (Unpublished master's thesis). Springfield College, MA.

Boselie, J.J.L.M., Vancleef, L.M.G., Smeets, T., & Peters, M.L. (2014). Increasing optimism abolishes pain-induced impairments in executive task performance. *Pain, 155,* 334–340. doi:10.1016/j.pain.2013.10.014

Boyce, D., & Brosky, J.A. (2008). Determining the minimal number of cyclic passive stretch repetitions recommended for an acute increase in an indirect measure of hamstring length. *Physiotherapy Theory and Practice, 24,* 113–120. doi:10.1080/09593980701378298

Braham, R.A., & Finch, C.F. (2004). Do community football players wear allocated protective equipment? Descriptive results from a randomised controlled trial. *Journal of Science and Medicine in Sport, 7,* 216–220. doi:10.1016/S1440-2440(04)80011-2

Braham, R.A., Finch, C.F., McIntosh, A., & McCrory, P. (2004). Community football players' attitudes towards protective equipment: A preseason measure. Descriptive results from a randomised controlled trial. *British Journal of Sports Medicine, 38,* 426–430. doi:0.1136/bjsm.2002.004051

Bramwell, S.T., Masuda, M., Wagner, N.N., & Holmes, T.H. (1975). Psychosocial factors in athletic injuries: Development and application of the Social and Athletic Readjustment Rating Scale (SARRS). *Journal of Human Stress, 1,* 6–20.

Bredemeier, B. (1985). Moral reasoning and the perceived legitimacy of intentionally injurious sport acts. *Journal of Sport Psychology, 7,* 110–124.

Bredemeier, B., Weiss, M., Shields, D., & Cooper, B. (1987). The relationship between children's legitimacy judgments and their moral reasoning, aggression tendencies, and sport involvement. *Sociology of Sport Journal, 4,* 48–60.

Brewer, B.W. (1993). Self-identity and specific vulnerability to depressed mood. *Journal of Personality, 61,* 343–364. doi:10.1111/j.1467-6494.1993.tb00284.x

Brewer, B.W. (1994). Review and critique of models of psychological adjustment to athletic injury. *Journal of Applied Sport Psychology, 6,* 87–100. doi:10.1080/10413209408406467

Brewer, B.W. (1999a). Causal attribution dimensions and adjustment to sport injury. *Journal of Personal and Interpersonal Loss, 4,* 215–224. doi:10.1080/10811449908409730

Brewer, B.W. (1999b). Adherence to sport injury rehabilitation regimens. In S.J. Bull (Ed.), *Adherence issues in sport and exercise* (pp. 145–168). Chichester: Wiley.

Brewer, B.W. (2001). Emotional adjustment to sport injury. In J. Crossman (Ed.), *Coping with sports injuries: Psychological strategies for rehabilitation* (pp. 1–19). Oxford: Oxford University Press.

Brewer, B.W. (2004). Psychological aspects of rehabilitation. In G.S. Kolt & M.B. Andersen (Eds.), *Psychology in the physical and manual therapies* (pp. 39–53). Edinburgh: Churchill Livingstone.

Brewer, B.W. (2007). Psychology of sport injury rehabilitation. In G. Tenenbaum & R.C. Eklund (Eds.), *Handbook of sport psychology* (3rd ed., pp. 404–424). New York: Wiley.

Brewer, B.W. (2010). The role of psychological factors in sport injury rehabilitation outcomes. *International Review of Sport and Exercise Psychology, 3,* 40–61. doi:10.1080/17509840903301207.

Brewer, B.W., Andersen, M.B., & Van Raalte, J.L. (2002). Psychological aspects of sport injury rehabilitation: Toward a biopsychosocial approach. In D.L. Mostofsky & L.D. Zaichkowsky (Eds.), *Medical and psychological aspects of sport and exercise* (pp. 41–54). Morgantown, WV: Fitness Information Technology.

Brewer, B.W., Avondoglio, J.B., Cornelius, A.E., Van Raalte, J.L., Brickner, J.C., Petitpas, A.J., Hatten, S.J. (2002). Construct validity and interrater agreement of the Sport Injury Rehabilitation Adherence Scale. *Journal of Sport Rehabilitation, 11,* 170–178.

Brewer, B.W., & Buman, M.P. (2006). Attentional focus and endurance performance: Review and theoretical integration. *Kinesiologia Slovenica, 12,* 82–97.

Brewer, B.W., Cornelius, A.E., Sklar, J.H., Van Raalte, J.L., Tennen, H., Armeli, S. Brickner, J.C. (2007). Pain and negative mood during rehabilitation after anterior cruciate ligament reconstruction: A daily process analysis. *Scandinavian Journal of Medicine and Science in Sports, 17,* 520–529. doi:10.1111/j.1600-0838.2006.00601.x

Brewer, B.W., Cornelius, A.E., Stephan, Y., & Van Raalte, J.L. (2010). Self-protective changes in athletic identity following ACL reconstruction. *Psychology of Sport and Exercise, 11,* 1–5. doi:10.1016/j.psychsport.2009.09.005

Brewer, B.W., Cornelius, A.E., & Van Raalte, J.L. (2010, October). *Preoperative effects of a multimedia CD-ROM for ACL surgery and rehabilitation: Results of a randomized clinical trial.* Paper presented at the annual meeting of the Association for Applied Sport Psychology, Providence, RI.

Brewer, B.W., Cornelius, A.E., Van Raalte, J.L., Brickner, J.C., Sklar, J.H., Corsetti, J.R., Emery, K. (2004). Rehabilitation adherence and anterior cruciate ligament reconstruction outcome. *Psychology, Health, & Medicine, 9,* 163–175. doi:10.1080/13548500410001670690

Brewer, B.W., Cornelius, A.E., Van Raalte, J.L., Brickner, J.C., Tennen, H., Sklar, J.H., Pohlman, M.H. (2004). Comparison of concurrent and retrospective pain ratings during rehabilitation following anterior cruciate ligament reconstruction. *Journal of Sport & Exercise Psychology, 26,* 610–615.

Brewer, B.W., Cornelius, A.E., Van Raalte, J.L., Petitpas, A.J., Sklar, J.H., Pohlman, M.H., Ditmar, T. (2003a). Protection motivation theory and sport injury rehabilitation adherence revisited. *The Sport Psychologist, 17,* 95–103.

Brewer, B.W., Cornelius, A.E., Van Raalte, J.L., Petitpas, A.J., Sklar, J.H., Pohlman, M.H., Ditmar, T.D. (2003b). Age-related differences in predictors of adherence to rehabilitation after anterior cruciate ligament reconstruction. *Journal of Athletic Training, 38,* 158–162.

Brewer, B.W., Cornelius, A.E., Van Raalte, J.L., Tennen, H., & Armeli, S. (2013). Predictors of adherence to home rehabilitation exercises following anterior cruciate ligament reconstruction. *Rehabilitation Psychology, 58,* 64–72. doi:10.1037/a0031297

Brewer, B.W., Daly, J.M., Van Raalte, J.L., Petitpas, A.J., & Sklar, J.H. (1999). A psychometric evaluation of the Rehabilitation Adherence Questionnaire. *Journal of Sport & Exercise Psychology, 21*, 167–173.

Brewer, B.W., & Helledy, K.I. (1998). Off (to) the deep end: Psychological skills training and water running. *Applied Research in Coaching and Athletics Annual, 13*, 99–118.

Brewer, B.W., Jeffers, K.E., Petitpas, A.J., & Van Raalte, J.L. (1994). Perceptions of psychological interventions in the context of sport injury rehabilitation. *The Sport Psychologist, 8*, 176–188.

Brewer, B.W., Linder, D.E., & Phelps, C.M. (1995). Situational correlates of emotional adjustment to athletic injury. *Clinical Journal of Sport Medicine, 5*, 241–245. doi:10.1097/00042752-199510000-00006

Brewer, B.W., Petitpas, A.J., & Van Raalte, J.L. (1999). Referral of injured athletes for counseling and psychotherapy. In R. Ray & D.M. Wiese-Bjornstal (Eds.), *Counseling in sports medicine* (pp. 127–141). Champaign, IL: Human Kinetics.

Brewer, B.W., Petitpas, A.J., Van Raalte, J.L., Sklar, J.H., & Ditmar, T.D. (1995). Prevalence of psychological distress among patients at a physical therapy clinic specializing in sports medicine. *Sports Medicine, Training, and Rehabilitation, 6*, 139–145. doi:10.1080/15438629509512045.

Brewer, B.W., & Petrie, T.A. (1995). A comparison between injured and uninjured football players on selected psychosocial variables. *Academic Athletic Journal, 10*, 11–18.

Brewer, B.W., & Petrie, T.A. (2014). Psychopathology in sport and exercise. In J.L. Van Raalte & B.W. Brewer (Eds.), *Exploring sport and exercise psychology* (3rd ed., pp. 311–335). Washington, DC: American Psychological Association.

Brewer, B.W., & Van Raalte, J.L. (Executive Producers). (2009). *Conquering ACL surgery and rehabilitation* [CD-ROM]. (Available from Virtual Brands, LLC, 10 Echo Hill Road, Wilbraham, MA 01095)

Brewer, B.W., Van Raalte, J.L., Cornelius, A.E., Petitpas, A.J., Sklar, J.H., Pohlman, M.H., Ditmar, T.D. (2000). Psychological factors, rehabilitation adherence, and rehabilitation outcome after anterior cruciate ligament reconstruction. *Rehabilitation Psychology, 45*, 20–37. doi:10.1037/0090-5550.45.1.20

Brewer, B.W., Van Raalte, J.L., & Linder, D.E. (1990). Effects of pain on motor performance. *Journal of Sport & Exercise Psychology, 12*, 353–365.

Brewer, B.W., Van Raalte, J.L., & Linder, D.E. (1991). Role of the sport psychologist in treating injured athletes: A survey of sports medicine providers. *Journal of Applied Sport Psychology, 3*, 183–190. doi:10.1080/10413209108406443

Brewer, B.W., Van Raalte, J.L., & Linder, D.E. (1993). Athletic identity: Hercules' muscles or Achilles heel? *International Journal of Sport Psychology, 24*, 237–254.

Brewer, B.W., Van Raalte, J.L., & Petitpas, A.J. (2007). Patient–practitioner interactions in sport injury rehabilitation. In D. Pargman (Ed.), *Psychological bases of sport injuries* (3rd ed., pp. 79–94). Morgantown, WV: Fitness Information Technology.

Brewer, B.W., Van Raalte, J.L., Petitpas, A.J., Sklar, J.H., & Ditmar, T.D. (1995). Predictors of perceived sport injury rehabilitation status. In R. Vanfraechem-Raway & Y. Vanden Auweele (Eds.), *IXth European Congress on Sport Psychology proceedings: Part II* (pp. 606–610). Brussels: European Federation of Sports Psychology.

Brewer, B.W., Van Raalte, J.L., Petitpas, A.J., Sklar, J.H., Pohlman, M.H., Krushell, R.J., Weinstock, J. (2000). Preliminary psychometric evaluation of a measure of adherence to clinic-based sport injury rehabilitation. *Physical Therapy in Sport, 1*, 68–74. doi:10.1054/ptsp.2000.0019

Broglio, S.P., & Puetz, T.W. (2008). The effect of sport concussion on neurocognitive function, self-report symptoms, and postural control: A meta-analysis. *Sports Medicine, 38*, 53–67.

Buckworth, J., & Dishman, R.K. (2007). Exercise adherence. In G. Tenenbaum & R.C. Eklund (Eds.), *Handbook of sport psychology* (3rd ed., pp. 509–536). New York: Wiley.

Burton, R.W. (2000). Mental illness in athletes. In D. Begel & R.W. Burton (Eds.), *Sport psychiatry* (pp. 61–81). New York: Norton.

Busanich, R., McGannon, K.R., & Schinke, R.J. (2014). Comparing elite male and female distance runner's experiences of disordered eating through narrative analysis. *Psychology of Sport and Exercise, 15*, 705–712. doi:10.1016/j.psychsport.2013.10.002

Byerly, P.N., Worrell, T., Gahimer, J., & Domholdt, E. (1994). Rehabilitation compliance in an athletic training environment. *Journal of Athletic Training, 29*, 352–355.

Bystad, M., Bystad, C., & Wynn, R. (2015). How can placebo effects best be applied in clinical practice? A narrative review. *Psychology Research and Behavior Management, 41*. doi:10.2147/PRBM.S75670

Caine, C.G., Caine, D.J., & Lindner, K.J. (1996). The epidemiologic approach to sports injuries. In D.J. Caine, C.G. Caine, & K.J. Lindner (Eds.), *Epidemiology of sports injuries* (pp. 1–13). Champaign, IL: Human Kinetics.

Caine, D.J., Caine, C.G., & Lindner, K.J. (Eds.). (1996). *Epidemiology of sports injuries.* Champaign, IL: Human Kinetics.

Campbell, C.J., Carson, J.D., Diaconescu, E.D., Celebrini, R., Rizzardo, M.R., Godbout, V., Cote, M. (2014). Canadian Academy of Sport and Exercise Medicine position statement: Neuromuscular training can decrease anterior cruciate ligament injuries in youth soccer players. *Clinical Journal of Sport Medicine, 24,* 263–267.

Caraffa, A., Cerulli, G., Projetti, M., Aisa, G., & Rizzo, A. (1996). Prevention of anterior cruciate ligament injuries in soccer. *Knee Surgery, Sports Traumatology, Arthroscopy, 4,* 19–21.

Carlson, C.R., & Hoyle, R.H. (1993). Efficacy of abbreviated progressive muscle relaxation training: A quantitative review of behavioral medicine research. *Journal of Consulting and Clinical Psychology, 61,* 1059–1067.

Carson, F., & Polman, R. (2010). The facilitative nature of avoidance coping within sports injury rehabilitation. *Scandinavian Journal of Medicine & Science in Sports, 20,* 235–240. doi:10.1111/j.1600-0838.2009.00890.x

Carson, F., & Polman, R. (2012). Experiences of professional rugby union players returning to competition following anterior cruciate ligament reconstruction. *Physical Therapy in Sport, 13,* 35–40. doi:10.1016/j.ptsp.2010.10.007

Carson, F., & Polman, R.C.J. (2008). ACL injury rehabilitation: A psychological case study of a professional rugby union player. *Journal of Clinical Sport Psychology, 2,* 71–90.

Cartoni, A.C., Minganti, C., & Zelli, A. (2005). Gender, age, and professional-level differences in the psychological correlates of fear of injury in Italian gymnasts. *Journal of Sport Behavior, 28,* 3–17.

Cartwright, R.D., & Wood, E. (1991). Adjustment disorders of sleep: The sleep effects of a major stressful event and its resolution. *Psychiatry Research, 39,* 199–209. doi: 10.1016/0165-1781(91)90088-7

Castillo, R.P., Cremades, J.G., & Butcher, M. (2002). Relaxation techniques as a method to reduce reinjury anxiety in athletes. *Journal of Sport & Exercise, 24,* S42.

Centers for Disease Control and Prevention. (2002). Nonfatal sports- and recreation-related injuries treated in emergency departments—United States, July 2000–June 2001. *Morbidity and Mortality Weekly Report, 51,* 736–740.

Centers for Disease Control and Prevention. (2006). Sports-related injuries among high school athletes—United States, 2005–06 school year. *Morbidity and Mortality Weekly Report, 55,* 1037–1040. www.cdc.gov/mmwr/preview/mmwrhtml/mm5538a1.htm.

Cerny, F.J., Patton, D.C., Whieldon, T.J., & Roehrig, S. (1992). An organizational model of sports medicine facilities in the United States. *Journal of Orthopaedic and Sports Physical Therapy,15,* 80–86.

Chaduneli, B., & Ibanez, M. (2014). Relationship between beliefs about protective equipment and the risky behaviour in rugby players [Abstract]. *Clinical Journal of Sport Medicine, 24,* e24.

Chan, C.S., & Grossman, H.Y. (1988). Psychological effects of running loss on consistent runners. *Perceptual and Motor Skills, 66,* 875–883.

Chan, D.K., & Hagger, M.S. (2012a). Transcontextual development of motivation in sport injury prevention among elite athletes. *Journal of Sport & Exercise Psychology, 34,* 661–682. doi:10.2466/pms.1988.66.3.875

Chan, D.K., & Hagger, M.S. (2012b). Theoretical integration and the psychology of sport injury prevention. *Sports Medicine, 42,* 725–732. doi:10.2165/11633040-000000000-00000

Chan, D.K., Lonsdale, C., Ho, P.Y., Yung, P.S., & Chan, K.M. (2009). Patient motivation and adherence to postsurgery rehabilitation exercise recommendations: The influence of physiotherapists' autonomy-supportive behaviors. *Archives of Physical Medicine & Rehabilitation, 90,* 1977–1982. doi:10.1016/j.apmr.2009.05.024

Chapman, C.R., Casey, K.L., Dubner, R., Foley, K.M., Gracely, R.H., & Reading, A.E. (1985). Pain measurement: An overview. *Pain, 22,* 1–31. doi: 10.1016/0304-3959(85)90145-9

Chapman, P.J. (1985). Orofacial injuries and the use of mouthguards by the 1984 Great Britain rugby league touring team. *British Journal of Sports Medicine, 19,* 34–36.

Charlesworth, H., & Young, K. (2006). Injured female athletes: Experiential accounts from England and Canada. In S. Loland, B. Skirstad, & I. Waddington (Eds.), *Pain and injury in sport: Social and ethical analysis* (pp. 89–106). New York: Routledge.

Chatterjee, M., & Hilton, I. (2007). A comparison of the attitudes and beliefs of professional rugby players from one club and parents of children playing rugby at an adjacent amateur club to the wearing of mouthguards. *Primary Dental Care, 14,* 111–116.

Chmielewski, T.L., Jones, D., Day, T., Tillman, S.M., Lentz, T.A., & George, S.Z. (2008). The association of pain and fear of movement/reinjury with function during anterior cruciate ligament reconstruction rehabilitation. *Journal of Orthopaedic & Sports Physical Therapy, 38,* 746–753. doi:10.2519/jospt.2008.2887

Chmielewski, T.L., Zeppieri, G., Jr., Lentz, T.A., Tillman, S.M., Moser, M.W., Indelicato, P.A., & George, S.Z. (2011). Longitudinal changes in psychosocial factors and their association with knee pain and function after anterior cruciate ligament reconstruction. *Physical Therapy, 91,* 1355–1366. doi:10.2522/ptj.20100277

Christakou, A., & Zervas, Y. (2007). The effectiveness of imagery on pain, edema, and range of motion in athletes with a grade II ankle sprain. *Physical Therapy in Sport, 8,* 130–140. doi:10.1016/j.ptsp.2007.03.005

Christakou, A., Zervas, Y., & Lavallee, D. (2007). The adjunctive role of imagery on the functional rehabilitation of a grade II ankle sprain. *Journal of Human Movement, 26,* 141–154. doi:10.1016/j.humov.2006.07.010

Christakou, A., Zervas, Y., Psychountaki, M., & Stavrou, N.A. (2012). Development and validation of the Attention Questionnaire of Rehabilitated Athletes Returning to Competition. *Psychology, Health, & Medicine, 17,* 499–510. doi:10.1080/13548506.2011.630402

Christakou, A., Zervas, Y., Stavrou, N.A., & Psychountaki, M. (2011). Development and validation of the Causes of Re-Injury Worry Questionnaire. *Psychology, Health, & Medicine, 16,* 94–114. doi:10.1080/13548506.2010.521565

Christian, L.M., Graham, J.E., Padgett, D.A., Glaser, R., & Kiecolt-Glaser, J.K. (2006). Stress and wound healing. *NeuroImmunoModulation, 13,* 337–346. doi:10.1159/000104862

Clarkson, P.M., Nosaka, K., & Braun, B. (1992). Muscle function after exercise-induced muscle damage and rapid adaptation. *Medicine and Science in Sports and Exercise, 24,* 512–520.

Clement, D., & Arvinen-Barrow, M. (2013, October). *Psychosocial responses during different phases of sport injury rehabilitation: A qualitative study.* Paper presented at the annual meeting of the Association for Applied Psychology, New Orleans, LA.

Clement, D., Arvinen-Barrow, M., Hamson-Utley, J.J., Kamphoff, C., Zakrajsek, R., Lee, S.L., Martin, S. (2012). Athletes' use of psychosocial strategies during sport injury rehabilitation. In *Association for Applied Sport Psychology—2012 conference proceedings & program* (p. 68). Indianapolis: Association for Applied Sport Psychology.

Clement, D., Granquist, M.D., & Arvinen-Barrow, M.M. (2013). Psychosocial aspects of athletic injuries as perceived by athletic trainers. *Journal of Athletic Training, 48,* 512–521. doi:10.4085/1062-6050-48.3.21

Clement, D., & Shannon, V. (2009). The impact of a workshop on athletic training students' sport psychology behaviors. *The Sport Psychologist, 23,* 504–522.

Clement, D., & Shannon, V. (2011). Injured athletes' perceptions about social support. *Journal of Sport Rehabilitation, 20,* 457–470.

Clement, D., & Shannon, V., & Connole, I.J. (2012a). Performance enhancement groups for injured athletes, part 1: Preparation and development. *International Journal of Athletic Therapy & Training, 17*(3), 34–36

Clement, D., & Shannon, V., & Connole, I.J. (2012b). Performance enhancement groups for injured athletes, part 2: Implementation and facilitation. *International Journal of Athletic Therapy & Training, 17*(5), 38–40.

Clover, J., & Wall, J. (2010). Return-to-play criteria following sports injury. *Clinics in Sports Medicine, 29,* 169–175. doi:10.1016/j.csm.2009.09.008

Cohen, S., & Wills, T.A. (1985). Stress, social support, and the buffering hypothesis. *Psychological Bulletin, 98,* 310–357.

Conn, J.M., Annest, J.L., & Gilchrist, J. (2003). Sports and recreation related injury episodes in the US population. *Injury Prevention, 9,* 117–123.

Corbillon, F., Crossman, J., & Jamieson, J. (2008). Injured athletes' perceptions of the social support provided by their coaches and teammates during rehabilitation. *Journal of Sport Behavior, 31,* 93–107.

Cornwell, H., Messer, L.B., & Speed, H. (2003). Use of mouthguards by basketball players in Victoria, Australia. *Dental Traumatology, 19,* 193–203.

Cottler, L.B., Abdallah, B., Cummings, A., Barr, S.M., Banks, J., & Rayna Forcheimer, R. (2011). Injury, pain, and prescription opioid use among former National Football League (NFL) players. *Drug and Alcohol Dependence, 116,* 188–194.

Coutu, D.L. (1995). *The effect of the presence of the coach on pain perception and pain tolerance of athletes* (Unpublished master's thesis). Springfield College, MA.

Crawford, J.J., Gayman, A.M., & Tracey, J. (2014). An examination of post-traumatic growth in Canadian and American parasport athletes with acquired spinal cord injury. *Psychology of Sport and Exercise, 15,* 399–406. doi:10.1016/j.psychsport.2014.03.008

Creighton, D.W., Shrier, I., Shultz, R., Meeuwisse, W.H., & Matheson, G.O. (2010). Return-to-play in sport: A decision-based model. *Clinical Journal of Sport Medicine, 20,* 379–385.

Crossman, J., Gluck, L., & Jamieson, J. (1995) The emotional responses of injured athletes. *New Zealand Journal of Sports Medicine, 23,* 1–2.

Crossman, J., & Jamieson, J. (1985). Differences in perceptions of seriousness and disrupting effects of athletic injury as viewed by athletes and their trainer. *Perceptual and Motor Skills, 61*, 1131–1134. doi:10.2466/pms.1985.61.3f.1131

Crossman, J., Jamieson, J., & Hume, K.M. (1990). Perceptions of athletic injuries by athletes, coaches, and medical professionals. *Perceptual and Motor Skills, 71*, 848–850. doi:10.2466/pms.1990.71.3.848

Crossman, J., & Roch, J. (1991, April). An observation instrument for use in sports medicine clinics. *The Journal of the Canadian Athletic Therapists Association*, 10–13.

Culley, S., & Bond, T. (2007). *Integrative counselling skills in action* (2nd ed.). London: Sage.

Cupal, D.D., & Brewer, B.W. (2001). Effects of relaxation and guided imagery on knee strength, reinjury anxiety, and pain following anterior cruciate ligament reconstruction. *Rehabilitation Psychology, 46*, 28–43. doi:10.1037/0090-5550.46.1.28

Curry, T.J. (1986). A visual method of studying sports: The photo-elicitation interview. *Sociology of Sport Journal, 3*, 204–216.

Curry, T.J. (1993). A little pain never hurt anyone: Athletic career socialization and the normalization of sports injury. *Symbolic Interaction, 16*, 273–290. doi:10.1525/si.1993.16.3.273

Curry, T.J., & Strauss, R.H. (1994). A little pain never hurt anybody: A photo-essay on the normalization of sport injuries. *Sociology of Sport Journal, 11*, 195–208.

Czuppon, S., Racette, B.A., Klein, S.E., & Harris-Hayes, M. (2014). Variables associated with return to sport following anterior cruciate ligament reconstruction: A systematic review. *British Journal of Sports Medicine, 48*, 356–364. doi:10.1136/bjsports-2012-091786

Daly, J.M., Brewer, B.W., Van Raalte, J.L., Petitpas, A.J., & Sklar, J.H. (1995). Cognitive appraisal, emotional adjustment, and adherence to rehabilitation following knee surgery. *Journal of Sport Rehabilitation, 4*, 23–30.

Darrow, C.J., Collins, C.L., Yard, E.E., & Comstock, R.D. (2009). Epidemiology of severe injuries among United States high school athletes: 2005–2007. *The American Journal of Sports Medicine, 37*, 1798–1805. doi:10.1177/0363546509333015

Davies, S.C., & Bird, B.M. (2015) Motivations for underreporting suspected concussion in college athletics. *Journal of Clinical Sport Psychology, 9*, 101–115. doi:10.1123/jcsp.2014-0037

Davis, J.O. (1991). Sports injuries and stress management: An opportunity for research. *The Sport Psychologist, 5*, 175–182.

Dawes, H., & Roach, N.K. (1997). Emotional responses of athletes to injury and treatment. *Physiotherapy, 83*, 243–247. doi:10.1016/S0031-9406(05)66215-3

DeFrancesco, C., Miller, M., Larson, M., & Robinson, K. (1994, October). *Athletic injury, rehabilitation, and psychological strategies: What do the athletes think?* Paper presented at the annual meeting of the Association for the Advancement of Applied Sport Psychology, Lake Tahoe, NV.

Deitrick, J., Covassin, T., Bleecker, A., Yang, J., & Heiden, E. (2013, October). *Time loss and fear of reinjury in athletes after return to participation.* Paper presented at the annual meeting of the Association for Applied Sport Psychology, New Orleans, LA.

De Nooijer, J., De Wit, M., & Steenhuis, I. (2004). Why young Dutch inline skaters do (not) use protective equipment. *European Journal of Public Health, 14*, 178–181.

Deroche, T., Woodman, T., Stephan, Y., Brewer, B.W., & Le Scanff, C. (2011). Athletes' inclination to play through pain: A coping perspective. *Anxiety, Stress, & Coping: An International Journal, 24*, 579–587. doi:10.1080/10615806.2011.552717

Derscheid, G.L., & Feiring, D.C. (1987). A statistical analysis to characterize treatment adherence of the 18 most common diagnoses seen at a sports medicine clinic. *Journal of Orthopaedic and Sports Physical Therapy, 9*, 40–46.

DeWitt, D.J. (1980). Cognitive and biofeedback training for stress reduction with university athletes. *Journal of Sport Psychology, 2*, 288–294.

Diekhoff, G.M. (1984). Running amok: Injuries in compulsive runners. *Journal of Sport Behavior, 7*, 120–129.

DiFabio, R.P. (1995). Efficacy of comprehensive rehabilitation programs and back school for patients with low back pain: A meta-analysis. *Physical Therapy, 75*, 865–878.

DiMatteo, M.R., Giordani, P.J., Lepper, H.S., & Croghan T.W. (2002). Patient adherence and medical treatment outcomes: A meta-analysis. *Medical Care, 40*, 794–811.

DiMatteo, M.R., Hays, R., & Prince, L.M. (1986). Relationship of physicians' nonverbal communication skill to patient satisfaction, appointment noncompliance, and physician workload. *Health Psychology, 5*, 581–594.

DiMatteo, M.R., & Martin, L.R. (2002). *Health psychology*. Boston: Allyn & Bacon.

DiMatteo, M.R., Taranta, A., Friedman, H.S., & Prince, L.M. (1980). Predicting patient satisfaction from physicians' nonverbal communication skill. *Medical Care, 18*, 376–387.

Dobbe, J.G., van Trommel, N.E., de Freitas Baptista, J.E., Ritt, M.J., Steenbeek, A., & Molenaar, H.A. (1999). A portable device for finger tendon rehabilitation that provides an isotonic training force and records exercise behaviour after finger tendon surgery. *Medical & Biological Engineering & Computing, 371*, 396–399.

Driediger, M., Hall, C., & Callow, N. (2006). Imagery use by injured athletes: A qualitative analysis. *Journal of Sport Sciences, 24*, 261–272. doi:10.1080/02640410500128221

Duda, J.L., Smart, A.E., & Tappe, M.K. (1989). Predictors of adherence in rehabilitation of athletic injuries: An application of personal investment theory. *Journal of Sport & Exercise Psychology, 11*, 367–381.

Dunn, E.C., Smith, R.E. & Smoll, F.L. (2001). Do sport-specific stressors predict athletic injury? *Journal of Science and Medicine in Sport, 4*, 283–291. doi:10.1016/S1440-2440(01)80037-2

Duymus, Z.Y., & Gungor, H. (2009). Use of mouthguard rates among university athletes during sport activities in Erzurum, Turkey. *Dental Traumatology, 25*, 318–322.

Dvorak, J., Junge, A., Chomiak, J., Graf-Baumann, T., Peterson, L., Rösch, D., & Hodgson, R. (2000). Risk factor analysis for injuries in football players. *The American Journal of Sports Medicine, 28*, S69–S74. doi:10.1177/28.suppl_5.S-69

Egan, G. (2014). *The skilled helper: A problem-management and opportunity-development approach to helping* (10th ed.). Belmont, CA: Brooks/Cole.

Eime, R., Finch, C., Wolfe, R., Owen, N., & McCarty, C. (2005). The effectiveness of a squash eyewear promotion strategy. *British Journal of Sports Medicine, 39*, 681–685. doi:10.1136/bjsm.2005.018366

Eime, R.M., Finch, C.F., Sherman, C.A., & Garnham, A.P. (2002). Are squash players protecting their eyes? *Injury Prevention, 8*, 239–241. doi:10.1136/ip.8.3.239

Ekenman, I., Hassmén, P., Koivula, N., Rolf, C., & Fellander-Tsai, L. (2001). Stress fractures of the tibia: Can personality traits help us detect the injury-prone athlete? *Scandinavian Journal of Medicine and Science in Sports, 11*, 87–93. doi:10.1034/j.1600-0838.2001.011002087

Ekman, P., & Friesen, W.V. (1974). Detecting deception from the body or face. *Journal of Personality and Social Psychology, 29*, 288–298. doi:10.1037/h0036006

El Ali, M., Marivain, T., Heas, S., & Boulva, A.H. (2008). Analysis of coping strategies used by male and female tennis players toward a severe athletic injury. *Annales Medico-Psychologiques, 166*, 779–788. doi:10.1016/j.amp.2005.06.013.

Elaziz, A.F.A.A. (2010). Impact of psychological rehabilitation program on self-confidence level and competition anxiety for soccer players of anterior cruciate ligament injury. *World Journal of Sport Sciences, 3*(S), 138–143.

Ellington, L., & Wiebe, D. (1999). Neuroticism, symptom presentation, and medical decision making. *Health Psychology, 18*, 634–643. doi:10.1037/0278-6133.18.6.634

Emery, C.A. (2003). Risk factors for injury in child and adolescent sport: A systematic review of the literature. *Clinical Journal of Sport Medicine, 13*, 256–268. doi:10.1097/00042752-200307000-00011

Emery, C.A. (2010). Injury prevention in paediatric sport-related injuries: A scientific approach. *British Journal of Sports Medicine, 44*, 64–69. doi:10.1136/bjsm.2009.068353

Emery, C.A., & Meeuwisse, W.H. (2010). The effectiveness of neuromuscular prevention strategy to reduce injuries in youth soccer: A cluster-randomised trial [Abstract]. *British Journal of Sports Medicine, 44*, 555–562. doi:10.1136/bjsm.2012.074377

Emery, C.A., Meeuwisse, W.H., & Hartmann, S.E. (2005). Evaluation of risk factors for injury in adolescent soccer: Implementation and validation of an injury surveillance system. *The American Journal of Sports Medicine, 33*, 1882–1991.

Emery, C.A., Rose, M.S., McAllister, J.R., & Meeuwisse, W.H. (2007). A prevention strategy to reduce the incidence of injury in high school basketball: A cluster randomized controlled trial. *Clinical Journal of Sport Medicine, 17*, 17–24. doi:10.1097/JSM.0b013e31802e9c05

Encarnacion, M.L.G., Meyers, M.C., Ryan, N.D., & Pease, D.G. (2000). Pain coping styles of ballet performers. *Journal of Sport Behavior, 23*, 20–32.

Engel, G.L. (1977). The need for a new medical model: A challenge for biomedicine. *Science, 196*, 129–136. doi:10.1126/science.847460

Engel, G.L. (1980). The clinical application of the biopsychosocial model. *American Journal of Psychiatry, 137*, 535–544.

Etzel, E.F., Zizzi, S., Newcomer-Appaneal, R.R., Ferrante, A.P., & Perna, F. (2007). Providing psychological assistance to college student-athletes with injuries and disabilities. In D. Pargman (Ed.),

Psychological bases of sport injuries (3rd ed., pp. 151–169). Morgantown, WV: Fitness Information Technology.

Evans, F.J., & McGlashan, T.H. (1967). Work and effort during pain. *Perceptual and Motor Skills, 25,* 794.

Evans, L., & Hardy, L. (1995). Sport injury and grief responses: A review. *Journal of Sport & Exercise Psychology, 17,* 227–245.

Evans, L., & Hardy, L. (1999). Psychological and emotional response to athletic injury: Measurement issues. In D. Pargman (Ed.), *Psychological bases of sport injuries* (2nd ed., pp. 49–64). Morgantown, WV: Fitness Information Technology.

Evans, L., & Hardy, L. (2002a). Injury rehabilitation: A goal-setting intervention study. *Research Quarterly for Exercise and Sport, 73,* 310–319. doi:10.1080/02701367.2002.10609025

Evans, L., & Hardy, L. (2002b). Injury rehabilitation: A qualitative follow-up study. *Research Quarterly for Exercise and Sport, 73,* 320–329. doi:10.1080/02701367.2002.10609026

Evans, L., Hardy, L., & Fleming, S. (2000). Intervention strategies with injured athletes: An action research study. *The Sport Psychologist, 14,* 188–206.

Evans, L., Hardy, L., Mitchell, I., & Rees, T. (2008). The development of a measure of psychological responses to injury. *Journal of Sport Rehabilitation, 16,* 21–37.

Evans, L., Hardy, L., & Mullen, R. (1996). The development of the Psychological Responses to Sport Injury Inventory. *Journal of Sports Sciences, 14,* 27–28.

Evans, L., Hare, R., & Mullen, R. (2006). Imagery use during rehabilitation from injury. *Journal of Imagery Research in Sport and Physical Activity, 1,* 1–19. doi:10.2202/1932-0191.1000

Evans, L., Wadey, R., Hanton, S., & Mitchell, I. (2012). Stressors experienced by injured athletes. *Journal of Sports Sciences, 30,* 917–927. doi:10.1080/02640414.2012.682078

Evans, T.A., & Lam, K.C. (2011). Clinical outcomes assessment in sport rehabilitation. *Journal of Sport Rehabilitation, 20,* 8–16.

Fawkner, H.J., McMurray, N.E., & Summers, J.J. (1999) Athletic injury and minor life events: A prospective study. *Journal of Science and Medicine in Sport, 2,* 117–124. doi:10.1016/S1440-2440(99)80191-1

Fields, J., Murphey, M., Horodyski, M., & Stopka, C. (1995). Factors associated with adherence to sport injury rehabilitation in college-age recreational athletes. *Journal of Sport Rehabilitation, 4,* 172–180.

Fields, K.B., Delaney, M., & Hinkle, J.S. (1990). A prospective study of type A behavior and running injuries. *The Journal of Family Practice, 30,* 425–429.

Finch, C., Valuri, G., & Ozanne-Smith, J. (1998). Sport and active recreation injuries in Australia: Evidence from emergency department presentations. *British Journal of Sports Medicine, 32,* 220–225. doi:10.1136/bjsm.32.3.220

Finch, C.F. (2006). A new framework for research leading to sports injury prevention. *Journal of Science & Medicine in Sport, 9,* 3–9. doi:10.1016/j.jsams.2006.02.009

Finch, C.F. (2011). No longer lost in translation: The art and science of sports injury prevention implementation research. *British Journal of Sports Medicine, 45,* 1253–1257. doi:10.1136/bjsports-2011-090230

Finch, C.F., & Donaldson, A. (2010). A sports setting matrix for understanding the implementation context for community sport. *British Journal of Sports Medicine, 44,* 973–978. doi:10.1136/bjsm.2008.056069

Finch, C.F., McIntosh, A.S., & McCrory, P. (2001). What do under 15 year old rugby union players think about protective headgear? *British Journal of Sports Medicine, 35,* 89–94. doi:10.1136/bjsm.35.2.89

Finney, J.W., Putnam, D.E., & Boyd, C.M. (1998). Improving the accuracy of self-reports of adherence. *Journal of Applied Behavior Analysis, 31,* 485–488. doi:10.1901/jaba.1998.31-485

Finnie, S.B. (1999, September). *The rehabilitation support team: Using social support to aid compliance to sports injury rehabilitation programs.* Paper presented at the annual meeting of the Association for the Advancement of Applied Sport Psychology, Banff, Alberta, Canada.

Fishbein, M., & Ajzen, I. (1975). *Belief, attitude, intention, and behavior: An introduction to theory and research.* Reading, MA: Addison-Wesley.

Fisher, A.C., Domm, M.A., & Wuest, D.A. (1988). Adherence to sports-injury rehabilitation programs. *The Physician and Sportsmedicine, 16*(7), 47–52.

Fisher, A.C., & Hoisington, L.L. (1993). Injured athletes' attitudes and judgments toward rehabilitation adherence. *Journal of Athletic Training, 28,* 48–54.

Fisher, A.C., Mullins, S.A., & Frye, P.A. (1993). Athletic trainers' attitudes and judgments of injured athletes' rehabilitation adherence. *Journal of Athletic Training, 28,* 43–47.

Flanigan, D.C., Everhart, J.S., Pedroza, A., Smith, T., & Kaeding, C.C. (2013). Fear of reinjury (kinesiophobia) and persistent knee symptoms are common factors for lack of return to sport after anterior cruciate ligament reconstruction. *Arthroscopy: The Journal of Arthroscopic and Related Surgery, 29,* 1322–1329. doi:10.1016/j.arthro.2013.05.015

Flint, F.A. (1991). *The psychological effects of modeling in athletic injury rehabilitation.* Unpublished doctoral dissertation, University of Oregon, Eugene.

Flint, F.A. (1998). Integrating sport psychology and sports medicine in research: The dilemmas. *Journal of Applied Sport Psychology, 10*, 83–102.

Flint, F.A., & Weiss, M.R. (1992). Returning injured athletes to competition: A role and ethical dilemma. *Canadian Journal of Sport Sciences, 17*, 34–40.

Flor, H. (2001). Psychophysiological assessment of the patient with chronic pain. In D.C. Turk & R. Melzack (Eds.), *Handbook of pain assessment* (2nd ed., pp. 76–96). New York: Guilford.

Ford, I.W., Eklund, R.C., & Gordon, S. (2000). An examination of psychosocial variables moderating the relationship between life stress and injury time-loss among athletes of a high standard. *Journal of Sports Sciences, 18*, 301–312. doi:10.1080/026404100402368

Ford, I.W., & Gordon, S. (1999). Coping with sport injury: Resource loss and the role of social support. *Journal of Personal and Interpersonal Loss, 4*, 243–256.

Fordyce, W.E. (1988). Pain and suffering: A reappraisal. *American Psychologist, 43*, 276–283. doi:10.1037/0003-066X.43.4.276

Forgione, A.G., & Barber, T.X. (1971). A strain gauge pain stimulator. *Psychophysiology, 8*, 102–106. doi:10.1111/j.1469-8986.1971.tb00441.x

Fox, B. (2004). Cognitive and motivational functions of imagery during injury rehabilitation and their relation to practice return affect [Abstract]. *Journal of Sport and Exercise Psychology, 26*(Suppl.), S74.

Francis, S.R., Andersen, M.B., & Maley, P. (2000). Physiotherapists' and male professional athletes' views on psychological skills for rehabilitation. *Journal of Science and Medicine in Sport, 3*, 17–29. doi:10.1016/S1440-2440(00)80044-4

Frey, J.H. (1991). Social risk and the meaning of sport. *Sociology of Sport Journal, 8*, 136–145.

Friedman, H., Thompson, R.B., & Rosen, E.F. (1985). Perceived threat as a major factor in tolerance for experimentally-induced cold-water pain. *Journal of Abnormal Psychology, 94*, 624-629.

Friedman, H. (2002). *Health psychology* (2nd ed.). Upper Saddle River, NJ: Prentice Hall.

Friedman, H.S., DiMatteo, M.R., & Taranta, A. (1980). A study of the relationship between individual differences in nonverbal expressiveness and factors of personality and social interaction. *Journal of Research in Personality, 14*, 351–364.

Friedman, H.S., Hall, J.A., & Harris, M.J. (1985). Type A behavior, nonverbal expressive style, and health. *Journal of Personality and Social Psychology, 48*, 1299–1315. doi:10.1037/0022-3514.48.5.1299

Friedman, R., & James, J.W. (2008). The myth of the stages of dying, death, and grief. *Skeptic, 14*(2), 37–41.

Friedrich, M., Cermak, T., & Maderbacher, P. (1996). The effects of brochure use versus therapist teaching on patients performing therapeutic exercise and on changes in impairment status. *Physical Therapy, 76*, 1082–1088.

Frontera, W.R. (2003). Preface. In W.R. Frontera (Ed.), *Rehabilitation of sports injuries: Scientific basis* (pp. viii–x). Malden, MA: Blackwell Science.

Gabbe, B.J., Bailey M., Cook, J.L., Makdissi, M., Scase, E., Ames, N., Orchard, J.W. (2010). The association between hip and groin injuries in the elite junior years and injuries sustained during elite senior competition. *British Journal of Sports Medicine, 44*, 799–802. doi:10.1136/bjsm.2009.062554

Gabbe, B.J., Bennell, K.L., Finch, C.F., Wajswelner, H., & Orchard, J.W. (2006). Predictors of hamstring injury at the elite level of Australian football. *Scandinavian Journal of Medicine & Science in Sports, 16*, 7–13.

Gagliano, M.E. (1988). A literature review on the efficacy of video in patient education. *Journal of Medical Education, 63*, 785–792.

Gagné, M., Ryan, R.M., & Bargmann, K. (2003). Autonomy support and need satisfaction in the motivation and well-being of gymnasts. *Journal of Applied Sport Psychology, 15*, 372–390. doi:10.1080/714044203

Gagnier, J.J., Morgenstern, H., & Chess, L. (2013). Interventions designed to prevent anterior cruciate ligament injuries in adolescents and adults: A systematic review and meta-analysis. *The American Journal of Sports Medicine, 41*, 1952–1962. doi:10.1177/0363546512458227

Galambos, S.A., Terry, P.C., Moyle, G.M., & Locke, S.A. (2005). Psychological predictors of injury among elite athletes. *British Journal of Sports Medicine, 39*, 351–354. doi:10.1136/bjsm.2005.018440

Gallagher, B.V., & Gardner, F.L. (2007). An examination of the relationship between early maladaptive schemas, coping, and emotional response to athletic injury. *Journal of Clinical Sport Psychology, 1*, 47–67.

Gallo, M.L., & Staskin, D.R. (1997). Cues to action: Pelvic floor muscle exercise compliance in women with stress urinary incontinence. *Neurourology and Urodynamics, 16*, 167–177. doi:10.1002/(SICI)1520-6777(1997)16:3 < 167::AID-NAU6 > 3.0.CO;2-C

Gapin, J., & Etnier, J.L. (2010a). Parental perceptions of the effects of exercise on behavior in children and adolescents with AD/HD. *Journal of Sport & Exercise Psychology, 32* (Suppl.), S165.

Gapin, J., & Etnier, J.L. (2010b). The relationship between physical activity and executive function performance in children with attention-deficit hyperactivity disorder. *Journal of Sport & Exercise Psychology, 32*, 753–763.

Garnham, A. (2007). Pharmacological agents in sport and exercise. In G.S. Kolt & L. Snyder-Mackler

(Eds.), *Physical therapies in sport and exercise* (pp. 541–557). Edinburgh: Churchill Livingstone.

George, S.Z., Lentz, T.A., Zeppieri, G., Jr., Lee, D., & Chmielewski, T.L. (2012). Analysis of shortened versions of the Tampa Scale for Kinesiophobia and Pain Catastrophizing Scale for patients after anterior cruciate ligament reconstruction. *Clinical Journal of Pain, 28*, 73–80. doi:10.1097/AJP.0b013e31822363f4

George, S.Z., Parr, J.J., Wallace, M.R., Wu, S.S., Borsa, P.A., Dai, Y., & Fillingim, R.B. (2014). Biopsychosocial influence on exercise-induced injury: Genetic and psychological combinations are predictive of shoulder pain phenotypes. *The Journal of Pain, 15*, 68–80. doi:10.1016/j.pain.2013.09.012

Gerdle, B., Ghafouri, B., Ernberg, M., & Larsson, B. (2014). Chronic musculoskeletal pain: Review of mechanisms and biochemical biomarkers as assessed by the microdialysis technique. *Journal of Pain Research, 7*, 313–326. doi:10.2147/JPR.S59144

Geva, N., & Defrin, R. (2013). Enhanced pain modulation among triathletes: A possible explanation for their exceptional capabilities. *Pain, 154*, 2317–2323. doi:10.1016/j.pain.2013.06.031

Gignac, M.A.M., Cao, X., Ramanathan, S., White, L.M., Hurtig, M., Kunz, M., & Marks, P.H. (2015). Perceived personal importance of exercise and fears of re-injury: A longitudinal study of psychological factors related to activity after anterior cruciate ligament reconstruction. *BMC Sports Science, Medicine, and Rehabilitation, 7*, 4. www.biomedcentral.com/2052-1847/7/4.

Gissane, C., White, J., Kerr, K., & Jennings, D. (2001). An operational model to investigate contact sports injuries. *Medicine & Science in Sports & Exercise, 33*, 1999–2003.

Glazer, D.D. (2009). Development and preliminary validation of the Injury-Psychological Readiness to Return to Sport (I-PRRS) Scale. *Journal of Athletic Training, 44*, 185–189. doi:10.4085/1062-6050-44.2.185

Goode, A.P., Reiman, M.P., Harris, L., DeLisa, L., Kauffman, A., Beltramo, D., Taylor, A.B. (2015). Eccentric training for prevention of hamstring injuries may depend on intervention compliance: A systematic review and meta-analysis. *British Journal of Sports Medicine, 49*, 349–356. doi:10.1136/bjsports-2014-093466

Gordon, S. (1986, March). Sport psychology and the injured athlete: A cognitive-behavioral approach to injury response and injury rehabilitation. *Science Periodical on Research and Technology in Sport*, 1–10.

Gordon, S., & Lindgren, S. (1990). Psycho-physical rehabilitation from a serious sport injury: Case study of an elite fast bowler. *The Australian Journal of Science and Medicine in Sport, 22*, 71–76.

Gordon, S., Milios, D., & Grove, J.R. (1991). Psychological aspects of the recovery process from sport injury: The perspective of sport physiotherapists. *Australian Journal of Science and Medicine in Sport, 23*, 53–60.

Gordon, S., Potter, M., & Ford, I. (1998). Toward a psychoeducational curriculum for training sport-injury rehabilitation personnel. *Journal of Applied Sport Psychology, 10*, 140–156. doi:10.1080/10413209808406382

Gould, D., Udry, E., Bridges, D., & Beck, L. (1997a). Stress sources encountered when rehabilitating from season-ending ski injuries. *The Sport Psychologist, 11*, 361–378.

Gould, D., Udry, E., Bridges, D., & Beck, L. (1997b). Coping with season-ending injuries. *The Sport Psychologist, 11*, 379–399.

Granito, V.J., Hogan, J.B., & Varnum, L.K. (1995). The performance enhancement group program: Integrating sport psychology and rehabilitation. *Journal of Athletic Training, 30*, 328–331.

Granquist, M.D., & Brewer, B.W. (2013). Psychological aspects of rehabilitation adherence. In M. Arvinen-Barrow & N. Walker (Eds.), *The psychology of sport injury and rehabilitation* (pp. 40–53). New York: Routledge.

Granquist, M.D., & Brewer, B.W. (2015). Psychosocial aspects of rehabilitation. In M.D. Granquist, J. Hamson-Utley, L. Kenow, & J. Stiller-Ostrowski (Eds.), *Psychosocial strategies for athletic training* (pp. 187–208). Philadelphia: Davis.

Granquist, M.D., Gill, D.L., & Appaneal, R.N. (2010). Development of a measure of rehabilitation adherence for athletic training. *Journal of Sport Rehabilitation, 19*, 249–267.

Granquist, M.D., & Kenow, L.J. (2015). Identification of psychosocial distress and referral. In M.D. Granquist, J. Hamson-Utley, L. Kenow, & J. Stiller-Ostrowski (Eds.), *Psychosocial strategies for athletic training* (pp. 145–164). Philadelphia: Davis.

Granquist, M.D., Podlog, L., Engel, J.R., & Newland, A. (2014). Certified athletic trainers' perspectives on rehabilitation adherence in collegiate athletic training settings. *Journal of Sport Rehabilitation, 23*, 123–133. doi:10.1123/JSR.2013-0009

Graugaard, P., & Finset, A. (2000). Trait anxiety and reactions to patient-centered and doctor-centered styles of communication: An experimental study. *Psychosomatic Medicine, 62*, 33–39.

Green, G.A., Uryasz, F.D., Petr, T.A., & Bray, C.D. (2001). NCAA study of substance use and abuse habits of college student-athletes. *Clinical Journal of Sport Medicine, 11*, 51–56.

Green, S.L., & Weinberg, R.S. (2001). Relationships among athletic identity, coping skills, social support, and the psychological impact of injury in recreational participants. *Journal of Applied Sport Psychology, 13,* 40–59. doi:10.1080/10413200109339003

Greenan-Fowler, E., Powell, C., & Varni, J.W. (1987). Behavioral treatment of adherence to therapeutic exercise by children with hemophilia. *Archives of Physical Medicine and Rehabilitation, 68,* 846–849.

Greenfield, S., Kaplan, S.H., Ware, J.E., Jr., Yano, E.M., & Frank, H.J.L. (1988). Patients' participation in medical care: Effects on blood sugar control and quality of life in diabetes. Journal of General Internal Medicine, 3, 448–457.

Greenwald, A.G., McGhee, D.E., & Schwartz, J.K.L. (1998). Measuring individual differences in implicit cognition: The Implicit Association Test. Journal of Personality and Social Psychology, 74, 1464–1480.

Grindley, E.J., Zizzi, S.J., & Nasypany, A.M. (2008). Use of protection motivation theory, affect, and barriers to understand and predict adherence to outpatient rehabilitation. *Physical Therapy, 88,* 1529–1540. doi:10.2522/ptj.20070076

Gunnoe, A.J., Horodyski, M., Tennant, K.L., & Murphey, M. (2001). The effect of life events on incidence of injury in high school football players. *Journal of Athletic Training, 36,* 150–155.

Gurevich, M., Kohn, P.M., & Davis, C. (1994). Exercise-induced analgesia and the role of reactivity in pain sensitivity. *Journal of Sports Sciences, 12,* 549–559.

Guskiewicz, K.M., Marshall, S.M., Bailes, J., McCrea, J., Harding, H.R., Jr., Matthews, A., Cantu, R.C. (2007). Recurrent concussion and risk of depression in retired professional football players. *Medicine & Science in Sports & Exercise, 39,* 903–909.

Habif, S.E. (2009). Examination of injury and the association between sport injury anxiety and injury severity and frequency among Olympic distance triathletes. *Dissertation Abstracts International: Section A Humanities and Social Sciences, 69*(8-A), 3048.

Hägglund, M., Atroshi, I., Wagner, P., & Waldén, M. (2013). Superior compliance with a neuromuscular training programme is associated with fewer ACL injuries and fewer acute knee injuries in female adolescent football players: Secondary analysis of an RCT. *British Journal of Sports Medicine, 47,* 974–979. doi:10.1136/bjsports-2013-092644

Hall, A.M., Kamper, S.J., Hernon, M., Hughes, K., Kelly, G., Lonsdale, C., Ostelo, R. (2015). Measurement tools for adherence to non-pharmacologic self-management treatment for chronic musculoskeletal conditions: A systematic review. *Archives of Physical Medicine and Rehabilitation, 96,* 552–562. doi:10.1016/j.apmr.2014.07.405

Hall, E.T. (1966). *The hidden dimension.* Garden City, NY: Doubleday.

Hammond, A., & Freeman, K. (2001). One-year outcomes of a randomized controlled trial of an educational–behavioural joint protection programme for people with rheumatoid arthritis. *Rheumatology, 40,* 1044–1051. doi:10.1093/rheumatology/40.9.1044

Hamson-Utley, J.J., Martin, S., & Walters, J. (2008). Athletic trainers' and physical therapists' perceptions of the effectiveness of psychological skills within sports injury rehabilitation programs. *Journal of Athletic Training, 43,* 258–264. doi:10.4085/1062-6050-43.3.258

Handegard, L.A., Joyner, A.B., Burke, K.L., & Reimann, B. (2006). Relaxation and guided imagery in the sport rehabilitation context. *Journal of Excellence, 10,* 146–164.

Hanson, S.J., McCullagh, P., & Tonymon, P. (1992). The relationship of personality characteristics, life stress, and coping resources to athletic injury. *Journal of Sport & Exercise Psychology, 14,* 262–272.

Hardy, C.J., Burke, K.L., & Crace, R.K. (1999). Social support and injury: A framework for social support-based interventions with injured athletes. In D. Pargman (Ed.), *Psychological bases of sport injuries* (2nd ed., pp. 175–198). Morgantown, WV: Fitness Information Technology.

Hardy, C.J., Richman, J.M., & Rosenfeld, L.B. (1991). The role of social support in the life stress/injury relationship. *The Sport Psychologist, 5,* 128–139.

Hare, R., Evans, L., & Callow, N. (2008). Imagery use during rehabilitation from injury: A case study of an elite athlete. *The Sport Psychologist, 22,* 405–422.

Harris, L.L., Demb, A., & Pastore, D.L. (2004). Perceptions and attitudes of athletic training students towards a course addressing psychological issues in rehabilitation. *Journal of Allied Health, 34,* 101–109.

Hays, R.D., Kravitz, R.L., Mazel, R.M., Sherbourne, C.D., DiMatteo, M.R., Rogers, W.H., & Greenfield, S. (1994). The impact of patient adherence on health outcomes for patients with chronic disease in the Medical Outcomes Study. *Journal of Behavioral Medicine, 17,* 347–360. doi:10.1007/BF01858007

Heaney, C. (2013). The impact of sport psychology education on the practice of physiotherapists. *British Journal of Sports Medicine, 47*(17), e4. doi:10.1136/bjsports-2013-093073.21

Heatherton, T.F., & Penn, R.J. (1995). Stress and the disinhibition of behavior. *Mind-Body Medicine, 1,* 72–81.

Heck, J.F., Clarke, K.S., Peterson, T.R., Torg, J.S., & Weis, M.P. (2004). National Athletic Trainers' Association position statement: Head-down contact and spearing in tackle football. *Journal of Athletic Training, 39,* 101–111.

Hegel, M.T., Ayllon, T., VanderPlate, C., & Spiro-Hawkins, H. (1986). A behavioral procedure for increasing compliance with self-exercise regimens in severely burn-injured patients. *Behavioral Research Therapy, 24,* 521–528. doi:10.1016/0005-7967(86)90032-X

Heidt, R.S., Jr., Sweeterman, L.M., Carlonas, R.L., Traub, J.A., & Tekulve, F.X. (2000). Avoidance of soccer injuries with preseason conditioning. *The American Journal of Sports Medicine, 28,* 659–662.

Heijne, A., Axelsson, K., Werner, S., & Biguet, G. (2008). Rehabilitation and recovery after anterior cruciate ligament reconstruction: Patients' experiences. *Scandinavian Journal of Medicine & Science in Sports, 18,* 325–335. doi:10.1111/j.1600-0838.2007.00700.x

Heil, J. (1993a). Conducting assessment and intervention. In J. Heil (Ed.), *Psychology of sport injury* (pp. 113–136). Champaign, IL: Human Kinetics.

Heil, J. (1993b). Mental training in injury management. In J. Heil (Ed.), *Psychology of sport injury* (pp. 151–174). Champaign, IL: Human Kinetics.

Heil, J. (1993c). Referral and coordination of care. In J. Heil (Ed.), *Psychology of sport injury* (pp. 251–266). Champaign, IL: Human Kinetics.

Heil, J. (1993d). Sport psychology, the athlete at risk, and the sports medicine team. In J. Heil (Ed.), *Psychology of sport injury* (pp. 1–13). Champaign, IL: Human Kinetics.

Heil, J., Hartman, D., Robinson, G., & Teegarden, L. (2002). Attention-deficit hyperactivity disorder in athletes. *Olympic Coach, 12*(2), 5–7.

Heil, J., & Podlog, L. (2012). Pain and performance. In S.M. Murphy (Ed.), *The Oxford handbook of sport and performance psychology* (pp. 618–634). New York: Oxford University Press.

Hendawy, H.M.F.M., & Awad, E.A.A. (2013). Personality and personality disorders in athletes. In D.A. Baron, C.L. Reardon, & S.H. Baron (Eds.), *Clinical sports psychiatry: An international perspective* (pp. 53–64). Chichester, UK: Wiley-Blackwell.

Heniff, C.B. (1998). *A comparison of life event stress, weekly hassles, and mood disturbances between injured and uninjured female university athletes.* Unpublished masters' thesis, University of Minnesota, Minneapolis.

Herring, S.A., Bergfeld, J.A., Boyd, J., Duffey, T., Fields, K.B., Grana, W.A....Sallis, R.E. (2002). The team physician and return-to-play issues: A consensus statement. *Medicine and Science in Sports and Exercise, 34,* 1212-1214.

Herring, S.A., Boyajian-O'Neill, L.A., Coppel, D.B., Daniels, J.M., Gould, D., Grana, W., Putukian, M. (2006). Psychological issues related to injury in athletes and the team physician: A consensus statement. *Medicine & Science in Sports & Exercise, 38,* 2030-2034.

Hewett, T.E., Ford, K.R., & Myer, G.D. (2006). Anterior cruciate ligament injuries in female athletes: Part 2, a meta-analysis of neuromuscular interventions aimed at injury prevention. *The American Journal of Sports Medicine, 34,* 490–498. doi:10.1177/0363546505282619

Hibberd, E.E., & Myers, J.B. (2013). Practice habits and attitudes and behaviors concerning shoulder pain in high school competitive club swimmers. *Clinical Journal of Sport Medicine, 23,* 450–455. doi:10.1097/JSM.0b013e31829aa8ff

Hidding, A., van der Linden, S., Gielen, X., Witte, L., Dijkmans, B., & Moolenburgh, D. (1994). Continuation of group physical therapy is necessary in ankylosing spondylitis. *Arthritis Care and Research, 7,* 90–96. doi:10.1002/art.1790070208

Hilliard, R.C., Brewer, B.W., Cornelius, A.E., & Van Raalte, J.L. (2014). Big five personality characteristics and adherence to clinic-based rehabilitation activities after ACL surgery: A prospective analysis. *The Open Rehabilitation Journal, 7,* 1–5. doi:10.2174/1874943701407010001

Hoar, S.D., & Flint, F. (2008). Determinants of help-seeking intentions in the context of athletic injury recovery. *International Journal of Sport and Exercise Psychology, 6,* 157–175. doi:10.1080/1612197X.2008.9671859

Hodge, D., Evans, L., Hanton, S., & Hardy, J. (2009, September). *Athletes' use of self-talk during injury rehabilitation.* Paper presented at the annual meeting of the Association for Applied Sport Psychology, Salt Lake City, UT.

Hokanson, R.G. (1994). *Relationship between sports rehabilitation practitioners' communication style and athletes' adherence to injury rehabilitation.* Unpublished master's thesis, Springfield College, MA.

Holmes, T.H. (1970). Psychological screening. In *Football injuries* (pp. 211–214). Paper presented at a workshop sponsored by the Subcommittee on Athletic Injuries, Committee on the Skeletal System, Division of Medical Science, National Research Council, February 1969. Washington, DC: National Academy of Sciences.

Holmes, T.H., & Rahe, R.H. (1967). The Social Readjustment Rating Scale. *Journal of Psychosomatic Research, 11,* 213–218. doi:10.1016/0022-3999(67)90010-4

Hootman, J., Dick, R., & Agel, J. (2007). Epidemiology of collegiate injuries for 15 sports: Summary and recommendations for injury prevention initiatives. *Journal of Athletic Training, 42,* 311–319.

Hopson, B. (1981). Response to the papers by Schlossberg, Brammer, and Abrego. *The Counseling Psychologist, 9*(2), 36–39. doi:10.1177/001100008100900204

Horton, A.S. (2002). *The impact of support groups on the psychological state of athletes experiencing con-*

cussions. Unpublished doctoral dissertation, McGill University, Montreal, Canada.

House, J.S., & Kahn, R.L. (1985). Measures and concepts of social support. In S. Cohen & S.L. Syme (Eds.), *Social support and health* (pp. 83–108). New York: Academic Press.

Howe, D.P. (2004). *Sport, professionalism, and pain: Ethnographies of anxiety.* London: Routledge.

Hughes, R.H., & Coakley, J. (1991). Positive deviance among athletes: The implications of overconformity to the sport ethic. *Sociology of Sport Journal, 8,* 307–325.

Hurley, O.A., Moran, A., & Guerin, S. (2007). Exploring athletes' experience of their injuries: A qualitative investigation. *Sport & Exercise Psychology Review, 3,* 14–22.

Hutchison, M., Comper, P., Mainwaring, L., & Richards, D. (2011). The influence of musculoskeletal injury on cognition: Implications for concussion research. *The American Journal of Sports Medicine, 39,* 2331–2337. doi:10.1177/0363546511413375

Hutchison, M., Comper, P., Mainwaring, L., Richards, D., & Bisschop, S.M. (2011). Differential emotional responses of varsity athletes to concussion cognition: Implications for concussion research. *Clinical Journal of Sport Medicine, 19,* 13–19. doi:10.1097/JSM.0b013e318190ba06

Ievleva, L., & Orlick, T. (1991). Mental links to enhanced healing: An exploratory study. *The Sport Psychologist, 5,* 25–40.

International Association for the Study of Pain. (1979). Pain terms: A list with definitions and notes on usage. Pain, 6, 249–252.

International Association for the Study of Pain Subcommittee on Taxonomy. (1986). Classification of chronic pain: Descriptions of chronic pain syndromes and definitions of pain terms. Amsterdam: Elsevier.

Ivarsson, A., & Johnson, U. (2010). Psychological factors as predictors of injuries among senior soccer players. A prospective study. *Journal of Sports Science & Medicine, 9,* 347–352.

Ivey, A.E., Ivey, M.B., & Zalaquett, C.P. (2013). *Intentional interviewing and counseling: Facilitating client development in a multicultural society* (8th ed.). Belmont, CA: Brooks/Cole.

Jackson, D.W., Jarrett, H., Bailey, D., Kausek, J., Swanson, M.J., & Powell, J.W. (1978). Injury prediction in the young athlete: A preliminary report. *The American Journal of Sports Medicine, 6,* 6–12.

Jackson, L.D. (1994). Maximizing treatment adherence among back-pain patients: An experimental study of the effects of physician-related cues in written medical messages. *Health Communication, 6,* 173–191. doi:10.1207/s15327027hc0603_1

Jacobson, E. (1938). *Progressive relaxation.* Chicago: University of Chicago Press.

Janda, D.H. (2003). The prevention of baseball and softball injuries. *Clinical Orthopaedics and Related Research, 409,* 20–28. doi:10.1097/01.blo.0000057789.10364.e3

Janelle, C.M., Kaminski, T.W., & Murray, M. (1999). College football injuries: Physical self-perception as a predictor. *International Sports Journal, 3,* 93–102.

Janssen, K.W., Hendriks, M.R.C., van Mechelen, W., & Verhagen, E. (2014). The cost-effectiveness of measures to prevent recurrent ankle sprains: Results of a 3-arm randomized controlled trial. *The American Journal of Sports Medicine, 42.* doi:10.1177/0363546514529642

Janssen, K.W., van Mechelen, W., & Verhagen, E.A.L.M. (2014). Bracing superior to neuromuscular training for the prevention of self-reported recurrent ankle sprains: A three-arm randomized controlled trial. *British Journal of Sports Medicine, 48,* 1235–1239. doi:10.1136/bjsports-2013-092947

Jaremko, M.E., Silbert, L., & Mann, T. (1981). The differential ability of athletes and nonathletes to cope with two types of pain: A radical behavioral model. *The Psychological Record, 31,* 265–275.

Jensen, M.P. (2011). Psychosocial approaches to pain management: An organizational framework. *Pain, 152,* 717–725. doi:10.1016/j.pain.2010.09.002

Jensen, M.P., Karoly, P., & Braver, S. (1986). The measurement of clinical pain intensity: A comparison of six methods. *Pain, 27,* 117–126.

Jensen, M.P., Karoly, P., O'Riordan, E.F., Bland, F., Jr., & Burns, R.S. (1989). The subjective experience of acute pain: An assessment of the utility of 10 indices. *The Clinical Journal of Pain, 5,* 153–159.

Jette, A.M. (1995). Outcomes research: Shifting the dominant research paradigm in physical therapy. *Physical Therapy, 75,* 965–970.

Jevon, S.M., & Johnston, L.H. (2003). The perceived knowledge and attitudes of governing-body-chartered physiotherapists towards the psychological aspects of rehabilitation. *Physical Therapy in Sport, 4,* 74–81. doi:10.1016/S1466-853X(03)00034-8

Johnson, U. (1997). Coping strategies among long-term-injured competitive athletes. A study of 81 men and women in team and individual sports. *Scandinavian Journal of Medicine & Science in Sports, 7,* 367–372. doi:10.1111/j.1600-0838.1997.tb00169.x

Johnson, U. (1998). Psychological risk factors during the rehabilitation of competitive male soccer players with serious knee injuries [Abstract]. *Journal of Sports Sciences, 16,* 391–392.

Johnson, U. (2000). Short-term psychological intervention: A study of long-term-injured competitive athletes. *Journal of Sport Rehabilitation, 9,* 207–218.

Johnson, U., Ekengren, J., & Andersen, M.B. (2005). Injury prevention in Sweden: Helping soccer players at risk. *Journal of Sport & Exercise Psychology, 27,* 32–38.

Johnson, U., & Ivarsson, A. (2011). Psychological predictors of sport injuries among junior soccer players. *Scandinavian Journal of Medicine & Science in Sports, 21,* 129–136. doi:10.1111/j.1600-0838.2009.01057.x

Johnston, L.H., & Carroll, D. (1998). The context of emotional responses to athletic injury: A qualitative analysis. *Journal of Sport Rehabilitation, 7,* 206–220.

Johnston, L.H., & Carroll, D. (2000). Coping, social support, and injury: Changes over time and the effects of level of sports involvement. *Journal of Sport Rehabilitation, 9,* 290–303.

Judge, L.W., Harris, B., & Bell, R.J. (2009, September). *Perceived social support from strength coaches among injured student-athletes.* Paper presented at the annual meeting of the Association for Applied Sport Psychology, Salt Lake City, UT.

Junge, A., Lamprecht, M., Stamm, H., Hasler, H., Bizzini, M., Tschopp, M., Dvorak, J. (2011). Countrywide campaign to prevent soccer injuries in Swiss amateur players. *The American Journal of Sports Medicine, 39,* 57–63. doi:10.1177/0363546510377424

Junge, A., Rosch, D., Peterson, L., Graf-Baumann, T., & Dvorak, J. (2002). Prevention of soccer injuries: A prospective intervention study in youth amateur players. *The American Journal of Sports Medicine, 30,* 652–659.

Kahanov, L., Dusa, M.J., Wilkinson, S., & Roberts, J. (2005). Self-reported headgear use and concussions among collegiate men's rugby union players. *Research in Sports Medicine: An International Journal, 13,* 77–89. doi:10.1080/15438620590956025

Kahanov, L., & Fairchild, P.C. (1994). Discrepancies in perceptions held by injured athletes and athletic trainers during the initial evaluation. *Journal of Athletic Training, 29,* 70–75.

Kamm, R.L. (2005). Interviewing principles for the psychiatrically aware sports medicine physician. *Clinics in Sports Medicine, 24,* 745–769. doi:10.1016/j.csm.2005.06.002

Kamphoff, C.S., Hamson-Utley, J.J., Antoine, B., Knutson, R., Thomae, J., & Hoenig, C. (2010). Athletic training students' perceptions of and academic preparation in the use of psychological skills in sport injury rehabilitation. *Athletic Training Education Journal, 5,* 109–116.

Karoly, P. (1985). The assessment of pain: Concepts and procedures. In P. Karoly (Ed.), *Measurement strategies in health psychology* (pp. 461–516). New York: Wiley.

Kazarian, A.E., Thompson, G.W., & Clark, R.D. (1995, September). *Type A vs. type B behavior patterns: Injury susceptibility and recovery time in college football players.* Paper presented at the Third International Olympic Committee World Congress on Sport Sciences, Atlanta, GA.

Keats, M.R., Emery, C.A., & Finch, C.F. (2012). Are we having fun yet? Fostering adherence to injury-preventive exercise recommendations in young athletes. *Sports Medicine, 42,* 175–184. doi:10.2165/11597050-000000000-00000

Kerns, R.D., Turk, D.C., & Rudy, T.E. (1985). The West Haven-Yale Multidimensional Pain Inventory. *Pain, 23,* 345–356. doi:10.1016/0304-3959(85)90004-1

Kerr, G., & Goss, J. (1996). The effects of a stress management program on injuries and stress levels. *Journal of Applied Sport Psychology, 8,* 109–117. doi:10.1080/10413209608406312

Kerr, K.M. (2000). Relaxation techniques: A critical review. *Critical Reviews in Physical and Rehabilitation Medicine, 12,* 51–89.

Kerr, Z.Y., Register-Mihalik, J.K., Kroshus, E., Baugh, C.M., & Marshall, S.W. (2016). Motivations associated with nondisclosure of self-reported concussions in former collegiate athletes. *American Journal of Sports Medicine, 44,* 220–225. doi:10.1177/0363546515612082

Kiecolt-Glaser, J.K., McGuire, L., Robles, T.F., & Glaser, R. (2002). Emotions, morbidity, and mortality: New perspectives from psychoneuroimmunology. *Annual Review of Psychology, 53,* 83–107.

Kiecolt-Glaser, J.K., Page, G.G., Marucha, P.T., MacCallum, R.C., & Glaser, R. (1998). Psychological influences on surgical recovery: Perspectives from psychoneuroimmunology. *American Psychologist, 53,* 1209–1218.

Kingen, E., Shapiro, J., Katz, H., & Mullan, M. (2013, October). An examination of the relationship between coping strategies, stress, mood, and adherence throughout injury rehabilitation in an active population. Paper presented at the annual meeting of the Association for Applied Sport Psychology, New Orleans, LA.

Kleiber, D.A., & Brock, S.C. (1992). The effect of career-ending injuries on the subsequent well-being of elite college athletes. *Sociology of Sport Journal, 9,* 70–75.

Kleinert, J. (2002). An approach to sport injury trait anxiety: Scale construction and structure analysis. *European Journal of Sport Science, 2,* 1–12. doi:10.1080/17461390200072305

Kleinert, J. (2007). Mood states and perceived physical states as short term predictors of sport injuries: Two prospective studies. *International Journal of Sport and Exercise Psychology, 5,* 340–351. doi:10.1080/1612197X.2007.9671840

Klinger, E. (1977). *Meaning and void.* Minneapolis, MN: University of Minnesota Press.

Klügl, M., Shrier, I., McBain, K., Shultz, R., Meeuwisse, W.H., Garza, D., & Matheson, G.O. (2010). The prevention of sport injury: An analysis of 12,000 published manuscripts. *Clinical Journal of Sport Medicine, 20,* 407–412. doi:10.1097/JSM.0b013e3181f4a99c

Knowles, S.B. (2010). Is there an injury epidemic in girls' sports? *British Journal of Sports Medicine, 44,* 38–44. doi:10.1136/bjsm.2009.065763

Kok, B.E., Coffey, K.A., Cohn, M.A., Catalino, L.I., Vacharkulksemsuk, T., Algoe, S., Fredrickson, B.L. (2013). How positive emotions build physical health: Perceived positive social connections account for the upward spiral between positive emotions and vagal tone. *Psychological Science, 24,* 1123–1132. doi: 10.1177/0956797612470827

Kolt, G.S. (2000). Doing sport psychology with injured athletes. In M.B. Andersen (Ed.), *Doing sport psychology* (pp. 223–236). Champaign, IL: Human Kinetics.

Kolt, G.S. (2004). Pain and its management. In G.S. Kolt & M.B. Andersen (Eds.), Psychology in the physical and manual therapies (pp. 141–161). Edinburgh: Churchill Livingstone.

Kolt, G.S. (2007). Pain. In G.S. Kolt & L. Snyder-Mackler (Eds.), Physical therapies in sport and exercise (pp. 133–148). Edinburgh: Churchill Livingstone.

Kolt, G.S., Brewer, B.W., Pizzari, T., Schoo, A.M.M., & Garrett, N. (2007). The Sport Injury Rehabilitation Adherence Scale: A reliable scale for use in clinical physiotherapy. *Physiotherapy, 93,* 17–22. doi:10.1016/j.physio.2006.07.002

Kolt, G.S., Hume, P.A., Smith, P., & Williams, M.M. (2004). Effects of a stress-management program on injury and stress of competitive gymnasts. *Perceptual & Motor Skills, 99,* 195–207. doi:10.1080/10413209608406312

Kolt, G.S., & Kirkby, R.J. (1994). Injury, anxiety, and mood in competitive gymnasts. *Perceptual and Motor Skills, 78,* 955–962. doi:10.2466/pms.1994.78.3.955

Kolt, G.S., & Kirkby, R.J. (1996). Injury in Australian female gymnasts: A psychological perspective. *Australian Journal of Physiotherapy, 42,* 121–126. doi:10.1016/S0004-9514(14)60444-X

Kolt, G.S., & Snyder-Mackler, L. (2007). The role of the physical therapies in sport, exercise, and physical activity. In G.S. Kolt & L. Snyder-Mackler (Eds.), *Physical therapies in sport and exercise* (pp. 1–5). Edinburgh: Churchill Livingstone.

Koltyn, K.F. (2000). Analgesia following exercise: A review. *Sports Medicine, 29,* 85–98. doi:10.2165/00007256-200029020-00002

Koltyn, K.F. (2002). Exercise-induced hypoalgesia and intensity of exercise. *Sports Medicine, 32,* 477–487.

Kontos, A.P. (2004). Perceived risk, risk taking, estimation of ability, and injury among adolescent sport participants. *Journal of Pediatric Psychology, 29,* 447–455. doi:10.1093/jpepsy/jsh048

Kottler, J.A. (2003). Introduction to therapeutic counseling: Voices from the field (5th ed.). Belmont, CA: Wadsworth.

Krasnow, D., Mainwaring, L., & Kerr, G. (1999). Injury, stress, and perfectionism in young dancers and gymnasts. Journal of Dance Medicine and Science, 3, 51–58.

Krosshaug, T., Andersen, T.E., Olsen, O.-E.O., Myklebust, G., & Bahr, R. (2005). Research approaches to describe the mechanisms of injuries in sport: Limitations and possibilities. *British Journal of Sports Medicine, 39,* 330–339. doi:10.1136/bjsm.2005.018358

Kübler-Ross, E. (1969). *On death and dying.* New York: Macmillan.

Kucera, K.L., Marshall, S.W., Kirkendall, D.T., Marchak, P.M., & Garrett, W.E. (2005). Injury history as a risk factor for incident injury in youth soccer. *British Journal of Sports Medicine, 39,* 462. doi:10.1136/bjsm.2004.013672

Kvist, J., Ek, A., Sporrstedt, K., & Good, L. (2005). Fear of re-injury: A hindrance of returning to sports after anterior cruciate ligament reconstruction. *Knee Surgery, Sports Traumatology, Arthroscopy, 13,* 393–397. doi:10.1007/s00167-004-0591-8

LaBella, C.R., Huxford, M.R., Grissom, J., Kim, K.Y., Peng, J., & Christoffel, K.K. (2011). Effect of a neuromuscular warm-up on injuries in female soccer and basketball athletes in urban public high schools: Cluster randomized controlled trial. *Archives of Pediatric and Adolescent Medicine, 165,* 1033–1040.

Labus, J.S., Keefe, F.J., & Jensen, M.P. (2003). Self-reports of pain intensity and direct observations of pain behavior: When are they correlated? *Pain, 102,* 109–124. doi:10.1016/s0304-359(02)003554-8

Ladyshewsky, R., & Gotjamanos, E. (1997). Communication skill development in health professional education: The use of standardised patients in combination with a peer assessment strategy. *Journal of Allied Health, 26,* 177–186.

Lafferty, M.E., Kenyon, R. & Wright, C.J. (2008). Club-based and non-club-based physiotherapists' views on the psychological content of their practice when treating sports injuries. *Research in Sports Medicine, 16,* 295–306. doi:10.1080/15438620802523378

Lampton, C.C., Lambert, M.E., & Yost, R. (1993). The effects of psychological factors in sports medicine rehabilitation adherence. *Journal of Sports Medicine and Physical Fitness, 33,* 292–299.

Langford, J.L., Webster, K.E., & Feller, J.A. (2009). A prospective longitudinal study to assess psychological changes following anterior cruciate ligament reconstruction surgery. *British Journal of Sports Medicine, 43*, 377–381. doi:10.1136/bjsm.2007.044818

Larson, G.A., Starkey, C.A., & Zaichkowsky, L.D. (1996). Psychological aspects of athletic injuries as perceived by athletic trainers. *The Sport Psychologist, 10*, 37–47.

Laubach, W.J., Brewer, B.W., Van Raalte, J.L., & Petitpas, A.J. (1996). Attributions for recovery and adherence to sport injury rehabilitation. *Australian Journal of Science and Medicine in Sport, 28*, 30–34.

Lauersen, J.B., Bertelsen, D.M., & Andersen, L.B. (2014). The effectiveness of exercise interventions to prevent sports injuries: A systematic review and meta-analysis of randomised controlled trials. *British Journal of Sports Medicine, 48*, 871–877. doi:10.1136/bjsports-2013-092538

Lavallee, L., & Flint, F. (1996). The relationship of stress, competitive anxiety, mood state, and social support to athletic injury. *Journal of Athletic Training, 31*, 296–299.

Lazarus, R.S., & Folkman, S. (1984). *Stress, appraisal, and coping.* New York: Springer.

Leddy, M.H., Lambert, M.J., & Ogles, B.M. (1994). Psychological consequences of athletic injury among high-level competitors. *Research Quarterly for Exercise and Sport, 65*, 347–354.

Lemberger, M.E. (2008). Systematic referrals: Issues and processes related to psychosocial referrals for athletic trainers. In J.M. Mensch & G.M. Miller (2008), *The athletic trainer's guide to psychosocial intervention and referral* (pp. 65–99). Thorofare, NJ: Slack.

Lentz, T.A., Tillman, S.M., Indelicato, P.A., Moser, M.W., George, S.Z., & Chimielewski, T.L. (2009). Factors associated with function after anterior cruciate ligament reconstruction. *Sports Health: A Multidisciplinary Approach, 1*, 47–53. doi:10.1177/1941738108326700

Lentz, T.A., Zeppieri, G., George, S.Z., Tillman, S.M., Moser, M.W., Farmer, K.W., & Chmielewski, T.L. (2015). Comparison of physical impairment, functional, and psychosocial measures based on fear of reinjury/lack of confidence and return-to-sport status after ACL reconstruction. *The American Journal of Sports Medicine, 43*, 345–353. doi:10.1177/0363546514559707

Leventhal, H., & Everhart, D. (1979). Emotion, pain, and physical illness. In C.E. Izard (Ed.), *Emotions in personality and psychopathology* (pp. 263–299). New York: Plenum.

Levin, M.F., & Riley, E.J. (1984). Effectiveness of teaching interviewing and communication skills to physiotherapy students. *Physiotherapy Canada, 36*, 190–194.

Levitt, R., Deisinger, J.A., Wall, J.R., Ford, L., & Cassisi, J.E. (1995). EMG feedback-assisted postoperative rehabilitation of minor arthroscopic knee surgeries. *The Journal of Sports Medicine and Physical Fitness, 35*, 218–223.

Levy, A.R., Polman, R.C.J., & Borkoles, E. (2008). Examining the relationship between perceived autonomy support and age in the context of rehabilitation in sport. *Rehabilitation Psychology, 53*, 224–230. doi:10.1037/00905550.53.2.224

Levy, A.R., Polman, R.C.J., & Clough, P.J. (2008). Adherence to sport injury rehabilitation programs: An integrated psycho-social approach. *Scandinavian Journal of Medicine and Science in Sport, 18*, 798–809. doi:10.1111/j.1600-0838.2007.00704.x

Levy, A.R., Polman, R.C.J., Clough, P.J., Marchant, D.C., & Earle, K. (2006). Mental toughness as a determinant of beliefs, pain, and adherence in sport injury rehabilitation. *Journal of Sport Rehabilitation, 15*, 246–254.

Lim, B., Lee, Y.S., Kim, J.G., An, K.O., Yoo, J., & Kwon, Y.H. (2009). Effects of sports injury prevention training on the biomechanical risk factors of anterior cruciate ligament injury in high school female basketball players. *The American Journal of Sports Medicine, 37*, 1728–1734. doi:10.1177/0363546509335220

Linder, D.E., Brewer, B.W., Van Raalte, J.L., & DeLange, N. (1991). A negative halo for athletes who consult sport psychologists: Replication and extension. *Journal of Sport & Exercise Psychology, 13*, 133–148.

Linder, D.E., Pillow, D.R. & Reno, R.R. (1989). Shrinking jocks: Derogation of athletes who consult a sport psychologist. *Journal of Sport and Exercise Psychology, 11*, 270–280.

Lisha, N.E., & Sussman, S. (2010). Relationship of high school and college sports participation with alcohol, tobacco, and illicit drug use: A review. *Addictive Behaviors, 35*, 399–407. doi:10.1016/j.addbeh.2009.12.032

Liston, K., Reacher, D., Smith, A., & Waddington, I. (2006). Managing pain and injury in non-elite rugby union and rugby league: A case study of players at a British university. *Sport in Society, 9*, 388–402. doi:10.1080/17430430600673407

Little, J.C. (1969). The athlete's neurosis—A deprivation crisis. *Acta Psychiatrica Scandinavia, 45*, 187–197. doi:10.1111/j.1600-0447.1969.tb10373.x

Loland, S., Skirstad, B., & Waddington, I. (Eds.) (2006). *Pain and injury in sport: Social and ethical analysis.* New York: Routledge.

Lombardo, J.A., & Wilkerson, L.A. (1996). Clinical sports medicine training and accreditation: The

United States experience. *Clinical Journal of Sport Medicine, 6*, 76–77.

Lord, R.H., & Kozar, B. (1989). Pain tolerance in the presence of others: Implications for youth sports. *The Physician and Sportsmedicine, 17*(10), 71–77.

Lord, R.H., Kozar, B., Whitfield, K.E., & Ferenz, C. (1994). Implicit goals and social facilitation effects on cold pressor pain tolerance in young athletes [Abstract]. *Research Quarterly for Exercise and Sport, 65*(Suppl.), A-88–A-99.

Loubert, P.V. (1999). Ethical perspectives in counseling. In R. Ray & D.M. Wiese-Bjornstal (Eds.), *Counseling in sports medicine* (pp. 161–175). Champaign, IL: Human Kinetics.

Lowry, S.F. (1993). Cytokine mediators of immunity and inflammation. *Archives of Surgery, 28*, 1235–1241.

Lu, F.J.H., & Hsu, Y. (2013). Injured athletes' rehabilitation beliefs and subjective well-being: The contribution of hope and social support. *Journal of Athletic Training, 48*, 92–98.

Lynch, G.P. (1988). Athletic injuries and the practicing sport psychologist: Practical guidelines for assisting athletes. *The Sport Psychologist, 2*, 161–167.

Lysens, R., Steverlynck, A., Vanden Auweele, Y., Lefevre, J., Renson, L., Claessens, A., & Ostyn, M. (1984). The predictability of sports injuries. *Sports Medicine, 1*, 6–10.

Macan, J., Bundalo-Vrbanac, D., & Romic, G. (2006). Effects of new karate rules on the incidence and distribution of injuries. *British Journal of Sports Medicine, 40*, 326–330. doi:10.1136/bjsm.2005.022459

Macchi, R., & Crossman, J. (1996). After the fall: Reflections of injured classical ballet dancers. *Journal of Sport Behavior, 19*, 221–234.

Maddison, R., & Prapavessis, H. (2005). A psychological approach to the prediction and prevention of athletic injury. *Journal of Sport & Exercise Psychology, 27*, 289–310.

Maddison, R., Prapavessis, H., & Clatworthy, M. (2006). Modeling and rehabilitation following anterior cruciate ligament reconstruction. *Annals of Behavior Medicine, 31*, 89–98. doi:10.1207/s15324796abm3101_13

Maddison, R., Prapavessis, H., Clatworthy, M., Hall, C., Foley, L., Harper, T., Brewer, B. (2012). Guided imagery to improve functional outcomes post-anterior cruciate ligament repair: Randomized-controlled pilot trial. *Scandinavian Journal of Medicine and Science in Sports, 22*, 816–821. doi:10.1111/j.1600-0838.2011.01325.x

Madrigal, L., Robbins, J., Gill, D.L., & Wurst, K. (2015). A pilot study investigating the reasons for playing through pain and injury: Emerging themes in men's and women's collegiate rugby.

The Sport Psychologist, 29, 310–318. doi:10.1123/tsp.2014-013

Maehr, M., & Braskamp, L. (1986). *The motivation factor: A theory of personal investment.* Lexington, MA: Lexington Books.

Mahler, H.I., & Kulik, J.A. (1998). Effects of preparatory videotapes on self-efficacy beliefs and recovery from coronary bypass surgery. *Annals of Behavioral Medicine, 20*, 39–45. doi:10.1007/BF02893808

Mainwaring, L. (1999). Restoration of self: A model for the psychological response of athletes to severe knee injuries. *Canadian Journal of Rehabilitation, 12*, 145–156.

Mainwaring, L.M., Bisschop, S.M., Green, R.E.A., Antoniazzi, M., Comper, P., Kristman, V., Richard, D.W. (2004). Emotional reaction of varsity athletes to sport-related concussion. *Journal of Sport and Exercise Psychology, 26*, 119–135.

Mainwaring, L.M., Hutchison, M., Bisschop, S.M., Comper, P., & Richards, D.W. (2010). Emotional response to sport concussion compared to ACL injury. *Brain Injury, 24*, 589–597. doi:10.3109/02699051003610508

Makarowski, L.M. (2007). Ethical and legal issues for sports professionals counseling injured athletes. In D. Pargman (Ed.), *Psychological bases of sport injury* (3rd ed., pp. 289–303). Morgantown, WV: Fitness Information Technology.

Malcom, N.L. (2006). "Shaking it off" and "toughing it out": Socialization to pain and injury in girls' softball. *Journal of Contemporary Ethnography, 35*, 495–525. doi:10.1177/0891241605283571

Malinauskas, R. (2010). The associations among social support, stress, and life satisfaction as perceived by injured college athletes. *Journal of Social Behavior and Personality, 38*, 741–752. doi:10.2224/sbp.2010.38.6.741

Mandelbaum, B.R., Silvers, H.J., Watanabe, D.S., Knarr, J.F., Thomas, S.D., Griffin, L.Y., Garrett, W., Jr. (2005). Effectiveness of a neuromuscular and proprioceptive training program in preventing anterior cruciate ligament injuries in female athletes: 2-year follow-up. *The American Journal of Sports Medicine, 33*, 1003-1010. doi:10.1177/0363546504272261

Manderino, M., & Bzdek, V. (1984). Effects of modeling and information on reactions to pain: A childbirth analogue. *Nursing Research, 33*, 9–14.

Maniar, S., Perna, F., Newcomer, R., Roh, J., & Stilger, V. (1999, September). *Athletic trainers' recognition of psychological distress following athletic injury: Implications for referral.* Paper presented at the annual meeting of the Association for the Advancement of Applied Sport Psychology, Banff, Alberta, Canada.

Maniar, S.D., Perna, F.M., Newcomer, R.R., Roh, J.L., & Stilger, V.G. (1999, August). *Emotional reactions to injury: With whom are athletes comfortable talking?* Paper presented at the annual meeting of the American Psychological Association, Boston.

Maniar, S.D., Perna, F.M., Newcomer, R.R., Roh, J.L., & Stilger, V.G. (2000, August). *Injured athletes' preferences for seeking help: A replication and extension.* Paper presented at the annual meeting of the American Psychological Association, Washington, DC.

Mankad, A., & Gordon, S. (2010). Psycholinguistic changes in athletes' grief response to injury after written emotional disclosure. *Journal of Sport Rehabilitation, 19*, 328–342.

Mankad, A., Gordon, S., & Wallman, K. (2009a). Psycho-immunological effects of written emotional disclosure during long-term injury rehabilitation. *Journal of Clinical Sport Psychology, 3*, 205–217.

Mankad, A., Gordon, S., & Wallman, K. (2009b). Psycholinguistic analysis of emotional disclosure: A case study in sport injury. *Journal of Clinical Sport Psychology, 3*, 182–196.

Mann, B.J., Grana, W.A., Indelicato, P.A., O'Neill, D.F., & George, S.Z. (2007). A survey of sports medicine physicians regarding psychological issues in patient-athletes. *The American Journal of Sports Medicine, 35*, 2140–2147. doi:10.1177/0363546507304140

Mann, E., & Carr, E. (2006). *Pain management.* Oxford, UK: Blackwell.

Manning, E., & Fillingim, R.B. (2002). The influence of athletic status and gender on experimental pain responses. *The Journal of Pain, 3*, 421–428.

Manning, E., Mack, D., Fettig, N., Gillespie, S., Meter, K., & Moss, J. (1997). Pain and the competitive athlete [Abstract]. *Journal of Applied Sport Psychology, 9*(Suppl.), S125.

Manuel, J.C., Shilt, J.S., Curl, W.W., Smith, J.A., DuRant, R.H., Lester, L., & Sinal, S.H. (2002). Coping with sports injuries: An examination of the adolescent athlete. *Journal of Adolescent Health, 31*, 391–393.

Marcolli, C., Schilling, G., & Segesser, B. (2001). Comeback: A mental training program to enhance the rehabilitation process after severe athletic injuries. In A. Papaioannou, M. Goudas, & Y. Theodorakis (Eds.), *International Society of Sport Psychology 10th World Congress of Sport Psychology programme & proceedings: In the dawn of a new millennium* (Vol. 1, p. 94). Thessaloniki, Greece: Christodoulidi.

Marshall, S.W., Covassin, T., Dick, R., Nassar, L.G., & Agel, J. (2007). Descriptive epidemiology of collegiate women's gymnastics injuries: National Collegiate Athletic Association injury surveillance system, 1988–1989. *Journal of Athletic Training, 42*, 234–240.

Martens, M.P., Dams-O'Connor, K., & Beck, N.C. (2006). A systematic review of college student-athlete drinking: Prevalence rates, sport-related factors, and interventions. *Journal of Substance Abuse Treatment, 31*, 305–316.

Martens, M.P., Dams-O'Connor, K., & Kilmer, J.R. (2007). Alcohol and drug use among athletes: Prevalence, etiology, and interventions. In G. Tenenbaum & R.C. Eklund (Eds.), *Handbook of sport psychology* (3rd ed., pp. 859–878). New York: Wiley.

Martens, R. (1987). *Coaches guide to sport psychology.* Champaign, IL: Human Kinetics.

Masters, K.S., & Ogles, B.M. (1998). The relations of cognitive strategies with injury, motivation, and performance among marathon runners: Results from two studies. *Journal of Applied Sport Psychology, 10*, 281–296.

Masters, K.S., Ogles, B.M., & Jolton, J.A. (1993). The development of an instrument to measure motivation for marathon running: The Motivations of Marathoners Scales (MOMS). *Research Quarterly for Exercise and Sport, 64*, 134–143.

Mather, R.C., Hettrich, C.M., Dunn, W.R., Cole, B.J., Bach, B.R., Huston, L.J., & Spindler, K.P. (2014). Cost-effectiveness analysis of early reconstruction versus rehabilitation and delayed reconstruction for anterior cruciate ligament tears. *American Journal of Sports Medicine, 42*, 1583–1591. doi:10.1177/0363546514530866

Matheson, G.O., Mohtadi, N.G., Safran, M., & Meeuwisse, W.H. (2010). Sport injury prevention: Time for an intervention? *Clinical Journal of Sport Medicine, 20*, 399–401. doi:10.1097/JSM.0b013e318203114c

May, S., & Potia, T.A. (2013). An evaluation of cultural competency training on perceived patient adherence. *European Journal of Physiotherapy, 15*, 2–10. doi:10.3109/14038196.2012.760647

May, S., & Taylor, A.H. (1994). The development and examination of various measures of patient compliance, for specific use with injured athletes [Abstract]. *Journal of Sports Sciences, 12*, 180–181.

McArdle, S. (2010). Psychological rehabilitation from anterior cruciate ligament-medial collateral ligament reconstructive surgery. *Sports Health: A Multidisciplinary Approach, 2*, 73–77. doi:10.1177/1941738109357173

McBain, K., Shrier, I., Shultz, R., Meeuwisse, W.H., Klügl, M., Garza, D., & Matheson, G.O. (2011). An overview of interventions designed to reduce risk factors for sport injury. *British Journal of Sports Medicine, 45*, 322.

McCaul, K.D., & Malott, J.M. (1984). Distraction and coping with pain. *Psychological Bulletin, 95*, 516–533.

McClay, M.H., Appleby, D.C., & Plascak, F.D. (1989). Predicting injury in young cross country runners with the self-motivation inventory. *Sports Train-*

ing, Medicine, and Rehabilitation, 1, 191-195. doi:10.1080/15438628909511875

McCrory, P., Meeuwisse, W., Aubry, M., Cantu, B., Dvorak, J., Echemendia, R. J., Turner, M. (2013). Consensus statement on concussion in sport: The 4th International Conference on Concussion in Sport, held in Zurich, November 2012. *British Journal of Sports Medicine, 47,* 250–258. doi:10.1136/bjsports-2013-092313

McCullagh, P., Ste-Marie, D., & Law, B. (2014). Modeling: Is what you see, what you get? In J. L. Van Raalte & B.W. Brewer (Eds.), *Exploring sport and exercise psychology* (3rd ed., pp. 139-162). Washington, DC: American Psychological Association.

McCullough, K.A., Phelps, K.D., Spindler, K.P., Matava, M.J., Dunn, W.R., Parker, R.D., Reinke, E.K. (2012). Return to high school- and college-level football after anterior cruciate ligament reconstruction: A Multicenter Orthopaedic Outcomes Network (MOON) cohort study. *The American Journal of Sports Medicine, 40,* 2523–2529. doi:10.1177/0363546512456836

McDonald, S.A., & Hardy, C.J. (1990). Affective response patterns of the injured athlete: An exploratory analysis. *The Sport Psychologist, 4,* 261–274.

McGlashan, A.J., & Finch, C.F. (2010). The extent to which behavioural and social science theories and models are used in sport injury prevention research. *Sports Medicine, 40,* 841–858. doi:10.2165/11534960-000000000-00000

McGowan, R.W., Pierce, E.F., Williams, M., & Eastman, N.W. (1994). Athletic injury and self diminution. *Journal of Sports Medicine and Physical Fitness, 34,* 299–304.

McGuine, T.A., Hetzel, S., Wilson, J., & Brooks, A. (2012). The effect of lace-up ankle braces on the injury rates in high school students. *The American Journal of Sports Medicine, 40,* 49–57. doi:10.1177/0363546511422332

McIntosh, A.S., Andersen, T.E., Bahr, R., Greenwald, R., Kleiven, S., Turner, M., McCrory, P. (2011). Sports helmets now and in the future. *British Journal of Sports Medicine, 45,* 1258–1265. doi:10.1136/bjsports-2011-090509

McKay, C., Campbell, T., Meeuwisse, W., & Emery, C. (2013). The role of risk factors for injury in elite youth ice hockey players. *Clinical Journal of Sport Medicine, 23,* 216–221. doi:10.1097/JSM.0b013e31826a86c9

McKay, C.D., Steffen, K., Romiti, M., Finch, C.F., & Emery, C.A. (2014). The effect of coach and player injury knowledge, attitudes, and beliefs on adherence to the FIFA 11 + programme in female youth soccer. *British Journal of Sports Medicine, 48,* 1281–1286. doi:10.1136/bjsports-2014-093543

McLean, S.M., Burton, M., Bradley, L., & Littlewood, C. (2010). Interventions for enhancing adherence with physiotherapy: A systematic review. *Manual Therapy, 15,* 514–521. doi:10.1016/j.math.2010.05.012

McManus, A., Stevenson, M., & Finch, C. (2006). Incidence and risk factors for injury in non-elite netball. *Journal of Science & Medicine in Sport, 9,* 119–124. doi:10.1016/j.jsams.2006.03.005

McNair, D., Lorr, M., & Droppleman, L. (1971). *Manual for Profile of Mood States.* San Diego: Educational and Industrial Testing Service.

Medibank Private. (2004). *Medibank Private sports injuries report.* Melbourne: Medibank Private.

Meeuwisse, W.H. (1994). Assessing causation in sport injury: A multifactorial model. *Clinical Journal of Sport Medicine, 4,* 166–170.

Meeuwisse, W.H., Tyreman, H., Hagel, B., & Emery, C. (2007). A dynamic model of etiology in sport injury: The recursive nature of risk and causation. *Clinical Journal of Sport Medicine, 17,* 215–219. doi:10.1097/JSM.0b013e3180592a48

Meichenbaum, D. (1985). *Stress inoculation training.* New York: Pergamon Press.

Meichenbaum, D., & Turk, D.C. (1987). *Facilitating treatment adherence.* New York: Plenum.

Melamed, B.G., Yurcheson, R., Fleece, E.L., Hutcherson, S., & Hawes, R. (1978). Effects of film modeling on the reduction of anxiety-related behaviors in individuals varying in level of previous experience in the stressful situation. *Journal of Consulting and Clinical Psychology, 46,* 1357–1367.

Melzack, R. (1975). The McGill Pain Questionnaire: Major properties and scoring methods. *Pain, 1,* 277–299. doi:10.1016/0304-3959(75)90044-5

Melzack, R. (1999). From the gate to the neuromatrix. *Pain, 82*(Suppl. 1), S121–S126. doi: 10.1016/S0304-3959(99)00145-1

Melzack, R., & Wall, P.D. (1965). Pain mechanisms: A new theory. *Science, 150,* 971–979. doi:10.1126/science.150.3699.971

Mendonza, M., Patel, H. & Bassett, S. (2007). Influences of psychological factors and rehabilitation adherence on the outcome post anterior cruciate ligament injury/surgical reconstruction. *New Zealand Journal of Physiotherapy, 35,* 62–71.

Mensch, J.M. (2008). Athletic training and psychosocial issues. In J.M. Mensch & G.M. Miller (2008), *The athletic trainer's guide to psychosocial intervention and referral* (pp. 1–30). Thorofare, NJ: Slack.

Messner, M. (1992). *Power at play: Sports and the problem of masculinity.* Boston: Beacon Press.

Meyer, J.D., Fink, C.M., & Carey, P.F. (1988). Medical views of psychological consultation. *Professional Psychology: Research and Practice, 19,* 36–358.

Meyers, M.C., & Barnhill, B.S. (2004). Incidence, causes, and severity of high school football injuries on FieldTurf versus natural grass: A 5-year prospective study. *The American Journal of Sports Medicine*, *32*, 1626–1638. doi:10.1177/0363546504266978

Meyers, M.C., Bourgeois, A.W., Stewart, S., & LeUnes, A. (1992). Predicting pain response in athletes: Development and assessment of the Sports Inventory for Pain. *Journal of Sport & Exercise Psychology*, *14*, 249–261.

Miles, M.P., & Clarkson, P.M. (1994). Exercise-induced muscle pain, soreness, and cramps. *Journal of Sports Medicine and Physical Fitness*, *304*, 203–216.

Miller, R.P., Kori, S., & Todd, D. (1991). The Tampa Scale: A measure of kinesiophobia. *Clinical Journal of Pain*, *7*, 51–52.

Milne, M., Hall, C., & Forwell, L. (2005). Self-efficacy, imagery use, and adherence to rehabilitation by injured athletes. *Journal of Sport Rehabilitation*, *14*, 150–167.

Misasi, S.P., Davis, C.F., Morin, G.E., & Stockman, D. (1996). Academic preparation of athletic trainers as counselors. *Journal of Athletic Training*, *31*, 39–42.

Mogk, C., Otte, S., Reinhold-Hurley, B., & Kröner-Herwig, B. (2006). Health effects of expressive writing on stressful or traumatic experiences—A meta-analysis [Die Wirkung expressiven Schreibens über belastende Erfahrungen auf die Gesundheit—eine Meta-analyse]. *GMS Psycho-Social-Medicine*, *3*, Doc06. www.egms.de/static/en/journals/psm/2006-3/psm000026.shtml.

Monsma, E., Mensch, J., & Farroll, J. (2009). Keeping your head in the game: Sport-specific imagery and anxiety among injured athletes. *Journal of Athletic Training*, *44*, 410–417. doi:10.4085/1062-6050-44.4.410

Moore, D.J., Keogh, E., & Eccleston, C. (2012). The interruptive effect of pain on attention. *Quarterly Journal of Experimental Psychology*, *65*, 565–586. doi:10.1080/17470218.2011.626865

Morgan, W.P. (1978, April). The mind of the marathoner. *Psychology Today*, 38–40, 43, 45–46, 49.

Morrey, M.A., Stuart, M.J., Smith, A.M., & Wiese-Bjornstal, D.M. (1999). A longitudinal examination of athletes' emotional and cognitive responses to anterior cruciate ligament injury. *Clinical Journal of Sport Medicine*, *9*, 63–69.

Morrongiello, B.A., Walpole, B., & Lasenby, J. (2007). Understanding children's injury-risk behavior: Wearing safety gear can lead to increased risk taking. *Accident Analysis & Prevention*, *39*, 618–623. doi:10.1016/j.aap.2006.10.006

Morse, E.D. (2013). Substance use in athletes. In D.A. Baron, C.L. Reardon, & S.H. Baron (Eds.), *Clinical sports psychiatry: An international perspective* (pp. 3–12). Chichester, UK: Wiley-Blackwell.

Moser, R.S. (2007). The growing public health concern of sports concussion: The new psychology practice frontier. *Professional Psychology: Research and Practice*, *38*, 699–704. doi:10.1037/0735-7028.38.6.699

Moulton, M.A., Molstad, S., & Turner, A. (1997). The role of athletic trainers in counseling collegiate athletes. *Journal of Athletic Training*, *32*, 148–150.

Mountjoy, M., Sundgot-Borgen, J., Burke, L., Carter, S., Constantini, N., Lebrun, C., Ljungqvist, A. (2014). The IOC consensus statement: Beyond the female athlete triad—Relative energy deficiency in sport (RED-S). *British Journal of Sports Medicine*, *48*, 491–497. doi:10.1136/bjsports-2014-093502

Murphy, G.C., Foreman, P.E., Simpson, C.A., Molloy, G.N., & Molloy, E.K. (1999). The development of a locus of control measure predictive of injured athletes' adherence to treatment. *Journal of Science and Medicine in Sport*, *2*, 145–152. doi:10.1016/S1440-2440(99)80194-7

Murphy, S.M. (1988). The on-site provision of sport psychology services at the 1987 U.S. Olympic Festival. *The Sport Psychologist*, *2*, 337–350.

Myer, G.D., Faigenbaum, A.D., Ford, K.R., Best, T.M., Bergeron, M.F., & Hewett, T.E. (2011). When to initiate integrative neuromuscular training to reduce sports-related injuries and enhance health in youth? *Current Sports Medicine Reports*, *10*, 157–166. doi:1537-890x/1003/157-166

Myer, G.D., Faigenbaum, A.D., Foss, K.B., Xu, Y., Khoury, J., Dolan, L.M., & Hewett, T.E. (2014). Injury initiates unfavourable weight gain and obesity markers in youth. *British Journal of Sports Medicine*, *48*, 1477–1481. doi:10.1136/bjsports-2012-091988

Myer, G.D., Ford, K.R., Brent, J.L., & Hewett, T.E. (2007). Differential neuromuscular training effects on ACL risk factors in "high-risk" versus "low-risk" athletes. *BMC Musculoskeletal Disorders*, *8*, 39. doi:10.1186/1471-2474-8-39

Myers, C.A., Peyton, D.D., & Jensen, B.J. (2004). Treatment acceptability in NCAA Division I football athletes: Rehabilitation intervention strategies. *Journal of Sport Behavior*, *27*, 165–169.

Myklebust, G., Engebretsen, L., Braekken, I.H., Skolberg, A., Olsen, O.E., & Bahr, R. (2003). Prevention of anterior cruciate ligament injuries in female team handball players: A prospective intervention study over three seasons. *Clinical Journal of Sport Medicine*, *13*, 71–78.

Naidu, M.U.R., Reddy, K.S.K., Rani, P.U., & Rao, T.R.K. (2011). Development of a simple radiant heat induced experimental pain model for evaluation of analgesics in normal healthy human volunteers. *Indian Journal of Pharmacology*, *43*, 632–637.

Naoi, A., & Ostrow, A. (2008). The effects of cognitive and relaxation interventions on injured athletes' mood and pain during rehabilitation. *Athletic Insight: The Online Journal of Sport Psychology*, *10*, 1–25.

Nathan, B. (1999). *Touch and emotion in manual therapy.* London: Churchill Livingstone.

National Athletic Trainers' Association. (2011). *Athletic training education competencies* (5th ed.). Dallas: Author.

National Collegiate Athletic Association. (2012). *National study of substance abuse trends among NCAA college student-athletes.* http://ncaapublications.com/p-4266-research-substance-use-national-study-of-substance-use-trends-among-ncaa-college-student-athletes.aspx.

Neeb, T.B., Aufdemkampe, G., Wagener, J.H.D., & Mastenbroek, L. (1997). Assessing anterior cruciate ligament injuries: The association and differential value of questionnaires, clinical tests, and functional tests. *Journal of Orthopaedic and Sports Physical Therapy*, *26*, 324–331.

Newcomer, R.R., & Perna, F.M. (2003). Features of posttraumatic stress among adolescent athletes. *Journal of Athletic Training*, *38*, 163–166.

Newsom, J., Knight, P., & Balnave, R. (2003). Use of mental imagery to limit strength loss after immobilization. *Journal of Sport Rehabilitation*, *12*, 249–258.

Nigorikawa, T., Oishi, E., Tasaukawa, M., Kamimura, M., Murayama, J., & Tanaka, N. (2003). Type A behavior pattern and sports injuries. *Japanese Journal of Physical Fitness and Sports Medicine*, *52*, 359–367.

Ninedek, A., & Kolt, G.S. (2000). Sport physiotherapists' perceptions of psychological strategies in sport rehabilitation. *Journal of Sport Rehabilitation*, *9*, 191–206.

Niven, A. (2007). Rehabilitation adherence in sport injury: Sport physiotherapists' perceptions. *Journal of Sport Rehabilitation*, *16*, 93–110.

Nixon, H.L., II. (1992). A social network analysis of influences on athletes to play with pain and injuries. *Journal of Sport & Social Issues*, *16*, 127–135. doi:10.1177/019372359201600208

Nixon, H.L., II. (1993a). Accepting the risks of pain and injury in sport: Mediated cultural influences on playing hurt. *Sociology of Sport Journal*, *10*, 183–196.

Nixon, H.L., II. (1993b). Social network analysis of sport: Emphasizing social structure in sport. *Sociology of Sport Journal*, *10*, 315–321.

Nixon, H.L., II. (1994a). Coaches' views of risk, pain, and injury in sport, with special reference to gender differences. *Sociology of Sport Journal*, *11*, 79–87.

Nixon, H.L., II. (1994b). Social pressure, social support, and help seeking for pain and injuries in college sports networks. *Journal of Sport & Social Issues*, *18*, 340–355. doi:10.1177/019372394018004004

Nixon, H.L., II. (1996a). Explaining pain and injury attitudes and experiences in sport in terms of gender, race, and sports status factors. *Journal of Sport & Social Issues*, *20*, 33–44. doi:10.1177/019372396020001004

Nixon, H.L., II. (1996b). The relationship of friendship networks, sports experiences, and gender to expressed pain thresholds. *Sociology of Sport Journal*, *13*, 78–86.

Nixon, H.L., II. (1998). Response to Martin Roderick's comment on the work of Howard L. Nixon II. *Sociology of Sport Journal*, *15*, 80–85.

Noh, Y.E., Morris, T., & Andersen, M.B. (2005). Psychosocial factors and ballet injuries. *International Journal of Sport and Exercise Psychology*, *3*, 79–90.

Noyes, F.E., Lindenfeld, T.N., & Marshall, M.T. (1988). What determines an athletic injury (definition)? Who determines an injury (occurrence)? *The American Journal of Sports Medicine*, *16*(Suppl. 1), S65–S68.

Noyes, F.R., Matthews, D.S., Mooar, P.A., & Grood, E.S. (1983). The symptomatic anterior cruciate-deficient knee. Part II: The results of rehabilitation, activity modification, and counseling on functional disability. *Journal of Bone and Joint Surgery*, *65-A*, 163–174.

O'Hair, D., O'Hair, M.J., Southward, G.M., & Krayer, K.J. (1987). Physician communication and patient compliance. *Journal of Compliance in Health Care*, *2*, 125–129.

Olivier, L.C., Neudeck, F., Assenmacher, S., & Schmit-Neuerburg, K.P. (1997). Acceptance of Allgower/Wenzl partial dynamic weight bearing orthosis. Results using a hidden step counting device. *Unfallchirurgie*, *23*, 200–204.

Olmedilla, A., Ortega, E., & Gómez, J.M. (2014). Influencia de la lesión deportiva en los cambios del estado de ánimo y de la ansiedad precompetitiva en futbolistas [Influence of sports injury changes in mood and precompetitive anxiety in soccer players]. *Cuadernos de Psicología Del Deporte*, *14*, 55–61.

Olmedilla, A., Prieto, J.G., & Blas, A. (2011). Relaciones entre estrés psicosocial y lesiónes deportivas en tenistas. *Universitas Psychologica*, *10*, 909–922.

Olsen, O.E., Myklebust, G., Engebretsen, L., Holme, I., & Bahr, R. (2003). Relationship between floor type and risk of ACL injury in team handball. *Scandinavian Journal of Science & Medicine in Sports*, *13*, 299–304. doi:10.1034/j.1600-0838.2003.00329.x

O'Malley, E., Murphy, J., Gissane, C., McCarthy-Persson, U., & Blake, C. (2014). Effective exercise based training interventions targeting injury prevention in team-based sports: A systematic review. *British Journal of Sports Medicine, 48,* 647. doi:10.1136/bjsports-2014-093494.231

O'Neill, D.F. (2008). Injury contagion in alpine ski racing: The effect of injury on teammates' performance. *Journal of Clinical Sport Psychology, 2,* 278–292.

Orchard, J., McCrory, P., Makdissi, M., Seward, H., & Finch, C.F. (2014). Use of rule changes to reduce injury in the Australian Football League. *Minerva Ortopedica E Traumatologica, 65,* 355–364.

Orr, B., Brown, C., Hemsing, J., McCormick, T., Pound, S., Otto, D., Beaupre, L.A. (2013). Female soccer knee injury: Observed coach knowledge gaps in injury prevention among players/parents/coaches and current evidence (the KNOW study). *Scandinavian Journal of Medicine and Science in Sports, 23,* 271–280. doi:10.1111/j.1600-0838.2011.01381.x

Orzel-Gryglewska, J. (2010). Consequences of sleep deprivation. *International Journal of Occupational Medicine and Environmental Health, 23,* 95–114. doi:10.2478/v10001-010-0004-9

Owen, O.G., & Goodge, P. (1981). Physiotherapists talking to patients. *Patient Counseling and Health Education, 3,* 100–102. doi:10.1016/S0738-3991(81)80003-1

Oztekin, H.H., Boya, H., Ozcan, O., Zeren, B., & Pinar, P. (2008). Pain and affective distress before and after ACL surgery: A comparison of amateur and professional male soccer players in the early postoperative period. *The Knee, 15,* 368–372. doi:10.1016/j.knee.2008.05.007

Pantano, K.J. (2009). Strategies used by physical therapists in the U.S. for treatment and prevention of the female athlete triad. *Physical Therapy in Sport, 10,* 3–11. doi:10.1016/j.ptsp.2008.09.001

Paparizos, A.L., Tripp, D.A., Sullivan, M.J.L., & Rubenstein, M.L. (2005). Catastrophizing and pain tolerance in recreational ballet dancers. *Journal of Sport Behavior, 28,* 35–50.

Pargman, D. (1996). Conversion blindness: A case report. *International Journal of Rehabilitation and Health, 2,* 57–65. doi:10.1007/BF02213564

Pargman, D., & Lunt, S.D. (1989). The relationship of self-concept and locus of control to the severity of injury in freshmen collegiate football players. *Sports Training, Medicine, and Rehabilitation, 1,* 203–208. doi:10.1080/15438628909511877

Parkkari, J., Kujala, U.M., & Kannus, P. (2001). Is it possible to prevent sports injuries? Review of controlled clinical trials and recommendations for future work. *Sports Medicine, 31,* 985–995. doi:10.2165/00007256-200131140-00003

Parr, J., Borsa, P., Fillingim, R., Kaiser, K., Tillman, M.D., Manini, T. M., George, S. (2014). Psychological influences predict recovery following exercise induced shoulder pain. *International Journal of Sports Medicine, 35,* 232–237. doi:10.1055/s-0033-1345179

Parry, J. (2006). The intentional infliction of pain in sport. In S. Loland, B. Skirstad, & I. Waddington (Eds.), *Pain and injury in sport: Social and ethical analysis* (pp. 144–161). New York: Routledge.

Pasanen, K., Parkkari, J., Pasanen, M., Hiilloskorpi, H., Makinen, T., Jarvinen, M., & Kannus, P. (2008). Neuromuscular training and the risk of leg injuries in female floorball players: Cluster randomised controlled study. *British Medical Journal, 337,* 96–99. doi:10.1136/bmj.a295

Passer, M.W., & Seese, M.D. (1983). Life stress and athletic injury: Examination of positive versus negative life events and three moderator variables. *Journal of Human Stress, 9,* 11–16.

Patel, D.R., & Nelson, T.L. (2000). Sports injuries in adolescents. *Medical Clinics of North America, 84,* 983–1007. doi:10.1016/S0025-7125(05)70270-4

Patterson, E.L., Smith, R.E., Everett, J.J., & Ptacek, J.T. (1998). Psychosocial factors as predictors of ballet injuries: Interactive effects of life stress and social support. *Journal of Sport Behavior, 21,* 101–112.

Payne, R.A. (2004). Relaxation techniques. In G.S. Kolt & M.B. Andersen (Eds.), *Psychology in the physical and manual therapies* (pp. 111–124). Edinburgh: Churchill Livingstone.

Pearson, L., & Jones, G. (1992). Emotional effects of sports injuries: Implications for physiotherapists. *Physiotherapy, 78,* 762–770. doi:10.1016/S0031-9406(10)61642-2

Pen, L.J., & Fisher, A.C. (1994). Athletes and pain tolerance. *Sports Medicine, 18,* 319–329.

Pen, L.J., Fisher, A.C., Storzo, G.A., & McManis, B.G. (1995). Cognitive strategies and pain tolerance in subjects with muscle soreness. *Journal of Sport Rehabilitation, 4,* 181–194.

Pennebaker, J.W. (1997). Writing about emotional experiences as a therapeutic process. *Psychological Science, 8,* 162–166. doi:10.1111/j.1467-9280.1997.tb00403.x

Penpraze, P., & Mutrie, N. (1999). Effectiveness of goal setting in an injury rehabilitation programme for increasing patient understanding and compliance [Abstract]. *British Journal of Sports Medicine, 33,* 60.

Peretz, D. (1970). Development, object-relationships, and loss. In B. Schoenberg, A.C. Carr, D. Peretz, & A.H. Kutscher (Eds.), *Loss and grief: Psychological management in medical practice* (pp. 3–19). New York: Columbia University Press.

Perna, F.M., Antoni, M.H., Baum, A., Gordon, P., & Schneiderman, N. (2003). Cognitive behavioral stress management effects on injury and illness among competitive athletes: A randomized clinical trial. *Annals of Behavioral Medicine, 25,* 66–73. doi:10.1207/S15324796ABM2501_09

Perna, F.M., & McDowell, S.L. (1995). Role of psychological stress in cortisol recovery from exhaustive exercise among elite athletes. *International Journal of Behavioral Medicine, 3,* 13–26. doi:10.1207/s15327558ijbm0201_2

Pero, S., Tracey, C., & O'Neil, A. (2000, October). *Sport psychology techniques utilized by certified athletic trainers at the collegiate level.* Paper presented at the annual meeting of the Association for the Advancement of Applied Sport Psychology, Nashville, TN.

Pero, S.F. (1995). *Development, implementation, and evaluation of an educational program in sport psychology for athletic trainers.* Unpublished doctoral dissertation, Temple University, Philadelphia, PA.

Petering, R.C., & Webb, C. (2011). Treatment options for low back pain in athletes. *Sports Health: A Multidisciplinary Approach, 3,* 550–555. doi:10.1177/1941738111416446

Petersen, K.L., & Rowbotham, M.C. (1999). A new human experimental pain model: The heat/capsaicin sensitization model. *Neuroreport, 10,* 1511–1516. doi:10.1097/00001756-199905140-00022

Peterson, K. (1997). Role of social support in coping with athletic injury rehabilitation: A longitudinal qualitative investigation [Abstract]. *Journal of Applied Sport Psychology, 9*(Suppl.), S33.

Peterson, L., & Renström, P. (2001). *Sports injuries: Their prevention and treatment* (3rd ed.). Champaign, IL: Human Kinetics.

Petitpas, A., & Cornelius, A. (2004). Practitioner–client relationships: Building working alliances. In G.S. Kolt & M.B. Andersen (Eds.), *Psychology in the physical and manual therapies* (pp. 57–70). Edinburgh: Churchill Livingstone.

Petitpas, A.J. (2000). Managing stress on and off the field: The Littlefoot approach to learned resourcefulness. In M.B. Andersen (Ed.), *Doing sport psychology* (pp. 33–43). Champaign, IL: Human Kinetics.

Petitpas, A.J. (2002). Counseling interventions in applied sport psychology. In J.L. Van Raalte & B.W. Brewer (Eds.), *Exploring sport and exercise psychology* (2nd ed., pp. 253–268). Washington, DC: American Psychological Association.

Petitpas, A.J., & Danish, S.J. (1995). Caring for injured athletes. In S.M. Murphy (Ed.), *Sport psychology interventions* (pp. 255–281). Champaign, IL: Human Kinetics.

Petrie, T.A. (1992). Psychosocial antecedents of athletic injury: The effects of life stress and social support on female collegiate gymnasts. *Behavioral Medicine, 18,* 127–138.

Petrie, T.A. (1993). Coping skills, competitive trait anxiety, and playing status: Moderating effects of the life stress–injury relationship. *Journal of Sport & Exercise Psychology, 15,* 261–274.

Petrie, T.A. (2007). Using counseling groups in the rehabilitation of athletic injury. In D. Pargman (Ed.), *Psychological bases of sport injuries* (3rd ed., pp. 193–216). Morgantown, WV: Fitness Information Technology.

Petrie, T.A., & Falkstein, D.L. (1998). Methodological, measurement, and statistical issues in research on sport injury prediction. *Journal of Applied Sport Psychology, 10,* 26–45. doi:10.1080/10413209808406376

Petrie, T.A., & Perna, F. (2004). Psychology of injury: Theory, research, and practice. In T. Morris & J. Summers (Eds.), *Sport psychology: Theory, applications, and issues* (pp. 547–571). Brisbane: Wiley.

Petrosenko, R.D., Vandervoort, B.M., Chesworth, B.M., Porter, M.M., & Campbell, G.J. (1996). Development of a home ankle exerciser. *Medical Engineering and Physics, 18,* 314–319. doi: 10.1016/1350-4533(95)00057-7

Pettersen, J.A. (2002). Does rugby headgear prevent concussion? Attitudes of Canadian players and coaches. *British Journal of Sports Medicine, 36,* 19–22. doi:10.1136/bjsm.36.1.19

Piaget, J. (1971). *Biology and knowledge.* Chicago: University of Chicago Press.

Pizzari, T., Taylor, N.F., McBurney, H., & Feller, J.A. (2005). Adherence to rehabilitation after anterior cruciate ligament reconstructive surgery: Implications for outcome. *Journal of Sport Rehabilitation, 14,* 201–214.

Plante, T.G., & Booth, J. (1997). Personality correlates of athletic injuries among elite collegiate baseball players: The role of narcissism, anger, and locus of control. *Journal of Human Movement Studies, 24,* 47–59.

Podlog, L., Dimmock, J., & Miller, J. (2011). A review of return to sport concerns following injury rehabilitation: Practitioner strategies for enhancing recovery outcomes. *Physical Therapy in Sport, 12,* 36–42. doi:10.1016/j.ptsp.2010.07.005

Podlog, L., & Dionigi, R. (2010). Coach strategies for addressing psychosocial challenges during the return to sport from injury. *Journal of Sport Sciences, 28,* 1197–1208. doi:10.1080/02640414.2010.487873

Podlog, L., & Eklund, R.C. (2005). Return to sport after serious injury: A retrospective examination of motivation and psychological outcomes. *Journal of Sport Rehabilitation, 14,* 20–34.

Podlog, L., & Eklund, R.C. (2006). A longitudinal investigation of competitive athletes' return to sport following serious injury. *Journal of Applied Sport Psychology, 18*, 44–68. doi:10.1080/10413200500471319

Podlog, L., & Eklund, R.C. (2007). The psychosocial aspects of a return to sport following serious injury: A review of the literature from a self-determination perspective. *Psychology of Sport and Exercise, 8*, 535–566. doi:10.1016/j.psychsport.2006.07.008

Podlog, L., & Eklund, R.C. (2009). High-level athletes' perceptions of success in returning to sport following injury. *Psychology of Sport and Exercise, 10*, 535–544. doi:10.1016/j.psychsport.2009.02.003

Podlog, L, & Eklund, R.C. (2010). Returning to competition after a serious injury: The role of self-determination. *Journal of Sports Sciences, 28*, 819–831. doi:10.1080/02640411003792729

Podlog, L., Gao, Z., Kenow, L., Kleinert, J., Granquist, M., Newton, M., & Hannon, J. (2013). Injury rehabilitation overadherence: Preliminary scale validation and relationships with athletic identity and self-presentation concerns. *Journal Of Athletic Training, 48*, 372–381. doi:10.4085/1062-6050-48.2.20

Podlog, L., Kleinert, J., Dimmock, J., Miller, J., & Shipherd, A.M. (2012). A parental perspective on adolescent injury rehabilitation and return to sport experiences. *Journal of Applied Sport Psychology, 24*, 175–190. doi:10.1080/10413200.2011.608102

Podlog, L., Lochbaum, M., & Stevens, T. (2010). Need satisfaction, well-being, and perceived return-to-sport outcomes among injured athletes. *Journal of Applied Sport Psychology, 22*, 167–182. doi:10.1080/10413201003664665

Podlog, L., Reel, J., & Greviskes, L. (2014, October). *Injury, body satisfaction, and disordered eating among dancers: Exploring potential relationships.* Paper presented at the annual meeting of the Association for Applied Psychology, Las Vegas, NV.

Pope, H.G., Gruber, A.J., Choi, P., Olivardia, R., & Phillips, K.A. (1997). Muscle dysmorphia: An underrecognized form of body dysmorphic disorder. *Psychosomatics, 38*, 548–557. doi:10.1016/S0033-3182(97)71400-2

Portenga, S.T., Sommer, T.L., & Statler, T. (2001). Establishing a psychological performance enhancement group for injured athletes. In A. Papaioannou, M. Goudas, & Y. Theodorakis (Eds.), *International Society of Sport Psychology 10th World Congress of Sport Psychology programme & proceedings: In the dawn of a new millennium* (Vol. 1, pp. 115–116). Thessaloniki, Greece: Christodoulidi.

Prentice, W.E. (2011). Principles of athletic training: A competency-based approach (14th ed.). New York: McGraw-Hill.

Prentice-Dunn, S., & Rogers, R.W. (1986). Protection motivation theory and preventive health: Beyond the health belief model. *Health Education Research, 1*, 153–161. doi:10.1093/her/1.3.153

Prieto, J.M., Labisa, A., & Olmedilla, A. (2014). Lesiónes deportivas y personalidad: Una revision sistemática. *Apunts Medicina de l'Esport, 49*(184), 139–149. doi:10.1016/j.apunts.2014.06.002

Prochaska, J.O., & DiClemente, C.C. (1983). Stages and processes of self-change of smoking: Toward an integrated model of change. *Journal of Consulting and Clinical Psychology, 51*, 390–395.

Prodromos, C.C., Han, Y., Rogowski, J., Joyce, B., & Shi, K. (2007). A meta-analysis of the incidence of anterior cruciate ligament tears as a function of gender, sport, and a knee injury-reduction regimen. *Arthroscopy, 23*, 1320–1325.

Prugh, J., Zeppieri, G., Jr., & George, S.Z. (2012). Impact of psychosocial factors, pain, and functional limitations on throwing athletes who return to sport following elbow injuries: A case series. *Physiotherapy Theory and Practice, 28*, 633–640. doi:10.3109/09593985.2012

Quackenbush, N., & Crossman, J. (1994). Injured athletes: A study of emotional response. *Journal of Sport Behavior, 17*, 178–187.

Quinn, A.M. (1996). *The psychological factors involved in the recovery of elite athletes from long-term injuries.* Unpublished doctoral dissertation, University of Melbourne, Australia.

Quinn, A.M., & Fallon, B.J. (1999). The changes in psychological characteristics and reactions of elite athletes from injury onset until full recovery. *Journal of Applied Sport Psychology, 11*, 210–229. doi:10.1080/10413209908404201

Rand, C.S., & Weeks, K. (1998). Measuring adherence with medication regimens in clinical care and research. In S.A. Shumaker, E.B. Schron, J.K. Ockene, & W.L. McBee (Eds.), *The handbook of health behavior change* (2nd ed., pp. 114–132). New York: Springer.

Rape, R.N., Bush, J.P., & Slavin, L.A. (1992). Toward a conceptualization of the family's adaptation to a member's head injury: A critique of developmental stage models. *Rehabilitation Psychology, 37*, 3–22.

Rathleff, M.S., Bandholm, T., Ahrendt, P., Olesen, J.L., & Thorborg, K. (2014). Novel stretch-sensor technology allows quantification of adherence and quality of home exercises: A validation study. *British Journal of Sports Medicine, 48*, 724–728. doi:10.1136/bjsports-2012-091859

Rathleff, M.S., Thorborg, K., Rode, L.A., McGirr, K.A., Sørensen, A.S., Bøgild, A., & Bandholm, T. (2015). Adherence to commonly prescribed, home-based strength training exercises for the lower extremity can be objectively monitored using the BandCizer. *Journal of Strength and Conditioning Research, 29,* 627–636. doi:10.1519/JSC.0000000000000675

Ray, R. (1999). Documentation in counseling. In R. Ray & D.M. Wiese-Bjornstal (Eds.), *Counseling in sports medicine* (pp. 143–160). Champaign, IL: Human Kinetics.

Ray, R., Terrell, T., & Hough, D. (1999). The role of the sports medicine professional in counseling athletes. In R. Ray & D.M. Wiese-Bjornstal (Eds.), *Counseling in sports medicine* (pp. 3–20). Champaign, IL: Human Kinetics.

Reardon, C.L., & Factor, R.M. (2010). Sport psychiatry: A systematic review of diagnosis and medical treatment of mental illness in athletes. *Sports Medicine, 40,* 961–980. doi:10.2165/11536580-000000000-00000

Rees, T., Mitchell, I., Evans, L., & Hardy, L. (2010). Stressors, social support, and psychological responses to sport injury in high- and low-performance standard participants. *Psychology of Sport & Exercise, 11,* 505–512. doi:10.1016/j.psychsport.2010.07.002

Rees, T., Smith, B., & Sparkes, A.C. (2003). The influence of social support on the lived experiences of spinal-cord-injured sportsmen. *The Sport Psychologist, 17,* 135–156.

Reinking, M.F., Austin, T.M., & Hayes, A.M. (2010). Risk factors for self-reported exercise-related leg pain in high school cross-country athletes. *Journal of Athletic Training, 45,* 51–57. doi:10.4085/1062-6050-45.1.51

Rejeski, W.J., & Sanford, B. (1984). Feminine-typed females: The role of affective schema in the perception of exercise intensity. *Journal of Sport Psychology, 6,* 197–207.

Reuter, J.M., & Short, S.E. (2005). The relationship among three components of perceived risk of injury, previous injuries, and gender in non-contact/limited-contact sport athletes. *Athletic Insight: The Online Journal of Sport Psychology, 7,* 20–42.

Rhudy, J.L. (2013). Does endogenous pain inhibition make a better athlete, or does intense athletics improve endogenous pain inhibition? *Pain, 154,* 2241–2242. doi:10.1016/j.pain.2013.07.034

Richman, J.M., Rosenfeld, L.B., & Hardy, C.J. (1993). The Social Support Survey: An initial evaluation of a clinical measure and practice model of the social support process. *Research on Social Work Practice, 3,* 288–311.

Riggio, R.E., & Friedman, H.S. (1983). Individual differences and cues to deception. *Journal of Personality and Social Psychology, 45,* 899–915.

Riley, J.L., III, Robinson, M.E., Wise, E.A., Myers, C.D., & Fillingim, R.B. (1998). Sex differences in the perception of noxious stimuli: A meta-analysis. *Pain, 74,* 181–187.

Ritter-Taylor, M.L. (1998). An exploration of identity, normative expectations, and the eating, pain, and injury risk behaviors of competitive gymnasts [Abstract]. *Journal of Applied Sport Psychology, 10*(Suppl.), 114.

Rivet, S., Brewer, B.W., Van Raalte, J.L., & Petitpas, A.J. (2013, October). *Preseason injury anxiety and kinesiophobia of intercollegiate athletes.* Paper presented at the annual meeting of the Association for Applied Sport Psychology, New Orleans, LA.

Robbins, J.E., & Rosenfeld, L.B. (2001). Athletes' perceptions of social support provided by their head coach, assistant coach, and athletic trainer, pre-injury and during rehabilitation. *Journal of Sport Behavior, 24,* 277–297.

Roberts, W.O., Brust, J.D., Leonard, B., & Hebert, B.J. (1996). Fair play rules and injury reduction in ice hockey. *Archives of Pediatric and Adolescent Medicine, 150,* 140–145.

Robinson, M.E., Wise, E.A., Riley, J.L., III, & Atchison, J.W. (1998). Sex differences in clinical pain: A multisample study. *Journal of Clinical Psychology in Medical Settings, 5,* 413–424. doi:10.1023/A:1026282210848

Robles, T.F., Brooks, K.P., & Pressman, S.D. (2009). Trait positive affect buffers the effects of acute stress on skin barrier recovery. *Health Psychology, 28,* 373–378. doi:10.1037/a014662

Rock, J.A., & Jones, M.V. (2002). A preliminary investigation into the use of counseling skills in support of rehabilitation from sport injury. *Journal of Sport Rehabilitation, 11,* 284–304.

Roderick, M. (1998). The sociology of risk, pain, and injury: A comment on the work of Howard L. Nixon II. *Sociology of Sport Journal, 15,* 64–79.

Rogers, C. (1957). The necessary and sufficient conditions of therapeutic personality change. *Journal of Consulting Psychology, 21,* 95–103.

Rogers, T.J., Alderman, B.L., & Landers, D.M. (2003). Effects of life-event stress and hardiness on peripheral vision in a real-life situation. *Behavioral Medicine, 29,* 21–27. doi:10.1080/08964280309596171

Rogers, T.J., & Landers, D.M. (2005). Mediating effects of peripheral vision in the life event stress/athletic injury relationship. *Journal of Sport & Exercise Psychology, 27,* 271–288.

Roh, J.L., & Perna, F.M. (2000). Psychology/counseling: A universal competency in athletic training. *Journal of Athletic Training, 35,* 458–465.

Rohe, D.E. (1988). Psychological aspects of rehabilitation. In A. Delisa (Ed.), *Rehabilitation medicine: Principles and practice* (pp. 66–82). Philadelphia: Lippincott.

Rose, J., & Jevne, R.F.J. (1993). Psychosocial processes associated with sport injuries. *The Sport Psychologist, 7*, 309–328.

Rosenfeld, L.B., Richman, J.M., & Hardy, C.J. (1989). Examining social support networks among athletes: Description and relation to stress. *The Sport Psychologist, 3*, 23–33.

Ross, M.J., & Berger, R.S. (1996). Effects of stress inoculation on athletes' postsurgical pain and rehabilitation after orthopedic injury. *Journal of Consulting and Clinical Psychology, 64*, 406–410.

Rotella, B. (1985). The psychological care of the injured athlete. In L.K. Bunker, R.J. Rotella, & A.S. Reilly (Eds.), *Sport psychology: Psychological considerations in maximizing sport performance* (pp. 273–287). Ann Arbor, MI: Mouvement.

Rotella, R.J., Ogilvie, B.C., & Perrin, D.H. (1993). The malingering athlete: Psychological considerations. In D. Pargman (Ed.), *Psychological bases of sport injuries* (pp. 85–97). Morgantown, WV: Fitness Information Technology.

Roter, D.L. & Hall, J.A. (1992). *Doctors talking with patients/patients talking with doctors: Improving communication in medical visits.* Westport, CT: Auburn House.

Rotter, J. (1966). Generalized expectancies for internal versus external control of reinforcements. *Psychological Monographs, 80*(1), 1–28.

Rubio, V.J., Pujals, C., de la Vega, R., Aguado, D., & Hernández, J.M. (2014). Autoeficiacia y lesiónes deportivas: ¿Factor protector o de riesgo? *Revista de Psicología del Deporte, 23*, 439–444.

Ruddock-Hudson, M., O'Halloran, P., & Murphy, G. (2012). Exploring psychological reactions to injury in the Australian Football League (AFL). *Journal of Applied Sport Psychology, 24*, 375–390. doi:10.1080/10413200.2011.654172

Ruddock-Hudson, M., O'Halloran, P., & Murphy, G. (2014). Long-term athletic injury: The psychological impact on Australian Football League (AFL) players. *Journal of Applied Sport Psychology, 26*, 377–394. doi:10.080/10413200.2014.897269

Ryan, E.D., Herda, T.J., Costa, P.B., Defreitas, J.M., Beck, T.W., Stout, J., & Cramer, J.T. (2009). Determining the minimum number of passive stretches necessary to alter musculotendinous stiffness. *Journal of Sports Sciences, 27*, 957–961. doi:10.1080/02640410902998254

Ryan, E.D., & Kovacic, C.R. (1966). Pain tolerance and athletic participation. *Perceptual and Motor Skills, 22*, 383–390. doi:10.1037/h0021226

Ryan, R.M., & Deci, E.L. (2000). Self-determination theory and the facilitation of intrinsic motivation, social development, and well-being. *American Psychologist, 55*, 68–78. doi:10.1037110003-066X.55.1.68

Sackett, D.L., Rosenberg, D.L., Gray, J.A., Haynes, R.B., & Richardson, W.S. (1996). Evidence-based medicine: What it is and what it isn't. *BMJ, 312*, 71–72. doi:10.1136/bmj.312.7023.71

Safai, P. (2003). Healing the body in the "culture of risk": Examining the negotiation of treatment between sport medicine clinicians and injured athletes in Canadian intercollegiate sport. *Sociology of Sport Journal, 20*, 127–146.

Safai, P. (2004). Negotiating the risk: Exploring the role of the sports medicine clinician. In K. Young (Ed.), *Sporting bodies, damaged selves: Sociological studies of sports related injury* (pp. 269–286). Oxford, England: Elsevier.

Safer, M.A., Tharps, Q.J., Jackson, T.C., & Leventhal, H. (1979). Determinants of three stages of delay in seeking care at a medical care clinic. *Medical Care, 17*, 11–29.

Salim, J., Wadey, R., & Diss, C. (2015). Examining the relationship between hardiness and perceived stress-related growth in a sport injury context. *Psychology of Sport and Exercise, 19*, 10–17. doi:10.1016/j.psychsport.2014.12.004

Salvador, H.F. (1985). The role of sport participation in the psychological response to physical injuries. *Dissertation Abstracts International, 45*(9-B), 3083.

San José, A. (2003). Injury of elite athletes: Sport- and gender- related representations. *International Journal of Sport and Exercise Psychology, 1*, 434–459. doi:10.1080/1612197X.2003.9671729

Sarafino, E.P., & Smith, T.W. (2011). *Health psychology: Biopsychosocial interactions.* Hoboken, NJ: Wiley.

Sarason, I.G., Johnson, J.H., & Siegel, J.M. (1978). Assessing the impact of life changes: Development of the Life Experiences Survey. *Journal of Consulting and Clinical Psychology, 46*, 932–946. doi:10.1037/0022-006X.46.5.932

Schaal, K., Tafflet, M., Nassif, H., Thibault, V., Pichard, C., Alcotte, M., Toussaint, J.-F. (2011). Psychological balance in high level athletes: Gender-based differences and sport-specific patterns. *PLoS ONE, 6*(5), e19007. doi:10.1371/journal.pone.0019007

Schafer, W. (1996). *Stress management for wellness* (3rd ed.). Fort Worth, TX: Harcourt Brace College.

Scherzer, C.B., Brewer, B.W., Cornelius, A.E., Van Raalte, J.L., Petitpas, A.J., Sklar, J.H., Ditmar, T.D. (2001). Psychological skills and adherence to rehabilitation after reconstruction of the anterior cruciate ligament. *Journal of Sport Rehabilitation, 10*, 165–172.

Schieber, R.A., Branche-Dorsey, C.M., Ryan, G.W., Rutherford, G.W., Jr., Stevens, J.A., & O'Neil, J. (1996). Risk factors for injuries from in-line skating and the effectiveness of safety gear. *New England Journal of Medicine, 335*, 1630–1635.

Schlenk, E.A., Dunbar-Jacob, J., Sereika, S., Starz, T., Okifuji, A., & Turk, D. (2000). Comparability of daily diaries and accelerometers in exercise adherence in fibromyalgia syndrome [Abstract]. *Measurement and Evaluation in Physical Education and Exercise Science, 4*, 133–134.

Schneiders, A.G., Zusman, M., & Singer, K.P. (1998). Exercise therapy compliance in acute low back pain patients. *Manual Therapy, 3*, 147–152. doi:10.1016/S1356-689X(98)80005-2

Schomer, H.H. (1990). A cognitive strategy training program for marathon runners: Ten case studies. *South African Journal of Research in Sport, Physical Education, and Recreation, 13*, 47–78.

Schuller, D.E., Dankle, S.K., Martin, M., & Strauss, R.H. (1989). Auricular injury and the use of headgear in wrestlers. *Archives of Otolaryngology—Head & Neck Surgery, 115*, 714–717.

Schwenk, T.L. (2000). The stigmatisation and denial of mental illness in athletes. *British Journal of Sports Medicine, 34*, 4–5. doi:10.1136/bjsm.34.1.4

Sechrest, R.C., & Henry, D.J. (1996). Computer-based patient education: Observations on effective communication in the clinical setting. *Journal of Biocommunication, 23*, 8–12.

Segerstrom, S.C., & Miller, G.E. (2004). Psychological stress and the immune system: A meta-analytic study of 30 years of inquiry. *Psychological Bulletin, 130*, 601–630. doi:10.1037/0033-2909.130.4.601

Sein, M.L., Walton, J., Linklater, J., Appleyard, R., Kirkbride, B., Kuah, D., & Murrel, G.A.C. (2010). Shoulder pain in elite swimmers: Primarily due to swim-volume-induced supraspinatus tendinopathy. *British Journal of Sports Medicine, 44*, 105–113. doi:10.1136/bjsm.2008.047282

Sepah, S.C., & Bower, J.E. (2009). Positive affect and inflammation during radiation treatment for breast and prostate cancer. *Brain, Behavior, and Immunity, 23*, 1068–1072. doi:10.1016/j.bbi.2009.06.149

Shaffer, S.M. (1996). Grappling with injury: What motivates athletes to wrestle with pain? [Abstract]. *Journal of Applied Sport Psychology, 8*(Suppl.), S57.

Shapiro, J.L. (2009, September). *A qualitative pilot study of an individualized multimodal mental skills intervention for injured college athletes*. Paper presented at the annual meeting of the Association for Applied Sport Psychology, Salt Lake City, UT.

Shaw, L., & Finch, C.F. (2008). Injuries to junior club cricketers: The effect of helmet regulations. *British Journal of Sports Medicine, 42*, 437–440. doi:10.1136/bjsm.2007.041947

Shealy, J.E., Ettlinger, C.F., & Johnson, R.J. (2005). How fast do winter sports participants travel on Alpine slopes? *Journal of ASTM International, 2*(7), 1–8. doi:10.1520/JAI12092

Shelbourne, K.D., & Wilckens, J.H. (1990). Current concepts in anterior cruciate ligament rehabilitation. *Orthopaedic Review, 19*, 957–964.

Sherman, C.P., & Poczwardowski, A. (2000). Relax! It ain't easy (or is it?). In M.B. Andersen (Ed.), *Doing sport psychology* (pp. 47–60). Champaign, IL: Human Kinetics.

Shertzer, B., & Stone, S. (1966). *Fundamentals of counseling*. Boston: Houghton Mifflin.

Short, S.E., Reuter, J., Brandt, J., Short, M.W., & Kontos, A.P. (2004). The relationships among three components of perceived risk of injury, previous injuries, and gender in contact sport athletes. *Athletic Insight, 6*, 38–46.

Shuer, M.L., & Dietrich, M.S. (1997). Psychological effects of chronic injury in elite athletes. *Western Journal of Medicine, 166*, 104–109.

Shultz, R., Bido, J., Shrier, I., Meeuwisse, W.H., Garza, D., & Matheson, G.O. (2013). Team clinician variability in return-to-play decisions. *Clinical Journal of Sport Medicine, 23*, 456–461. doi:10.1097/JSM.obo13e318295bb17

Shumaker, S.A., & Brownell, A. (1984). Toward a theory of social support: Closing concetual gaps. *Journal of Social Issues, 40*, 11–36. doi: 10.1111/j.1540-4560.1984.tb01105.x

Sibold, J.S. (2005). A comparison of psychosocial and orthopedic data in predicting days missed due to injury. *Dissertation Abstracts International, 65*(11-A), 4145.

Silkman, C., & McKeon, J. (2010). The effectiveness of electromyographic biofeedback supplementation during knee rehabilitation after injury. *Journal of Sport Rehabilitation, 19*, 343–351.

Silver, R.L., & Wortman, C.B. (1980). Coping with undesirable events. In J. Garber & M.E.P. Seligman (Eds.), *Human helplessness: Theory and applications* (pp. 279–375). New York: Academic Press.

Silvers, H., Mandelbaum, B., Bizzini, M., & Dvorak, J. (2014). The efficacy of the FIFA 11+ program in the collegiate male soccer player (USA). *British Journal of Sports Medicine, 48*, 662. doi:10.1136/bjsports-2014-093494.272

Singer, R.N., & Johnson, P.J. (1987). Strategies to cope with pain associated with sport-related injuries. *Athletic Training, 22*, 100–103.

Smith, A.M., & Milliner, E.K. (1994). Injured athletes and the risk of suicide. *Journal of Athletic Training, 29*, 337–341.

Smith, A.M., Scott, S.G., O'Fallon, W.M., & Young, M.L. (1990). Emotional responses of athletes to injury. *Mayo Clinic Proceedings, 65*, 38–50.

Smith, A.M., Scott, S.G., & Wiese, D.M. (1990). The psychological effects of sports injuries: Coping. *Sports Medicine, 9*, 352–369.

Smith, A.M., Stuart, M.J., Wiese-Bjornstal, D.M., Milliner, E.K., O'Fallon, W.M., & Crowson, C.S. (1993). Competitive athletes: Preinjury and postinjury mood state and self-esteem. *Mayo Clinic Proceedings, 68*, 939–947.

Smith, A.M., Young, M.L., & Scott, S.G. (1988). The emotional responses of athletes to injury. *Canadian Journal of Sport Sciences, 13*(Suppl.), 84P–85P.

Smith, R.E., Ptacek, J.T., & Smoll, F.L. (1992). Sensation seeking, stress, and adolescent injuries: A test of stress-buffering, risk-taking, and coping skills hypotheses. *Journal of Personality and Social Psychology, 62*, 1016–1024. doi:10.1037/0022-3514.62.6.1016

Smith, R.E., Smoll, F.L., & Ptacek, J.T. (1990). Conjunctive moderator variables in vulnerability and resiliency research: Life stress, social support and coping skills, and adolescent sport injuries. *Journal of Personality and Social Psychology, 58*, 360–370. doi:10.1037/0022-3514.62.6.1016

Smyth, J.M. (1998). Written emotional expression: Effect sizes, outcome types, and moderating variables. *Journal of Consulting and Clinical Psychology, 66*, 174–184. doi:10.1037/0022-006X.66.1.174

Snyder-Mackler, L., Delitto, A., Stralka, S.W., & Bailey, S.L. (1994). Use of electrical stimulation to enhance recovery of quadriceps femoris muscle force production in patients following anterior cruciate ligament reconstruction. *Physical Therapy, 74*, 901–907. doi:10.1037/0022-3514.62.6.1016

Snyder-Mackler, L., Schmitt, L.A., Rudolph, K., & Farquhar, S. (2007). Electrophysical agents in sport and exercise injury management. In G.S. Kolt & L. Snyder-Mackler (Eds.), *Physical therapies in sport and exercise* (pp. 220–235). Edinburgh: Churchill Livingstone.

Soisson, E.L., VandeCreek, L., & Knapp, S. (1987). Thorough record keeping: A good defense in a litigious era. *Professional Psychology: Research and Practice, 18*, 498–502. doi:10.1037/0735-7028.18.5.498

Soligard, T., Grindem, H., Bahr, R., & Andersen, T.E. (2010). Are skilled players at greater risk of injury in female youth football. *British Journal of Sports Medicine, 44*, 1118–1123. doi:10.1136/bjsm.2010.075093

Soligard, T., Myklebust, G., Steffen, K., Holme, I., Silvers, H., Bizzini, M., Andersen, T.E. (2008). Comprehensive warm-up programme to prevent injuries in youth football. *BMJ, 337*, a2469. doi:10.1136/bmj.a2469

Soligard, T., Nilstad, A., Steffen, K., Myklebust, G., Holme, I., Dvorak, J. Andersen, T.E. (2010). Compliance with a comprehensive warm-up programme to prevent injuries in youth football. *British Journal of Sports Medicine, 44*, 787–793. doi:10.1136/bjsm.2009.070672

Sordoni, C.A., Hall, C.R., & Forwell, L. (2000). The use of imagery by athletes during injury rehabilitation. *Journal of Sport Rehabilitation, 9*, 329–338.

Sordoni, C.A., Hall, C.R., & Forwell, L. (2002). The use of imagery in athletic injury rehabilitation and its relationship to self-efficacy. *Physiotherapy Canada, 54*, 177–185.

Sparkes, A.C. (1998). An Achilles heel to the survival of self. *Qualitative Health Research, 8*, 644–664. doi:10.1177/104973239800800506

Stadden, S.A., & Gill, D.L. (2008). Examining athletes' help-seeking tendencies for pains and injuries experienced during sport participation [Abstract]. *Journal of Athletic Training, 43*(Suppl.), S-79.

Stasinopoulos, D. (2004). Comparison of three preventive methods in order to reduce the incidence of ankle inversion sprains among female volleyball players. *British Journal of Sports Medicine, 38*, 182–185. doi:10.1136/bjsm.2002.003947

Steffen, K., Emery, C.A., Romiti, M., Kang, J., Bizzini, M., Dvorak, J., Meeuwisse, W.H. (2013). High adherence to a neuromuscular injury prevention programme (FIFA 11 +) improves functional balance and reduces injury risk in Canadian youth female football players: A cluster randomized trial. *British Journal of Sports Medicine, 47*, 794–802. doi:10.1136/bjsports-2012-091886

Steffen, K., Meeuwisse, W.H., Romiti, M., Kang, J., McKay, C., Bizzini, M., Emery, C.A., (2013). Evaluation of how different implementation strategies of an injury prevention programme (FIFA 11 +) impact team adherence and injury risk in Canadian female youth football players: A cluster-randomised trial. *British Journal of Sports Medicine, 47*, 480–487. doi:10.1136/bjsports-2012-091887

Steffen, K., Myklebust, G., Andersen, T.A., Holme, I., & Bahr, R. (2008). Self-reported injury history and lower limb function as risk factors for injuries in female youth soccer. *The American Journal of Sports Medicine, 36*, 700–708. doi:10.1177/0363546507311598

Steffen, K., Pensgaard, A.M., & Bahr, R. (2009). Self reported psychological characteristics as risk factors for injuries in female youth football. *Scandinavian Journal of Medicine Science and Sports, 19*, 442–451. doi:10.1111/j.1600-0838.2008.00797.x

Steptoe, A., Wardle, J., Pollard, T.M., & Canaan, L. (1996). Stress, social support, and health-related behavior: A study of smoking, alcohol consumption, and physical exercise. *Journal of Psychosomatic Research, 41*, 171–180.

Sternbach, R.A., Deems, L.M., Timmermans, G., & Huey, L.Y. (1977). On the sensitivity of the tourniquet pain test. *Pain, 3,* 105–110.

Sternberg, W.F. (2007). Pain: Basic concepts. In D. Pargman (Ed.), *Psychological bases of sport injuries* (3rd ed., pp. 305–317). Morgantown, WV: Fitness Information Technology.

Sternberg, W.F., Bailin, D., Grant, M., & Gracely, R.H. (1998). Competition alters the perceptions of noxious stimuli in male and female athletes. *Pain, 76,* 231–238.

Stetter, F., & Kupper, S. (2002). Autogenic training: A meta-analysis of clinical outcome studies. *Applied Psychophysiology and Biofeedback, 27,* 45–98.

Stevinson, C.D., & Biddle, S.J.H. (1998). Cognitive orientations in marathon running and "hitting the wall." *British Journal of Sports Medicine, 32,* 229–235. doi:10.1136/bjsm.32.3.229

Stiles, W.B., Putnam, S.M., Wolf, M.H., & James, S.A. (1979). Interaction exchange structure and patient satisfaction with medical issues. *Medical Care, 17,* 667–681.

Stiller-Ostrowksi, J.L., Gould, D.R., & Covassin, T. (2009). An evaluation of an educational intervention in psychology of injury for athletic training students. *Journal of Athletic Training, 44,* 482–489. doi:10.4085/1062-6050-48.3.21

Stiller-Ostrowski, J.L., & Hamson-Utley, J.J. (2010). The ATEP educated athletic trainer: Educational satisfaction and technique use within the psychosocial intervention and referral content area. *Athletic Training Education Journal, 5*(1), 4–11.

Stiller-Ostrowksi, J.L., & Ostrowski, J.A. (2009). Recently certified athletic trainers' undergraduate educational preparation in psychosocial intervention and referral. *Journal of Athletic Training, 44,* 67–75. doi:10.4085/1062-6050-44.1.67

Stoltenburg, A.L., Kamphoff, C.S., & Bremer, K.L. (2011). Transitioning out of sport: The psychosocial effects of career-ending injuries on collegiate athletes. *Athletic Insight, 13*(2), 1–12.

Stracciolini, A., Casciano, R., Friedman, H.L., Meehan, W.P., III, & Micheli, L.J. (2013). Pediatric sports injuries: An age comparison of children versus adolescents. *American Journal of Sports Medicine, 41,* 1922–1929. doi:10.1177/0363546513490644

Straub, R.O. (2012). *Health psychology: A biopsychosocial approach* (3rd ed.). New York: Worth.

Strauss, R.H., & Curry, T.J. (1983). Social factors in wrestlers' health problems. *The Physician & Sportsmedicine, 11*(11), 86–90, 95, 99.

Streator, S., Ingersoll, C.D., & Knight, K.L. (1995). Sensory information can decrease cold-induced pain perception. *Journal of Athletic Training, 30,* 293–296.

Strein, W., & Hershenson, D.B. (1991). Confidentiality in nondyadic counseling situations. *Journal of Counseling and Development, 69,* 312–316. doi:10.1002/j.1556-6676.1991.tb01512.x

Sugimoto, D., Myer, G.D., Bush, H.M., Klugman, M.F., Medina McKeon, J.M., & Hewett, T.E. (2012). Compliance with neuromuscular training and anterior cruciate ligament injury risk reduction in female athletes: A meta-analysis. *Journal of Athletic Training, 47,* 714–723. doi:10.4085/1062-6050-47.6.10

Sullivan, M.J.L., Rodgers, W.M., Wilson, P.M., Bell, G.J., Murray, T.C., & Fraser, S.N. (2002). An experimental investigation of the relation between catastrophizing and activity intolerance. *Pain, 100,* 47–53.

Suls, J., & Fletcher, B. (1985). The relative efficacy of avoidant and nonavoidant coping strategies. *Health Psychology, 4,* 249–288.

Suls, J., & Wan, C.K. (1989). Effects of sensory and procedural information on coping with stressful medical procedures and pain: A meta-analysis. *Journal of Consulting and Clinical Psychology, 57,* 372–379. doi:10.1037/0022-006X.57.3.372

Sundgot-Borgen, J. (1994). Risk and trigger factors for the development of eating disorders in female elite athletes. *Medicine and Science in Sports and Exercise, 26,* 414–419. doi:10.1249/00005768-199404000-00003

Swanik, C., Covassin, T., Stearne, D.J., & Schatz, P. (2007). The relationship between neurocognitive function and noncontact anterior cruciate ligament injuries. *The American Journal of Sports Medicine, 35,* 943–948.

Swart, E.F., Redler, L., Fabricant, P.D., Mandelbaum, B.R., Ahmad, C.S., & Wang, Y.C. (2014). Prevention and screening programs for anterior cruciate ligament injuries in young athletes: A cost-effectiveness analysis. *Journal of Bone & Joint Surgery, American Volume, 96,* 705–711. doi:10.2106/JBJS.M.00560

Swenson, D., & Dargan, P. (1994, June). *A group approach to counseling injured athletes.* Workshop presented at the 11th Annual Conference on Counseling Athletes, Springfield, MA.

Swirtun, L.R., & Renström, P. (2008). Factors affecting outcome after anterior cruciate ligament injury: A prospective study with a six-year follow-up. *Scandinavian Journal of Medicine & Science in Sports, 18,* 318–324. doi:10.1111/j.1600-0838.2007.00696.x

Symbaluk, D.G., Heth, C.D., Cameron, J., & Pierce, W.D. (1997). Social modeling, monetary incentives, and pain endurance: The role of self-efficacy and pain perception. *Personality and Social Psychology Bulletin, 23,* 258–269.

Szasz, T.S., & Hollender, M.H. (1956). A contribution to the philosophy of medicine. *Archives of Internal Medicine, 97*, 585–592. doi:10.1001/archinte.1956.00250230079008

Tan, B., Carnduff, R., McKay, C., Kang, J., Romiti, M., Nasuti, G., Emery, C. (2014). Risk factors for sport injury in elementary school children: Are children with developmental coordination disorder or attention deficit hyperactivity disorder at greater risk of injury? [Abstract]. *British Journal of Sports Medicine, 48*, 663–664. doi:10.1136/bjsports-2014-093494.277

Tate, A., Turner, G.N., Knab, S.E., Jorgensen, C., Strittmatter, A., & Michener, L.A. (2012). Risk factors associated with shoulder pain and disability across the lifespan of competitive swimmers. *Journal of Athletic Training, 47*, 149–158.

Tatsumi, T. (2013). Development of Athletic Injury Psychological Acceptance Scale. *Journal of Physical Therapy Science, 25*, 545–552. doi:10.1589/jpts.25.545

Taylor, A.H., & May, S. (1995). Physiotherapist's expectations and their influence on compliance to sports injury rehabilitation. In R. Vanfraechem-Raway & Y. Vanden Auweele (Eds.), *IXth European Congress on Sport Psychology proceedings: Part II* (pp. 619–625). Brussels: European Federation of Sports Psychology.

Taylor, A.H., & May, S. (1996). Threat and coping appraisal as determinants of compliance to sports injury rehabilitation: An application of protection motivation theory. *Journal of Sports Sciences, 14*, 471–482. doi:10.1080/02640419608727734

Taylor, J., Stone, K.R., Mullin, M.J., Ellenbecker, T., & Walgenbach, A. (2003). *Comprehensive sports injury management: From examination of injury to return to sport* (2nd ed.). Austin, TX: Pro-Ed.

Taylor, J., & Taylor, S. (1997). *Psychological approaches to sports injury rehabilitation.* Gaithersburg, MD: Aspen.

Taylor, S.E. (2012). *Health psychology* (8th ed.). New York: McGraw-Hill.

The team physician and the return-to-play decision: A consensus statement—2012 update. (2012). *Medicine and Science in Sports and Exercise, 34*, 1212–1214.

Tedder, S., & Biddle, S.J.H. (1998). Psychological processes involved during sports injury rehabilitation: An attribution-emotion investigation [Abstract]. *Journal of Sports Sciences, 16*, 106–107.

Terry-McElrath, Y.M., O'Malley, P.M., & Johnston, L.D. (2011). Exercise and substance abuse among American youth, 1991–2009. *American Journal of Preventive Medicine, 40*, 530–540. doi:10.1016/j.amepre.2010.12.021

Tesarz, J., Schuster, A.K., Hartmann, M., Gerhardt, A., & Eich, W. (2012). Pain perception in athletes compared to normally active controls: A systematic review with meta-analysis. *Pain, 153*, 1253–1262. doi:10.1016/j.pain.2012.03.005

te Wierike, S.C. M., van der Sluis, A., van den Akker-Scheek, I., Elferink-Gemser, M.T., & Visscher, C. (2013). Psychosocial factors influencing the recovery of athletes with anterior cruciate ligament injury: A systematic review. *Scandinavian Journal of Medicine & Science in Sports, 23*, 527–540. doi:10.1111/sms.12010

Thatcher, J., Kerr, J., Amies, K., & Day, M. (2007). A reversal theory analysis of psychological responses during sport injury rehabilitation. *Journal of Sport Rehabilitation, 16*, 343–362.

Thayer, J.F., & Sternberg, E. (2006). Beyond heart-rate variability: Vagal regulation of allostatic systems. *Annals of the New York Academy of Science, 1088*, 361–372. doi:10.1196/annals.1366.014

Theodorakis, Y., Beneca, A., Malliou, P., Antoniou, P., Goudas, M., & Laparidis, K. (1997). The effect of a self-talk technique on injury rehabilitation [Abstract]. *Journal of Applied Sport Psychology, 9*(Suppl.), S164.

Theodorakis, Y., Beneca, A., Malliou, P., & Goudas, M. (1997). Examining psychological factors during injury rehabilitation. *Journal of Sport Rehabilitation, 6*, 355–363.

Theodorakis, Y., Malliou, P., Papaioannou, A., Beneca, A., & Filactakidou, A. (1996). The effect of personal goals, self-efficacy, and self-satisfaction on injury rehabilitation. *Journal of Sport Rehabilitation, 5*, 214–223.

Thomeé, P., Thomeé, R., & Karlsson, J. (2002). Patellofemoral pain syndrome: Pain, coping strategies, and degree of well-being. *Scandinavian Journal of Medicine & Science in Sports, 12*, 276–281. doi:10.1034/j.1600-0838.2002.10226.x

Thomeé, P., Wahrborg, M., Börjesson, R., Thomeé, R., Eriksson, B.I., & Karlsson, J. (2007a). Determinants of self-efficacy in the rehabilitation of patients with anterior cruciate ligament injury. *Journal of Rehabilitation Medicine, 39*, 486–492. doi:10.2340/16501977-0079

Thomeé, P., Wahrborg, M., Börjesson, R., Thomeé, R., Eriksson, B.I., & Karlsson, J. (2007b). Self-efficacy, symptoms, and physical activity in patients with an anterior cruciate ligament injury: A prospective study. *Scandinavian Journal of Medicine & Science in Sports, 17*, 238–245. doi:10.1111/j.1600-0838.2006.00557.x

Thomeé, P., Wahrborg, P., Börjesson, M., Thomeé, R., Eriksson, B.I., & Karlsson, J. (2008). Self-efficacy of knee function as a preoperative predictor of outcome one year after anterior cruciate ligament reconstruction. *Knee Surgery, Sports Traumatology, Arthroscopy, 16*, 118–127. doi:10.1007/s00167-011-1669-8

Thompson, N.J., & Morris, R.D. (1994). Predicting injury risk in adolescent football players: The importance of psychological variables. *Journal of Pediatric Psychology, 19*, 415–429. doi:10.1093/jpepsy/19.4.415

Thompson, S.C., Nanni, C., & Schwankovsky, L. (1990). Patient-oriented interventions to improve communication in a medical office visit. *Health Psychology, 9*, 390–404.

Timpka, T., Jacobsson, J., Dahlström, Ö., Kowalski, J., Bargoria, V., Ekberg, J., Renström, P. (2014). Psychological risk factors for overuse injuries in elite athletics: A cohort study in Swedish youth and adult athletes [Abstract]. *British Journal of Sports Medicine, 48*, 666. doi:10.1136/bjsports-2014-093494.284

Timpka, T., Janson, S., Jacobsson, J., Kowalski, J., Ekberg, J., Mountjoy, M., & Svedin, C.G. (2014). Lifetime sexual and physical abuse among elite athletic athletes: A cross-sectional study of prevalence and correlates with athletics injury [Abstract]. *British Journal of Sports Medicine, 48*, 667. doi:10.1136/bjsports-2014-093494.285

Timpka, T., Lindqvist, K., Ekstrand, J., & Karlsson, N. (2005). Impact of social standing on sports injury prevention in a WHO safe community: Intervention outcome by household employment contract and type of sport. *British Journal of Sports Medicine, 39*, 453–457. doi:10.1136/bjsm.2004.014472

Tod, D., Hardy, J., & Oliver, E. (2011). Effects of self-talk: A systematic literature review. *Journal of Sport & Exercise Psychology, 33*, 666–687.

Tracey, J. (2003). The emotional response to the injury and rehabilitation process. *Journal of Applied Sport Psychology, 15*, 279–293. doi:10.1080/714044197

Tranaeus, U., Johnson, U., Engström, B., Skillgate, E., & Werner, S. (2014). A psychological injury prevention group intervention in Swedish floorball. *Knee Surgery, Sports Traumatology, Arthroscopy*. Advance online publication. doi:10.1007/s00167-014-3133-z

Tranaeus, U., Johnson, U., Ivarsson, A., Engström, B., Skillgate, E., & Werner, S. (2014). Sports injury prevention in Swedish elite floorball players: Evaluation of two consecutive floorball seasons. *Knee Surgery, Sports Traumatology, Arthroscopy*. Advance online publication. doi:10.1007/s00167-014-3411-9

Treacy, S.H., Barron, O.A., Brunet, M.E., & Barrack, R. (1997). Assessing the need for extensive supervised rehabilitation following arthroscopic ACL reconstruction. *The American Journal of Orthopedics, 26*, 25–29.

Tripp, D.A., Stanish, W.D., Coady, C., & Reardon, G. (2004). The subjective pain experience of athletes following anterior cruciate ligament surgery. *Psychology of Sport and Exercise, 5*, 339–354. doi:10.1016/S1469-0292(03)00022-0

Tripp, D.A., Stanish, W., Ebel-Lam, A., Brewer, B.W., & Birchard, J. (2007). Fear of reinjury, negative affect, and catastrophizing predicting return to sport in recreational athletes with anterior cruciate ligament injuries at 1 year postsurgery. *Rehabilitation Psychology, 52*, 74–81. doi:10.1037/2157-3905.1.S.38

Tripp, D.A., Sullivan, M.J.L., Stanish, W.D., Reardon, G., & Coady, C. (2001). Comparing pain, affective distress, catastrophizing, and pain medication consumption following ACL reconstruction in adolescents and adults [Abstract]. *Association for the Advancement of Applied Sport Psychology 2001 conference proceedings* (p. 17). Denton, TX: RonJon.

Turk, D.C., Meichenbaum, D., & Genest, M. (1983). *Pain and behavioral medicine: A cognitive-behavioral perspective*. New York: Guilford.

Uchino, B.N., Cacioppo, J.T., & Kiecolt-Glaser, J.K. (1996). The relationships between social support and physiological processes: A review with emphasis on underlying mechanisms and implications for health. *Psychological Bulletin, 119*, 488–531.

Uchino, B.N., Uno, D., & Holt-Lunstad, J. (1999). Social support, physiological processes, and health. *Current Directions in Psychological Science, 8*, 145–148. doi:10.1111/1467-8721.00034

Udry, E. (1997). Coping and social support among injured athletes following surgery. *Journal of Sport & Exercise Psychology, 19*, 71–90.

Udry, E. (1999). The paradox of injuries: Unexpected positive consequences. In D. Pargman (Ed.), *Psychological bases of sport injuries* (2nd ed., pp. 79–88). Morgantown, WV: Fitness Information Technology.

Udry, E., Gould, D., Bridges, D., & Beck, L. (1997). Down but not out: Athlete responses to season-ending injuries. *Journal of Sport & Exercise Psychology, 19*, 229–248.

Uitenbroek, D.G. (1996). Sports, exercise, and other causes of injuries: Results of a population survey. *Research Quarterly for Exercise and Sport, 67*, 380–385.

Upson, N. (1982) Dental injuries and the attitudes of rugby players to mouthguards. *British Journal of Sports Medicine, 16*, 241–244. doi:10.1136/bjsm.16.4.241

Valliant, P. (1981). Personality and injury in competitive runners. *Perceptual and Motor Skills, 53*, 251–253. doi:10.2466/pms.1981.53.1.251

van Beijsterveldt, A., Krist, M., van de Port, I., & Backx, F. (2011a). Compliance with an injury prevention program in Dutch adult male amateur soccer. British Journal of Sports Medicine, 45, 379–380. doi:10.1136/bjsm.2011.084038.196

van Beijsterveldt, A.M.C., Krist, M.R., Schmikli, S.L., Stubbe, J.H., de Wit, G.A., Inklaar, H., Backx, F.J.G. (2011a). Effectiveness and cost-effectiveness of an injury prevention programme for adult male amateur soccer players: Design of a cluster-randomised controlled trial. Injury Prevention, 17(1), e2. doi:10.1136/ip.2010.027979

van Beijsterveldt, A., Krist, M., van de Port, I., & Backx, F. (2011b). Cost effectiveness of an injury prevention program in Dutch adult male amateur soccer. British Journal of Sports Medicine, 45, 331. doi:10.1136/bjsm.2011.084038.60

van Beijsterveldt, A., Krist, M., van de Port, I., & Backx, F. (2011c). Compliance with an injury prevention program in Dutch adult male amateur soccer. *British Journal of Sports Medicine, 45*, 379-380. doi:10.1136/bjsm.2011.084038.196

van Mechelen, D.M., van Mechelen, W., & Verhagen, E. (2014). Sports injury prevention in your pocket?! Prevention apps assessed against the available scientific evidence: A review. *British Journal of Sports Medicine, 48*, 878–882. doi:10.1136/bjsports-2012-092136

van Mechelen, W., Hlobil, H., & Kemper, H.C.G. (1992). Incidence, severity, aetiology, and prevention of sports injuries: A review of concepts. *Sports Medicine, 14*, 82–99. doi:10.2165/00007256-199214020-00002

van Mechelen, W., Twisk, J., Molendijk, A., Blom, B., Snel, J., & Kemper, H.C.G. (1996). Subject related risk factors for sports injuries: A 1-yr perspective in young adults. *Medicine & Science in Sports & Exercise, 28*, 1171–1179.

Van Raalte, J.L. (2010). Self-talk. In S.J. Hanrahan & M.B. Andersen, *Routledge handbook of applied sport psychology: A comprehensive guide for students and practitioners* (pp. 510–517). Abingdon, Oxon, United Kingdom: Routledge.

Van Raalte, J.L., & Andersen, M.B. (2014). Referral processes in sport psychology. In J.L. Van Raalte & B.W. Brewer (Eds.), *Exploring sport and exercise psychology* (3rd ed., pp. 337–350). Washington, DC: American Psychological Association.

Van Raalte, J.L., Brewer, B.W., Brewer, D.D., & Linder, D.E. (1992). NCAA Division II college football players' perceptions of an athlete who consults a sport psychologist. *Journal of Sport & Exercise Psychology, 14*, 273–282.

Van Raalte, J.L., Brewer, B.W., & Cornelius, A.E. (2012, October). *Postrehabilitation perceptions of a psychoeducational multimedia CD-ROM for ACL surgery and rehabilitation.* Paper presented at the annual meeting of the Association for Applied Sport Psychology, Atlanta, GA.

Van Raalte, J.L., Brewer, B.W., & Petitpas, A.J. (1992). *Correspondence between athlete and trainer appraisals of injury rehabilitation status.* Paper presented at the annual meeting of the Association for the Advancement of Applied Sport Psychology, Colorado Springs, CO.

Van Reeth, O., Weibel, L., Spiegel, K., Leproult, R., Dugovic, C., & Maccari, S. (2000). Interactions between stress and sleep: From basic research to clinical situations. *Sleep Medicine Reviews, 4*, 201–219. doi:10.1053/smrv.1999.0097

Van Tiggelen, D., Wickes, S. Stevens, V., Roosen, P., & Witvrouw, E. (2008). Effective prevention of sports injuries: A model integrating efficacy, efficiency, compliance, and risk-taking behavior. *British Journal of Sports Medicine, 42*, 648–652. doi:10.1136/bjsm.2008.046441

Van Wilgen, C.P., Kaptein, A.A., & Brink, M.S. (2010). Illness perceptions and mood states are associated with injury-related outcomes in athletes. *Disability and Rehabilitation, 32*, 1576–1585. doi:10.3109/09638281003596857

Vergeer, I. (2006). Exploring the mental representation of athletic injury: A longitudinal study. *Psychology of Sport and Exercise, 7*, 99–114. doi:10.1016/j.psychsport.2005.07.003

Verhagen, E., van der Beek, A., Twisk, J., Bouter, L., Bahr, R., & van Mechelen, W. (2004). The effect of a proprioceptive balance board training program for the prevention of ankle sprains: A prospective controlled trial. *The American Journal of Sports Medicine, 32*, 1385–1393.

Verhagen, E.A.L.M., Hupperets, M.D.W., Finch, C.F., & van Mechelen, W. (2011). The impact of adherence on sports injury prevention effect estimates in randomised controlled trials: Looking beyond the CONSORT statement. *Journal of Science and Medicine in Sport, 14*, 287–292. doi:10.1016/j.jsams.2011.02.007

Visser, L. (2010, May 12). Ten years after leaving field, Haley on more solid ground. CBS Sports. Retrieved from www.cbssports.com

Vriend, I., Coehoorn, I., & Verhagen, E. (2015). Implementation of an app-based neuromuscular training programme to prevent ankle sprains: A process evaluation using the RE-AIM framework. *British Journal of Sports Medicine, 49*, 484–488. doi:10.1136/bjsports-2013-092896

Waddington, I. (2006). Ethical problems in the medical management of sports injuries: A case study of English professional football. In S. Loland, B. Skirstad, & I. Waddington (Eds.), *Pain and injury in sport: Social and ethical analysis* (pp. 89–106). New York: Routledge.

Wadey, R., Clark, S., Podlog, L., & McCullough, D. (2013). Coaches' perceptions of athletes' stress-related growth following sport injury. *Psychology of Sport and Exercise, 14*, 125–135. doi:10.1016/j.psychsport.2012.12.005

Wadey, R., & Evans, L. (2011). Working with injured athletes: Research and practice. In S. Hanton & S.D. Mellalieu (Eds.), *Professional practice in sport psychology: A review* (pp. 107–132). Abingdon, Oxon, United Kingdom: Routledge.

Wadey, R., Evans, L., Evans, K., & Mitchell, I. (2011). Perceived benefits following sport injury: A qualitative examination of their antecedents and underlying mechanisms. *Journal of Applied Sport Psychology*, *23*, 142–158. doi:10.1080/10413200.2010.543119

Wadey, R., Evans, L., Hanton, S., & Neil, R. (2012a). Examination of hardiness throughout the sport-injury process. *British Journal of Health Psychology*, *17*, 103–128. doi:10.1111/j.2044-8287.2011.02025.x

Wadey, R., Evans, L., Hanton, S., & Neil, R. (2012b). An examination of hardiness throughout the sport-injury process: A qualitative follow-up study. *British Journal of Health Psychology*, *17*, 872–893. doi:10.1111/j.2044-8287.2012.02084.x

Wadey, R., Evans, L., Hanton, S., & Neil, R. (2013). Effect of dispositional optimism before and after injury. *Medicine and Science in Sports and Exercise*, *45*, 387–394. doi:10.1249/MSS.0b013e31826ea8e3

Wadey, R., Podlog, L., Hall, M., Hamson-Utley, J., Hicks-Little, C., & Hammer, C. (2014). Reinjury anxiety, coping, and return-to-sport outcomes: A multiple mediation analysis. *Rehabilitation Psychology*, *59*, 256–266. doi:10.1037/a0037032

Wadsworth, L.T. (2006). Acupuncture in sports medicine. *Current Sports Medicine Reports, 5*, 1–3.

Wager, T.D., Atlas, L.Y., Lindquist, M.A., Roy, M., & Woo, C.-W. (2013). An fMRI-based neurologic signature of physical pain. *New England Journal of Medicine*, *368*, 1388–1397. doi:10.105/NEJMoa1204471

Walk, S.R. (1997). Peers in pain: The experiences of student athletic trainers. *Sociology of Sport Journal*, *14*, 22–56.

Walker, H., Gabbe, B., Wajswelner, H., Blanch, P., & Bennell, K. (2012). Shoulder pain in swimmers: A 12-month prospective cohort study of incidence and risk factors. *Physical Therapy in Sport*, *13*, 243–249. doi:10.1016/j.ptsp.2012.01.001

Walker, J. (1971). Pain and distraction in athletes and non-athletes. *Perceptual and Motor Skills*, *33*, 1187–1190. doi:10.2466/pms.1971.33.3f.1187

Walker, N. (2006). *The meaning of sports injury and re-injury anxiety assessment and intervention.* Unpublished doctoral thesis, University of Wales, Aberystwyth.

Walker, N., & Heaney, C. (2013). Relaxation techniques in sport injury rehabilitation. In M. Arvinen-Barrow & N. Walker (Eds.), *The psychology of sport injury and rehabilitation* (pp. 86–102). Abingdon, Oxon, United Kingdom: Routledge.

Walker, N., & Hudson, J. (2013). Self-talk in sport injury rehabilitation. In M. Arvinen-Barrow & N. Walker (Eds.), *The psychology of sport injury and rehabilitation* (pp. 103–116). Abingdon, Oxon, United Kingdom: Routledge.

Walker, N., Thatcher, J., & Lavallee, D. (2010). A preliminary development of the Re-Injury Anxiety Inventory (RIAI). *Physical Therapy in Sport*, *11*, 23–29. doi:10.1016/j.ptsp.2009.09.003

Walsh, M. (2005). Injury rehabilitation and imagery. In T. Morris, M. Spittle, & A.P. Watt (Eds.), *Imagery in sport* (pp. 267–284). Champaign, IL: Human Kinetics.

Wasley, D., & Lox, C.L. (1998). Self-esteem and coping responses of athletes with acute versus chronic injuries. *Perceptual and Motor Skills*, *86*, 1402. doi:10.2466/pms.1998.86.3c.1402

Waters, A.G. (2005). *The role of confidence in rehabilitation and the recovery of motor performance.* Unpublished doctoral thesis, University of Wales, Bangor, UK.

Waters, W.F., Adams, S.G., Binks, P., & Varnado, P. (1993). Attention, stress, and negative emotion in persistent sleep-onset and sleep-maintenance insomnia. *Sleep*, *16*, 128–136.

Waumsley, J.A., & Katz, J. (2013). Using a psychological model and counseling skills in sport injury rehabilitation. In M. Arvinen-Barrow & N. Walker (Eds.), *The psychology of sport injury and rehabilitation* (pp. 171–184). London: Routledge.

Webbe, F.M., & Ochs, S.R. (2007). Personality traits relate to heading frequency in male soccer players. *Journal of Clinical Sport Psychology*, *1*, 379–389.

Webbe, F.M., & Salinas, C.M. (2011). When science and politics conflict: The case of soccer heading in adults and children. In F.M. Webbe (Ed.), *The handbook of sport neuropsychology* (pp. 275–294). New York: Springer.

Webber, W.B., & Rinehart, G.C. (1992). Computer-based multimedia in plastic surgery education. *Proceedings of the Annual Symposium on Computer Applications in Medical Care*, 829–830.

Webborn, A.D.J., Carbon, R.J., & Miller, B.P. (1997). Injury rehabilitation programs: "What are we talking about?" *Journal of Sport Rehabilitation*, *6*, 54–61.

Webster, K.E., Feller, J.A., & Lambros, C. (2008). Development and preliminary validation of a scale to measure the psychological impact of returning to sport following anterior cruciate ligament reconstruction surgery. *Physical Therapy in Sport*, *9*, 9–15. doi:10.1016/j.ptsp.2007.09.003

Weeks, D.L., Brubaker, J., Byrt, J., Davis, M., Hamann, L., & Reagan, J. (2002). Videotape instruction versus illustrations for influencing quality of performance, motivation, and confidence to perform simple and complex exercises in healthy subjects. *Physiotherapy Theory and Practice, 18,* 65–73. doi:10.1080/09593980290058454

Weinberg, R. (2010). Activation/arousal control. In S.J. Hanrahan & M.B. Andersen (Eds.), *Routledge handbook of applied sport psychology: A comprehensive guide for students and practitioners* (pp. 471–480). Abingdon, Oxon, United Kingdom: Routledge.

Weinberg, R.S. (2002). Goal setting in sport and exercise: Research to practice. In J.L. Van Raalte & B.W. Brewer (Eds.), *Exploring sport and exercise psychology* (2nd ed., pp. 25–48). Washington, DC: American Psychological Association.

Weinberg, R. S., Vernau, D., & Horn, T. S. (2013). Playing through pain and injury: psychosocial considerations. *Journal of Clinical Sport Psychology, 7,* 41-59.

Weiss, M.R., & Troxel, R.K. (1986). Psychology of the injured athlete. *Athletic Training, 21,* 104–109, 154.

Wesch, N., Hall, C., Prapavessis, H., Maddison, R., Bassett, S., Foley, L., Forwell, L. (2012). Self-efficacy, imagery use, and adherence during injury rehabilitation. *Scandinavian Journal of Medicine & Science in Sports, 22,* 695–703. doi:10.1111/j.1600-0838.2011.01304.x

Wesch, N.N., Hall, C.R., Polgar, J., & Forwell, L. (2008). An examination of imagery use and self-efficacy during rehabilitation [Abstract]. *Journal of Sport and Exercise Psychology, 30,* S210.

Wiese, D.M., & Weiss, M.R. (1987). Psychological rehabilitation and physical injury: Implications for the sportsmedicine team. *The Sport Psychologist, 1,* 318–330.

Wiese, D.M., Weiss, M.R., & Yukelson, D.P. (1991). Sport psychology in the training room: Implications for the treatment team. *The Sport Psychologist, 5,* 15–24.

Wiese-Bjornstal, D.M. (2004). From skinned knees and peewees to menisci and masters: Developmental sport injury psychology. In M.R. Weiss (Ed.), *Developmental sport psychology: A lifespan perspective* (pp. 525–568). Morgantown, WV: Fitness Information Technology.

Wiese-Bjornstal, D.M. (2009). Sport injury and college athlete health across the lifespan. *Journal of Intercollegiate Sports, 2,* 64–80.

Wiese-Bjornstal, D.M., Gardetto, D.M., & Shaffer, S.M. (1999). Effective interaction skills for sports medicine practitioners. In R. Ray & D.M. Wiese-Bjornstal (Eds.), *Counseling in sports medicine* (pp. 55–74). Champaign, IL: Human Kinetics.

Wiese-Bjornstal, D.M., & Smith, A.M. (1993). Counseling strategies for enhanced recovery of injured athletes within a team approach. In D. Pargman (Ed.), *Psychological bases of sports injuries* (pp.

149–182). Morgantown, WV: Fitness Information Technology.

Wiese-Bjornstal, D.M., Smith, A.M., & LaMott, E.E. (1995). A model of psychologic response to athletic injury and rehabilitation. *Athletic Training: Sports Health Care Perspectives, 1,* 17–30.

Wiese-Bjornstal, D.M., Smith, A.M., Shaffer, S.M., & Morrey, M.A. (1998). An integrated model of response to sport injury: Psychological and sociological dimensions. *Journal of Applied Sport Psychology, 10,* 46–69. doi:10.1080/10413209808406377

Wilde, G.J.S. (1998). Risk homeostasis theory: An overview. *British Medical Journal, 4,* 89–91.

Williams, J. (2011, December 28). More evidence supporting injury prevention training: Cost effectiveness. The Science of Soccer Online. www.scienceofsocceronline.com/2011/12/more-evidence-supporting-injury.html.

Williams, J.M., & Andersen, M.B. (1997). Psychosocial influences on central and peripheral vision and reaction time during demanding tasks. *Behavioral Medicine, 26,* 160–167.

Williams, J.M., & Andersen, M.B. (1998). Psychosocial antecedents of sport injury: Review and critique of the stress and injury model. *Journal of Applied Sport Psychology, 10,* 5–25. doi:10.1080/10413209808406375

Williams, J.M., & Andersen, M.B. (2007). Psychosocial antecedents of sport injury and interventions for risk reduction. In G. Tenenbaum & R.C. Eklund (Eds.), *Handbook of sport psychology* (3rd ed., pp. 379–403). New York: Wiley.

Williams, J.M., Hogan, T.D., & Andersen, M.B. (1993). Positive states of mind and athletic injury risk. *Psychosomatic Medicine, 55,* 468–472.

Williams, J.M., Tonymon, P., & Andersen, M.B. (1990). Effects of life-event stress on anxiety and peripheral narrowing. *Behavioral Medicine, 16,* 174–181.

Williams, J.M., Tonymon, P., & Andersen, M.B. (1991). Effects of stressors and coping resources on anxiety and peripheral narrowing in recreational athletes. *Journal of Applied Sport Psychology, 3,* 126–141. doi:10.1080/10413209108406439

Williams, J.M., Tonymon, P., & Wadsworth, W.A. (1986). Relationship of life stress to injury in intercollegiate volleyball. *Journal of Human Stress, 12,* 38–43.

Williams-Avery, R.M., & MacKinnon, D.P. (1996). Injuries and use of protective equipment among college in-line skaters. *Accident Analysis & Prevention, 28,* 779–784. doi:10.1016/S0001-4575(96)00040-1

Wills, T.A. (1985). Supportive functions of interpersonal relationships. In S. Cohen & L. Syme (Eds.), *Social support and health* (pp. 61–82). New York: Academic Press.

Wise, A., Jackson, D.W., & Rocchio, P. (1979). Preoperative psychologic testing as a predictor of success in knee surgery. *The American Journal of Sports Medicine, 7,* 287–292. doi:10.1177/036354657900700503

Wittig, A.F., & Schurr, K.T. (1994). Psychological characteristics of women volleyball players: Relationships with injuries, rehabilitation, and team success. *Personality and Social Psychology Bulletin, 20,* 322–330. doi:10.1177/0146167294203010

Wong, P.T.P., & Weiner, B. (1981). When people ask "why" questions, and the heuristics of attributional search. *Journal of Personality and Social Psychology, 40,* 650–663. doi:0.1037/0022-3514.40.4.650

Wood, A.M., Robertson, G.A., Rennie, L., Caesar, B.C., & Court-Brown, C.M. (2010). The epidemiology of sports-related fractures in adolescents. *Injury, 41,* 834–838. doi:10.1016/j.injury.2010.04.008

Woods, S.E., Zabat, E., Daggy, M., Diehl J., Engel A., & Okragly, R. (2007). Face protection in recreational hockey players. Family Medicine, 39, 473–476.

Wooten, H.R. (2008). Mental health issues for athletic trainers. In J.M. Mensch & G.M. Miller (Eds.), *The athletic trainer's guide to psychosocial intervention and referral* (pp. 197–216). Thorofare, NJ: Slack.

Wortman, C.B., & Silver, R.C. (1987). Coping with irrevocable loss. In G.R. VandenBos & B.K. Bryant (Eds.), *Cataclysms, crises, and catastrophes: Psychology in action* (pp. 189–235). Washington, DC: American Psychological Association.

Wraga, M., & Kosslyn, S. (2002). Imagery. In L. Nadel (Ed.), *Encyclopedia of cognitive science* (Vol. 2, pp. 466–470). London: Nature Group.

Wright, B.J., Galtieri, N.J., & Fell, M. (2014). Non-adherence to prescribed home rehabilitation exercises for musculoskeletal injuries: The role of the patient–practitioner relationship. *Journal of Rehabilitation Medicine, 46,* 153–158. doi:10.2340/16501977-1241

Yang, J., Bowling, J.M., Lewis, M.A., Marshall, S.W., Runyan, C.W., & Mueller, F.O. (2005). Use of discretionary protective equipment in high school athletes: Prevalence and determinants. *American Journal of Public Health, 95,* 1996–2002. doi:10.2105/AJPH.2004.050807

Yang, J., Cheng, G., Zhang, Y., Covassin, T., Heiden, E.O., & Peek-Asa, C. (2014). Influence of symptoms of depression and anxiety on injury hazard among collegiate American football players. *Research in Sports Medicine: An International Journal, 22,* 147–160. doi:10.1080/15438627.2014.881818

Yang, J., Peek-Asa, C., Lowe, J.B., Heiden, E., & Foster, D.T. (2010). Social support patterns of collegiate athletes before and after injury. *Journal of Athletic Training, 45,* 372–379. doi:10.4085/1062-6050-45.4.372

Young, J.A., Pain, M.D., & Pearce, A.J. (2007). Experiences of Australian professional female tennis players returning to competition from injury. *British Journal of Sport Medicine, 41,* 806–811. doi:10.1136/bjsm.2007.036541

Young, K. (1991). Violence in the workplace of professional sport from victimological and cultural studies perspectives. *International Review for the Sociology of Sport, 26,* 3–14.

Young, K. (1993). Violence, risk, and masculinity in male sports culture. *Sociology of Sport Journal, 10,* 373–396.

Young, K. (Ed.). (2004). *Sporting bodies, damaged selves: Sociological studies of sports-related injury.* Oxford: Elsevier Press.

Young, K., & White, P. (1995). Sport, physical danger, and injury: The experiences of elite women athletes. *Journal of Sport and Social Issues, 19,* 45–61. doi:10.1177/019372395019001004

Young, K., White, P., & McTeer, W. (1994). Body talk: Male athletes reflect on sport, injury, and pain. *Sociology of Sport Journal, 11,* 175–194.

Young, M.E. (2012). *Learning the art of helping: Building blocks and techniques* (5th ed.). Upper Saddle River, NJ: Pearson.

Yung, P.S.-H., Chan, R.H.-K., Wong, F.C.-Y., Cheuk, P.W.-L., & Fong, D.T.-P. (2007). Epidemiology of injuries in Hong Kong elite badminton athletes. *Research in Sports Medicine, 15,* 133–146.

Zebis, M.K., Andersen, L.L., Bencke, J., Kjær, M., & Aagaard, P. (2009). Identification of athletes at future risk of anterior cruciate ligament ruptures by neuromuscular screening. *The American Journal of Sports Medicine, 37,* 1967–1973. doi:10.1177/0363546509335000

Zemper, E.D. (1993). Epidemiology of athletic injuries. In D.B. McKeag & D.O. Hough (Eds.), *Primary care sports medicine* (pp. 63–73). Dubuque, IA: Brown and Benchmark.

Zemper, E.D. (2010). Catastrophic injuries among young athletes. *British Journal of Sports Medicine, 44,* 13–20. doi:10.1136/bjsm.2009.069096

Index

Note: The italicized *f* and *t* following page numbers refer to figures and tables, respectively.

About the Authors

Britton W. Brewer, PhD, is a professor of psychology at Springfield College, where he has taught graduate and undergraduate classes and conducted research on psychological aspects of sport injury since 1991. He is a fellow of the American Psychological Association and the Association of Applied Sport Psychology and a certified consultant with the Association of Applied Sport Psychology. He has edited four books on sport psychology, authored or coauthored more than 100 articles in refereed journals (approximately 40 percent of which are on topics related to the psychology of sport injury), and authored or coauthored 28 book chapters (more than half of which are on topics related to the psychology of sport injury). He has been awarded more than $1,000,000 in grant funding from the National Institute of Arthritis and Musculoskeletal and Skin Diseases for his research on psychological aspects of anterior cruciate ligament (ACL) surgery and has received research awards from Divisions 22 (Rehabilitation Psychology) and 47 (Exercise and Sport Psychology) of the American Psychological Association.

Charles J. Redmond, MS, MEd, ATC, LAT, PT, is professor emeritus of exercise science and sport studies and retired dean of the School of Health, Physical Education and Recreation at Springfield College, where he has been a member of the faculty since 1969. He has extensive clinical, teaching, and administrative experience in athletic training and has served in multiple leadership positions in the National Athletic Trainers' Association. He received the Most Distinguished Athletic Trainer Award from the NATA in 1994 and was inducted into the NATA Hall of Fame in 2004. He has also been inducted into the Athletic Trainers of Massachusetts Hall of Fame and the Springfield College Athletic Hall of Fame. He served on the editorial advisory board of *Athletic Therapy Today* from 1995 to 2005, during which he was theme editor for issues such as eating and exercise disorders, psychosocial factors and athletic therapy, and advances in the management of patellofemoral pain. He has given presentations and conducted workshops on a variety of topics in sport health care, including the psychology of sport injury.